EXISTENCE AND CONSOLATION

REINVENTING ONTOLOGY, GNOSIS, AND VALUES IN AFRICAN PHILOSOPHY

PARAGON ISSUES IN PHILOSOPHY

African Philosophy: The Essential Readings
Critical Theory and Philosophy
Critical Theory: The Essential Readings
Existence and Consolation: Reinventing...African Philosophy
Foundations of Cognitive Science: The Essential Readings
Foundations of Philosophy of Science: Recent Developments
Global Ethics
Global Justice
Life, Liberty, and the Pursuit of Happiness, Version 4.0
Living Philosophy
Meaning and Truth: Essential Readings in Modern Semantics
Metaphysics: A Contemporary Introduction
Philosophy and Cognitive Science
Philosophy and Feminist Criticism
Philosophy of Science
Philosophy of Human Rights
Philosophy of Sex and Love: An Introduction
Philosophy of Sport
Philosophy of Technology: An Introduction
Philosophy of the United States
Postmodern Rationality, Social Criticism, and Religion
Problems in Personal Identity
Self-Interest and Beyond
Social and Political Philosophy
The US Supreme Court and Medical Ethics
Woman and the History of Philosophy
World Religions in a Postmodern Age

THE PARAGON ISSUES IN PHILOSOPHY SERIES

At colleges and universities, interest in the traditional areas of philosophy remains strong. Many new currents flow within them, too, but until recently many of these went largely unnoticed in undergraduate philosophy courses. The Paragon Issues in Philosophy Series responds to both perennial and newly influential concerns by bringing together a team of able philosophers to address the fundamental issues in philosophy today and to outline the state of contemporary discussion about them.

More than twenty-five volumes have been published; they are organized into three major categories. The first covers the standard topics—metaphysics, theory of knowledge, ethics, and political philosophy—stressing innovative developments in those disciplines. The second focuses on more specialized but still perennial concerns in the philosophies of science, religion, history, sport, and other areas. The third category explores work that relates philosophy to specialized fields such as feminist criticism, medicine, economics, technology, and literature.

The level of writing is aimed at undergraduate students who have little previous experience studying philosophy. The books provide brief but accurate introductions that appraise the state of the art in their fields and show how the history of thought about their topics has developed. Each volume is complete in itself but also complements others in the series.

Traumatic change characterizes recent decades. All of our pivotal issues involve philosophical questions. We remain grateful to the late Professor Frederick Sontag for helping to design this series. It has now secured a place among philosophy departments throughout the English-speaking world. As we continue to locate and update new texts for this series, we hope that it will help to encourage the understanding needed to chart a future that will be as complicated and problematic as it is promising.

John K. Roth
Claremont McKenna College

Gordon L. Anderson
Paragon House

EXISTENCE AND CONSOLATION

REINVENTING ONTOLOGY, GNOSIS AND VALUES IN AFRICAN PHILOSOPHY

ADA AGADA

A Jonathan Chimakonam Book

PARAGON HOUSE ✦ ST. PAUL

PARAGON ISSUES IN PHILOSOPHY

First Edition 2015

Published in the United States by
Paragon House
in the Paragon Issues in Philosophy Series

www.ParagonHouse.com

"A Jonathan Chimakonam Book"

Editorial production in West Africa by 3rd Logic Option Publishing
West African edition, Studies in African Philosophy, Science, Logic, and Mathematics, Volume Three

The aim of studies in African Philosophy, Science, Logic and Mathematics is to publish important original works in the areas so specified and to present the ideas of contemporary African scholars to the world. Intending contributors wishing to publish their works under this series should write the editors: studiesinafrica@gmail.com

Library of Congress Cataloging-in-Publication Data

Agada, Ada.
Existence and consolation : reinventing ontology, gnosis, and values in African philosophy / by Ada Agada. -- First [edition].
pages cm -- (The Paragon issues in philosophy series)
"(A Jonathan Chimakonam Book)."
ISBN 978-1-55778-914-3 (pbk. : alk. paper) 1. Philosophy, African--20th century. 2. Philosophy, African--21st century. 3. Consolation. 4. Philosophy and religion. 5. Philosophical theology. I. Title.
B5320.A33 2015
199'.6--dc23
2014039408

The paper used in this publication meets the minimum requirements of American National Standard for Information Sciences—Permanence of Paper for Printed Library Materials, ANSIZ39.48-1984.

Manufactured in the United States of America
10 9 8 7 6 5 4 3 2 1

Dedicated to

L.S. SENGHOR, whose original epistemology set me on the road to unraveling a 21st century African synthesis. In memoriam.

PROF. INNOCENT ASOUZU, whose work in complementary reflection confirmed that I was on the right path in searching for a constructive alternative program to ethno-philosophy.

PROF. KWASI WIREDU, who has tirelessly served the cause of African philosophy.

PROF. KWAME APPIAH, for his work in projecting the black intellect.

CHINUA ACHEBE, who revealed the soul of Africa to the 20th century. In memoriam.

BENEDICT SPINOZA, whose thoughts continue to inspire me. In memoriam.

Studies in African Philosophy, Science, Logic, and Mathematics

VOLUME THREE

The aim of the series Studies in African Philosophy, Science, Logic, and Mathematics is to publish important original works in the areas so specified and to present the ideas of contemporary African scholars to the world. Intending contributors wishing to publish their works under this series should write the editors: studiesinafrica@gmail.com.

Contents

FOREWORD

The title *Existence and Consolation: Reinventing Ontology, Gnosis and Values in African Philosophy* speaks of a reconstruction following the deconstructed African episteme that V. Y. Mudimbe, in his book *The Invention of Africa: Gnosis, Philosophy and the Order of Knowledge,* says was not purely African but rather an invention of Europe. Ada Agada, in this work, attempts to reinvent a thorough-going African episteme. This makes the terms Existence, Consolation and Reinvention as they appear in the title very insightful. First, let me dwell on the focus of this work.

African philosophy as a systematic discipline is only a recent development. Its history cannot be traced to an era before the 1920s. Yet the beginning of this subject was fraught with controversies if not outright confusion. The initial thoughts produced came to be disparaged as substandard by those who regarded themselves as professional African philosophers. This special tag only magnifies the unstated assumption that those who produced earlier thoughts were unprofessional philosophers to say the least. The illustrious Ghanaian philosopher Kwasi Wiredu describes such early thoughts as nothing more than "community thoughts." But it was the Benin philosopher Paulin Hountondji who was to become their greatest antagonist. He gave them the unenviable name "ethnophilosophers." His intention was clear; there had to be a line between actual philosophy in Africa and non-philosophies. Ethno-philosophy thus became an umbrella term not only for those who tried to excavate the African cultural episteme but also for all those who dwelt on nationalist and ideological concerns. Some of these scholars include the Belgian missionary Tempels Placide, his Rwandan admirer Alexis Kagame, the Ghanaian statesman Kwame Nkrumah credited with the theory of consciencism, and the Tanzanian politician Julius Nyerere noted for his ideology of ujamaa. Others include William Abraham, the Kenyan Theologian John Mbiti, the Nigerian Philosopher Innocent Onyewuenyi, and his compatriot C. S. Momoh. The list is endless, but I must not fail to mention the Senegalese poet and statesman Leopold Senghor in whose thought Ada Agada has found germs of philosophic wisdom.

Over the years, and especially since after the great debate, these two rival groups have come to be known as traditional and modern philosophers respectively. Senghor eminently belonged to the former group whose ideas are denigrated as ethno-philosophy and accused of containing no rigors or any modern tools of philosophizing such as analysis. Like Hume's book-burning crusade against metaphysics, many so-called modern African philosophers like Peter Bodunrin, Ebousi Boulaga, and Wamba Dia Wamba have joined Paulin Hountondji in calling for its rejection. Peter Bodunrin, it is important to mention, has done for this group in their fight to deconstruct ethno-philosophy what A. J. Ayer did for the logical empiricists against metaphysics.

However, just as the last line of defense for African traditional philosophy was heaving under immense pressure and disillusionment, Ada Agada emerges to tell us that we cannot simply wish away ethno-philosophy if we are to construct a true and authentic African episteme. He goes on to demonstrate that ethno-philosophy is the proper foundation of authentic African philosophy even though it is not the definitive African philosophy. For any philosophy to count as African philosophy, he says, it must look away from ancient Greece for inspiration and find this vital inspiration in ethno-philosophy and the traditional African community. His argument is that, since ethno-philosophy amounts to tribal philosophy and cannot of itself earn universal respect for African philosophy, the challenge before African thinkers in the 21st century is to develop constructive alternative programs to ethno-philosophy, which are inspired by the African experience and are yet in solidarity with other philosophical traditions of the world.

Consolation philosophy therefore becomes such a constructive alternative program. He describes it as metaphysics of terror and a morality of consolation. It is a doctrine of the mood. It is a philosophy that interprets the mood of the 21st century fraught with existential challenges. Consolation philosophy condenses the aspirations, hopes, and fears of the 21st century human in a construction that seeks to constitute the answers to two fundamental questions: Is the universe pointless? And, is human life futile? Ada's insistence that authentic African episteme draws inspiration from ethno-philosophy or if you like from African life-world is an idea that will be difficult to dethrone for, if the alternative constructive program were to have a background influence from Greece or some culture in the West, what then would make it African philosophy? Hountondji has extrapolated that merely being produced by an African is the only criterion a thought has to meet in order to qualify as African philosophy. Odera Oruka added to this, the idea that such a thought should necessarily address African issues. I do not agree with either. Hountondji shot himself in the foot by raising a criterion whose implication is that non-Africans cannot do African philosophy. If non-Africans can do such philosophy then Hountondji's criterion becomes grossly inadequate; if on the other hand they cannot, then such a philosophy lacks the property of universal applicability which makes it non-philosophy anyway. This is what I call Hountondji's dilemma. As for Oruka's submission, I think a discourse can still be African philosophy even if it does not address the so-called African issues. The most important thing is the cultural background which could be methodic and therefore logical. This is, for sure, what Ada Agada stresses when he says that ethno-philosophy should be the foundation of the reconstructed African episteme. And, he is correct.

His theory of consolation philosophy has taken off from Senghor's affective and black "rational" emotionality articulated in his ideology of Négritude. Senghor's failure to develop a concept freed from ethnocentric commitments meant that he could not break from ethno-philosophy. The contemporary Nigerian philosopher Innocent Asouzu has gone beyond Senghor to accomplish this liberation. According to Ada the struggle to liberate a universal idea that traces its roots to the African experience of life, flowed into Asouzu's concept of complementary reflection otherwise known as ibuanyidanda philosophy. What makes Asouzu unique among contemporary African philosophers is that he has not only moved away from ethno-philosophy in search of the radical concept but has also sought to highlight his system as universally applicable. However, Ada faults Asouzu's complementary reflection on the ground that it has liberated the long imprisoned African concept but has not quite succeeded in elevating this concept to the status of a synthesis. This lacuna paves the way for the emergence of consolation philosophy. Here, the human being is considered from the religious, scientific, and philosophical perspectives. A being in the world is not sufficient unto itself because it is that being who must appeal to something greater than itself and external to itself to fully realize its joy. What it appeals to may be characterized as God, science, nature, love, or other form of transcendental appeal. Developing Senghor's famous notion of black emotionality and white rationality further, Ada identifies Senghor's error in his inability to universalize his theory of reason. He therefore, asserts that "psycho-logic" is different from "logic" although the former yields the latter. The human phenomenon is a "melancholy" being. Humans of all races converge in the *melancholy being* for whom there is no meaning to human existence beyond the spheres of joy and sadness. This becomes the doctrine of mood—humans are in pursuit of joy, when they miss it they become sad. Under this condition, they seek the alternative from different sources which is consolation. Hence, consolation philosophy pursues the cause of African philosophy from where Senghor and Asouzu stopped, thus correcting and completing according to the author the thoughts of two of the most outstanding thinkers in African philosophy.

So, it is to Ada Agada that we owe the gratitude for evolving consolation philosophy. This theory derives inspiration from African traditional thought substituting the Western categories of omniscience and omnipotence for the African categories of power and glory for example; Ada Agada revisits the African life-world where poverty, disease, and all sorts of existential problems make sense not only of the concept of God but that of evil and despair. Consolation then becomes the only option where the mood of sadness has overshadowed that of joy.

Ada Agada has articulated a position that has more far reaching commitments than readily observed. The theory of consolation philosophy is not just a doctrine in African philosophy; it is the very template of authentic African philosophy—the reinvention of an African episteme by an African uninfluenced by Eurocentricism. It is arguably one of the the first rigorously complete original systems after the noble attempts by the likes of Innocent Asouzu and of course, the imaginative Pantaleon Iroegbu. Thus this work has not only a thematic importance but additionally, a historical significance.

Perhaps I should point out also that Ada Agada was not the first to employ the terms consolation and philosophy together but he certainly is the first to build it into a system. The idea of consolation has been implied in the works of early philosophers like Plato and such schools as Stoicism and Epicureanism. In the modern time, the works of thinkers like St. Augustine, Kant, and schools such as Existentialism, Pragmatism, and even religious movements like Buddhism, Catholicism, and Taoism to name just a few all imply some form of consolation. However, it was the Medieval philosopher Boethius who had in 524 A.D. written a book which he titled *Philosopiea Consolationis* (*The Consolation of Philosophy*) thus becoming the first philosopher to employ the terms in this technical sense. Written while awaiting execution in prison, Boethius suggested that, in the presence of despair, philosophy could offer consolation. Recently in 2011, the Irish Philosopher Paul O'Grady edited a collection that he titled *The Consolations of Philosophy: Reflections in an Economic Downturn*. Like Boethius did in his book, O'Grady seeks to establish that in the presence of harsh economic realities questions such as the point of the universe, existence and life have become banal. Hence, with the presentment of despair, the consolation that philosophy has to offer becomes an important option. I reckon this is similar to what Ada Agada set out to do with regard to African philosophy and African condition, but went beyond intellectual sermonizing to construct a rigorous system. This feat obviously stands his work out from the rest before it. But the question is, can philosophy ultimately offer consolation?

Paal Antonsen has argued in an essay entitled "Against Philosophical Consolation" that philosophy does not bring consolation in any important sense and that philosophy should not aim at bringing consolation except the pursuit of truth. I want to disagree with this position. Philosophy does and should bring consolation. We are told by Karl Jaspers that every philosophical answer quickly evolves into a new question but arriving at an answer at all assuages the pain of emptiness and the extent to which it is applied in solving the problem of humanity, it also consoles, at least there is some solution. Thus one of the important reasons philosophers seek solutions to problems is to annihilate despair even in the absence of a definitive solution. This is why humanity sees the philosopher as the last resort. History has it that Diogenes, a renowned Greek philosopher, once gave a lecture in the Egyptian City of Alexandria, in which he bared the philosopher's inability to offer consolation anymore. We are told that many of his listeners went home and committed suicide believing as he had told them that the philosopher cannot help humanity anymore. This shows the important role philosophy and philosophers play in the society.

Ada Agada is an ingenious African philosopher who has combined what Janheinz Jahn calls the "valuable past" and Bogumil Jewsiewicki refers to as "usable past" with the resources of his rich imagination to offer us a rigorously complete episteme in African philosophy. This is a work borne out of what Wilson Moses calls "creative conflict" in which the author struggled with the apparent contradictions in his mind first, as an African and second, as one brought up under an atmosphere pervaded by Western thought system. W. E. Du Bois in his *Souls of Black Folk* makes reference to such condition which he calls an uncomfortable two-ness in one black body. For the author to walk his way through this maze of conflicting shadows, a system that has produced what Tempels calls "evolués," Colin King calls it "deracinés," while Gloria Chuku refers to it as *Oyibo-oji* (meaning an African who by his training lost his Africanness and is yet not a European and is therefore lost and confused) and produce an authentic African episteme is a rare feat. This is because the problem of the two-ness in one black body has been the bulwark that inhibited the free expression of creativity and originality among the first eleven African philosophers who thrived in deconstructing, but could not reconstruct.

The author therefore, has emerged for some time now as a revolutionary force in African philosophy. Many of his essays bear testimony to what he represents in the contemporary history of African philosophy—a new order beyond ethno-philosophy and indeed, beyond the mongering of perverse dialogue. His work "Is African Philosophy Progressing?" is as incisive as "The Future Question in African Philosophy." Ada Agada has taken his place among the greats of African thought. As a man who has spent much of his academic life in the vineyard of African philosophy, we cannot expect any less. His wealth of experience in the discipline has eminently come to the fore in this masterpiece creation. This work holds a great promise not only for African philosophy but for African studies in general. With this feat, he has decolonized and reopened the African mind closed in the strangle-grip of Eurocentricism. The doors of creativity and originality have been thrown wide open in African philosophy; he has smashed the chains of copycat, commentating and transliteration philosophy in Africa.

One other interesting thing to note is that the author marshaled his thoughts in such an audacious and intellectually sophisticated diction that make such an elegant reading. My impression is that if you read a line, you would read a page; and if you read a chapter, you would inexorably read the entire work. It is rare to come by such a book that constantly beckons.

Personally, as the general editor of this work, it is a great honor to have invested some ideas in it; to have tinkered it to this shape; and to have processed it from a raw brilliant manuscript to a book of great promise. This book would make an important companion to a pastime reader just as it would make a dependable resource to researchers in all areas of African philosophy and studies. The author's emergence marks a silver lining on the discipline's horizon which has been populated for far too long by old names and where the recycling of the same old ideas of perverse dialogue has outlived its use. Ada Agada is without doubt the very evolution of contemporary African philosophy.

Jonathan O. Chimakonam Ph.D, MCPA, MNYAS, MNPA
Bloemfontein, S.A
January, 2014

PREFACE

The possibility of a philosophy of *mood* or a coherent system of thought founded on a philosophical understanding of human emotion has intrigued me since I was a boy. Human life has always struck me as consisting wholly in our capacity for joy and sadness. Indeed, the science of ethics can be regarded as the further explication of the foundational elements of joy and sadness epistemologically grasped as pleasure and pain. Thus virtually all the great philosophers who ventured to formulate ethical theories conceived happiness as the aim of human life, the realization of the *summum bonum*. The notions of duty and perfection suggested by a handful of philosophers like Kant and Plato are integral to the hope of happiness. However, I had to go further. I asked myself whether a thoroughgoing ontology, radical in its originality and therefore distinct from Western thought, cannot be explicated on the foundation of a new conception of human emotion that seeks reconciliation with the scheme of universal existence for us to have what we may call 'nature' in the truest sense of the word. I set about interrogating the great Western philosophers, from Democritus to Derrida. I compared their basic submissions with what the great African philosophers had to say about God, nature, the human person, and those conceptual schemes developed by human beings in their effort to structure a seemingly chaotic universe. L.S. Senghor, Kwasi Wiredu, Innocent Asouzu, and Jonathan Okeke Chimakonam particularly gave me cause for profound reflection on the achievements of the Western philosophical mind and the promise of the African mind. The product of this reflection is the work under consideration, *Existence and Consolation: Reinventing Ontology, Gnosis and Values in African Philosophy*.

My system, appropriately dubbed *consolation philosophy*, is not an existentialist system *per se*, in spite of the solid reference to concrete human conditions in this book. It should rather be seen as a work of African rationalism. If I have referred frequently to concrete human situations it is because I do not desire a system that loses itself in meaningless abstraction, a system that turns out to be a mere logic-chopping exercise. We are in an age of great economic, social, and political turmoil. With the continued threat to world peace posed by humanity's seeming inability to learn from past mistakes, with the political and economic turmoil ravaging the early 21st century and the heightened emotionality of the 21st century human who insists on having a say in how they are ruled, a new phenomenon has made its appearance: the phenomenon of the *melancholy being*. The *melancholy being* is the techno-emotive human. Just as this being is fascinated with machine, so does it dread the negative potentialities of the machine which it creates. The *melancholy being* rejoices in the glory of making the nuclear bomb, for instance, but also suffers from the anxiety that comes with the knowledge of the destructive capability of the nuclear bomb.

The task before me was at once simple and complex. Having recognized the *melancholy being*, it was important for me to construct a thought system that is not only genuinely African but one that adequately mirrors the mood of the century. Consolation philosophy had to be a doctrine of the century. In my struggle to explicate such concepts as nature, God, freedom, optimism, pessimism, determinism, fatalism, joy, sadness, etc, I came to the conclusion that panpsychism of one type or the other cannot be avoided by philosophy, science, and religion. Consequently, I linked the mind of the human person with the mind of the universe, declaring the impossibility of the elimination of the idea of God from the human mind. As many great thinkers had noted before me, if God did not exist man and woman would create Him.

This work is by no means perfect. The bulk of whatever shortcomings one may find in this book is due to the fact that I worked in an environment profoundly hostile to the ambitious intellectual goal I had set for myself. Of course, there will always be future editions to take care of these shortcomings. I must profusely thank Dr Jonathan O. Chimakonam the general editor for his insistence on finding an international audience for this book. He went through my manuscript and recommended corrections, additions, and subtractions. Without him the project of *consolation philosophy* would have suffered severe setback. My gratitude goes to my Ghanaian friend Jude Edze Davids for graciously agreeing to read a third of the manuscript of *Existence and Consolation* and offering useful suggestions. I also thank Professor Gerard Walmsley Vice President/Head of Philosophy, St. Augustine College of South Africa whose thorough review of the manuscript has been especially insightful. I pay homage to my teachers at the University of Nigeria, Nsukka, Prof. J.O. Eneh and Dr F.O.C. Njoku whose commitment to African philosophy renewed my belief that African philosophy must be the central focus of philosophical thought in Africa. I pay tribute to my friend the late Jud Evans who had looked forward to the day my book would be published but sadly did not live to see his dream come true. To my father Aba Agada I owe much gratitude. His great passion for education instilled in me the love of learning. I thank my brothers Akogwu Agada and Idoko Agada for their inexhaustible faith in me. I wish to acknowledge all the authors, living and dead, whose works I cited to buttress my theses. Finally, I thank the editorial staff of my Nigerian publishers 3rd Logic Option Publishing especially Goodness Mbonu for his warm assistance and the editors of Paragon House especially Dr. Gordon L. Anderson for going through my work with a fine-tooth comb.

Ada Agada
Otukpo, Nigeria
Janaury 2014

General Introduction to the African Synthesis and the Plan of *Existence and Consolation*

Background of Our Research

What is African philosophy?

In the centuries of the dominance of Greek thought through the Greco-Roman and Christian periods and on to the rise of European philosophy, with the surpassing of Greek philosophical genius by the European philosophical genius, the question we have just submitted was still in the womb of time. The Greek, Greco-Roman, and European centuries (with the Egyptian past downgraded in its philosophical worth or conveniently forgotten) knew and heard of Africa only as a dark continent. Again we submit the question: what is African philosophy? The question rang weakly in the German philosophical world in the time of Christian Wolff and before the ascendancy of Immanuel Kant, when a Ghanaian called Antony William Amo completed a dissertation on René Descartes and invited history to remember the lonely black thinker in Europe with the immortal statement: "These words Antony William Amo, an African, Master and University Lecturer in Philosophy and the Liberal Arts, has set down in everlasting memory of himself."[1] Amo sought to justify himself as a human and a philosopher, and in justifying himself he had to go outside the Western tradition. He had to find his inspiration in Africa.

What is African philosophy?

An answer had to be found, which would, in the process of clarifying itself, also clarify who an African was. The question was first asked by those who had the right to ask it. It was first mooted by black Africans like Nnamdi Azikiwe, J. B. Danquah, and Kwame Nkrumah. But these nationalists and statesmen lacked the intellectual and intuitive capacity of genuine philosophers. Thus they understood philosophy basically as political ideology. Hence, all the fuss about Marxism and African socialism. L.S. Senghor went farther than his fellow political activists and freedom fighters in search of the solution to the question we have just submitted. Négritude conceived and incubated but never hatched an original African epistemology. The trajectory of originality négritude blazed was never completed. It was terminated by ideological commitment. And so the world lost the opportunity of being in possession of the most original system of philosophy ever to come out of Black Africa (since philosophers like St. Augustine, Origen, and other Western greats of African origin must be excluded from the list of black African philosophers, their inspiration being essentially a Western inspiration).

After the freedom fighters turned their backs on philosophy with the collapse of bare-faced colonialism and became intoxicated with political power, the real technically competent philosophers emerged, creeping out of European and American universities and finding their way back home to Africa to mastermind the official outing of the tradition now known as African philosophy. Placide Tempels' *Bantu Philosophy* was already being widely read and debated. The returnee African philosophers like Kwasi Wiredu, J.O. Sodipo, H.O. Oruka, Paulin Hountondji, Kwame Gyekye, John Mbiti, Alexis Kagame, C.A. Diop, Moses Makinde, I.C. Onyewuenyi, to mention but a few, shrewdly realized that for them to be worthy of the title "philosophers" they must bring something new to world philosophy. It was not going to be enough for them to be called scholars of Western philosophy. They were human beings all right, but the qualification for their humanity was their membership of the African race. The attainment of transcendence which is called universality would only be realized by the transformation of the African particular through sublime thinking into a transcendent mode everywhere recognizable as a creation and achievement of the human spirit. These illustrious thinkers, to whom we cannot get tired of paying homage, insisted that there could be no universal without the particular. African philosophy must remain distinct from Western philosophy. There was no running away from this insistence that they must make an original contribution to world philosophical knowledge. With this realization came the urgency of answering the question: "What is African philosophy?" In their wisdom these pioneer thinkers dispersed and went to their villages to investigate the worldviews of their various tribes and subject their languages to philosophical analysis in the hope of distilling a true system of philosophy, which distillation, though counting as philosophy of a coherent kind, will not amount to an individual's system. This move which *ab initio* ruled out robust individualism is understandable because there was no African Plato or an African Immanuel Kant, Edmund Husserl, Jean-Paul Sartre,

Jacques Derrida, etc, to project the independence of the black intellect in a way that would leave the world nodding its head in admiration.

The school of African philosophy called ethno-philosophy necessarily became the foundation of African philosophy, marking the first victory for African philosophical thought. Ethno-philosophy did not emerge as the originality of the individual mind, but it did establish itself as the originality of the collective mind, the tribal or ethnic consciousness, a limitless reservoir of intellectual inspiration to inflame the minds of individual African thinkers for all time. Ethno-philosophy became for African philosophy what early and middle Greek philosophy was and still is for Western philosophy. Thus John Mbiti wrote *African Religions and Philosophy*. Moses Makinde wrote *African Philosophy, Culture and Traditional Medicine*. Segun Gbadegesin wrote *African Philosophy: Traditional Yoruba Philosophy and Contemporary African Realities*. Henry Odera Oruka wrote *Sage Philosophy and the Modern Debate on African Philosophy*. Emmanuel Edeh wrote *Towards an Igbo Metaphysics*. Martin Anshi wrote *Tiv Philosophy*. Etc. The list is lengthy, for almost all African philosophical thinkers sought to put their various ethnic groups on the map of world philosophy. The radical originality that would have liberated the individual thinker from the superficial egotism of the tribe was not available in the beginning. Indeed, this radical originality was never going to be available in the beginning. So ethno-philosophy emerged as the foundation of African philosophy. As it emerged it became a preparatory school for those thinkers who would go on to liberate themselves from the selfish and philosophically hollow demand of the tribe. As the foundation of African philosophy, providing the first content by which African philosophy is to be defined, ethno-philosophy recorded an immortal achievement, one that would not be diminished by the accusation of unanimism often leveled at ethno-philosophy.[2] The collectivization which Hountondji sees as the essence of ethno-philosophy—and this is obvious enough—became the most original trend in African philosophy since Senghor's négritude and before Innocent Asouzu's complementary reflection and now our own consolation philosophy. In spite of the loss of the individual initiative promised by négritude in the ethno-philosophical movement, a semblance of originality was won, an originality which Hountondji the "universalist" never attained with his critical perspective on ethno-philosophy.

Thus the question of who could be validly called an African philosopher began to lose its urgency and mystery. The African philosopher had effected his separation from the African scholar of Western philosophy. The African philosopher was no longer simply a black person, inhabiting Africa as an 'indigene' but one whose inspiration is African or whose inspiration at least traces itself to Africa. For this reason, non-Africans like Tempels, Marcel Griaule, Barry Hallen, Lucius Outlaw, and others were considered to have made contributions to African philosophy.

While it is true that the first noticeable achievement of African philosophy is the victory of ethno-philosophy, this achievement became ordinary with its devaluation by the tribe which was egotistical. African philosophers quickly forgot that ethno-philosophy (Wiredu sometimes uses the term "decolonization" to encompass the ethno-philosophical frenzy) was permitted to exist as the beginning, as the foundation, of African philosophy. It was never going to be the totality of African philosophy nor even its essence. Ethno-philosophy had to be a foundation only. Yet decades after the emergence of ethno-philosophy African philosophy was not making noticeable progress. The tradition was still equated with ethno-philosophy, the big scandal of African thought. Instead of African thinkers coming out to project their own voices, they were still comically speaking for their tribes. They betrayed their hero who had warned that:

> It is worth emphasizing, besides, that African philosophers in our time cannot live by decolonization alone but also by the direct interrogation of reality. What is truth, goodness, freedom, time, causality, justice? What is the origin of the universe, the meaning of life, the destiny of the human soul (whatever it is)? What are the principles of correct reasoning? What are the best ways of acquiring knowledge? ... We contemporary African philosophers have a duty to venture suggestions on these matters. In doing so we will, of course, have to take due account of our own heritage, as philosophers in other cultures routinely do.[3]

African philosophy stagnated so much that in a paper delivered at the 1998 conference of the World Council of Philosophy held in Boston, Makinde shocked African philosophers by urging the Western world to help stop the looming obliteration of African philosophy.[4] What does Makinde expect the West to do for African thought? Are Western philosophers now expected to bottle-feed African philosophers four decades after the official proclamation of African philosophy as a tradition distinct from Western and Eastern philosophies? Not satisfied with the outrageous technological dependence on the West, must we now import Western philosophical experts to do the thinking we are too lazy and uninspired to do ourselves? There certainly was a cause for lamentation, but Makinde's tearful appeal was directed at the wrong audience. The appeal that promises a solution to the dilemma of African philosophy must not be directed to Europe and America but to Africa itself, to the African mind, which, flattened by indolence and a spirit of anti-progress, was waiting for the white imagination to undertake the task of radical thinking sufficient to dignify African philosophy and continue the search for the answer to the monumental question: "What is African philosophy?"

While Makinde preferred to shock Africa and invite foreign experts (themselves ignorant of the problem they are being invited to solve), other African philosophers like Olufemi Taiwo put the blame for this stagnation of African philosophy on the doorstep of Hegel and a racist West bent on denying Africa the right to have a unique system of thought.[5] In the eloquent paper, "Exorcizing Hegel's Ghost: Africa's Challenge to Philosophy", Taiwo accuses the West of intellectual racism, of bracketing the African experience and giving the nod to a (Western) tradition Westerners have created and elevated to the status of the universal. Taiwo writes with pain: "The West, in constructing the universal, instead of truly embracing all that there is, or at least what of it can be so embraced, has merely puffed itself up and invited the rest of humanity, or the educated segment of it, to be complicit in this historical swindle."[6]

We refuse to dismiss Taiwo's grave accusation given the evil inherent in human nature which surely accounts for the possibility and reality of intellectual racism. But if we refuse to dismiss Taiwo's fears, we also refuse to accept his submission hook, line, and sinker, convinced that we African thinkers constitute the trouble with African philosophy. We have not dared to think with the kind of radicality that alone can earn the respect of the West whose approbation we desire since we lack an intellectual culture robust enough to provide this much desired approbation. For four decades we were content equating African philosophy with ethno-philosophy, a monumental error. Philosophers like Wiredu and Hountondji who saw with commendable acuity that ethno-philosophy could not be the essence of African philosophy did not, unfortunately, provide an alternative rich and radical enough to earn the universal acclaim we crave. In the African philosophical environment itself there are three types of thinkers, namely:

1. Scholars of Western philosophy.

2. Ethno-philosophers.

3. African philosophers.

We have presented our classification in an increasing order of eminence. The scholars of Western philosophy are the least eminent, being the least original, while the African philosophers are the most eminent, the most original, and the fewest. The ethno-philosophers are less eminent than the African philosophers and more eminent than the scholars of Western philosophy. Every serious African thinker in the field of philosophy is understandably a scholar of Western philosophy. Not all African philosophical thinkers are ethno-philosophers. Some, like Hountondji, have refused to be ethno-philosophers. We do not wish here to specifically argue who has qualified to be called an African philosopher in the strict sense that we now define an African philosopher (that is, a thinker whose inspiration is African but whose mind is universal and whose imagination is radical enough to capture the attention of a creativity-starved world).

Afrocentric thinkers like Diop have sought to appropriate the achievements of ancient Egyptian thought and science for Africa and demonstrate the ancient superiority of Africa over Europe. The issue of where ancient Egypt belongs, whether Black Africans can lay claim to the Egyptian heritage, is far from being settled. However, we will not delve into the barren arguments this issue has generated. Let us suppose that there was some sort of racial solidarity between ancient Egypt and Black Africa. If we go by this supposition we are struck by the similarity of the outcome of early philosophical commitment in both ancient Egypt and modern Black Africa. As was the case with Egypt, ethno-philosophy could not pass into philosophy in Black Africa. The pregnant Egyptian philosophical concept of *maat* was stifled by the complacence of the Egyptian mind which was content mythologizing the Egyptian imagination instead of radicalizing it. The failure of the cultural concept of *maat* to transform into a philosophical concept has its contemporary African analogy in the failure of the cultural concept of négritude to metamorphose into a full-blown philosophy in the hands of Senghor and other ethno-philosophers, at least until the coming of Asouzu who is, perhaps, the first African philosopher to liberate himself from the tiresome and often negative tutelage of the tribe.[7] The *maat* concept quarantined an original philosophical inspiration (ethno-philosophy) but failed to liberate the idea hidden in this inspiration as African philosophy. The same fate befell négritude. The inspiration connecting the concept of *maat* with négritude, the struggle to liberate a universal idea that traces its roots to the African experience of life, flowed into Asouzu's concept of complementary reflection. What makes Asouzu unique among modern African philosophers is that he has not only moved away from ethno-philosophy in search of the radical concept but has also sought to highlight his system as universally applicable, having acknowledged that the rage of thinkers like Taiwo, who threaten to unleash an African challenge to philosophy but settle back in their armchairs to theorize about tribal worldviews, is pure hypocrisy.[8]

Yet the radical promise of complementary reflection has not been fully realized by its main apostle. We dare say that it cannot be realized in a more complete form by Asouzu because this completion is, in the first place, not in the agenda of Asouzu. To complete the African concept a radical constructive philosophy must be conjured out of ethno-philosophy, as an extension of ethno-philosophy, yet independent ontologically of the ethno-philosophical context to which it refers for its inspiration. Therefore complementary reflection remains essentially a methodology, a prolegomena, in a broader African philosophical tradition in dire need of a synthesis, the synthesis that eluded the ancient Egyptian doctrine of *maat* and the modern idea of négritude. In our time complementary reflection has unveiled the concept that eluded the doctrines of *maat* and négritude. However, this unveiling by complementary reflection is, in fact, nothing more than the *liberation* of the concept that eluded the ancient Egyptians and Senghor. The *maat* doctrine and the idea of négritude indicated the possibility of the emergence of a distinctly African philosophical system that will owe no allegiance to Greece while embracing the whole of humanity. Complementary reflection realized this possibility and understood plurality as missing links of a reality that is itself the joy of all being. In this concept our philosophical fatalism has been foreshadowed. Not having been programmed to be a constructive system, complementary reflection has stagnated as a method of thinking within the African philosophical tradition instead of going further to constitute a body of constructive or synthetic knowledge at a time the African philosophical environment yearns for a synthesis.

If complementary reflection has liberated the long imprisoned African concept but has not quite succeeded in elevating this concept to the status of a synthesis, it has at least paved the way for the emergence of consolation philosophy which we believe can become Africa's first constructive philosophy, owing no allegiance to Greece but acknowledging solidarity with the world. In the celebrated work *The Invention of Africa: Gnosis, Philosophy, and the Order of Knowledge*, the historian of African ideas V.Y. Mudimbe asserts trenchantly that Africa's cultural and intellectual productions constitute a mere reaction to the Western intellectual imagination, that the post-colonial African knowledge-universe is severely deficient in originality. Consequently, he sees the West as the alien Other and Africa the entity in search of self-invention.[9] Scholars like D.A. Masolo and Hallen have rightly noted that while Mudimbe has brilliantly analyzed the African situation vis-à-vis authenticity, he has, nevertheless, failed to provide what I am going to call constructive alternative programs to the inherited and foreign Western episteme.[10] One of my aims in writing this book is to fill the gaping hole that Mudimbe's incisive criticism exposed at the heart of African philosophy and African thought in general without shying away from the insistence on the solidarity of the African mind and the Western mind by virtue of their shared participation in the great project of humanity. For Black humanity and white humanity are abstracted from one and the same phenomenon: the appearance of the *melancholy being*—man and woman—in the world, for whom anxiety signposts the fundamental emotionality that roots all rationality for the enlightenment of the human intellect that cheekily appropriates reason to itself.

Stating the Problem of Our Research

The African intellect stands indicted in the field of philosophy for failing to win for African philosophy international acclaim, for choosing to allow African philosophical thought to stagnate as ethno-philosophy—the very attitude that denied ancient Egyptian thinkers the honor of becoming philosophers after conceiving what we may call the *mythopoeic* dream of existence and admirably hatching the sublime concept of *maat*. While we have noted the great contributions of the ethno-philosophers, the inspirational Senghor and the compelling Asouzu, we have also shown why it is necessary for our consolation philosophy to emerge and build a new intellectual edifice on past achievements that the indictment of the African intellect may be lifted. Consolation philosophy desires to be Africa's most direct and eloquent challenge to philosophy.

As an essentially metaphysical system, albeit one that owes allegiance to the African experience of life, consolation philosophy seeks to come to grips with the main practical and theoretical questions that have troubled the Western philosophical mind since Thales of Miletus. We are going to be concerned with such questions as the concrete conditions of temporal existence and the justification of this existence with recourse to the phenomenon of the spirit in its desperate search for answers to the questions whether existence (and human existence in particular) was in the first place avoidable and what form fatalism should take in the face of the necessity of existence—for existence considered from whichever theoretical angle must be a necessity, since eternity itself is inevitability. Our concern will range over the question of the external world and its relation to mind and humanity as a whole, the notions of power, illusion, and reality. We will get down to work and try to find a solution to the problem of evil in the world and the connection with the structure of consciousness. We will need to show that morality belongs fundamentally to metaphysics and consequently proclaim its objectivity on grounds derived from our African inspiration. Thus, consolation philosophy is a monistic system set to reconstruct a theoretical universe on a model different from the Western model while at the same time remaining in solidarity with the Western model. Our task will be supported by our theory of reason which has evolved from Senghor's failed attempt to project an original African epistemology to support an ontology whose articulation he was not equal to.

Presented first as a practical doctrine of being, consolation philosophy goes on to seek metaphysical support in the realization that what remains is not the proof of our existence or the proof of the existence of other minds (incidentally a big problem in Western philosophy) but the justification of this being existence and the interpretation of fatalism through his understanding of *amor fati*, the love of fate. It is this inescapability of this justificatory exercise that draws consolation philosophy into engaging the metaphysical questions of time, God, the world, freedom, etc. Consolation philosophy is compelled to leave the arena of bare existentialism and become a rationalist enquiry. As a non-absolutizing monistic system, consolation philosophy does not pretend to escape probability to which all human sciences must be subject given the wishfulness of the human mind that denies it an adequate objectivity, a wishfulness which, ironically, lays bare the limitation of nature itself, the world outside the mind. We dare to submit the following problems and questions thrown up by our research:

1. Can data from the researches of physicists be interpreted philosophically as suggesting the directionality rather than pointlessness of mechanism?

2. The directionality of mechanism, however, opposes a simple view of teleology by questioning the claim of mind or intelligence to priority over matter.

3. For every effect there is a cause; but can this rule dissolve under the microscope of analysis into chaos and finally *nothing* or can it reveal the reign of intelligence, supreme at a point beyond the penetration of the human intellect?

4. The foregoing scenario constitutes the human world and its existential conditions. Emerging from its successful appeal in the court of African ethnophilosophy, our consolation philosophy responds to the mechanism-teleology opposition by positing the yearning character of reality, and this character as the very nature of bare mechanicism and the boldest teleology.

5. This reality is defined as *yearning*.

6. Yearning realizes itself without ever attaining perfection. This means that beauty and terror as elements of the good and evil constitute *yearning*.

7. If we present the metaphysics of terror as the triumph of pessimism in the world, how can our dialectic of *mood* ever terminate in a morality of consolation as the basis initially and the reality ultimately of optimism?

8. Is it beyond dispute that all meanings of human existence compound themselves in the phenomena of joy and sadness?

9. If we stand our ground that human existence is nothing more than the unity of joy and sadness, how can this notion be grounded outside human subjectivity, precisely in the so-called inanimate world, without our being criticized for indulging in extreme anthropomorphism?

10. Arising from (9) above, if joy and sadness constitute the meaning of human existence, how is this primordial joy and this primordial sadness the constitution of the human mood and how can this primitivity be projected into the objective universe as the mood of eternity?

11. Is there a human path that cuts through anxiety to a transcendent Being we may call God?

12. What is the relation between the primitive mind as the constituting principle of the universe, God as this principle and as a personal principle of the universe, and, on the other hand, an eternally existing universe?

13. How can our monistic system account for the reality of evil in the world without pretending as monistic systems in the Western tradition (notably Benedict Spinoza's infinite causal system) do, that the appearance and stubborn reality of evil in the world is no tragedy at all but is simply a necessary part of the furniture of the universe?

14. What consolation can there be for us if the *illusion* we call freedom is taken away from us?

15. How do we justify consolation philosophy as African philosophy?

16. How does our 21st century African synthesis stand in relation to Western and Oriental philosophies?

Scope and General Plan of Our Research

This work intends to achieve a comprehensive or, at least, an adequate systematization and elucidation of the metaphysics of terror, a philosophical vision of the doctrine of consolation, which asserts that the goal of consciousness as it lifts itself from an unconsciousness directed by primitive intelligence, is not the attainment of happiness but the fulfillment of consolation or the deepening of human joy and sadness as these two elements cut a path through anxiety to the concept of a transcendent Being.

The philosophical project of *Existence and Consolation: Reinventing Ontology, Gnosis and Values in African Philosophy* is expected to terminate in an original work that looks back to ethno-philosophy or the worldviews of the African tribe for its inspiration, thereby casting itself in the shape of a work in African rationalism, in the unfolding of the consolationist vision of humanity and the universe. Our research methodology follows the existentialist, analytical, critical, synthetic, hermeneutic, and evaluative patterns. A relatively intensive analysis of literature in African philosophy and the Western and Eastern traditions is inevitable in a work like *Existence and Consolation*. The first part of the project will focus critically on the works and contributions of African philosophical thinkers. This work claims to be an expression of African philosophy, after all, in the strictest sense of the term which we have already contrasted with ethno-philosophy and Western philosophy (still the dominant philosophy in Africa). Our critical attention to the giants and masters of African philosophical thought such as the nearly forgotten Ethiopian philosopher Zera Yaqub, L.S. Senghor, Kwasi Wiredu, Kwame Gyekye, Segun Gbadegesin, Kwame Anthony Appiah, Joseph Achike Agbakoba, Francis Njoku, Innocent Asouzu, Jonathan Chimakonam Okeke, etc, will reveal that, though highly original, consolation philosophy is not the eccentric idea of an unknown Nigerian thinker. Truly, our criticism, analysis, evaluation, and interpretation of the works of the old masters will reveal the emergence of consolation philosophy as an important stop—by no means the ultimate terminus—on the road of African philosophy, as integral to the evolution of African thought.

Consolation philosophy is the culmination of loose developments and outgrowths in African philosophical thought, from the mythologizing age of ancient Egypt and the era of Senghor to the rationalism of Asouzu. The concept was always waiting to be liberated from the jealous custody of the African community of sages and find rehabilitation in an individual's mind. Senghor could not liberate this concept, which, as concept, must become universal and therefore be qualified to claim the paternity of African philosophy. Unlike Senghor, the academic ethno-philosophers never really bothered to attempt the liberation of the concept, as they were proud to be called tribal thinkers or intellectual champions of their various tribes. The scholars of Western philosophy like Paulin Hountondji who saw the ultimate futility of the ethno-philosophical enterprise did not help matters. They criticized the only outstanding philosophical landmark of their time with unjustified disdain but failed to throw Africa's challenge to world philosophy by pointing at the way forward. What these scholars of Western philosophy did was amuse themselves with foundationless analysis in addition to the pastime of lambasting ethno-philosophy. Mercifully, Asouzu emerged in the first decade of the 21st century to liberate the concept that tortured the mind of the magnificent Senghor, although Asouzu himself did not arrive with the long-awaited synthesis, the unity Senghor discovered. But Asouzu did liberate the African concept. He formulated Africa's first universal philosophical doctrine in his notion of "complementary reflection," for which reason we adopt him as the father of modern African philosophy ahead of the illustrious Kwasi Wiredu.

Our research also borrows from the existentialist and rationalist methods. The word existentialism easily evokes the important achievements of European masters like Kierkegaard, Unamuno, Heidegger, and Sartre. Perhaps we owe a debt to these philosophers. Yet borrowing does not paint a true picture. Ultimately, there is only a universal philosophy, not tribal or racial philosophies. Our research makes use of the existentialist method to unfold consolation philosophy not because we admire the Western existentialists but because we are in solidarity with them as philosophers who clearly saw the precarious perch of human beings in the world and came to grips with the human condition using the instrument of philosophy. We discovered that the questions which agitated the Western existentialists also torment us, and we were pleased to note the oneness of a humanity that must forever seek the justification of its existence. However, we make a bold claim to originality for the reason that our philosophy of life was incubated and hatched in the womb of Africa. In other words, our metaphysics is supported by a theory of reason that owes no allegiance to ancient Greece. Our theory of reason which is the final universalization of Senghor's much misunderstood notion of black emotionality and white rationality has empowered our 21st century African existentialism, such that its resemblance to 20th century Western existentialism is a resemblance of form, not of content. Thus while Heidegger conceives anxiety as the ontic phenomenon of Dasein that brings this being face to face with nothingness (in part the loss of being through death), while the less metaphysical but by no means less obscure Sartre considers anxiety or anguish in a cavalier way to indicate our unlimited and ultimately meaningless freedom, while the analysis of human anxiety by these masters of Western existentialism leads them to agnosticism and atheism, the analysis of anxiety in consolation philosophy will lead us to a horizontal and vertical (ontological and metaphysical) justification of the existence of God.[11]

The hermeneutic method comes in handy to link the core doctrines of consolation philosophy with earlier theories as we try to demonstrate that African philosophy is ultimately an unbroken unity. We have already submitted the claim of having completed (as far as completion can go) the African philosophical unity Senghor discovered. Our interpretation of Senghor's négritude in a more philosophical perspective will provide the thread linking consolation philosophy to négritude through Asouzu's complementary reflection. From the Anglo-American analytic tradition we have borrowed the passion for clarity. We are addressing the century and we see no need to indulge in any Heideggerian obscurantism.

Consequently, the first part of this work will be devoted entirely to the justification of consolation philosophy as African philosophy. It is absolutely necessary for us to show beyond the thinnest doubt that consolation philosophy is not a development of Western philosophy. There is no need to defend the work against any possible ethno-philosophical charge since the work will speak for itself as a rationalist research. In spite of our confidence in the African authenticity of our long-awaited work, which will support our right to be called African philosophers, we still deem it necessary to show the African origin of the inspiration that launched this project. The entire work itself will be divided into four parts. Part One will serve introductory and justificatory purposes. Part Two which presents the doctrine of God and nature will support some of the core arguments of Part One with constructive thinking. This second part, together with the third part, will constitute the bulk of *Existence and Consolation*, as it will determine our claim to originality and confirm our right to be called African philosophers in the strict sense of this revered title. Part Three will present the doctrine of humanity and discuss such issues as one's relationship with fellow humans, with God, and with nature. In an inverted mimicry of Part One, the fourth and final part of our project will seek to justify consolation philosophy as a universal philosophy, as philosophy beyond African philosophy, to borrow Asouzu's famous phrase. This last part will compare and contrast some of the leading ideas in Western philosophy and Oriental philosophies with the core doctrines of consolation philosophy.

PART ONE

CONSOLATION PHILOSOPHY AS AFRICAN PHILOSOPHY

Chapter 1

INTRODUCTION TO CONSOLATION PHILOSOPHY

A Brief Reconsideration of the Old Debate on the Existence of African Philosophy

With Hegel putting the possibility of African philosophy into question, the responsibility of proving him awfully mistaken fell on African thinkers. Before Hegel became the lion of German philosophy an African called Antony William Amo—precisely a Ghanaian—had proved that Africans could think philosophically, and radically so, by winning the respect of the German scholars of his generation.[1] But then Amo was a scholar of Western philosophy, not an African philosopher in the strict and truest sense of that famous and revered appellation. It was a European, Placide Tempels, who had the first real shot at producing a work that could come close to being put in the category of "African Philosophy." His much debated work *Bantu Philosophy* alerted the world to the possibility, nay, reality, of African philosophy. The excitement the book created, however, was an exaggeration because it seemed to be making a big deal of something that should have been taken for granted: the fact that as long as a people exist and share in humanity they will produce philosophers. For they will have to justify their existence. A race that cannot justify its existence or does not seek to justify its existence in the face of the mighty question of why there is being instead of *nothing*, or, in our consolationist perspective, the question of human joy and sadness—such a race has no share in humanity. The question remains for the blacks as it remains for whites and the yellow people. This is the question so admirably put by Martin Heidegger against the background of his Greco-German inspiration: "Why is there anything at all, rather than nothing?"[2]

African philosophy can win universal respect only when its champions have labored sufficiently to answer this question. Why is there something instead of nothing? Tempels merely scratched the surface of the philosophical problem on behalf of the Bantu people and, alas, from a European perspective. While Tempels can be lauded for making an important contribution to African philosophy by showing obliquely the response of an African tribe to the fundamental question of philosophy, the mother of all problems, it must be pointed out that this contribution is far from sufficient. It is not on account of Tempels' identification of being with force in the African universe that we say his advance is an insufficient advance (after all quantum physics tends to show that phenomenal reality is essentially force or an interplay of force-fields) but rather because his inspiration is a European inspiration that stagnated at the level of ethno-philosophy.[3]

Tempels' work ushered in the long but not very fruitful debate over what African philosophy is and who can be called an African philosopher. It is as if these debaters, derided by M.A. Makinde as cynical intellectuals without faith in the promise of the African mind,[4] forgot that African philosophy will have to fight to earn its right to be called what it presumes itself to be. In *Primitive Mentality* Lucien Levy-Bruhl had ignorantly declared that the African was incapable of using concepts,[5] instead of admitting that the African had not immersed himself fully in intellectual activities at the time colonialism overtook him. African scholars soon launched into the debate on the African's intellectual competence with the enthusiasm of inexperienced recruits marching happily to their first war. D.A. Masolo notes with admirable insight that, "At the centre of this debate is the concept of reason, a value which is believed to stand as the great divide between the civilized and the uncivilized, the logical and the mystical."[6] For the debaters to successfully counter the foul moves of the European bigots they would have to formulate a theory of reason original enough to launch African metaphysics, from which metaphysics a praxis can be conveniently deduced. It was a testimony to the rich promise of the future that such a theory was almost found. It was found or almost found not by returnee Western-trained scholars bragging about their first-class degrees and research honors received in Western universities but by a poet-politician, the inimitable L.S. Senghor. Senghor stumbled upon his supreme epistemological theory, the famous notion of black emotionality and white rationality, but could not universalize it. If he had theoretically demonstrated that emotionality and rationality were two sides of the same coin and therefore intimate with the structure of the human mind (neither the one for blacks nor the other for whites) he would have finally had the last laugh on Hegel to the satisfaction of the black anti-Hegel indignation that still resounds today and the bewilderment of all white bigots. If Senghor had won this victory for Africa he would have become the father not of Senegalese politics but of African philosophy. Failing this, Senghor remained a promise waiting to be remembered by the future. Happily, we think that consolation philosophy has found the theory of reason that eluded Senghor. We think that we have found a key to the solution of the puzzle of African philosophy.

Since it is self-evident that African philosophy exists for the very reason that Africans exist, the debate over the existence of African philosophy had to lose its urgency and pass into the derivative debate over who can be rightly called an African philosopher. The derivative debate is tied to the question of the African identity. Who is an African? Being black should have been the decisive criterion of our Africanness. But then Africa is home to whites and Arabs who lay claim to the continent and have adopted it as their own, even as there are black people in North and South America who will have nothing to do with Black Africa. There is probably no single necessary and at the same time sufficient condition for being an African, as Njoku has noted.[7] Nevertheless, the question of who the African is may be resolved in favor of the black person first and then any other human being deeply involved or concerned with Africa and its affairs and who has adopted the continent as their father. This understanding of the identity of the African holds out much promise in our further comprehending the identity of the African philosopher. We have already seen that African philosophy is that philosophical tradition of a universal character seeking answers to the question, "Why is there something instead of nothing?" from a perspective inspired by the African experience. African philosophy can no longer be content with ethno-philosophy and the neo-ethno-philosophy of the Africana thinkers in the diaspora, especially African-American thinkers.

It is at once obvious that there is solidarity between African philosophy and Africana philosophy. The latter, according to Lucius T. Outlaw, is "meant to facilitate the organizing of past, present, and future philosophical articulations and practices by and in the interests of African-descended peoples."[8] Indeed, Africana philosophy claims such accomplished black thinkers as Wiredu, Gyekye, Appiah, Hountondji, and V.Y. Mudimbe in its fold. The Africa-inspired solidarity notwithstanding, we think Africana philosophy will always keep a psychological distance from African philosophy because of the divergence of the intimate experiences of the African in Africa, the African in the diaspora (or the migrant African), and the African-American who seems unable to shake off the psychological trauma of slavery, a very grave historical crime. Africana philosophy is still evolving; it has evolved enough for a discerning mind to guess that its black-consciousness obsession consigns it to the fate of ethno-philosophy, or a certain neo-ethno-philosophy, for a long time to come. This is a contradiction given that ethno-philosophical fixation has been the bane of African philosophy, stunting the latter's development and making a dwarf of it. The African experience and the African-American experience are not the same and not even the diaspora black Africans who have come to understand the race conflict in the West can completely bridge the two worlds.[9] It will seem, therefore, that African philosophy and Africana philosophy will develop along different paths, always maintaining a certain level of cooperation on account of the black-consciousness factor but developing apart all the same. Thus while African philosophy can legitimately claim Barry Hallen in view of the important contribution of Hallen to ethno-philosophy,[10] African philosophy cannot readily, in fact, should not, claim Outlaw, although both African philosophy and Africana philosophy can claim Hallen.

In the end the great debate produced two classes of African philosophical thinkers, namely, the ethno-philosophers and scholars of philosophy. Into the latter class we put the scholars of Western philosophy and the hermeneutic thinkers like Tsenay Serequeberhan and Marcien Towa. Into this second class too falls the renowned Ghanaian statesman and author of *Consciencism* Kwame Nkrumah. Nkrumah is not original enough to be grouped with the ethno-philosophers. He cannot be called an African philosopher for this very reason. His socialist convictions never really referred to Africa for inspiration, unlike the socialism of Julius Nyerere and the outstanding L.S. Senghor. Wiredu, who we must always approach with respect as a man who worked tirelessly in the service of African philosophy, is both an ethno-philosopher and an accomplished scholar of Western philosophy. He qualifies to be called an African philosopher in the strict sense of the appellation and could have beaten Asouzu to the title of "Father of Modern African Philosophy" if he had spoken less with the voice of his Akan ethnic group and more with his own voice.

Of the two classes mentioned above only the ethno-philosophers located the future trajectory of African philosophy (as distinct from African thought). We say this because applied philosophy, including the philosophy of culture, in the African context can only be validated by the prior existence of an African philosophy sustained by metaphysical, logical, and epistemological principles that are not Western in origin. Ethno-philosophy tried to constitute itself as this much desired African metaphysics and epistemology. It did succeed, but only partially. Ethno-philosophy succeeded by transforming into the foundation of African philosophy, much in the same manner that early Greek speculation became the foundation of Western philosophy. While it is true that Senghor belonged to the ethno-philosophical school, we hasten to point out that he is the most original of all the ethno-philosophers. In his voice humanity spoke to the world, not just the tribe. Humanity spoke to the world through Senghor who stumbled upon a unique epistemology, the doctrine of black emotionality and European rationality, for which J.O. Sodipo generously commends him, in spite of the universalization deficit.[11]

Lamenting the scientific and intellectual backwardness of Africa relative to Europe, Asia and North America, the brilliant African logician Jonathan Chimakonam Okeke finds fault with the educational system in Africa that ignores the element of cultural determinism in technological innovation. He writes with the passion of a man truly concerned about the bastardization of Africa by Africans. He notes that:

> A westernized approach to education cannot do an African any good beyond putting food on his table. Africa has through this method of education produced innumerable physicians and pharmacists who have not invented any new drug or diagnostic pattern, uncountable mechanical engineers who have not produced any automobile, many electronic and electrical engineers who have not invented any gadgets, many philosophers who have neither invented any idea nor solved any problem. Everything they teach in African schools to this day are ideas of Whiteman.[12]

While we must disagree with Chimakonam that cultural determinism is decisive in technological innovation—different cultural and racial groups all over the world have cracked the riddle of technology, the Iranians, the Japanese, the Chinese, Koreans, Indians, and the Latinos—we express admiration for him as an African thinker courageous enough to confess that Africa's current problems are mostly self-inflicted. Chimakonam is actually calling for initiative and originality in African scientific and intellectual circles. We have languished too long in a disastrous intellectual slumber, from which we are yet to fully rouse ourselves, even as the rest of the world has continued to kick us in the behind. Science, the enterprise of science, is a universal venture; being such it can be a success anywhere human beings dwell, among any race, regardless of their cultural beliefs and the level of external repression they have suffered at one time or the other.

Westernization is not a sufficient excuse for Africa's technological and intellectual backwardness. It is not primarily the fact that we are in awe of Western genius that we will not dare to beat virgin paths in our struggle with ourselves and with our environment. The trouble with Africa is simply intellectual laziness, that is, the effeminacy of the black mind that we recognize in its refusal to be original in the belief that the West and Asia will always be there to make the cars the African will ride in, to bottle-feed him, a mere dwarf rather than a baby, to grant him political asylum when his corrupt leadership style must have instigated violent political instability in his country. In the remarkable book *Bad Samaritans: The Myth of Free Trade and the Secret History of Capitalism*, Ha-Joon Chang has shown that the now wealthy nations of Europe and Asia did not incubate a strictly indigenous technological culture but raided each other's physical and intellectual territories to lift themselves to technological advancement, a complex process of technology "theft" that is ongoing in today's borderless computer age.

In the philosophical arena a similar situation persists. Western philosophy traces its birthplace to the glorious Greece of Thales, Democritus, Plato, and Aristotle. But it is as clear as daylight that Greek philosophy "stole" ideas from the ancient Egyptians, Phoenicians, Persians, etc. Indeed, Afrocentric thinkers like Cheikh Anta Diop have controversially insisted that ancient Egyptian thought was the original of Greek philosophy, the primitive archetype of the philosophical pride of the West.[13] The struggle of African philosophical thought is the aspiration towards originality initiated by the ethno-philosophical enterprise. The challenge before African philosophers is not a literal interpretation of Wiredu's decolonization cry—we have to "steal" ideas from Western philosophy in the same way that ancient Greek philosophers "stole" Egyptian mytho-philosophy and transformed it on Greek soil into an indisputably original and magnificent intellectual edifice of genius, again in the same way that South Korea "stole" Western technological secrets, including indulging in piracy, and became a technological giant—and the resulting search for a foundation already given. Ethno-philosophy is already this foundation, and it thrived, still thrives, as, in many ways, comparative philosophy. The ethno-philosophical project has "stolen" and will continue to "steal" ideas from Western philosophy. If it has been caught out and sneered at it is because it has not gone about its "adaptation" project with radicality, that is, with originality and absolute confidence—being essentially the analysis of tribal worldviews in the light of Western philosophy.

Yet the absence of radical originality does not equate the complete absence of originality. We will not tire to praise the ethno-philosophical enterprise for the level of originality it achieved that qualified it as the foundation of African philosophy. This originality is lacking in the hermeneutics of the Marxist thinkers and other scholarly investigators. Senghor and Nyerere not only borrowed ideas from Henri Bergson, Pierre Teilhard de Chardin, Jean-Paul Sartre, and Karl Marx but adapted borrowed ideas to the African experience to match the African inspiration. But what did we get when Kwame Nkrumah, anxious to be called a "revolutionary" Marxist, connected Marxism with Africa? We got scholarship without originality, second-rate plagiarism. Africa's challenge to philosophy is a return to the African experience (thanks to Wiredu's insight) supported by a consistent and unyielding aspiration towards originality at the individual level.

Preliminary Outline of Our Metaphysics of Terror and the Morality of Consolation

We call our system consolation philosophy because the metaphysics that underlies it is a metaphysics of terror while the morality that enlivens it is a morality of consolation. The vision of the universe is revealed as pessimistic. But the praxis of this vision is optimistic. In other words, consolation philosophy is a philosophy of fatalism. Our fatalism is not the uncritical fatalism that says fate reigns supreme and that human beings have no option but to receive it with passivity. Our fatalism is a philosophical fatalism. It follows from the recognition that mechanicism and teleology jostle with each other to explain the phenomenon of existence but fail apart from each other to give a satisfactory explanation of why something is. Fatalism then brings teleology and mechanicism together to give us an explanation which, though not wholly adequate and perhaps far from adequate, satisfies the yearning of a consciousness that may have its beginning in nature and is therefore nature, submitting a compelling argument for a kind of panpsychism endorsed by the possibility that teleology is only another term for mechanicism and vice versa.

This may not be a radically new suggestion, but our understanding of fatalism as inevitability simply, the *yearning of mood*, is certainly radical. It is an understanding supported by an epistemology that makes reason a feeling, merely the refinement of the emotion. The monistic whole called the universe we conceive as the totality of *mood*, the externally existing expression and work of an Intelligence which is also this work as its principle. Thus we say that the eternity of God translates to the eternity of the universe. Whence comes the terror of existence on which our metaphysics dwell? The terror of existence does not arise because existence is without any real purpose as bare mechanicism seems to lead us; the terror arises from the fact that the universe has a goal which is not the attainment of happiness for conscious beings and perfection for revealed nature but the realization of *consolation*. This consolation points at an impossible happiness that is nevertheless indicated by the yearning character of *mood*. Fatalism is this realization that consolation is enough for humanity, God, and the nature God renews. This is our 21st century doctrine of *mood*. If consolation is the goal of life and perfection is unattainable, then eternity is the totality of yearning. This is the terror and the vertical investigation of this terror is the metaphysics of terror.

Our philosophy will compel us, of course, to modify existing theories of existence, God, evil, freedom, etc. With regard to God we have overlooked the classical Western understanding of the Supreme Being as omnipotent, omniscient, and omnipresent and have favored a theory of God that regards Him as a Being of power and glory. We have been able to do this from a theistic perspective since we believe that a world without a God is logically impossible in a universe expressed as consolation. The doctrine of *mood* has enabled us to explain the phenomenon of evil as intimate with the universe, as the development of the pessimism or sadness component of *mood*. Freedom we have recognized as an illusion. Illusion for us is not delusion, not falseness. Illusion is the consolation for that which is impossible but which seems indicated by its very impossibility. When the consolationist says freedom is an illusion he is actually saying that *liberty* is the consolation granted us for the absence and impossibility of a freedom that equates happiness.

One may ask how moral responsibility is possible if there is no freedom. Morality is possible in the absence of freedom precisely because morality is objective, as we intend to demonstrate in the second and third parts of this work. Morality subsists in the human mind as well as in the external world as a development of the joy-principle that co-constitutes the mood of the universe from which the human mood arises. Evolution then is true, but this evolution is directional as consolatory and is therefore no valid grounds for atheism. Obviously, we do not accept the notion that society invents morality for the purpose of social progress, a social progress in the first place determined by the intensity of the joy and sadness of a given society.

But where is our starting point? The horizontal or everyday analysis of the human mood is our starting point. *Mood*, we have already seen, is the yearning of eternity. The human mood is a reflection of the mood of the universe. The human mood exhibits the complexities of the constituents of existence which once apprehended we call feelings, precisely joy and sadness. Whereas many a Western metaphysician goes back into his mind in search of "being" (a physical substance perhaps) that is everywhere revealed but is nowhere eternally substantial (as quantum physics has informed us), the consolationist thinker gropes for *mood* and finds it in the human mood even though he too cannot seize it with his hands and marvel at it. The horizontal analysis of the human mood yields the constituent elements of sadness and joy. Outside these elements comes the realization that there is absolutely no meaning to existence. All things matter to us only to the extent that they connect to this cosmic construction of sadness and joy. And if all things matter because they satisfy this condition, is it not likely that all things, living and non-living, are connected to consciousness, that what we call the inanimate is in fact disorganized consciousness still slumbering as the silence of *mood*? Is it not possible to reduce the physical appearance of a material object, for example a space rocket, to the formulae and calculations that go into its construction and direct its functioning and then to the person who thinks and works out the formulae, then to this person's concrete existence as a scientist or technologist seeking glory, then to the mood of joy in the absence of which the idea of glory loses its meaning to the scientist? This reduction is allowable. We see then that what is basic is the scientist's joy, not his space rocket. If he fails as a scientist he suffers sadness since glory will elude him. On the other hand, the space rocket can be resolved into the invisible atoms that constitute it, which are never at rest but move constantly in search of something we may assume to be consciousness, seeking the intelligent spark that will set it on its way to becoming human.

If evolution is plausible, and we do confess that it is plausible and possible, then we can project the aspiration of consciousness into the external world or the relatively unconscious world without the charge of anthropomorphism intimidating us. It is then possible to regard the unconscious as the silence of *mood*, the silence of the conscious whole. On this basis too we can argue for the existence of God as the principle of this eternal silence which in its moment of personality is the intelligence that animates the silence of its own eternity and releases it outside itself as mortal time-bound animation, that is, as a created thing.

Thus from the horizontal analysis of the human mood we are led further up to the vertical analysis of the mood of the world. The terror we encounter is the realization that if teleology points to intelligence as its guide mechanicism demands to know the origin of intelligence, asserting that intelligence follows the blind working of chance. Yet teleology points towards evolution. Evolution must be animated with intelligence, whether active or passive, as its starting point or its guide if it is ever to terminate in the kind of complexity that human existence is, and the revealed universe too. Bare mechanicism may after all be a fraud. Any conception of mechanicism that deviates from its bare fact becomes a mechanical theory of the universe obedient to the law of cause and effect and synchronizes with the idea of intelligence operative in the universe. An active intelligence must come either before or after this passive intelligence. If it is only this passive intelligence that endures we may equate nature with God and be permanently satisfied with pantheistic deism. Yet this active intelligence we talk about cannot be ruled out if evolution is to be believed. This active intelligence is a necessity preceding or succeeding the passive intelligence. The conclusion is that there is a God. He is either the age of the universe or is younger than the universe but is not older than the universe. He is either perfect or not perfect. But how can He be perfect if our theory has already ruled out perfection as the goal of the universe? How can we argue for a God who is not perfection (the classical Western idea of omnipotence, omniscience, and omnipresence cannot be defended by philosophy just as it cannot lead us to the idea of a personal God) but who is yet a Being of power and glory? We have discarded the Greek concept of God's perfection and substituted it with our notion of God's *consolation* which is an original African perspective and agrees with the Christian notion of God. Aristotle himself, whose teleology identifies form or reason as the goal of existence, admitted in his *Metaphysics* that the attainment of this form (perfection) is impossible for anything tainted with matter, consequent upon which he proclaimed the eternity of the world's existence. Only God is pure reason or form or perfection, but this God is an Unmoved Mover, a Being that creates and yet, paradoxically, does not create.[14] For us God is not the form of the universe *per se* but rather the consolation of the universe, not a self-contained Prime Mover.

We are unable to provide a purely existential account of humanity as Heidegger and Sartre did because the horizontal analysis shares borders with the vertical analysis. The simplest practice such as the tears of a lovelorn woman points us towards metaphysics with the most fundamental problem of philosophy, the question of God, taking the centre stage.

With terror evolving out of the structure or furniture of the universe, consciousness is left with nothing but resignation in its joy and sadness. This resignation is a simple faith in God as the consolation of the universe. It does not matter whether one is a believer or not. Fatalism asserts the impossibility of a God-less universe without yet succeeding in demonstrating conclusively why there has to be a God, leaving consolation philosophy open to probability. Part One of *Existence and Consolation* is introductory and justificatory. In this first part our preoccupation is showing that consolation philosophy is African philosophy, not Western scholarship and not ethno-philosophy, although ethno-philosophy is recognized and lauded as the ultimate source of our endeavor, providing the much needed inspiration following our turning away from Greek philosophical inspiration.

Existential Background of Consolation Philosophy

We earlier mentioned the tears of a lovelorn woman. Certainly, the microscopic examination of these tears will yield elements and atoms invisible to the naked eyes. In a similar way, minute analysis of the importance of these tears yields the element of grief. This grief is a deepening of a joy that must surely follow when grief exhausts itself. It is obvious that whatever practice we select as our starting point, this very practice will resolve itself under analysis to the two basic elements of joy and sadness, the elements of a theory of everything—fatalism. Humanity, our immediate focus, is thus left with terror and its compensatory or consolatory element, beauty. But what makes the metaphysics of terror and the morality of consolation so appropriate a philosophy for the 21st century? We will answer this question by referring to the real world lest someone accuses us of abstract idealism and sheer logic-chopping.

It is beyond doubt that at no time in the history of human society has technology so comprehensively proclaimed its triumph. At no time in human history, ironically, has emotion been as intense and victorious as in the 21st century, our contemporary and post-postmodern world. We use the unfamiliar term "post-postmodern" because the rise of emotionality in the 21st century clearly shows that the world is tired of the despair and the destructive enquiry of postmodernism, desiring instead consolation. It is an amazing thing to jump into a world characterized by the reign of technology side by side with the victory of the human emotion, both constructive and destructive (as in the rise of international terrorism). So pronounced is this development that we must describe our time as a techno-emotive age. To emphasize the technological aspect and overlook the emotive aspect just because of the success of technology, as in the case of the Mars Exploration Rover Mission and other scientific triumphs, is to make a grave mistake, for "rogue" nations and terrorists seeking technological secrets to unleash destruction on human beings are always nearby to remind success-intoxicated scientists that the earth itself is threatened by the irritable *mood* out of which leaps the phenomenon of evil. We have already reduced a spacecraft to its most basic level of existence, the silence of *mood*.

Continuing, we note that modern technological triumphs have been put to the service of *mood* in order that one's joy may be more deeply realized in a process that, alas, allows too much room for terror and the sadness terror engenders. We will provide as many instances as is required to show how technology has been a passive servant of emotion. Let us start with the field of philosophy. Impressed by the scientific triumph of the Enlightenment and the Industrial Revolution and the blow they seemed to have dealt the European's faith in God, Friedrich Nietzsche announced the death of God. The author of *Thus Spake Zarathustra* pioneered the postmodernist project of the highlighting of cynicism and the surrender to despair in the guise of a revaluation of all values to terminate in the rejection of all "grand narratives." The God-question as a philosophical, religious, and cultural proposition is of course a "grand narrative." While Christianity waned in the West to the satisfaction of the God-is-dead prophets, this stubborn "narrative" which is nothing more than a necessity of *mood*; this "narrative" was gathering speed and strength in a different ideological vehicle. This other "grand narrative" we are talking about is Islamic fundamentalism, a violent affirmation of faith which is today threatening to devour a Western world with no faith but the tenuous support of technology which is itself the slave of *mood*. With a stronger faith for support, Islamic fundamentalism is less prone to the mass hysteria, the anxiety, terror breeds in a highly technological and sophisticated age. As the West begins to realize that a faith is needed to successfully ward off a violent faith, the return of the "grand narrative" of a weakened Christianity, contemporary Western philosophers have lent their ears once again to the entreaties of religion. This is particularly true of analytic philosophers in Europe and America like Antony Flew, Peter van Inwagen, and Alvin Plantinga.[15]

The coming of motion pictures was welcomed and hailed as one more example of the resounding impact of technology on art. But which victory are we talking about? Is it the victory of technology over human passion? Clearly, it is human passion that has triumphed. The technology input in movie-making serves only to enhance the intensity of human emotion. In the area of human sexuality it is emotion that has trumped technology. For the mere sake of deepening or intensifying the human orgasm—a mere satisfying feeling of release that is expected to make for our joy—strange objects called toys such as vibrators and dildos have been developed. There is in fact a real possibility that robot wives will make their appearance in the future. As *mood* commands technology the latter is content to serve.

The biggest intellectual task for the compulsorily moral consciousness of human beings is the task of comprehending the phenomenon of evil, both moral and physical. Belief in God has been built and destroyed on the foundation of this comprehension. Humanity and nature have been overrated and at the same time devalued based on this comprehension. Evil proceeding straight from *mood* has had its fair share of the domination of technology. When Albert Einstein and his fellow physicists helped create the world's first atomic bomb it never occurred to these worthy intellects that the crudest terror would be frozen in history in Hiroshima and Nagasaki. It never occurred to them that an arms race had started in the name of national pride, for the mere massaging of the irritable human mood. People are both good and bad, it is said. The bad and the good are emotions. That they are emotions is the only reason for their existence. The good person today would remember the first outing of weapons of mass destruction in Japan and exclaim, "how terrible, how terrible!" The bad person in the shape of an Osama bin Laden would say, "good, very good; let us lay our hands on that Hiroshima bomb and I swear by Allah that the Great Satan will cease to exist on the surface of the earth!" Thus emotion laughs at technology. Science boasts that it is a rational enterprise, but emotion reminds science that the truth of emotionality is the supreme rationality of the universe. The African master Leopold Sedar Senghor was trying to formulate this very statement with his négritude doctrine of black emotionality and white rationality.

We are still on the issue of the subordination of technology to emotion and therefore the powers of good and evil. It must not be forgotten that the Nazi tested the potency of their technological creativity by determining how many Israelis they could kill in large numbers in an outburst of the terror now solemnized in history as the Holocaust. In the first, and now the second, decade of the 21st century, Iran the successor nation of the ancient Persian Empire has been accused of trying to acquire weapons of mass destruction for evil purposes, for the sake of national pride, and for deterrent purpose. Iran forgets that in seeking to utterly destroy another nation it will be destroying itself. Emotion in the service of evil (denounced as sheer terror) refuses to listen to the wisdom of emotion in the service of good, which we call rationality or reason. North Korea expends its resources on military technology and regularly tests the potency of its weapons of mass destruction while its dehumanized citizens starve.

In Africa dictatorship and dictatorial democracies have impoverished the continent, looting national treasuries and transferring stolen wealth to financial and tax havens in Europe for the benefit of Europeans. It is true that the problem of evil, the evidential problem of evil, is as old as homo sapiens. The point we have been trying to make is that technological progress has not altered the eternal order, the determined path of *mood*. Evil was, is, and will always be. The difference technological advance has made is to revolutionize the practice of evil. Unassisted by technology, there is still the pain mankind suffers from the assault of diseases, age, death, trauma, etc. In the midst of suffering one stands witness to terror. Yet how may it be that humans can be called a witness to *liberty*?

This brings us to the consolatory value of existence. Human beings are a witness to *liberty* (morality or the emotion of good) because of the undeniable beauty that continually challenges the terror of existence. For every Hitler there is a Mandela. For every North Korea there is a South Korea. There are nuclear bombs in the nuclear arsenals of nuclear-armed nations, products of technology; yet there are two rovers now on Planet Mars investigating the geological history of an alien planet in a positive victory for science and technology. Nature punishes with floods, earthquakes, hurricanes, etc, but it also blesses with rainfall, sunshine, etc. Existence throws up both terror and beauty. Our metaphysics of terror arises out of the practical examination of everyday terror. The morality of consolation is affirmative of the beauty of existence. The dialectic of *mood*, that is, consolation philosophy, with its existential root in everyday living seeks a place in world philosophy as a doctrine of the century.

Chapter 2

COUNTDOWN TO CONSOLATION PHILOSOPHY

On the Necessity of the Justification of Consolation Philosophy as Authentic African Philosophy

It is agreed that the only way an African can earn the appellation "philosopher" and then the revered title "African philosopher" is to make an original contribution to philosophy. Until this contribution is made, the African traversing the terrain of Western philosophy remains a scholar, the dignified term for an intellectual licensed to plagiarize. Until African thinkers discharge their intellectual debt to philosophy by making this original contribution, the world will not take African philosophy seriously and the Taiwos of Africa will continue to lament the fate of African philosophy when those who have worked very hard with racial and national pride (the West and the East) condescend to classify available works in African philosophy under the headings of Anthropology, Political Science, African Studies, and, most insulting of all, Folklore. Thus laments Taiwo:

> What is worse, even the limited presence in the form of libel that members of Hegel's generation represented in their writings has been expunged ... hence the peculiar absence. Africa is not overtly condemned as it was in Hegel's day; it is simply ignored or made to suffer the ultimate insult of having its being unacknowledged. One is right to wonder whether it is worse to be libeled than to be passed over in silence.[1]

Consider the righteous rage vibrating through the lines of the quotation above from Taiwo's very eloquent essay, "Exorcizing Hegel's Ghost: Africa's Challenge to Philosophy." Is it possible that Taiwo is unaware that African philosophy in the strict and most proper sense is just beginning to emerge in the aftermath of Innocent Asouzu's work? Is it possible that he is unaware that the late emergence is attributable to the inability or refusal of his generation to recognize ethno-philosophy as merely the foundation of African philosophy, not African philosophy itself, in the same way that early Greek philosophy cannot claim to be Western philosophy itself but rather the foundation and inspiration of Western philosophy? We ask these questions because, among the first generation thinkers, only Wiredu seems to have understood this problem. He warned that the postcolonial reconstructive project called decolonization (another term synonymous with ethno-philosophy) must not drag on forever.[2]

Obviously, there is a tendency for African intellectuals to be sucked into the race debates that dominate the writings of Black American writers, the black-consciousness phenomenon nurtured on the staple of the historical wrong of slavery which no act of penance could right, presumably. The romanticization of Africa by these African intellectuals who, in the first place, left Africa because of the harsh anti-intellectual African environment, avails little. There can be no doubt that racism is alive and kicking in Europe and America, but so is its African equivalent: ethnicity or tribalism. We cannot hold up our challenge to philosophy when we lack elevated racial pride and indulge in narrow tribal chauvinism. In fact, the phenomenon of racism in the West and ethnic chauvinism in Africa invites us to be sober and solemnly consider the fundamental philosophical question of evil as the most striking tendency of human nature, indicative of the ethical failure of humanity, which must ultimately be blamed on the failure of reality itself (not God, we think). The perpetual presentation of blackness as the victim of whiteness has lost its emotional entertainment value in the light of our insight into the metaphysics of terror. There is tragedy enough in the African predicament, no doubt, but there is a far greater tragedy in the existential predicament of humanity as a whole. Unlike ethno-philosophy which is particular, our consolation philosophy which seeks to become a universal philosophy can provide us with the moral tool that will enable us to transcend particular limitations and arrive at truly universal values in its commitment to an elevated concept of humanity on the grounds of the necessity of consolation. We speak of humanity, not just the African, the Westerner or the Easterner. While ethno-philosophy favors balkanization with its obvious obsession with the narrow ethnic group consolation philosophy seeks the reconciliation of group loyalty with the concerns of humanity without discarding particular values. Group loyalty which ethno-philosophy promotes all too easily leads to ethnic chauvinism, authoritarianism, and the resulting ethnic conflict that has been the curse of Africa. This tendency of group glorification arising from the absence of a deeper appreciation of universal values extends to the Western world where rival political parties, activist groups, and ideological societies contest claims and counter-claims.

A Brief Preparatory Analysis of the Egyptian Principle of *Maat* as Philosophically Contemporaneous with the *Ujamaa* and *Ubuntu* Communal Wisdom of the People of Black Africa

The philosophical aspect of *maat* reduces a way of thinking and acting to ethics, to the idea of justice, truth, balance or responsibility, and goodness, a human ideal in one's struggle through life. In its more metaphysical sense, *maat* provides insight into the eternity of the world in the notion of an eternally existing chaos out of which the orderly world emerged. In pointing ancient Egyptian mythology towards receptivity to the idea of immortality, the general concept of *maat* is recognized as a teleological vision of humanity in the cosmos. *Maat* grapples with the question of existence, why there should be something instead of nothing. It rules out the idea of nothing as a conceptual absurdity and lays the foundation of being on chaos. From this chaos a dialectical and evolutionary process directed by intelligence reveals the "something" of existence, the phenomenal reality. Since the question of the "nothing," whether theoretically absurd or not, must always threaten the revealed "something," the ancient Egyptians recognized a *metaphysics of terror*. By eliminating the necessity of the "nothing" and uniting metaphysics with ethics as a condition for living a life of general moral equilibrium with the sure reward in a life beyond death, the continuing elimination of the "nothing" through the progressive annihilation of its necessity, the ancient Egyptians found existential strength in a *morality of consolation*.

One intellectual poignancy of the ideal represented by *maat* is its closeness to the African space, its intellectual contemporaneity with the African moral wisdom of *ujamaa* and *ubuntu* (both express the same ethical ideal). "In truth, *Maat* is a way of life," Théophile Obenga confesses.[3] But so is *ubuntu* (and *ujamaa*) which captures African communal morality so well. *Ubuntu* is conceived both as a collective worldview of the tribe and an individual morality, thus qualifying itself as an African humanism.[4] The humanistic vision that strikes a balance between individualism and collectivism while recognizing the collectivist claim to eminence on the grounds of its providing for the continued existence of the race easily links *maat* to the *ubuntu* and the *ujamaa* concepts. The assertion of the eminence of the community and the moral equality of all men amounting to true humanism in *maat* wisdom and *ubuntu* socio-political philosophy is underlined by Julius Nyerere the apostle of *ujamaa* who insists on an African and universal brotherhood, the up-gathered humanity that we bring under the umbrella of the big family whose practice is *familyhood*.[5]

It is erroneous to classify Nyerere's *ujamaa* doctrine under socio-political philosophy and regard it chiefly as an ideology. It is less a socio-political philosophy and more a wisdom of life like its sister doctrines *maat* and *ubuntu*. Nyerere himself rejects any conception of *ujamaa* in the light of communism or "doctrinaire socialism."[6] While Nkrumah swallowed Western socialism hook, line, and sinker, Nyerere tried to adapt an African wisdom to contemporary social realities. He spoke glowingly about an African socialism, but the term "socialism" was almost superfluous for him. *Ujamaa* belongs to ethno-philosophy as much as the researches of the class of African thinkers called ethno-philosophers.

Now that we have related *maat* with *ujamaa* and *ubuntu* doctrines and shown them to be worldviews of the African people pregnant with the pure concept of philosophy, how do we link *maat* to our consolation philosophy? Is there any basis for a linkage? There certainly is. *Maat* as an African humanism is a nod to consolation philosophy or, better still, it indicates the possibility of an African philosophy that will not worship at the altar of Greek philosophical genius. *Maat* is the mytho-philosophical system that failed to transform into a universal philosophy, a transformation that was undoubtedly its goal. Following in the footsteps of Diop, Onyewuenyi employed textual analysis of the Pyramid Texts, the Book of the Dead, the Leiden Papyrus, etc, to be able to distil a coherent Egyptian philosophy.[7] A literal reading of these texts will not instantly reveal any serious philosophical merit. As mytho-philosophical texts they come under the heading of ethno-philosophy. They are pregnant with the invasive concept of *maat*. Now this concept of *maat* is a universal ideal aspiring towards universal philosophical formulation. The Egyptian mytho-philosophers, perhaps impressed by their advanced mathematics, believed they had arrived at true philosophy with the ingenious concept of *maat* and were content to sit on their laurels. In other words, the ancient Egyptians who were as gifted as the ancient Greeks equated mytho-philosophy with philosophy, in the same way that contemporary African thinkers like Taiwo and Makinde equated ethno-philosophy with philosophy and still went ahead to boldly demand the admiration of the philosophical world.

In his time Diop claimed to have identified similarities between the thought system of the ancient Egyptians and the structure of the Wolof language.[8] We are modest and see only a link between the *maat* concept and consolation philosophy in terms of aspiration. What the ancient failed to complete we wish to fulfil. Onyewuenyi writes: "*Maat* is the Egyptian concept of the principle which underlies and governs the interrelationship of antithetical pairs of opposites and brings about harmony, balance, and justice among aspects of existence which otherwise should be antagonistic, and makes them complementary in the mutual production of an effect."[9] The fundamental demand of *maat* is the demand for perfection from a universe which cannot be perfect. With this impossibility reality is revealed as the striving of a yearning spirit. This spirit is nature too. So all is yearning. From chaos the world leaps into order. How was this leap accomplished? *Maat* philosophy froze too early to give a non-mythical account of this leap. It is not that the exact cosmic picture of the beginning can ever be arrived at, but it would have amounted to an intellectual victory if Egyptian philosophy had gone ahead to provide us with a rich hypothesis of the leap from chaos into phenomenal reality or, at least, a fertile and original outline of the metaphysics and ethics *maat* promised.

Ethno-philosophy as the Foundation of Our Late and Early Synthesis

The Idoma Concept of Mind and the Consolationist Theory of Reason as a Peculiar Emotion

Paulin Hountondji, sometimes regarded as the inventor of the term "ethno-philosophy," has graciously acknowledged his debt to Kwame Nkrumah who mentioned in his autobiography his desire to pursue a doctorate in ethno-philosophy at the University of Pennsylvania.[10] We may be sure that the usage of the term predates Nkrumah. Whichever way we see the matter, it is beyond dispute that the term "ethno-philosophy aptly describes literatures that seek to distil a philosophical content from tribal worldviews. Ethno-philosophy is not exactly mytho-philosophy because the former is a conscious critical enterprise determined to squeeze out a coherent theory out of the theoretically incoherent, out of disorganized thinking. In this sub-section I will attempt to show how my understanding of the Idoma dualistic and semi-materialistic conception of the mind influenced my theory of reason even before I had come into contact with Senghor's crude but insightful epistemology and the writings of the ethno-philosophers on the African concept of mind. However, I will not dare to speak for the Idoma people of Central Nigeria to which I belong, knowing such a claim to be too presumptuous, and having marvelled myself at the boldness with which African scholars declared themselves philosophical spokesmen for tribal philosophies.

Now the Idoma distinguish between the mind and the soul. The mind's physical moment is biological and perishable. This mind or *otu* has two moments, the material or physical moment and the spiritual and timeless moment. Thus we encounter a semi-materialistic theory of mind. While the living phenomenon is temporally active, the spiritual moment of *otu* is not exactly the soul, or *o'do*. As soon as physical death occurs the capacities and powers of *otu's* physical moment disappear even as consciousness passes into the spiritual moment of *otu*. Now an independent entity, the spiritual moment of *otu* becomes the soul, that entity which embraces immortality. This interactionist and semi-materialistic conception of the mind seems to be the standard notion in the African traditional worldview. We have *otu* which is both physical and non-physical and *o'do* which is immaterial and immortal.

The heart certainly is a biological organ. It is capable of degeneration and perishes with the physical death of the organism. In popular, non-scientific, usage an analogy is drawn between the heart as the warehouse of the body's life-blood and the peculiar character of mental phenomena, that is, the non-locality and irreducibility of emotions and thoughts to a physical substratum. The Idoma response to this peculiarity is the formulation of the interactionist theory of mind independent of Western influences. The rejection of the bodily basis of the mind would be futile. To dismiss the non-physical dimension of the mind would be incredible. Therefore it is plausible to divide *otu* into moments or phases of thought, with the physical moment going with the brain and the non-physical moment going with what is traditionally called mind, which non-physical moment transforms into *o'do* at death. The heart analogy of *otu* is understandable. It is not the heart as an organ that is being directly referred to in social discourse but rather the emotional symbolism of the heart as the warehouse and distributor of the body's life-blood, as the sustainer of life. So, although *otu* may refer directly to the heart, the term actually covers thought and mental phenomena in general. Thus an Idoma man may describe a mean person as *ikp'otu*, the hard heart or the heart of stone. Thoughts and feelings co-habit in the same mental field. Logic and psycho-logic (thought bound to the emotional component of our vast material life) are not poles apart. They interact in *otu*. Logic is the light of thought cast in the shadow of thought. By this I mean that logic asserts its independence of psycho-logic only when it has successfully hidden psycho-logic within itself.

When a person becomes very excited the emotion (psycho-logic) hidden in reason (logic) restores its perpetual unity with reason. When emotion reunites with reason and morality is alive we have the phenomenon called rationality. When emotion leads reason in the absence of a strong morality we have the phenomenon called irrationality. The state of mind different from madness but which manifests itself in inhumane or cold behavior does not mean an absence of emotion or loss of reason; it means the active presence of emotion and reason but the absence of morality or its suspension. Logicians know this to be the case. Hence, they contrive esoteric symbols and formulae to escape the living warmth natural to the mind that *yearns*. But since logicians are human beings and not robots they must rejoice to have successfully transformed psycho-logic to logic. The more one translates the symbols of mathematics and advanced logic into ordinary language the bolder the hidden emotion becomes and the more frantically it seeks its natural state, the restoration of its unity with reason.

We have encountered at last the origin of Senghor's famous idea of the emotionality of blacks and the rationality of whites. We have found the key to the discovery of the philosophical synthesis that eluded Senghor, the synthesis which is arguably late for the world but indisputably early for Africa—our consolation philosophy. Senghor, an original mind, imagined he was providing a phenomenological description of the black person, not knowing that he was actually attempting to unveil the *melancholy being*—man and woman as Human. The masterstroke failed for Senghor, but we have discovered the link that eluded him, the link between white and black and other races.

I meditated long on the Idoma conception of the mind and the emotionality of *otu* and later hit on the emotion theory of reason upon which I constructed the metaphysics of terror and arrived at the morality of consolation. The given, the beginning and the end, is yearning. The mind is a point of this yearning. It is *mood*. Being essentially yearning the mind is comprehensively emotional. As *mood* the mind is a unity of sadness and joy, the basic elements of existence. Optimism and pessimism are epistemological correlates of joy and sadness. What we call the intellect which is accompanied by reason is the mind in its pessimistic phase. Being pessimistic, this phase is sluggish, skeptical, and so highly critical as to pursue existence into "nothingness." The second phase of the mind is the optimistic phase of greater spontaneity, the phase of joy and faith. I arrived at this theory without any reference to Greek philosophy. My inspiration is an entirely African inspiration. My intellectual encounter with Senghor was a confirmation of my early conviction. Later encounter with the ethno-philosophers, Asouzu and the African logician Chimakonam strengthened this conviction.

The Essential Agreement of the Different Formulations of the Mind-Body Problem in African Ethno-philosophy

Our brief analysis of the Idoma conception of the human mind (better still, my understanding of this conception) revealed the source of our theory of human reason and submitted a quasi-materialistic and interactionist theory of mind. To what extent does the Idoma collective mind (let us be excused this presumptuousness on the grounds of the basic commonality of worldviews) agree with the African collective mind?

The Akan understand human reality as composed of the *ōkra*, or soul, the *sumsum* or spirit or ego, and the *honam* or body. According to Gyekye the *ōkra* is the immaterial principle of life corresponding to the immortal soul in Western philosophy.[11] He is ever ready to grant the *ōkra* a pretemporal, eternal existence. The *sumsum* is the ego constituting the basis of personality and determining the character of a person. As the subject of experience it is immaterial.[12] Wiredu disagrees somewhat with Gyekye, insisting that the notion of *ōkra* enables the Akan to comprehend the phenomenon of life rather than thought. Gyekye seems to identify the soul with the mind as the unity of consciousness. This is all right. The original Wiredu seems to favor a semi-materialistic conception of the mind, what he calls quasi-physicalism.[13] This too is valid. The two Akan ethno-philosophers are not really in opposition, for their difference has been accounted for in the analysis of the Idoma conception of the mind that we have already presented. It is not only the human body that is material but also the physical moment of the human mind identified with the brain. The non-physical moment of *otu* is the principle of life, considered immortal. Its separation from the physical moment, that is, the human brain, means the death of the individual. Consciousness survives with the non-physical moment of the mind. When separation occurs the non-physical moment of the human mind becomes the *ōkra* as conceived by Gyekye. The physical moment corresponds with the *sumsum* rather than the *ōkra*. The *sumsum* is the physical moment of the human mind. We disagree with Gyekye that it is immaterial. Ultimately, Wiredu is right in arriving at a quasi-physicalist conception of the mind as understood by Africans. Gyekye's dualistic theory is also correct.

The notion of person in Yoruba traditional thought yields results similar to what we have just discovered. The *okan* which is the heart may also refer to the brain in Yoruba thought.[14] We are obliged to go beyond the direct organ reference and focus on the indirect mind reference. The mind's non-physical moment is either the *ori* or the *emi*. Both the *emi* and the *ori* are believed to be non-physical. This agrees well with our basic premise that the African conception of the mind is quasi-materialistic. M.W. Anshi in the paper "The Concept of the Person in Tiv Philosophy" identifies the *ishima* as the heart. We have already explained that the "heart" almost always indicates the brain when used in the mind-body discourse in African languages. The heart is indicated as the seat of thought and feelings rather than as the physical organ that pumps blood to all parts of the body. This heart is actually the mind in its physical moment, that is, the brain as a biological organ. Anshi's analysis is instructive given its near exact similarity with our submission on the Idoma concept of mind.

The *ishima*, though material, is linked to the immaterial and immortal *jijingi*. The *ishima* is the seat of the finer emotions like joy, love, and sympathy as well as the cruder emotions like hate, envy, and spite. To bring Anshi's thoughts in harmony with ours, we only need to identify the *ishima* with *otu* and the *jijingi* with *o'do*. When Anshi notes that the *jijingi* and the *ishima* interact and that the former actualizes its potency through the latter, he is in fact forwarding our basic proposition. The *ishima* or brain is the mind in its physical moment while the *jijingi* is the mind in its non-physical moment. The one is material and perishable while the other is immaterial and imperishable. The immortal component goes away with consciousness when the material component dissolves. How this can be proved is a philosophical dilemma. For we now encounter the fundamental question of immortality which has challenged the ingenuity of Western and Oriental philosophers. We will take a more critical look at this matter in the third part of this book.

Thus interactionism and quasi-physicalism are entrenched in the African worldview with regard to the mind-body problem. The notion of immortality cannot be dismissed since human reality defies the full explanatory power of undiluted materialism, or physicalism. If mortality has to come into being as a threat to consciousness it is not logically impossible or absurd to assert that immortality can realize itself in being or has already realized itself. If consciousness is destined to be with the independent human essence that interacts with the human brain to make the complete worldly person, then immortality is not an absurd notion after all. This is the submission of the African tribe. We have listened to the voice of the tribe and there seems to be no reason for us to go into rebellion against the tribe in this regard. This being the case, we take up the task of completing what the tribe started but could not complete in the absence of original individual thinkers whose duty it is to complete what the tribe has given them as an inspiration.

Consolationist Salutation to Ethno-philosophy

In the beginning of this work we divided African philosophical thinkers into three groups, namely:

1. Scholars of Western philosophy.
2. Ethno-philosophers.
3. African philosophers.

The scholars of Western philosophy are learned men with absolutely no originality. Their works are footnotes to Western philosophy. They can quote every important Western philosopher from Plato to Richard Swinburne but can barely form a single original philosophical sentence. The men and women in this group constitute the majority of African philosophical thinkers. Every competent African with a postgraduate degree in philosophy is automatically a scholar of Western philosophy. It is very easy to break into this group, the easiest group in fact. The ethno-philosophers are first scholars of Western philosophy since they studied Western philosophy as undergraduates and as research students (they may also have some level of competence in Oriental philosophies). The ethno-philosophers are more worthy to be called African philosophers than the scholars of Western philosophy, although it is obvious that the narrow research of many an ethno-philosopher is sloppy, anthropological, and generally lacking in rigorous intellectual merit (as when an African thinker wastes time describing the phenomenon of witchcraft or traditional festivals). Hountondji has noted this sloppiness and has severely criticized the enterprise of ethno-philosophy,[15] even suggesting, wrongly I think, that ethno-philosophy might have served the neocolonialist purposes of Europe.[16]

Hountondji, arguably the greatest critic of ethno-philosophy, called for a philosophy addressed to Africans. He believed only such a philosophy, critical and reconstructive, can truly qualify as African philosophy. While it is true that ethno-philosophy has a tendency to address a European audience, the fact remains that only the less gifted ethno-philosophers do so blatantly. The renowned foundation thinkers of the ethno-philosophical school such as Kwasi Wiredu, Alexis Kagame, Henry Odera Oruka, Barry Hallen, John Sodipo, and others, addressed themselves both to the European audience and the African audience. The foundation thinkers were tellingly jealous for the pride of African philosophy. They saw more clearly than Hountondji that African philosophy had to start somewhere and that this important starting point cannot be the critical project Hountondji's intellectualist temperament demanded. Such a critical and reconstructive endeavor, if it had been realized during the earliest years of African philosophy, and it was never realized even by Hountondji—Wiredu came closest to realizing this ambitious dream—if it had been realized it would have amounted to a philosophical miracle. It would have taken the genius of an original African thinker to perform this miracle because such a thinker would have referred to the African experience in the African community for his inspiration while at the same time producing a philosophy that could command the respect of the world. In other words, such a philosopher would have been a scholar of Western philosophy who overleaped ethno-philosophy to position himself in the class of African philosophers.

But how could such a thinker have emerged in the infancy of African intellectualism, without a foundation on which to stand? Senghor was the most original African thinker of his era although not the most dedicated. The essence of his originality was of such a high quality that he could have launched a bid to be precisely this wonderful African philosopher. Apart from the fact that Senghor was first and foremost a poet and politician, there was no foundation for him to stand on and proceed with his critical and reconstructive work on behalf of Africa. There was no inspiration for him to fall back on. Thus he became his own inspiration by going back directly to the tribe. In becoming his own inspiration, he was transformed into an ethno-philosopher instead of an African philosopher, for what he got from the tribe was not the concept but the myth that hid the concept. In becoming an ethno-philosopher, he had to address himself directly to foreigners, since the pride of Black Africa was at stake, and then indirectly to the Africans, since the Africans needed a report or feedback before preparing for the next project which is masterminding the transition from ethno-philosophy to the age of radical individual synthesis and analysis.

Ethno-philosophy as a project, therefore, was an emphatic triumph for African thought. In later years, after the foundation thinkers had completed the work of ethno-philosophy, Asouzu was able to emerge, bringing with him the kind of originality Senghor was blessed with, and dedication in addition. Though Asouzu has harshly criticized the ethno-philosophical project, he clearly benefitted from the work of ethno-philosophy, as we will soon see. If any aspect of ethno-philosophy is to be criticized at all, it is not the striving of the ethno-philosophical thinkers to secure the foundation of African philosophy in the first three decades following the announcement of the coming of the tradition called African philosophy. If harsh criticism is required, such criticism is to be directed at the professors, the doctors of learning, the masters of knowledge, who are still equating African philosophy with ethno-philosophy in the first and second decades of the 21st century. While the revered early ethno-philosophers regarded the whole of Africa (or Black Africa) as their country or philosophical constituency, the contemporary ethno-philosophers, who richly deserve Asouzu's contempt, regard their tribes as their countries or philosophical constituencies. These inferior ethno-philosophers are not even addressing Europe; they are addressing their tribesmen. This aberration has ensured that African philosophy in the 21st century remains primitive and polemical instead of constructive and critical.

We are not saying that ethno-philosophy should be completely abandoned. Such a demand would be ridiculous. The past must always be revisited, just as it is important not to prescribe a rigid program of action for African philosophical thinkers.[17] We may look back from time to time at what a particular tribe has said or thought about some or all of the fundamental questions of philosophy. What is not in doubt is the fact that the tribe has spoken too long. The tribe spoke when Tempels wrote his famous *Bantu Philosophy* and Mbiti his *African Religions and Philosophy*. In Nigeria, Hallen and Sodipo tried to systematize Yoruba epistemology through, chiefly, the instrument of linguistic analysis. Gbadegesin and Makinde followed in the footsteps of Hallen and Sodipo. Claude Sumner unearthed the work of the almost forgotten Ethiopian philosopher of originality, Zera Yaqub. In Ghana, Wiredu, Gyekye, and others studied the thought systems of the Akan and other Ghanaian tribes. In Mali, Marcel Griaule researched the metaphysical beliefs of the Dogon people.[18] In Kenya, Oruka investigated the possibility of the "concept" having already developed in the mind of individuals he called sages. In Uganda,Victor Ocaya investigated Acholi traditional logic system. Diop, Obenga, Onyewuenyi, and other Afrocentric ethno-philosophers dedicated themselves to showing that ancient Egypt with all its glory was black in essence.

The achievements of these thinkers cannot be lightly dismissed on account of the criticism of Hountondji, Serequeberhan, Towa, Mudimbe, and others. Hountondji gave Africa polemic in the place of philosophy, an African meta-philosophy before African philosophy. There was no foundation for him to stand on and he was not willing to join the ethno-philosophers in establishing the foundation that later thinkers would stand on. He called for a culture of criticism and analysis when there was little or nothing to be analyzed and criticized. He insisted that the mill of African philosophy must grind, but there was no grain in the mill. In the absence of grains the mill merely produced the quite unpleasant sound that is uninspiring polemic. The Marxist-leaning works of Serequeberhan and the hermeneutics of Marcien Towa and Okonda Okolo are failed exercises in ethno-philosophy. Serequeberhan, for instance, neither contributed originally to revolutionary thought since there was no African foundation for him to stand on nor advanced African philosophy since he had rejected ethno-philosophy.[19]

While Hountondji recognized the fact that ethno-philosophy was very inadequate philosophically, he failed to realize that African philosophy cannot mature just as it is being born. Wiredu's vision was sharper, and for this sharpness of vision he became a scholar of Western philosophy, an ethno-philosopher, and an African philosopher all at once. Wiredu used the term "decolonization" to validate the ethno-philosophical enterprise, having realized that there could be no African philosophy if this tradition was not in some way different from other traditions, the Western tradition in particular. This difference does not entail the dilution of intellectual rigor. It does not mean embracing the myth and undermining the concept. This difference simply underlines the importance of originality. In the infancy of African philosophy, this difference could only have been achieved in two ways without harm to the black pride. Firstly, a thinker or more than one thinker would have emerged owing no loyalty to Greece, whose originality was so great that he would become the founder of African philosophy by the sheer power of his genius. No such thinker was forthcoming. Senghor aspired and failed. Secondly, African thinkers could go back to the tribe to build a foundation from scratch. This second way was the easiest way to actualize the difference. Expectedly, most African thinkers in the field of philosophy opted for the second way, a wise decision, for which the consolationist salutes them today.

Thus Wiredu was not harsh on the ethno-philosophical project. In his famous essay "Toward Decolonizing African Philosophy and Religion," Wiredu notes, "Although at the present time we are still in an era of postcolonial reconstruction which calls for a large dose of decolonization, we ought not to be oblivious to the other imperatives of philosophical thinking."[20] Wiredu insists that the forward march of African philosophy will not mean that ethno-philosophical investigations will be abandoned altogether, pointing to the fact that to this day Western philosophers still go back to their philosophical roots in Greece to historically locate a concept or discuss the ideas of some ancient Greek philosopher or the other. In a similar manner, African philosophical thinkers will feel the need to go back to their philosophical roots, back to tribal wisdom, to investigate what the Idoma, Akan, Luo, or whichever tribe, have said about something with a philosophical relevance. Making it clear that ethno-philosophy cannot be equated with African philosophy in view of its being tribal philosophy that is unsure of itself, Wiredu cautions that "such discussions [ethno-philosophical analyses] will eventually not have quite the special urgency that they now have in African philosophy. The time would come when there would be, for the most part, no pressing need for the kind of particularism discussed above here."[21]

The time has come for this momentous shift of emphasis. Most African philosophical thinkers are still going back to their villages to interrogate old men when everything they need to have to move the African tradition forward is already available, thanks to the works of the committed early ethno-philosophers. This mass return to the past is retrogression, the refusal or inability to throw Africa's challenge to world philosophy. We must not be in a hurry to forget Taiwo's war cry of exorcizing the ghost of Hegel. Taiwo himself did little by way of preparing for the war, having sent forth the war cry and retreated into the undemanding territory of ethno-philosophical investigations. In the place of rigorous constructive and analytical thinking, we see such widespread concerns with such themes as the philosophy of development, the philosophy of business and technology, conflict resolution, widowhood practices, etc.[22] It is not true that science and technology need philosophy. The philosophical attribute of incisive and critical thinking will definitely help an African scientist who has encountered philosophy in one form or the other; yet the immersion of philosophy in science, apart from leading to the loss of the philosophical spirit itself, will also not achieve a single victory for science. With regard to philosophy, science is self-sufficient. Fears that philosophy will lose its relevance if it does not become the handmaid of science is unfounded, precisely because metaphysics, which is the spirit of philosophy, permeates life so thoroughly that it will always have a grip on humans, like religion, music, literature, and art in general. Philosophy must always have a humanistic focus. To subject itself to science in any humiliating manner will spell philosophy's disappearance and the emergence of a technical farce masquerading as philosophy. What we are saying is that philosophy must remain an inspiration for humanity even in our highly computerized 21st century.

Wiredu has shown us the path to our dream. The decolonization work has to be done in two stages. The first stage has been completed. This is the stage of ethno-philosophical preoccupation. This stage juxtaposed the academic ethno-philosophers with Senghor. While Senghor worked with relative independence of the tribe, the academic ethno-philosophers insisted that they were speaking for the tribe. Ultimately, the work of decolonization, conceptual or otherwise, was successfully accomplished. Both Senghor and the academic ethno-philosophers pointed a visionary finger towards the future.

The second stage of conceptual decolonization, the call for the sustaining of "difference" in a manner sympathetic to "otherness"—that is, the insistence that African philosophy is not the handmaid of Western philosophy—was kick-started by Asouzu, regardless of his misgiving about Wiredu's great call for conceptual decolonization.[23] For what the call represents is a demand for originality, not fundamentally a call for a radical break with the Western tradition. Such a radical break, amounting to what Mudimbe will call the "invention" of Africa, is impossible, although a "reinvention" of Africa is possible through the affirmation of "difference" and the reconciliation of this "difference" with "otherness"—the very task we intend to achieve in this treatise. As radical and original as the ethno-philosophical enterprise is, a reading of Kagame or Gbadegesin or Wiredu himself will clearly reveal the lasting influence of Western philosophical thought on the black mind. The cruder and less talented ethno-philosophers were actually directly translating Western thought into the languages of the African people. The second stage of the decolonization of African philosophy will see the complete emergence of the individual whose reference to the tribe will serve only as an appeal to inspiration. For the philosopher in this second stage cannot hope to attain any level of originality if he draws his inspiration from Greece. His inspiration has to come from Africa.

Wiredu provides an interesting list of those Western philosophical concepts in need of decolonization or reinterpretation from an African perspective, which is simply a call for originality, as we keep saying. This is in harmony with Asouzu's philosophical project and our own consolationist endeavor of the second stage of the decolonization project. These concepts include reality, being, existence, entity, substance, truth, property, quality, knowledge, faith, doubt, proposition, statement, idea, mind, soul, spirit, thought, matter, sensation, person, individuality, community, subjectivity, objectivity, reason, cause, chance, freedom, responsibility, democracy, justice, God, world, nature, space, time, nothingness, creation, life, death, morality, universe, and supernature.[24] This exhaustive list is impressive. The first stage of the decolonization process has attempted to take a second look at these concepts from an African perspective while speaking for the tribe. The voice of the individual upon which philosophical progress depends was largely silenced in this first stage. The second stage has commenced. It will be a disaster for our struggling tradition if the 21st century philosophers return to ethno-philosophy en masse or take the easy way out of the challenge of African philosophy to write papers on development, conflict resolution, widows' rights, technology in Africa, etc. These simple matters can be resolved by political scientists, sociologists, and other social scientists. Let us return to the vision of Wiredu and undertake the task he has outlined for us. Undertaking this task will ennoble our tradition and usher in African philosophy in the strict and most proper sense. A rich harvest of exciting intellectualism must be underway.

Transition from Ethno-philosophy to the Metaphysical Vision of Leopold Sedar Senghor

It is beyond dispute that Senghor was a great poet and politician, perhaps Africa's greatest poet ever. But it is possible to contest his philosophical relevance. Yet we wish to reveal that before the emergence of Asouzu, Senghor incubated the most radical idea in the whole of African philosophy, even if he never nursed this idea to maturity. As a matter of fact, the originality of Senghor in its promise of constructive thinking surpasses Asouzu's originality, the latter's chief advantage over the former being a much higher level of dedication to the philosophical enterprise. Senghor has been grouped with nationalist philosophers or political ideologists; yet in his works are scattered profound metaphysical and epistemological insights. As a political thinker Senghor is of little relevance to African philosophy and much less to consolation philosophy, since there is hardly anything he said with political or ideological merit which his fellow politician-philosophers like Nkrumah, Nnamdi Azikiwe, Kenneth Kaunda, and Nyerere did not say. Senghor is a perpetual object of interest for us because of the core message of négritude, its philosophical import, which qualified him to be called an ethno-philosopher, and, what is more, an inspiration for consolation philosophy.

We have said quite a lot about ethno-philosophy and its link with our 21st century African synthesis, that is, ethno-philosophy as the foundation of consolationism. It is more than proper for us to now effect the transition from academic ethno-philosophy to the individualism of Senghor's metaphysical vision. The academic ethno-philosophers ordinarily should be given precedence over Senghor in view of their superior intellectual rigor. However, in our scale of originality, Senghor takes precedence, and so the countdown to consolation philosophy begins with the transition from academic ethno-philosophy to Senghorian ethno-philosophy, the latter advancing the former. Négritude arrived as an ideology and proclaimed itself as an African humanism and therefore a universal humanism. The vision before Senghor was the vision no longer of an ideology beneficial only to the African people but a philosophy embracing humanity. Négritude was *ujamaa* taken to a higher conceptual level. While the academic ethno-philosophers traversed the length and breadth of Black Africa trying to unveil the universal concept (the key to an African philosophy of universal value) Senghor had already conceived the universal idea in his mind. Black Africa had already bestowed the concept upon him. Unlike the academic ethno-philosophers who conveniently forgot that they would find the concept within them if they searched their minds diligently instead of seeking it wholeheartedly in the minds of community sages, Senghor knew that the greatness was already within him, that as a black man in touch with the continent he already carried an African conception of the universe that owes no allegiance to Greece. The uniqueness of African philosophy claimed by both Senghor and the academic ethno-philosophers is nothing more than the universalizability of the particular, that uniqueness which made Western and Oriental philosophies what they are. Unfortunately, neither Senghor nor the academic ethno-philosophers succeeded in liberating the idea from the custody of mythology which became formidable by claiming the identity of custom. But the great struggle was ever present in the works of these pioneer thinkers, the struggle for the liberation of the concept. The claim of the uniqueness of African philosophy is not the denial of active reason to Black Africa but the proclamation of the emotionality of reason, the call for a closer scrutiny of the very alluring phenomenon called reason.

It never occurred to the academic ethno-philosophers that Senghor had stumbled on an idea destined to revolutionize African philosophy in our time, not in his time, although with admirable acuity Sodipo recognized the immortal worth of Senghor's insight.[25] Although Senghor's insight was early for Africa, it was not early for the West. A critical examination of the epistemology of Western greats like Immanuel Kant (for whom logic correctly identifies itself with psycho-logic, this identification being ultimately inevitable), Henri Bergson, David Hume, Jean-Jacques Rouseau, Teilhard de Chardin, the phenomenologists, the existentialists, and even some of the analytical thinkers like Peter Strawson reveals that these thinkers may have struggled with the strong suspicion that human reason is a dimension of human emotionality. Kant, the greatest of them all, in his metaphysical and ethical works grounded objectivity in subjectivity, traced freedom to reason, and eventually lost reason in the depths of the human mind, being unable to find its grounds and understand its essence. It cannot be doubted, therefore, that Senghor had put forward a theory sanctioned not only by the mind of Africa but also by the mind of humanity. Thus while ethno-philosophy proper concerned itself with such particular values as communal well-being and observances that conduce to the happiness of the community, Senghor was reaching out for the universal and declaring négritude an African humanism. Consolation philosophy, on its part, has endeavored to realize universal values through the analysis of such concepts as human anxiety and the philosophical grounds of empathy from a vigorously individualistic perspective, thereby challenging the iron grip of the community or state on the individual.

Senghor was trying to announce that reason is not isolated from emotion and vice versa. Instead of announcing the emotionality of reason, Senghor scandalously contrasted the emotionality of the African mind with the rationality of the Western mind, leaving out the Asian mind and the Arab mind. But this was expected. In the infancy of Senghor's genius mythology dominated philosophy. To have arrived at the universal truth of his inspiration he needed a relatively developed theory of reason and the metaphysics of the *melancholy being*. Lacking both, Senghor remained a promise he himself could not fulfil. But being a promise, he became the father of African philosophy.

Senghor tells us that négritude as an idea expresses a distinctly African way of life. Though a distinction from Westernism, it does not have to fundamentally oppose Westernism because it is in its essence a vision of humanity, an African humanism. For Senghor négritude is animated by "intuitive reason, because this sentient reason ... expresses itself emotionally, through that self-surrender, that coalescence of subject and object, through myths, by which I mean the archetypal images of the collective soul, synchronized with those of the cosmos ... the sense of communion, the gift of myth-making, the gift of rhythm ... the essential elements of *Négritude*, which you will find indelibly stamped on all the works and activities of the black man."[26] To Senghor Black Africa's portion is the sympathetic or emotional reason, what he calls the "reasoning embrace," the Greek *logos* rather than the Latin *ratio*, the dynamic intimacy that refuses to divide things into independent and sufficient essences.[27] In Asouzu this notion became complementary reflection. We must insist that Senghor underrated humanity by unduly particularizing a universal truth and leaving it in the particular. The quotation above is not mere poetizing, for it is pregnant with the concept. Senghor tries to present the African as a hospitable and welcoming being incapable of hurting himself and the foreigner. Now, there is this tendency to exaggerate the warmth of the black person by African scholars, to extol the communal spirit of the black people in a manner suggestive of the black person not being a *melancholy being*, and therefore incapable of evil. This African warmth which Senghor romanticizes as the gift of rhythm and a love of communion is a universal quality of man and woman, the *melancholy being*, although it may be argued that blacks express this capacity in their own fashion. To make this capacity the sole prerogative of the black person is to be guilty of ignoble sentimentality given that the African is capable of great brutality as past and recent history clearly shows. We only need to remember how our ancestors foolishly sold their children and relatives to Western slave traders and contemporary problems harassing the African continent such as fratricidal wars and financial corruption to agree with F.O.C. Njoku that the African communal spirit was never so benevolent as to deserve the adulation bestowed on it by people not in any position to reconstruct the past. "The people whose ideas reigned in the clan were the domineering or influential individuals. There was an obsessive fear of the juju man, the rich, the strong wrestler ... there was no egalitarian society therein but a society of projected interests of some individuals.... There is the saying among the Igbo of Onitsha area of Eastern Nigeria that *azu na-erighi ibe ya etobeghi*—which means: a fish that has not eaten a fellow fish has not yet started to grow."[28]

Obviously, Senghor overlooked a fundamental problem of the *melancholy being* that he was trying to reveal, the problem of evil in the world. The consolationist interpretation of Senghor is this, that the communion he praised so much as an African phenomenon is a rejection of the dualistic conception of the universe and the insistence on monism of some sort. This preference for monism is underlined by the reference to the African reason as that which includes, that embraces things, and penetrates them to their depths. This emphasis on complementarity re-echoes in Asouzu's philosophy of complementary reflection which we will soon examine to determine how far African philosophy has radically progressed. According to Senghor, the African is certainly gifted with reason. But his kind of reason is an emotional reason analogous to the Greek *logos*, which touches, penetrates, and synthesizes, and is therefore not rigid in its logical categorization.[29] It is easy to see why Senghor prefers the Greek *logos* to the Latin *ratio*. The *logos* is always threatened by what we may call the emotion of reason that inspires the flight of mythology. Here we see Senghor being led in a particular determined direction by his profoundly poetic spirit. On the other hand, the *ratio* is supposedly disinterested, clinical, and incisive. Yet the disinterestedness of the *ratio* is an illusion, for the *ratio* is enhanced by the reason of emotion, the ethical imperative of human existence which impresses itself on human consciousness as rationality, full blown rationality. And this rationality has its logical, ethical, aesthetic, and psychological dimensions; yet it is fundamentally an emotion, the yearning character that puzzled the mighty Kant in his struggle to unravel the profound problem of human freedom while at the same time thoroughly neglecting the metaphysics of terror, without which logic can produce no insight. If rationality is a development of the *ratio* from the *logos*, of discursive reason from sympathetic or symbolic reason, it is ethical. If rationality is ethical it is an emotion. If this is the case, Senghor is correct to have spoken about a reasoning emotion, for which he deserves the technical philosopher's respect. Where he goes wrong is his insistence on the Africanity of this phenomenon of consciousness, that is, rationality.

Unable to liberate the concept from his profoundly poetic mind, Senghor failed to work out the metaphysical implication of his original epistemological insight. With this philosophical failure staring him in the face, Senghor had to take refuge in the knowledge that he was a poet first and then a politician. Philosophy came a distant third. Thus he found satisfaction in négritude as a political ideology. Expectedly, he took the easy way out of the intimidating philosophical task ahead of him, preferring politics and political philosophy to metaphysics and epistemology. Négritude as a political ideology does not interest us, therefore.

Now that we have rediscovered the African philosophical unity that eluded Senghor most spectacularly and all the academic ethno-philosophers, what do we make of Senghor's inspiration which has clearly underlined the pregnant proposition that without the emotion there is no mind and without the mind there is no life? How can we radicalize Senghor by taking off in another direction—a direction different from Senghor's—while flying on the same trajectory that announced the discovery of the African philosophical synthesis? Radicalizing Senghor will mean universalizing his insight which, after all, is not so strange to the world, since elements of the Senghorian inspiration are inchoate in the thoughts of some of the great philosophers of the Occident and in the religio-philosophical traditions of the Orient, India in particular. Now, what way is there for us to show that Senghor was a promise of a universal philosophy ripe for today and for the 21st century?[30]

This work emerged as a response to the questions posed above. We think that in consolation philosophy we have found a bridge, a way, linking Senghor's inspiration to the new century. "Whither philosophy in Africa on the eve of the 21st century?" Makinde appears to ask facetiously. "How can we exorcize the ghost of Hegel and compel the world to stop sneering at African philosophy?" Taiwo seems to be asking in bewilderment. "Hegel can be exorcized only when African philosophers take a critical, personal stand," Asouzu appears to be saying triumphantly. We endorse Asouzu's position but call for the metaphysical foundation of our tradition to be firmly entrenched before we bother ourselves with the much easier aspect of analysis and applied philosophy. In universalizing Senghor, we will show that Senghor's emotional "negro" is nothing more than Man and Woman—the *melancholy being* of emotion and reason. Being the existential human, the white human, the black human, the yellow human, the red human, being all these, the *melancholy being* is not racially limited, but a *human* being. The second part of our work is fast approaching. Before we launch into the constructive part of this work we must pause to pay homage to Asouzu whose work extends the trajectory of Senghor into the 21st century. The fact that we have been able to trace the history of the struggle of the African concept for intellectual liberation, from the academic ethno-philosophers through Senghor, and now over to Asouzu, clearly indicates that African philosophy is making progress.

Transition from the Metaphysical Vision of Senghor to the Rationalism of Asouzu

Methodological Preamble

Asouzu has been harsh in his criticism of the ethno-philosophical enterprise in African philosophical thought.[31] He denounces all forms of intellectual bigotry, railing not only at the ethno-philosophical enterprise but also at Eurocentrism, the tribalism ravaging the African continent, and the general favoritism that arises from the intense suspicion that the finer the affirmation of sameness the more secure one is. This is the immoral notion that inclusivity should be restricted to the primary group at all levels.[32] But then the work of Asouzu is more an exercise in the methodology of contemporary African philosophy than it is a work of synthesis, although there are synthetic tendencies in Asouzu. Consequently, Asouzu indulges in the intense polemical debate that had consumed African philosophy in its early years. The harsh criticism of ethno-philosophy follows from his conviction that in complementary reflection or *ibuanyidanda* philosophy he has found a platform from which African philosophy can launch itself on another philosophical trajectory. Since Asouzu's success is the liberation of the African concept imprisoned by ethno-philosophical thinking, it must be obvious that Asouzu's inspiration lies in ethno-philosophy. Our preparatory analysis has so far shown that this is the case. Asouzu had to return to the tribe, in this case his Igbo community, to find inspiration for his work. He did find this inspiration. Thus he conceived the doctrine of *ibuanyidanda*, the doctrine of complementarity, precisely the doctrine that "no task is insurmountable for *danda*."[33]

Danda means ant. Everyone knows how cooperative a colony of ants can be. Through an admirable system of division of labor and cooperation these tiny insects are able to accomplish difficult tasks. The idea is that complementarity provides the most acceptable answer to the riddle of existence, that it is in the working of complementarity that a fuller meaning of existence is extracted from the gigantic puzzle that this existence represents. Asouzu borrows the Igbo expression *mkpuchi anya* (the phenomenon of concealment) to describe the puzzle of existence. At this stage Asouzu is at the same level as the academic ethno-philosophers and not yet at Senghor's level. At this point Asouzu is an ethno-philosopher like the thinkers he stridently criticizes. But as soon as he introduces his notion of the *joy of being* he surpasses the ethno-philosophers. As soon as he begins to reflect on the problem of missing links he surpasses Senghor.

As I said earlier, the biggest part of Asouzu's work is about methodology, what I like to call his long prolegomena to any African philosophical engagement after him. His distaste for ethno-philosophy is not simply informed by the fact that he considers the enterprise as pseudo-philosophy but chiefly because he thinks the ethno-philosophers lost sight of the matter of the unity of being in their search for uniqueness. He sternly asserts, "Contrary to the pretensions of ethnophilosophic inspired method of investigations that the essence of philosophy lies solely in documentation of differences, all philosophies resemble themselves in the point where the philosopher is a bridge between reality, in its most sublime form, and humanity, as this becomes evident even in given localities."[34]

The above observation can hardly be disputed. However, Asouzu seems to forget that the academic ethno-philosophers addressed themselves more to the West than to Africa in their philosophical research, which is a clear indication that they had a rough idea of the universal solidarity that Senghor advanced as mytho-philosophy, which Asouzu improves upon by advancing as pure thought. In the absence of originality the academic ethno-philosophers just could not make any progress with the concept by liberating it from the custody of tribal wisdom and applying it to humanity. If they felt that the work of philosophy, their ordinary-language analysis, lay with the "documentation of differences" alone, they would not have bothered addressing themselves to the West and the rest of the world. They were groping for the African concept, a uniquely African way of seeing the world that, possessing real intellectual vigour, would amount to the universalization of the particular. They were struggling to transform particular values like the supremacy of the community or tribe into universal values like the rights of the individual in his relation with the community. The less talented ethno-philosophers groped in vain for the African concept. The foreign investigators like Tempels and Griaule also groped in vain. They thought they found the African concept, but they never did. They could not have found it with their Western mindset, having prostrated before Greece. Only an African could carry the cross of the black intellect. To find the African concept, an African had to arise who was not in awe of Greece. Senghor was that African. He saw how difference could be equated with uniqueness without the exclusion of universal solidarity.

Hence, he declared négritude an African humanism. Certainly, Nyerere did promote *ujamaa* as an African humanism, as familyhood, but he lacked the depth and originality of Senghor and therefore failed to consciously unveil the African concept. By asserting that blacks have a conception of the universe that reads emotion into all things—a conception essentially in agreement with human nature—Senghor became the most audacious black thinker of the 20th century, as original as Asouzu and in fact more audacious and deeper than Asouzu. The failure of Senghor is the failure to universalize the African particular. Wiredu, another outstanding African thinker, noted this failure and called for conceptual decolonization, the practice of which would seem to negate the idea behind this loud call since this practice would have finely merged with the project of the universalization of African philosophy. Decolonization would mean the stout refusal to bow the knees to Greece since the Greek inspiration is not an African inspiration, although this Greek inspiration is universally applicable. It is the destiny of African philosophy to be a comparative philosophy because of the circumstances of the absence of a written philosophical tradition before the dawn of colonialism, because of the reality of colonialism itself, and finally because of the fact that African philosophical thinkers start off as scholars of Western philosophy. This comparative character of African philosophy will always ensure that difference does not exclude solidarity.

Asouzu is the first thinker to seriously pursue the reconciliation of difference with universal solidarity working with the instrument of complementarity which asserts reality to be a convergence and divergence of missing links. Hence, the phenomenon of "concealment" or the puzzle of existence. He writes:

> For Ibuanyidanda philosophy, therefore, to be is to be in mutual complementary relationship (*ka s? m? adina*) and its negation is to be alone (*ka s? m? di*) and not nothingness. This is why it is a tragedy to locate the essence of existence in the capacity to act outside of the framework provided by all missing links of reality. In this sense, the act of being and with it existence, is all it takes to affirm that anything that exists serves a missing link of reality towards the joy of being.[35]

Here Asouzu is reacting to Aristotle's static conception of being, the essentialist view of being as that which is, categorically being as being. Asouzu favors a more dynamic notion of being, yet not a merely dynamic notion but a dynamism with a future reference within a complementary framework, a dynamism desiring completion in the convergence of all the links belonging to diverse backgrounds and natures. It is in the possibility of this completion that Asouzu reads joy into being. The consolationist thinker believes that this completion is indeed always indicated but never attained because the possibility is dissipated in the tortuous process of completion. Thus, while Asouzu is basically optimistic we carry the burden of pessimism. In emphasizing the joy of being as consequent upon the completion towards which the missing links converge, Asouzu delivers a masterstroke and confirms himself as an African philosopher. Here, in the idea of the joy of being, Asouzu unveils the African concept just as Senghor did in the 20th century with his theory of reason. While Senghor failed to see that he was using an African instrument to explain a fundamental phenomenon of the world,

Asouzu saw farther and universalized the particular by introducing the elements of missing links and complementarity.

The optimism of Asouzu announces an early rejection of nihilism. He has not developed this idea, but he has hinted at it in the quotation above. He has rejected solipsism which hides the claims of nihilism in all its aspects and in its various degrees. Thus, for Asouzu the problem of the existence of the other does not arise. The individual is a missing link, and as a missing link he is already part of a community of *others* or other minds. To deny this is to plunge into a conceptual error, the error of solipsism which translates ultimately into the existential error of nihilism. The nihilism referred to here is not restricted to its more virulent aspects expressed in the rejection of all moral and religious beliefs or the belief in nothing. The denial of the complementarity of missing links counts automatically as nihilism, for this denial puts one on the road to pessimism and skepticism (which are valid metaphysical notions in themselves as we will demonstrate in the second and third parts of this book) and then the complete surrender to a despair that is full-blown nihilism. For Asouzu there is no nothingness, only the rejection of the complementary framework of existence, a rejection equivalent to existential solitude. This solitude is a tragedy. We will return to this matter later, in the next section, when we engage in a brief comparative analysis of consolation philosophy and complementary reflection.

Asouzu's definition of a missing link is broad. We see the individual as a missing link. The tree in front of my house is a missing link; so is my house itself, the black person, the white person, the thoughts of black and white men and women, cultures, beliefs, religions, etc. Precisely, missing links are "finite beings and their different modes of expression in history in so far they are fragments that cannot be conceptualized except in complementary relationship to each other ... finite beings in their diverse modes of expression and the categories of such beings ... the mind can grasp and intuit as missing links units and units of units, things and things of things, ideas and ideas of ideas, thoughts and thoughts of thoughts."[36] This insight informs and animates the project of complementary reflection. The unique character of African philosophy seeks reconciliation with foreign thought systems in order to validate itself. Asouzu is saying that African philosophy cannot claim to be philosophy if the complementary interpretation of difference escapes it. The bigotry of the African thinker who convinces himself that the uniqueness of African philosophy does not only lie in the originality of the African philosophical inspiration but also in an essentialist conception of difference is as reprehensible as the bigotry of the Western thinker who may see elements of the thought systems of the great Western philosophers in African thinkers and conclude at once that there has been an intellectual plagiarism.

The tendency of the mind to totalize means that philosophies of diverse cultures manifest a certain commonality. This point provides Asouzu's main justification for condemning the ethno-philosophical project. He writes:

> Thus complementary reflection explores the condition for the validation of our claims and assertions which it understands as being fundamentally rooted in the sense of the acquisition of a complementary, unified, emancipated and transcendental mindset. This is the dispositional precondition for ratiocination as it enables the philosopher to attain the full consciousness of himself or herself as a typical instance of being seeking full and comprehensive actualization in history irrespective of local constraints.[37]

The way which Asouzu has opened up is a hard way, but then this hard way is the only way for the African philosophical thinker, and for Africa as a continent, unless we want to keep playing second fiddle to Western and Oriental philosophers and sell ourselves into an intellectual but historically significant slavery.

The Shadow of a Synthesis

The moment Asouzu surpassed Senghor African philosophy looked up to him to bring with him Black Africa's first thoroughly worked synthesis. While it is disputable that Asouzu brings with him a synthesis, it is more than obvious that the Asouzian synthesis is basically the shadow of a synthesis, given the glaring incompleteness of the synthesis. We have noted that Asouzu is all too often guilty of over-indulging in the dry polemic that renders the works of Hountondji so barren. The polemical character of analytical African philosophy is due mainly to the relative absence of synthetic thinking in African philosophy. Ethno-philosophy which still remains the biggest synthetic enterprise in African philosophical thought lacks the individualized fecundity and the intellectual rigor to feed a truly rewarding analysis. It is disappointing that Asouzu indulges a great deal in polemics, railing at the ethno-philosophers who made a very important contribution to African thought and sparing, or ignoring, the hermeneutic and meta-philosophical thinkers who made very little contribution to African philosophy.

Asouzu's synthesis remains in the region of shadows for the following reasons:

1. He fails to develop certain important metaphysical concepts and show how these concepts fit into the framework of *ibuanyidanda* philosophy, e.g., the concept of nothingness which he only hints at as superfluous and in fact impossible since the denial of complementarity equates solitude rather than nothingness.

2. Asouzu's philosophy is optimistic in character. This is clearly indicated by the very important notion of the *joy of being* that points towards the futurity of an increasingly complete complementarity. The concept of the *joy of being* which universalizes Senghor's idea of the African's gift of rhythm and sense of communion is greatly underutilized. This notion is pivotal to the optimism of Asouzu. Yet it has been denied a house in which to live. Why must the optimistic vision of the universe stand given that human life provides enough materials to feed pessimism and put forward the claim of pessimism to metaphysical priority over optimism? Is optimism not a missing link in the chain of complementarity? If yes, what is its relationship with pessimism? What significance can be attached to a notion such as the *sadness of being*?

3. The phenomenon of missing links is not given adequate metaphysical depth, coming over to us mostly in the socio-cultural and ethical contexts.

4. Wiredu has given an exhaustive list of concepts requiring conceptual decolonization, concepts like being, universe, evil, freedom, reality, time, cause, etc. As the most original African philosopher since Senghor, Asouzu should have taken the pains to construct an intellectual edifice around some of these concepts. Such a construction would have given world philosophy the complete *ibuanyidanda* vision of the universe and put Innocent Asouzu in the top rank of the great philosophers of the world.

The above notwithstanding, our purpose here is to bring out the continuing link in African philosophy from the ethno-philosophers and Senghor to Asouzu and finally our research in consolation philosophy. We have taken all the pains to show that Senghor was indeed right to have boasted that there is a distinctly African way of seeing the world not one bit inferior to the Western approach. This distinct way of conceiving the world is the African vision of existence. As a vision it is simply *character* or form, not content *per se*. Since this is the case, the African vision can be expressed in a rigorous intellectual language, as much as the Western and Oriental visions. To be sure, the academic ethno-philosophers also recognized this possibility. But unlike Senghor they made no conscious effort to liberate the African concept and transform it through thought into the universal concept. The genius of Asouzu is the fact that he became the first African thinker to liberate the African concept by transforming it into the universal concept in the expansive notion of the *joy of being*. This honor could have easily gone to the brilliant Wiredu if he had not preferred to be a scholar than a thinker in an intellectual environment sorely in need of original thinkers. Since the credit has gone to Asouzu, let us now briefly examine his metaphysics, on the strength of which he makes his claim to greatness.

Asouzu favors a monistic conception of the universe like Senghor before him and indeed all the major ethno-philosophers. But the universe conceived as a totality is not a Hegelian Absolute that unfolds itself to human consciousness as perfect rationality. Something is always concealed in Asouzu's dialectic. Something is always hidden from the human mind. This mind indeed totalizes and therefore conceives the universe as an absolute. Yet the absolute is only the totality as given, which is not the same as a perfect absolute. The diverse elements of plurality then constitute missing links. To sustain the authenticity of the plural unity "actors have to encounter all missing links in full awareness of their relativity, historicity and fragmentation, while at the same time bearing in mind their ultimate determination to absoluteness, universality, comprehensiveness, unity, totality, and future reference."[38] All forms of knowledge converge in the given totality. Monism provides the grounds of the ultimate unity of philosophy (in this case African, Western, and Oriental philosophies), science, and religion (all religious modes). For this reason we must not exaggerate uniqueness. "This structural constitution is characteristic of universal human experience of reality, as relative subjects, everywhere and every time," adds Asouzu. "It is along this line that the mind always seeks to capture reality in complementary contraries ... day and night, male and female, being and non-being, truth and falsehood, good and evil, up and down, etc."[39]

Consequently, Asouzu triumphantly formulates the principles and imperatives of complementary reflection, namely:

1. The principle of integration which states that *anything that exists serves a missing link of reality*.

2. The principle of progressive transformation which states that *all human actions are geared towards the joy of being*.

3. The imperative of *ibuanyidanda* philosophy which states that *allow the limitations of being to be the cause of your joy*.

4. The truth and authenticity criterion which states that *never elevate any world immanent missing link to an absolute instance.*[40]

For one reason or the other, Asouzu has avoided the exploration of the metaphysical consequences of his ontology. He has avoided transcendent metaphysics. For instance, Asouzu asserts that to be is to be in mutual complementarity, to be independent in dependence.[41] According to Asouzu, the denial of this complementarity is to be alone. Asouzu distinguishes this existential solitude from the concept of nothingness without going further to construct a mini-philosophy of nothingness (or discredit it with reasons) which will give us an idea of an African philosopher's thought on nothingness as demanded rightly by the great Wiredu.

If Asouzu had been consumed by the urgency of the need for an African synthesis he would have spent less time on polemic against the ethno-philosophers (with Tempels receiving extra volley). He would have more deeply analyzed the concept of nothingness, the idea of nihilism, and the justification (if there is any) for solipsism. A conflict yawns in Asouzu, the conflict of the totalizing demand of the human mind and the glaring incompleteness of the world. He gave African philosophy the key to the possible resolution of this conflict (to which the great Western philosophers also responded) but did not himself resolve it. The task before the consolationist thinker is to fill the gaps left deliberately by Asouzu for reasons we think do not require examination here. Having been shown the way to go, we will move from everyday life to ontology and up to metaphysics, then back again to the everyday life which is our starting point.

Transition from the Rationalism of Asouzu to the Doctrine of *Mood* as the Synthesis of the Philosophy of Consolation

The master doctrine, the key to the solution of the questions we have posed, is the doctrine of *mood*. The assertion of the essential *moodiness* (that is, the yearning essence of existence, the totality of being) may leave us open to the accusation of idealism. Mercifully, this will not be the accusation that we are German idealists. Our idealism, which, paradoxically, destroys and resurrects universal idealism, is an African idealism. Thus we have devoted a significant portion of *Existence and Consolation* to the justification of consolationism by neatly tracing the source of our inspiration from the African community that endures, through the African light shed by the academic ethno-philosophers and the vision of Senghor to the rationalism of Asouzu.

Consolationism constitutes an idealistic paradox, we say. It is idealistic, yet it destroys idealism before seeking to resurrect it again. It destroys idealism by erecting a primary doctrine of pessimism as accounting for the foundation of existence. Here we are different from Asouzu who never explores the phenomenon of metaphysical nihilism and appears to overlook the problem of evil like the monists and absolute idealists of Western philosophy. Where Asouzu talks about the *joy of being* as a realizable in the convergence of missing links we talk of the sadness of existence as the foundation of being and the *joy of being* as the supreme recognition of the eternal sway of fatalism. In elevating the place of sadness in human consciousness and in constructing a pessimistic metaphysics that accommodates nihilism, consolation philosophy destroys idealism. In elevating the position of joy in human consciousness and in building an optimistic metaphysics on the doctrine of fatalism and, in the process, showing that nihilism is an exaggeration misunderstood by anarchists, consolation philosophy resurrects idealism.

Consolation philosophy is the doctrine of *mood*, the system of thought shadowed by the emotion of life. A cursory examination of the process of perception indicates the burden of the mind as its emotion. The emotional burden of the mind has been denied by the class of thinkers called logicians who, even as they are denying, have to contend with cynicism and skepticism, the first symptoms of the emotional burden of the intellect. All disciplines are substantially the creations of the human intellect, but because this intellect is itself an emotion its processes terminate ultimately in conscious or unconscious surrender to nihilism in its many forms. The logic of life is the emotionality of existence and the logic of the mind is the detachment of the intellect, which logicians isolate from the other vaster logic. We insist that this same intellect is nothing more than a refined emotion. How then can the intellect mock the emotive faculty? Why must science denigrate poetry? Why must we think that one philosophy can be emotional or romantic (e.g. the philosophy of Unamuno or the philosophy of Senghor or even the philosophy of Spinoza) while another is logical or unsentimental (e.g. the philosophy of Descartes or the philosophy of Russell)?

If the logic of the intellect has its origin in the primal logic of existence, precisely in emotion, then the intellect can never escape its emotional origin. In plainer words, the intellect can never reject the idea of God (which is at once concept and emotion). The rejection of this idea already entails its acceptance as we will soon see. The choice of believing is the emotional decision of the intellect. Emotion may be stronger at everyday levels of eating, drinking, mating, and social interaction, but it is not absent at higher levels of abstraction. Let us take the example of the philosopher or scientist who thinks that the logic of the intellect is able to detach itself from the logic of life in rigorous reasoning and analysis. René Descartes and Bertrand Russell were both philosophers and mathematicians who arrived at different conceptions of God through rigorous thinking. While Descartes famously concluded that there is a God, Russell thought it is more likely that there is no God. So we have broadly identified two doctrines, theism or deism and atheism. Agnosticism is either theism or atheism; so we must ignore it.

As the positive affirmation of faith in the logic of existence, theism is a display of emotion. As positive affirmation it is inspired by joy. The first demand of emotion, the primal energy of that which yearns, is the demand that God should exist. Atheists correctly suspect that theism is a kind of emotional outburst, an unreasoning and therefore foolish emotion. Atheism is an emotion but not a foolish emotion, in the same way that theism is not a foolish emotion. When the atheist accuses the theist of inventing a god who is silent and invisible in order not to be shamed by the eternal postponement of the appearance of his god he does not gloat for too long. His polemical triumph is terminated abruptly because the theist responds that in inventing his god he desires his invention, and desires it so earnestly from the top to the bottom of his being, so completely, that a possibility emerges which is asserted as a reality, the denial of which will amount to the denial of a concrete life that exists beyond doubt. This of course is the triumph of probability, upon which science itself depends. As soon as we begin to ask the questions, "What is matter?" and, "Why is there something?" the coherence of science dissolves and this same science is revealed as a body of beliefs, a dogma that seizes certainty for itself out of probability. Atheism is an emotion because it is the withdrawal of the affirmation of the theist, the refusal to affirm faith in the logic of life which, we say, insists on the demand that God should exist. The God-concept is already a given in consciousness. It only remains for this concept to be affirmed or denied. Its denial takes its first premise from the positive affirmation of the theist.

First Fundamental	Derivative
God exists.	God exists.
Yes, He exists.	No, He does not exist.

The first fundamental belongs to the theist. The derivative is the atheist's. So the atheist, unfortunately, comes last. Before the atheist makes his denial, his supreme act of nihilist emotionalism, he goes through the three stages of skepticism, cynicism, and despair. He is skeptical because he doubts. He is cynical because he thinks. He despairs because he is dissatisfied with the *absence* he thinks exists instead of the *presence* of the theist. The proclamation of the non-existence of God brings satisfaction in the aftermath of the first spontaneous dissatisfaction. Both dissatisfaction and satisfaction are emotions. The satisfaction comes as the intellect's vindication of its cynicism. The dissatisfaction is due to the collapse of an illusion. Thus despair corrupts the intellect by making it cynical and skeptical. The cynicism and skepticism of the intellect do not constitute a rebellion against the God-concept *per se* but rather indicate the intellect's recognition of the fundamental tragedy of existence. This tragedy reveals emotion in its creative sway (the mythopoeic element of existence). The unending struggle of the intellect with despair underlines its emotionality. The height of this despair is atheism.

We had to show that the intellect itself is emotional to pre-empt detractors who may want to dismiss consolationism as a philosophy of emotion or as mere intellectual romanticism. Our analysis has once again demonstrated the originality of our philosophy which looks back to the African community for inspiration. Consolation philosophy is a continuation of the African synthesis discovered by Senghor and advanced by Asouzu. Consolation philosophy propagates the doctrine of *mood* as the key to the unraveling of the notion of fatalism. It is a doctrine of *mood* in the recognition of the fact that emotion shadows thought. Emotion is the given logic of life which baffles the intellect in the despair of the intellect, for which fatalism is not enough. Yet surrender it must to fatalism. If existence has no reason to be what it is beyond the fact that yearning characterizes it, then this existence is a *fatality*. Yet it cannot be that existence is superfluous because it is characterized by yearning. Yearning is not a *reason* but a *determinant*, not the blind will of Arthur Schopenhauer but originary intelligence. As characterized by yearning, the meaning of existence is *consolation*. At the level of human existence consolation resolves itself as joy and sadness meditated upon by human consciousness as optimism and pessimism. The sadness is basic, but the joy is real for that which yearns. The sadness is fundamental since the cosmic goal is consolation rather than perfection. The pessimism is basic, but the optimism constantly denies nihilism because of what Asouzu calls the future reference, the indication of the possibility of a realizable progress, even as it is necessarily indicated, within a totality that is yearning. Asouzu condenses this insight into the imperative of complementary reflection: *Allow the limitations of being to be the cause of your joy*.

What content, synthetic or analytic, does Asouzu give to the principle above? "Thus, Ibuanyidanda philosophy seeks to show how the essential and accidental, how being and its various modes of expression form an integrated complementary whole," writes Asouzu by way of promise. "Here, we wish to show how being becomes manifest as the authentic mutual joyous experience that unifies all missing links."[42] While it is true that Asouzu has given some analytical content to the matter under consideration, he has left the surroundings and the general intellectual environment of *ibuanyidanda* philosophy bare. This is so because his philosophy lacks adequate construction. Perhaps we are not sufficiently immersed in his vision yet since Asouzu is still writing actively. Yet we have seen enough to know that there is a constructive lacuna in Asouzu. As a pathfinder he has been called to be a constructive thinker basically. All the same, he has rendered great service to African philosophy, from which we cannot but benefit.

Consolation philosophy seeks to find in philosophical fatalism the grounds of the universe's sufficiency. The question arises: "Can the doctrine of *mood* lead us to a conception of fatalism which in turn yields a notion of sufficiency that entails the necessity of the inevitable and therefore the compulsory existence of the universe?" Again this: "Can fatalism entail determinism?" How can we argue that sufficient conditions are prior to necessary conditions, that what suffices produces what is necessary? Granted, the point I am trying to make is complex as I seek to render more intelligible the matter of infinite regress raised by the supposition that determinism can give us a satisfactory explanation of the origin of the universe. The rule of causality says every event has a cause. This is necessity. But is it really true that for every effect there must be a cause? Let us assume that the phenomena of the world can be traced to God as First Cause. How do we account for God's existence? Thus we see that the chance element previously discarded rears its head just when we think it has been permanently shut out. Here tychism (the notion that chance plays an important role in the evolution of the universe) threatens theological determinism. Yet dignifying chance by conferring creativity on it makes it an intelligent force, a directional cosmic impulse. The battle line is therefore drawn between determinism and indeterminism, with the one losing its character now and taking the form of the other again.

My way out of this difficulty, the infinite causal regress, is to subordinate determinism to the notion of fatalism in the consolationist perspective. Fatalism then becomes the highest *necessity*, as that which throws up sufficiency and is itself sufficiency. For something to exist it must meet the conditions of sufficiency. That which is must be sufficient, either in itself or in something which is sufficient in itself. The necessity of a thing's existence can be abstracted from its sufficiency. We cannot generalize about a set of instances if we do not isolate particular instances. In causation this isolation of particular instances gives priority to sufficiency. If standing in the hot sun for a long period causes headache and having malaria fever also causes headache, we have two causes producing the same effect and standing as conditions. Both conditions are sufficient rather than necessary if considered together. It is enough to have malaria to get a headache, yet standing in the sun also gives one a headache. But when we isolate these instances and critically analyze them in their isolation the conditions previously seen as sufficient become necessary. That is to say, sufficiency passes into necessity. Let us reconsider the example of headache caused by malaria. Moving from plurality to singularity, one gets a headache if and only if one has malaria. Applied to the puzzle of existence, this point we have made indicates that logical certainty is extracted from existential probability. The universe must necessarily exist only because it is sufficient unto itself. Logic demands certainty (rigid determinism), but existence which is expressed in plurality gives us probability. Probability encompasses the inevitability of events as a person's limited intellect grasps them. Existence gives us not a precisely determined universe but rather an imperfectly expressed universe, whose imperfection nevertheless indicates the possibility, nay necessity, of progress. That which is probable is an imperfection that yet points compulsorily towards progress by virtue of its existing essentially as consolation, fatalistically, having no reason for existing accessible to the human mind beyond the realization that it yearns and is in motion. Existence indeed is an absolute unity, but this absolutism is perceived by the human intellect as pluralism. The entailment of necessity by sufficiency supplies the only genuine reason for the validity of dialectic.

As the grounds of all actualities and possibilities, fatalism is the sufficient condition for the existence of the universe. It accounts for the puzzle of necessity as an inevitability rooted in a yearning essence. Thus we say the universe, existence itself, is a *fatality* and that the human mood mirrors an objective external state with which it is intimate. The clarification of this African monistic dialectic is the supreme struggle of the consolationist perspective. While it is true that we have taken notice of the merits and demerits of the dominant Western philosophical traditions (in particular, rationalism, phenomenology, existentialism, and philosophical analysis), we must insist that our system is neither a development from Western existentialism nor a product of philosophical analysis. Our system, that is, consolationism, is African philosophy. Existentialism takes full account of one's concrete situation, which is interesting, but fails to account for the fatality of the universe, thus preparing the way for the despair-laden postmodernist tradition. The almost entirely bleak vision of existentialism and postmodernism is contrary to the optimistic African spirit (Afro-optimism) which Senghor hinted at ahead of Asouzu's declaration of this optimism. The analytical tradition dominant in England and America relies too much on the power of language and seeks unjustly to subordinate philosophy to science as if sounding "scientific" will ever make the philosopher a scientist of notable scientific achievements. Linguistic analysis alone cannot achieve our task which is the interpretation of the mood of the 21st century, the satisfaction of the rigorous standard philosophy as a discipline demands, the development of a doctrine that is practical by providing humanity with intellectual hope, and the promotion of African speculative thought. If truly language is contemporaneous with thought (for it cannot be prior to thought) it is because the former is a development of thought and, through thought, the *mood* of eternity. Language is subordinate to this *mood*. Thought itself is an evolutionary fragment of *mood*. Language cannot create a pain. Thought may express this pain, but *mood* is this pain itself. Consequently, consolation philosophy is not particularly enamoured of the Anglo-American analytic tradition while taking note of its emphasis on clarity and rigor.

EXISTENCE AND CONSOLATION

PART TWO

THE DOCTRINE OF GOD AND NATURE

Chapter 3

CONSOLATIONIST METAPHYSICS

General Preamble

What was the universe like in the beginning? Did matter detach itself from mind or did mind evolve from matter? If monism must triumph over dualism, can it be insisted upon that there was any real detachment of matter from mind or that the notion of mind evolving from matter marks any real victory for abiogenesis and mechanicism?

The creative will of a mind which is eternal issues out of itself as external reality within the fullest reality consisting of itself and everything in itself and outside itself of which it is the principle. The universe is already a given. This given is striving, yearning. As yearning mind has emerged. This mind is either conscious or unconscious. As yearning this mind is *mood*, and the eternal constituents of *mood* are joy and sadness. It is not only human consciousness that comprehends joy and sadness. There must be cosmic joy and sadness for things to develop from their infancy. The joy-component of existence is affirmative and optimistic while the sadness-component is restrictive and pessimistic. The moodiness of the universe is asserted because here is a universe that exists for no other reason than that it yearns for a completion that is never possible. Purpose is indicated, but a stubborn mechanical theory of the universe frustrates the hopes of teleology. We theorize that matter is the weight of sadness in the Eternal Mood, which is the same as saying that matter and mind have their origin in the Eternal Mood, the primitive mind and origin of all things. A stone, for instance, is a piece of matter not because its essence is alien to mind but because it sleeps under the weight of sadness. The chief claim of radical biological evolution or abiogenesis is that this sleep of cosmic sadness can be so shaken that awareness will arise out of this sleep, thereby gifting what may pass as non-life with a sentient life and therefore mind. But if mind comes to be as a consequence of evolution, it is reasonable to assume that matter was already intimate with mind, that the sadness-component of existence had from the beginning bestowed the capacity for feeling on that which seems dead. The *sadness* we are talking about and making contemporaneous with the primitive mind is what Western existentialist philosophers celebrated as the "nothing." Henri Bergson correctly assumed that the nothing is a cosmic impossibility.[1] As the sadness-component of existence, the nothing (as emptiness) is impossible. It is truly a primitive emotion burdened by the reality of existence as a fatality. If my readers are uncomfortable with what may seem to them anthropomorphic thinking I will substitute the words "sadness" and "joy" with the words "terror" and "beauty" to capture the essence of cosmic yearning. However, I want to make it clear at this point in my treatise that what holds for humanity holds for nature, more or less, that humanity and nature are in solidarity. If humans yearn nature yearns too. If nature or the objective universe did not yearn there would be no universe in the first place and no one to observe its motions.

Existence is a perpetual grieving for its fatality, the necessity of its being real and not being able to attain perfection, gifted only with consolation which is also its essence. To be nothing means to be in a state of oblivion. This oblivion does not mean non-existence but rather means existence slumbering under the weight of cosmic grief without yet being aware of this condition of cosmic grief. Wherever consciousness emerges its triumph automatically becomes its curse, for it will become aware of the condition of cosmic grief that compels matter to detach itself from mind or causes mind to evolve out of matter. Cosmic sleep is what it is: potential awareness. Silence is what it is: preparation for the emergence of consciousness. If we sound a bit mystical it is not because we seek to mystify but because the problem of origin itself is *mythopoeic*, that is, shrouded behind the existential veil of cosmic emotion. Any attempt to theorize in this terrain will yield something that looks mystical. Quantum physics is a branch of physics that has contended with the mythopoeic character of existence with the blurring of determinist and indeterminist borders within force-fields characterized by yearning. We are far from playing Plotinus here. To run away from our African inspiration on account of encountering the dense darkness of the *mythopoeic* is to betray the cause of African philosophy. We will have to go back to the doctrine of *mood* and gradually make our way through the dark labyrinths of thought and arrive at a more luminous understanding of God and nature.

Life is the entry into awareness of mind and matter. Matter when raised to awareness becomes life and mind when deadened into silence becomes matter. To this extent we may say that without the mind there is no life and without life there is no mind. We are at a loss how mechanicism, active and self-directed, can be possible without a modicum of intelligence guiding the directional activities of the universe. If mechanism is itself a miracle, as Santayana will say, we are still faced with the profound mystery of the appearance of the *mythopoeic*. The *mythopoeic* is in all things. It is the emotion of the universe, fatality itself as the coming into existence of terror and beauty. Our own analysis will take a non-scientific path while not ignoring scientific developments. Let us return to the idea of matter as the silence of existence, as mind not yet come to awareness. We hope to show that the realm of human subjectivity mirrors the realm of nature's objectivity. We are to show that mind and matter are in solidarity—as quantum physics seems to be doing today with the project of the "dematerialization" of matter—by appealing to the consolationist doctrine of *mood*, by revealing the dialectic phases of the evolution of cosmic sadness as the building block of existence, all through its metamorphosis as fear and anxiety in human consciousness, to its dream of joy and the emergence of intellect. As the host of despair the intellect can be said to be anti-life, for it is closer to the sadness-component of existence than the joy-component. It is this pessimistic tendency of the intellect that compelled Bergson to denigrate the intellect and identify it with inert matter in his masterpiece *Creative Evolution*.

In the beginning (could this ever have been?) intelligence was a mood, the primitive mood of melancholy. Creation cannot be possible where there is no silence to be shattered. And where there is silence there will be the emotion of grief, struggling to become consciousness on its way to full maturity once the necessary conditions are there, and they are always there. For *mood* is a fatalistic miracle which must evolve. A creative process cannot be blind because it is itself an emotion struggling to unravel intelligence and complete cosmic joy in an exercise of freedom. This freedom is impossible for any existent that characterizes itself as yearning. It is definitely not bestowed on the created thing. Freedom remains to be won by the fatalistic principle which creates and comprehends creation as an expression of its conquest of cosmic fear, the completion of its consolation, which then qualifies it to be called Consolation. We propose God as this fatalistically willing principle, as the consolation of the universe. And if freedom can be predicated of any being in the universe at all, then God is this being. The Eternal Mood or the principle of fatalism (external to the creation that has come out of the nothing of silence) we say is emotional in its life. Being emotional it is the totality of joy and sadness, represented to itself as optimism and pessimism. Creation or the willing of worlds outside the Eternal Mood is an act of optimism. The idea of creation is perfect from the viewpoint of optimism but its execution is imperfect because pessimism broods at the root of the eternal life which the Eternal Mood is the principle. The idea of the world, perfect in its moment of conception, issues out of its principle as imperfection. The world carries this imperfection because its birth did not escape the essence of cosmic existence which we keep saying is yearning, the striving towards a perfection which, being impossible, must make a final stop with consolation and desire contentment. The inspiration of the world is pure emotion. Instead of using the categories of perfection and necessity it is fitting for us to talk about consolation and sufficiency.

So the world comes to be as an idea out of the will of an inspirer. This inspiration may remain the silence of eternity as matter. We call matter silent sadness because matter is not conscious enough to comprehend the fatality in which it subsists. Matter is solid *mood* because unawakened. On the other hand, *mood* emerging as an idea from its inspirer may retain its advanced character of mentality and develop into the intellect, such as we find in homo sapiens. But this intellect once formed is not to be regarded as alien to matter, as perpetually opposed to nature. It is not even to be opposed with life. Matter points immediately to the failure of reality. Reality is supposed to be the perfect idea, perfect joy, but its eternal existence is already imperfect, a yearning. The pessimism of the human intellect which expresses itself in nihilist impulses and despair arises from its glimpse of the terrible dialectic operative throughout all existence and in the fatalistic principle. The realization here is the intellect's ultimate emotionalization. Henceforth, it is grief-stricken. Henceforth, it remains in amazement at the imperfection of things and turns to nihilism in search of a negative consolation. Yet this same intellect is the refinement of the emotion, terrible as its final knowledge is and regardless of the tendency towards nihilism. But, then, the intellect lacks the simple faith of the emotion in which it is born and finds it difficult to come to terms with the consolation which is the highest aspiration of a yearning totality. Failing to find perfection, the human intellect tends towards the conclusion that "nothing" is better than a "yearning something." The intellect is embittered into rebellion against life and its principle and yearns for the nothing which is just as impossible as perfection.

Clarification of the Nature of the Eternal Mood

Since my system will have as its foundation the Eternal Mood, it will be necessary to clarify its nature, what I think it is, and how it can be efficient at all as the fatalistic principle and account for origins and destinies. I bring a uniquely African intuition to this clarification, such that instead of regarding the Eternal Mood as the principle of rationality I make it the principle of emotionality which is the basis of life and later deduce rationality from emotionality. Developing the Senghorian idea of the essential emotionality of the universe and the complementary reflection of Asouzu further,[3] I say that the universe is not a rational universe *per se*. The rationality of the universe, which we grasp in our minds and in the very fact that the universe aligns itself to mathematical laws, follows from a deep-rooted emotionality, a yearning. It is in postulating this thesis of emotionality that we can found subjectivity or consciousness and objective nature on the primordial elements of joy and sadness, the constituents of *mood*. There is nothing absurd here, for what the human mind grasps as optimism and pessimism are actually epistemic correlates of joy and sadness. By assuming *mood* to be the totality of joy and sadness we hit upon a philosophy able to show the universe as a fatality, able to demonstrate why reality has to fail by falling short of perfection and exhibiting the dimensions of the tragic.

In this system alone can we be able to explore a metaphysics of terror preparatory to a morality of consolation which fascinated the Western existentialist philosophers from a distance but finally eluded them. Why, for example, is there evil in the world? We can show that evil is real both in human affairs (and the lower grades of living things) and in the order of seemingly non-living nature. For while not wholly embracing a panpsychic conception of life and the universe, we must hold that everything breathed upon by *mood* is potentially alive. A rational universe such as that propagated by Plato, Aristotle, and Kant cannot issue out of *mood*. The important question for humans as they try to comprehend the fatality of existence is not the reality of evil itself but this: why is there evil at all? Here we are talking about physical and moral evil, not moral value. This question becomes the most important question for the mind privileged with a questioning intellect when we realize that "inanimate" nature manifests a capacity for rapacity or destruction; for example, in the cases of volcanic eruptions (regardless of their identified benefits), earthquakes, and hurricanes. In other words, nature too yearns. It struggles to attain consciousness, the attainment of which is the epistemic encounter of mind with the meaning of the tragedy of existence. That our universe is in one dimension clearly a deformed universe indicates that a radical element underlies its apparent rationality, the element of the emotional. In accepting this submission alone can we make yearning the character of the Eternal

Mood, and, by transmission, the essence of all things, from which it follows that the goal of the universe is the realization of *consolation*, not reason nor form nor freedom *per se*. Reason in the absence of yearning is impossible and freedom is an illusion. Freedom here equates happiness. It is not granted to the created thing to ever attain this perfect state as hard as it struggles for this ultimate realization.

The Eternal Mood as the Mood of Melancholy

Senghor dimly realized the great truth that our universe would have been a perfect universe if its rationality claimed independence of emotionality. In a rational universe the mechanism of cause and effect would have validated radical determinism, such that it would be possible for not only God but also humans to predict the future with exact precision. It would have been possible to have one billion Nostradamuses, all seeing tomorrow in one sweeping act of vision with such precision as would have amazed Nostradamus himself. What is more, it would have been possible for us to avert all future calamities from the beginning. Such superhuman capacity would at once transform mechanism in nature into freedom in nature. It would have been the perfection of determinism, the final solution to the problem of evil: the final solution, we say, because evil would not exist in a perfectly rational universe.

Since our world is an emotive world that throws up rationality necessarily, we now go back in search of the principle informing this paradox that makes consolation the goal of conscious and unconscious existence. I have spoken of the Eternal Mood, but this too is the *mood* of melancholy, by which I mean that it is the principle of fatalism. The fatal is that whose occurrence challenges causal deterministic explanation, whose existence would seem gratuitous because the only reason for its existing is that it yearns. It is like Sartre's *being-in-itself*, which simply is. But unlike Sartre's *being-in-itself*, the Eternal Mood existing gratuitously becomes effective as the reason for everything posterior to it. Whatever it inspires into being carries the stamp, however lightly, of its nature. The Eternal Mood is not simply Reason or Thought or Thought of Thought. If it were all these only, its eternity would not be a given and its existence would not be fatal, requiring the postulation of a spontaneous act of its emergence. The Eternal Mood is a primal emotion carrying within itself the sufficient grounds of the universe. To say it exists fatalistically is the same as saying it came into being undetermined and without any reason beyond the fact that it is *yearning*. The Eternal Mood is the mythopoeic dream of existence and the origin of illusion. This illusion is the truth of a fatalistic existence realized and continuously being realized in the unfolding of reason out of cosmic emotion. The Eternal Mood is more than an impersonal principle. It is not perfection in the sense conveyed by the categories of omnipotence and omniscience. The categories applicable to it are those of power and glory. It is *mood* before becoming mind. The difficulty involved in the clarification of this principle is due to the fact that its emergence is not determined *per se* but fatalistic. The rule of causality cannot account for its beginning, or any beginning at all; and there has to be a beginning, even of that which is eternal. When the straight course is rejected in favor of cyclical evolution the first cycle must still be accounted for.

Yet we say it is the *mood* of melancholy. How is this the case? Melancholy in human terms or in its ordinary meaning refers to the state of unhappiness. At the risk of being accused of anthropomorphism (which incidentally is the character of all thinking directed towards the mythopoeic dream of existence from which everything springs, as we will try to justify later), we extend this attribute to the Eternal Mood that we may properly show that it is *mood*. Our metaphysical system recognizes two elements of *mood* which constitute melancholy, for to be melancholic and thereby illusory is the nature of *mood*. These two constituents of *mood* are joy and sadness. Consciousness identifies these objective metaphysical realities as optimism and pessimism. Sadness is a tendency towards nihilism or negation while joy is a tendency towards affirmation. Joy is the creative impulse in the Eternal Mood. Sadness and joy constitute differences in the Eternal Mood and their interplay accounts for the dialectic of *mood* and the unfolding of a rational universe out of a given principle of cosmic emotion.

I say that the Eternal Mood is not simply an impersonal principle. As primal yearning it cannot be impersonal although it is conceived as impersonality when taken as the moving principle of the universe, one contemporaneous with the universe. It is the origin of desire which Buddhism calls *tanha*. This yearning has a content that is primal emotion but a form that is reason. Thus I say that rationality follows from an underlying emotionality and that determinism does not provide the sufficient condition for the existence of the universe.

The Eternal Mood as the Mythopoeic Dream of Existence

The Eternal Mood is the mythopoeic dream of existence for the very reason that it is the first principle of melancholy. The dream-like character, the apprehension of an imperfect objective reality by consciousness, is traceable to the emotional veil of existence, the sadness of *mood* which also accounts for the malaise of evil in the world. That human consciousness struggles to comprehend reality and ends up having the sense of dream or illusion is not something to be disputed. Philosophers argue about the objectivity of the universe outside the mind and endorse probabilism and skepticism precisely because of this dream state of consciousness relative to reality. When we say the world sometimes looks unreal, usually in our more pessimistic or skeptical moments, we do not mean that it does not exist. What is happening is that human consciousness which itself is a fragment of *mood* is seeing its very nature reflected back to it in external nature. Mind and matter are in solidarity and the yearning of *mood* characterizes both. The *mythopoeic* is the insubstantial reality of *mood*. This dream is not static. It would be static only if it is nothingness. But the Eternal Mood which expresses this dream is not nothingness. It thinks not only of itself but outwardly, and in thinking outwardly it creates the tension of activity that terminates in plurality. Pluralization is the realization of the yearning essence of *mood*, an act of optimism, which nevertheless does not unveil perfection but consolation. Reality must fail because it is born in emotion rather that in reason. However, its objective expression is already its consolation. Thus the Eternal Mood alternates between the impersonal principle of fatalism and the personal principle of creation. There is a "love of creation" in the Eternal Mood necessitated by its being the yearning of the joy-principle for freedom.

By virtue of its constitution the Eternal Mood is already the mythopoeic dream of existence, realizing itself as the power in all the possibilities of joy and sadness and imparting this character of illusion—the emotionality suppressing and yet realizing rationality—to the outcome of its creative impulses. *Mood* is yearning and the driving force of that which yearns is intellectual love, the desire for creation and replication. This love wills the good when intention becomes externalized, but it contends with its own foundation principle, the sadness element of melancholy. This element tugs at the joy of creation and in pulling it backwards create the malaise of being in the externalized world. The *joy of being* which Innocent Asouzu celebrates in his *ibuanyidanda* philosophy is an incomplete joy. Cosmic joy perpetually contemplates the limitation imposed on it by its origin, the cosmic sadness that tugs at it. Realizing itself as incomplete, the joy of being seeks completion in a higher unity, in complementarity. The highest *complement* is the Eternal Mood which exists as the yearning of eternity. It is the closest thing to freedom, yet it is not freedom because of its inner joy-sadness contradiction. No *complement* in everyday human affairs can isolate joy from sadness. Human society can, of course, aspire towards progress in widening the sphere of inclusiveness but it is true that conflict will continue to threaten *complements*. Therefore the Asouzian immanent philosophy of optimism must refer to a metaphysics of terror. In making this referral we return to the task of explicating consolationist metaphysics.

The completion the joy element of *mood* seeks is never attained because being carries the silence of sadness, that which has been celebrated in the history of philosophy as the "nothing" by Western thinkers like Plato, Hegel, and Heidegger. The sadness of the world was famously reconsidered phenomenologically in relation to "anxiety" by such existentialist philosophers as Kierkegaard, Heidegger, and Sartre. So, then, by revealing its constitution as melancholy the Eternal Mood reveals itself as the mythopoeic dream, and in being the foundation of existence it is the mythopoeic dream of existence. The nature of the *mythopoeic* is simply the character of emotionality which creates illusion and determines truth as the pursuit of illusion. This illusion is *consolation*. For we can only talk about truth, and absolute truth indeed, if happiness or freedom is realizable. Freedom and happiness being impossible, existence is left with the consolatory elements of joy and sadness, the yearning which is the totality of existence. As hard as *mood* tries to attain freedom it stares consolation perpetually in the face. This consolation, existence itself, is the "something" in view of the impossibility of the "nothing" which is in fact the sadness of being. It is possible that there was a beginning, but this possibility is no longer essential to fatalism since our universe is already expressed, and expressed as an imperfection.

The Dialectic of Mood and the Inevitability of Creation External to the Eternal Mood

Having established cosmic sadness and joy or terror and beauty (of which human sadness and joy are developments) as the building blocks of existence and constituents of *mood*, how to we proceed to show that a second reality dependent on the eternal reality had to come into animated existence? This inevitability can be demonstrated by the explication of the dialectic of *mood*, involving its constituents. This is not a tension of opposites *per se* but one of complements which, nevertheless, are doomed never to arrive at a perfect complementarity. The tension involves a unity that discriminates within itself and recognizes the tendencies of cosmic sadness and joy. Recognition of the tendency of sadness in the Eternal Mood is pessimism while recognition of the tendency of joy is optimism. While sadness deepens the character of impersonality in *mood* given its pessimistic character, joy accentuates the character of personality given its optimism. The cosmic tension involves a swing from impersonality and indifference to personality and love and back again, in perpetuity. This is yearning. This tension creates activity such that the Eternal Mood, already the impersonal principle of fatalism, recognizes itself as the personal God of creation. From principle to creativity and back again, endlessly. The drying up of emotion into the static indifference of eternal perfection is arrested by the filling up of emotion into the active benevolence of intellectual love which finds peace in consolation. Creation is an activity of love, and not merely an activity of love but indeed intellectual love, for the Eternal Mood is conscious of an outburst of optimism which yet is doomed from the beginning to imperfection from the originating principle. God as the originating principle of creation is to be deemed the Being that has conquered the eternal despair of *mood* within Himself and therefore has become the Being of power and glory rather than omnipotence and omniscience. Creation is contemplated in God as perfect. But issuing out of His will in an act of intellectual love it resonates with imperfection because a reality distinct from the Being of power and glory now claims independence without having won the victory God won for Himself as the Eternal Mood transiting from impersonal principle to personality.

The "nothing" of sadness is thinnest as "silence," the state of unawareness of the terrible dialectic at play in *mood* which embraces all reality and is indeed reality. If by "nothing" we mean a nil that was never started or opened up, this is impossible. If it is possible, then we cannot comprehend this possibility. It is beyond human consciousness to comprehend a nil below silence, for everything is yearning. Yet even as yearning is eternal there must have been a spontaneous beginning of this cyclical intimation, the outburst of yearning in an unconditioned act. Imagining this cosmic scenario is sheer horror, but, then, the idea of a beginningless eternity is just as terrible to contemplate.

What we regard as nothingness is in the perspective of our consolationist philosophy the silence of sadness. The awakening of this sadness to the state of creativity and the energization of the sadness that hides it results in the joy of creation, the joy of being. So creation grasped as the totality of matter and energy, matter and mind, issues out of a higher mind which transits from impersonal principle to personal God by virtue of intellectual love which the joy element of *mood* activates, the rationality of its emotionality, the activity of optimism. This primordial mind becomes personal because it is first an impersonality subject to the dictates of an eternal dialectic of *mood*. The dialectic of *mood* isolates the tendencies of joy and sadness. With joy goes the formation of the world, the outburst of emotion as mind and matter. Since the balance of creation favors joy and optimism, creation itself is not an act of malignity or irresponsibility. Creation is an act of a good will perfect in the mind of the creator but imperfect outside the creator's mind. Creation carries the silence of sadness which dominates it as fear. Creation as matter slumbers under the weight of cosmic fear, unable to have knowledge of the terrible dialectic of *mood* that throws it up. The ignorance of matter is its salvation. But mind having gained consciousness suffers from the dominance of this fear which it clearly discerns. This fear is latent in the Eternal Mood, latent because it lacks any real effectiveness. In God who is the personality of the Eternal Mood this fear has been overcome by intellectual love.

Thus I say that the categories of omnipotence and omniscience are not appropriate to God. These Western categories cannot give us the God of Paul the Apostle. They cannot give us the Christian God, only the God of Aristotle and Plato. Such categories would be ideal in a rational universe. A rational universe is a perfect universe in which perfect determinism reigns so that effects are clearly adequate to causes, completely erasing real novelty. But this universe would be a static universe, one in which motion is a mere illusion, a universe frozen forever, the impossible universe of Parmenides and Zeno. The hope of such a perfect but lifeless universe is just an emotional demand of the intellect for eternal peace. The demand arises from anthropomorphic thinking. And when this eternal peace is attained, what must we find and have? Nothing but an eternal peace in eternal melancholy. The eternal rest sought is eternal melancholy, the latter being the first and the last, the beginning and the end. The testimony of common sense with regard to the impossibility of a static universe is amply supported by the reconciliation rationalism of Plato the father of Western idealism, the unsteady dualism of Kant, the creative evolutionism of Bergson, and developments in quantum physics. The setting aside of the problematic categories of omnipotence and omniscience will subtract nothing from God's majesty. The demand of infinite perfection is a mere emotional requirement of an intelligence that has not yet come to terms with the essence of *mood*. What the consolationist perspective demands is not an infinitely powerful God but a sufficiently powerful God defined by His glory as the conqueror of cosmic silence. God is eternity itself and therefore a yearning with no determinate frontier, a perpetual realization of the possibilities of *mood*, the finding and further seeking of consolation.

It has been shown that there is a creation out of eternity or out of nothing but in time. The release of matter and mind, creation, should be regarded as the moment time and space came into play, unfolding out of the silence of *mood*. Matter carried space within it as silence into the world at the birth of the world. Mind carried time within itself as the conscious acknowledgment of the presence of silence, and the world was born. But time is not the product of mind nor space the product of matter. Time and eternity are already one in the Eternal Mood. Space is already united with the silence of cosmic sadness in the Eternal Mood. Consequently, time as perceived by consciousness is objective. It is prior to human consciousness and survives it. All the talk about the immanent limitations of time and space, its singular application only to the "natural" world, misses the point. Time and space are not this-worldly while eternity and the silence it carries are other-worldly. If the conditions of space and time imply a certain metaphysical and epistemological limitation it is because *mood* informs this limitation. At the bottom of yearning lies a negativizing force inclined to pessimism—cosmic sadness. Time is at once in things and outside things. It is the immanent side of eternity. This is perhaps what Kant was trying to realize in the transcendental aesthetic of *Critique of Pure Reason* when he talked about the transcendental ideality and empirical reality of time. Time has to be outside things because it is merely the perspective of eternity grasped by consciousness. A sufficiently optimistic consciousness, that is, a superior mind, can comprehend eternity in the very act of comprehending time. The human intellect is not sufficiently powerful to execute this operation.

We return now to the dialectic of *mood* which yields reality outside the Eternal Mood. The question now is, how did matter and mind go their separate ways? Quantum physics has revealed the insubstantiality of matter at the micro level of electrical interactions. If we hold that mind and matter proceed from *mood*, it stands to reason that they are of the same essence, the one differing from the other only in the degree of the possession of consciousness and therefore latent and active life. Everything is potentially alive, being a fragment of *mood* which is characterized as yearning. The active life may never be awakened, but it is still there in the belly of silence. Our theory is not a universal panpsychism *per se* although same is implied, since silence unawakened constitutes an unbridgeable gulf between life and what we may call potential life. The creative impulse must realize itself outside its originating principle, the Eternal Mood. This impulse is still yearning and so develops into life and consciousness. When this impulse deadened by the weight of silence fails to attain to life and consciousness we refer to it as matter. Matter is that which fails to attain the life-potential and reach the knowledge of the fatality of the universe. That which attains consciousness immediately grasps the tragic dimension of existence. However, it is not clear why matter had to petrify into the state of unawareness in the form we see it in the world and why mind should go on to attain consciousness and be tormented by the pessimism of the human intellect. A stone is what it is and a human being is also what it is. While both are potentially alive, starting from the beginning, the human phenomenon possesses an intellect given to doubt, despair, and pessimism. The stone having become a petrified impulse of *mood* ceases to strive towards consolation and the terrible knowledge of fatalism which reaches its peak in the anxiety that belongs to the human phenomenon. In humans the impulse carried by joy realizes a fuller being with a full-functioning mind which, tragically, finds that its very nature is its curse. The human phenomenon carries matter too, but the matter it carries possesses life. The matter here is *body*. This mind, intimate with anxiety, is *otu oche*, the human mind. It carries the stamp of *Otu Owoicho*, the Eternal Mood. In the third part of this work we will provide a fuller discussion of human anxiety which is an important fact of consciousness and has already been noted in Western philosophy.[4]

Creationism and Evolutionism

At the heart of the claims of creation lies the God-factor. Scientific evolutionism seeks to eliminate the God-factor and regard the course of the development of organic phenomena from inorganic phenomena as undirected or as a mechanical process directed by some nebulous power called chance. Some philosophers and scientists like Jacques Loeb will say that the origin of life and indeed the world itself do not constitute any riddle at all, that as soon as we study physico-chemical mechanism under the microscope of the searching intellect the jigsaw puzzle of existence falls into place and we announce the triumph of mechanism working through evolution.[5] For Loeb since the processes of the formation of human sex cells and fertilization—ontogeny and phylogeny— can be reduced to physical and chemical bases the riddle of human life and life in general stands solved. Faith in the sufficiency of mechanism is complete when Ernst Haeckel proclaims his belief in the unity of all nature and the natural laws of development. This way he thinks we can avoid the difficulty involved in invoking a "supernatural creation, although he does not reject the idea of a pantheistic God similar to Spinoza's Substance.[6] He is putting forward a theory of abiogenesis, what he calls spontaneous generation or *archigony*, using the very simple organism *monera* as a case study. For him this organism is so simple that it could have arisen from inorganic elements by spontaneous generation. All the same, Haeckel confesses that the process of *autogeny* (the origin of a simple organic individual in an inorganic formative fluid) and *plasmogeny* (the origin of the organism in an organic formative fluid or fluid which already contains life-forming elements like albumen and hydrate of carbon) that constitutes the mother process of spontaneous generation has not been demonstrated to be true. Before we comment on the observation of Loeb and Haeckel let us look at what an atheist turned deist has to say about abiogenesis. Confronted with the mind-boggling magnitude of the complexity of the physical universe and its conformity to natural laws, a complexity matched, if not surpassed, by the mechanism of the human DNA and brain, Antony Flew asked, "How can a universe of mindless matter produce beings with intrinsic ends, self-replication capabilities, and 'coded chemistry'?"[7] The DNA is a highly complex coded system yielding meaningful information. How could a mechanism of chance have brought about this intricate arrangement, this complex coding? Continuing, Flew writes, "It is true that protobiologists do have theories of the evolution of the first living matter, but they are dealing with a different category of problem. They are dealing with the interaction of chemicals, whereas our questions have to do with how something can be intrinsically purpose-driven and how matter can be managed by symbol processing. But even at their own level, the protobiologists are still a long way from any definite conclusions."[8] After appealing to the apparent finetuning of the universe which ensures the exact quantitative balance of fundamental constants like the speed of light and the mass of an electron that make the evolution of life possible at all, Flew sees the need for a creative factor like Bergson before him. Is evolution creative? Bergson answers in the affirmative. He believes that only in bringing in the creative element (what he calls the *élan vital* which may roughly approximate primal intelligence or mind) can we account for the rich diversity of organized life and the divergent evolutionary path life took at some decisive point. He notes:

> Vegetative torpor, instinct, and intelligence—these, then, are the elements that coincided in the vital impulsion common to plants and animals, and which in the course of a development in which they were made manifest

> in the most uniform forms, have been dissociated by the very fact of their growth. *The cardinal error which, from Aristotle onwards, has vitiated most of the philosophies of nature, is to see in vegetative, instinctive, and rational life three successive degrees of the development of one and the same tendency, whereas they are three divergent directions of an activity that has split up as it grew.*[9]

The problem men like Loeb and Richard Dawkins[10] have with any explanation of the evolution of life and non-living matter that introduces or hints at the creative factor is this, that a personal creator of the world and life will turn out an idle postulate since mechanical processes need must go on whether this personal creator is there or not. Biologists in particular have been emboldened to tow this line because the processes of life continue on their course without any apparent need for a First Cause. Yet, focusing on the course of these processes while ignoring their complexities oversimplifies the problem of origin and, to a lesser extent, of destiny. Determinism cannot account for the universe in which we find ourselves. Physical necessity is entailed by a prior condition which is sufficient for the emergence of the universe. Thus physicists who see farther than biologists are beginning to give up the hope of escaping the positing of an initial intelligence, a creative factor.[11] It is difficult to attribute the complexity of life and nature to the ingenuity or caprice of chance. The order in the world is still a marvel even when put side by side with the disorder in it. To give chance this power of creativity is to hypostasize it *ab initio* and propose a *mind*. To endow chance with this creative power is to deprive it of the nature of caprice, that is to say, to replace caprice with some form of intelligence. Mechanical processes cannot regress forever. The universe may well be eternal, but this eternity has to be accounted for as the moment of the spontaneous springing into being of matter and energy. This spontaneity would be altogether gratuitous, wholly pointless, unless eternity as a totality was regarded as the very expression of yearning.

Showing how this is the case is precisely the great task of consolation philosophy. The eternal regression of mechanical processes will lead the world and everything in it to dissolution and disappearance into nothingness. The condition of nothingness which logicians consider a mere quantifier indicative of a failed expectation but to which existentialists attribute a kind of substantiality seems an impossibility. The Western existentialists were not so naive, though. Their nothing did not stand alone. Heidegger linked it with *care* while Sartre linked it with freedom. But then we demand to know whether there was never a state of nothingness in the beginning. It is difficult for the mind to comprehend a substantial nothing, for a substantial nothing is already something. But was there never a beginning? The positive answer to this question is just as frightening as the negative answer. The nothing state must not be dismissed by us simply because we are fortunate enough to exist in an age infinitely remote from a mysterious beginning. Our metaphysics is aptly entitled the metaphysics of terror because we desire to investigate this difficult question using the theoretical instrument of fatalism in the unfolding of the dialectic of *mood*. We will revisit this problem of the nothing in the third part of this book which records our doctrine of humanity.

So mechanism must have its terminus or proclaim its beginning as the commencement of the action of intelligence. Mechanicists and atheists face this dilemma, for they are confronted with a terminus much like a full stop. Yet this full stop can be what it is in the absence of a primordial mind if what the full stop encloses is "nothing." But can anyone assert that life and the world are nothing? The Hindu may cry *maya*, *maya*! but the illusion still reveals something. We have already said the universe is the truth of *mood*. The unbelieving thinker, a great nihilist, suspects that God cannot exist and that even if He exists He must be superfluous as far as the processes of the world are concerned. Yet he cannot account for the complexity of these processes, nor can he endow chance with being, for this will mean positing a God or some kind of primordial mind the way Haeckel did. If the unbelieving thinker takes account of the complexity of the world and life and begins to suspect that there may be a God after all he is again confronted with the problem of the terminus, which is also the problem of the beginning. Why is there a beginning at all? Why should something be said to be eternal? Can there be an end (Planet Earth, for instance, is projected to die in the distant future along with its sun) without a beginning? In other words, he confronts fatalism and is bewildered. Fatalism as the ultimate explanation, the beginning and the terminus, is that beyond which human intelligence cannot search. The human intellect stops where determinism stops. But determinism cannot account for the eternity of the world. So it is superseded by fatalism which asserts that all things happen as they do happen but that this happening is consequent upon yearning. This yearning under scrutiny yields the cosmic elements of joy and sadness which are active in the physical world as the laws of nature and which have attained awareness of the entire meaning of human life.

Fatalism also confronts the believing thinker since he cannot help asking himself how God came into being. This question can only be answered by fatalism. Beyond the verdict of fatalism there is no appeal. The mechanicist takes note of the believing thinker's dilemma in the existential confrontation with fatalism and tells himself that if God's existence cannot be explained he may safely embrace mechanicism doctrinally and posit its eternal operation, the permanence of physico-chemical processes going on in a cycle and needing no explanation. The atheist elevates chance to the level of mind in the process and remains troubled. This is the point Loeb and Haeckel (who is curiously not a clear-cut theist, deist, agnostic, pantheist, or atheist) make when they speak of a mechanistic conception of life and the unity of all nature. For them mechanism must rule, God or no God. Unfortunately for the unbelieving determinist, the mechanism that rules is either a mind or is subservient to mind. In vain they try to leave out the creative factor. We have no problem with the idea of the unity of all nature and the natural laws of development. Our system is a monism, after all, but not an all-embracing Spinozistic or Hegelian monism. We opt for a serrated monism which distances God from humans while retaining the notion that they are a fragment of God.

Flew had wondered how mindless matter could encrypt information of the type decoded in the human DNA. This is a legitimate question, one which defies a purely mechanistic conception of the world and life. We have already seen that matter has the quality of mind in being the interplay of *mood* in the continuing dialectic of *mood*. Matter and mind are products of *mood*. Since our hypothesis upholds this point the idea of a mind-matter is not ridiculous. A certain degree of panpsychism in the world is admissible if intelligence rather than an impossible chance is put at the foundation of existence. After all, it is the mind-matter combination that produces the animated phenomenon of the higher animals, which is to say that mechanical processes can so order and rearrange themselves that mind emerges out of matter. In other words, Haeckel's idea of spontaneous generation, and abiogenesis in general, is in principle not impossible. We are different from the mechanicists, however, in placing a fatalistic principle, the emotive principle of rationality, at the beginning of the causal chain, thereby accounting for the eternity of the world. While agreeing that evolution is possible and that the production of life from inorganic elements is not an absurdity, we hold up this bold caveat: *mechanicism is to be considered as a viable solution to the problem of the evolution of life and the development of nature if and only if a prior intelligence is posited as the force behind mechanism, which force is to be accounted for as a fatality*. In accepting this caveat we are certain to encounter the issue of the conditions necessary and sufficient for proclaiming the end of the causal regress. We will have to ask why the argument must not continue beyond

God, in which case God's emergence from nothing is a miracle of the order of the emergence of life from non-life. That is to say, if God is an absolute necessity antecedent to the existence of the universe, this universe itself could have come into existence as an absolute necessity requiring no further explanation. Yet one may wonder: If a God-created universe is admissible why should an uncreated universe not be admissible?

Let us call the above the "fatal" question for theism, deism, and atheism. It gives us two options. Either we agree that an uncaused God created the world or we admit, on the other hand, that an uncaused universe evolved entirely by mechanical means. Going with either viewpoint is an emotional requirement of the intellect as both doctrines bring us face to face with a confrontation with fatalism. Mechanicism must lead us back to the creative factor Bergson and Flew demanded. With the complex directionality of the human DNA and the physical universe as revealed by scientific investigations the "thingification" and eventual "ensouling" of chance becomes inevitable. This reification of chance is done willy-nilly, either consciously like Spinoza, Haeckel, and other pantheists or unconsciously like most agnostics. Reified, chance (and the mechanical processes that go with it) becomes a living mind, active and conscious as the principle of motion. Thus a God is made and we confront the question of the origin of God, the question why He should be the All in All if chance cannot account for itself. We are confronted by fatalism, the inescapable burden of philosophy and existence, the basis of the consolation of human consciousness in a universe of terror.

Evidence from the human genome mapping and scientific knowledge of the dependence of life on physical constants cannot tell the whole story of organic complexity or even the most significant part of it. The cosmic terror the bogey of determinism points to is already exhibited in the practical sphere of human conduct. We do not need to understand the processes of the DNA and the laws governing the motion of planets before we recognize or suspect that human capacity for good and evil is as much a marvel of complexity as the arrangement and functioning of the DNA and the physical mechanism of the cosmos. The tension between fatalism as the unraveling of the dialectic of *mood* and determinism as merely the rule of physical necessity rises again in the analysis of evil. A single human act of evil is as profound a mystery as the problematic of the origin of God. This latest consideration brings us to the element of the ethical and a shift away from the vertical metaphysics I have been struggling with so far. I will return to the problem of evil in a later section.

Early Explication of the Question of Fatalism

It is generally believed that fatalism is an inferior version of necessity, a mystical determinism. For most people the very notion of fatalism invokes some supernatural power who has decided from eternity the minute details of a person's life. Consequently, one ought to tamely accept circumstances beyond one's control. This is the general impression people have of the concept of fatalism. Everything that happens is predestined and the individual is powerless in the vast space of life into which he has been thrust. Determinism may or may not involve an overwhelming necessity such as we find postulated in the more familiar notions of fatalism. The necessity involved in determinism is not an overwhelming necessity, as compatibilists will insist, because it does not vitiate individual initiative. Determinism only states that for every effect there is a cause and once the cause is given the effect follows compulsorily if the law of causality must remain inviolable. This is regardless of the fact that indeterminism asserts the violability of the rule of causality. What is this inviolable law? It is necessity itself. Let us ask another question. Why should a law, supposedly a law of nature, be inviolable? We have already seen that natural causality, the mechanism of cause and effect, offers no real explanation of the essence and therefore origin of mind and matter. The analogy of a machine is often put forward to explain the mechanistic process, but why should there be a machine and how can it construct itself? Determinism cannot answer. It turns to fatalism for help. Therefore fatalism as the consolationist thinker conceives it enjoys a dignity higher than determinism. It is therefore no surprise that we have sought to show that fatalism entails determinism by promoting fatalism as the mother of all necessities.

The denigration of the concept of fatalism arises from its identification first with superstition as the religion of primitive peoples and then with religion as the consolation of unscientific minds. The justification of fatalism in whatever form it has been held by the peoples of the world is on a sound metaphysical footing. Its justification is the realization that terror stands between humanity and its existential apotheosis (freedom), the terror that eternally condemns him to never knowing freedom, the freedom of being the personification of power and glory. The justification is rooted in the dialectic of *mood* which is terror at play, the formation of the universe around the human phenomenon for reasons beyond the full grasp of humans whose only consolation is consciousness of the realization of joy and sadness in (moral) acts. Between an impossible "nothing" and a failed "something" one has to strive towards the meaning of individual existence. Fatalism offers the only template for the interpretation of his life. To denigrate fatalism and honor determinism begs the question. Between fatalists and determinists there is hardly any difference. They are identical twins of one mother claiming to have different fathers. When the determinist rules out the transcendental element, and he does so often in the name of a science that is not its own foundation, he cries out: "There is a grief in my intellect!" And rightly so since the human intellect is prone to pessimism, and pessimism itself is a never-failing symptom of sadness. After uttering this pessimistic cry of the determinist the fatalist moves on to combat nihilism with faith. In fatalism, the fatalist finds his consolation. The determinist does follow him but with a gnashing of teeth because he lacks the faith of the fatalist.

The Western-interpreted notion of determinism strives to leave out transcendental matters in the erroneous belief that mechanism is sufficient. Determinism is opposed to freedom, although soft determinism considers the opposing concepts complementary and reversible. The question of free will and determinism is no doubt a lively topic in contemporary Western philosophy with analytical philosophers of the Anglo-American axis outdoing themselves in the formulation of all sorts of scholastic subtleties to uphold the views they favor. In African philosophy, which is still struggling to grow, a profounder notion of determinism holds sway even if it has not been formulated with rigor and originality in view of the fact that African philosophy contends with the ever looming shadow of Western philosophy. In traditional African thought, which is unfortunately still equated with African philosophy, determinism is conceived at two levels: the level of naturalistic processes requiring no account of the origin of the world and the level of fatalism requiring precisely this account. The resort to fatalism is a last resort, very much similar to the resort of modern physics to the possibility of indeterminism to understand the uncanny behavior of micro-reality which supports everyday existence. The African standpoint is not a rejection of scientific determinism but a recognition of the truth that a mechanical cause is no explanation and that an explanation is always desired even though its possibility cannot go beyond what we have called fatalism.

Again, what do I mean by fatalism?

Fatalism is an umbrella notion for both determinism and freedom since the latter cannot complete themselves. Determinism and freedom are emotional demands of *mood* for intellectual satisfaction and therefore reversible concepts.

While determinism is often threatened by indeterminism and has to have recourse to fatalism for revalidation, freedom is a vanishing illusion under scrutiny. The analysis of fatalism always yields the ideas of determinism and freedom because the former is the terminus of intelligence and feeling. In fatalism the human intellect is finally satisfied with necessity since the worst consequence of necessity is sadness and the best result of this same necessity is joy. While determinism may be threatened by indeterminism and freedom declared a mere ideality under the power of intellectual analysis human joy and sadness are substantial, intimate with the whole person and justifiably projected into external nature as cosmic impulses or laws of nature. This is no mere subjectivization of nature, for humanity is nature and nature arises from the same source as humanity—the Eternal Mood. Panpsychism is no new philosophical discovery. It is entrenched in both African and Western thought. I have only formulated it in a more unique manner by discarding the Greek category of being and replacing it with the African category of *mood*.

Spontaneity liberates the initial determining condition upon which all subsequent conditions must depend. That which is eternal first began to exist as a spontaneity. There are difficulties involved here, of course. The spontaneous act is free; yet being uncaused it will seem to have been an act of caprice, something gratuitous. If we look for a cause we must look for a reason. But the coming into existence of the eternal, be this eternal God, the universe, mind, or matter, is uncaused. If chance is at the root of existence is the universe and human life not pointless? Clearly there is value in the world. Evil which we agree is abundant is also a value. The very existence of physical and moral evil confounds any extreme pessimistic notion of universal existence because the evil manifestation is the failure to complete a fundamental moral act, as we will discover later. The only comfortable solution to the problem posed by a spontaneous coming into being of the universe is the appeal to the doctrine of *mood*. The eternity of the world does not preclude its answering to a sufficient condition which is itself a free springing into being. For this uncaused act not to be capricious the sufficient condition of all things must be characterized by yearning. The doctrine of *mood* may not resolve the question completely, but we may find its solution satisfactory.

Our decisions about what to believe are essentially emotion-driven, and determinism is an intellectual construct demanded by the emotive faculty. So we have a determinism that is freedom when spontaneity takes the place of the elusive initial cause. Granting character or form to this nebulous spontaneity returns freedom to determinism as spontaneity becomes the cause carrying within itself the initial conditions from which later conditions can be deduced. Fatalism now comes in as a superior explanation, claiming to know the trick the intellect plays on us in distinguishing determinism from freedom when in fact both are actually the same thing, a causality whose foundation is rooted in the mythopoeic dream of existence, and therefore unintelligible beyond its emotive and practical significance. We are thus compelled to tackle the ethical question the ideas of determinism and freedom always bring up, since what really counts is not the forced dichotomy of freedom and determinism—neither of these theoretically complementary notions is accurate as what truly subsists is a causality neither free nor determined but *fatal*—but the emotional and intellectual significance of these notions. Fatalism is the recognition of the emotional and intellectual significance of freedom and determinism, the resolution of the existential conflict in the causality of *mood*. For freedom is the causality of spontaneity while determinism is the causality of this same spontaneity reified. The interchangeability and opposition of these two concepts lead us further to the question of origin through mechanism and teleology, up to fatalism, beyond which there is no light for the intellect born in emotion. The intellect cannot go beyond its origin, search as far as it can go. The impression that fatalism is indifferent to the ethical consequences of our actions because of a supposed tyranny of fate or God is not on a sound basis. The problem of evil, the question of the rightness and wrongness of actions, is most passionately engaged by our theory of fatalism. Fatalism is a richer statement of the aspiration of freedom and determinism and so cannot be indifferent to the question of morality which in fact pours out of its own essence to clarify the emotional and intellectual significance of a subjective existence that mirrors objective existence.

Fatalism is not a denial of moral responsibility but an affirmation of the moral character of the world. It does not reject the ethical preoccupations of freedom but demotes freedom from the position of reality to the status of an aspiration. Humans are not free. Nature is not free. Yet freedom is an aspiration. Fatalism does not uphold the claims of rigid determinism to having worked out an almighty formula in which causes correspond perfectly to effects, such that an initial condition strictly accounts for subsequent behavior of nature and living consciousness. Fatalism acknowledges, like determinism, that there is a given, a whole. It disagrees with the determinist viewpoint that this whole is perfectly structured and undeviating in its course, be this course a straight line from a beginning or a circle expanding from eternity. The fatalist declares that the whole is given in advance of a perfection impossible. The whole advances without ever arriving. Perfection is still an aspiration. At every point of advance of the unity of existence the whole expands without being able to complete itself. This is probably what Bergson means when he says repeatedly in *Creative Evolution* that existence is in fact duration, although he did not attempt a metaphysical exposition of the character of the *élan vital* beyond proposing it as a kind of dim and distant intelligence. Our sympathy for Spinoza (a believer in the completeness of the world and the necessity of evil) does not prevent us from admitting our kinship with William James (a *meliorist* believer in possibilities). We disagree that all is well with existence but think all may still be well with it. One may hasten to declare that we are projecting the demand of human consciousness into inert nature. We respond that nature is not inert, that mind is already factored into the structure of matter, and that this same matter will arrive at the conclusion of mind that all is not well with it if only it can be energized enough by the principle of feeling received by mind from *mood*. Of course we are still open to the criticism that matter has not yet been shown to possess even the most dormant feeling or intelligence. This is true. Yet if we do not insist on the solidarity between matter and mind the ideas of evolution and creation lose all meanings whatsoever. Science and religion become null.

For we do not see how evolutionism and creationism can escape the conclusion of the solidarity of mind and matter. It seems to us that these two theories of origin must refer to a theory of abiogenesis grudgingly before going their separate ways again in the schism of the God question. Biological evolution asserts the gradual production of species from simple life-forms through the mutations or variations that come with natural selection, hence the doctrine of the survival of the fittest which in the end is compatible with Jean Lamarck's theory of use and disuse. The pillars of evolution are graduality and adaptation, development and conformity to patterns suggested by the change inherent in development. On the other hand, the idea of creation promotes the active role of a primal intelligence in the coming into existence of things, an idea compelling in its metaphysical non-dogmatic purity. Creation does not have to follow the pattern described in the Book of Genesis—believing Christians today agree that a literal reading of the creation story of Genesis is not essential to the basic truth of the role of a creative principle immanent in the world. The Genesis story is a myth just like the creation stories that abound in African folklore. And myths are truth travestied. They hide truth by virtue of their direct contact with reality which is *mythopoeic*—illusory, emotional, and therefore consolatory. The myth is the intuitive revelation of a reality that cannot succeed as perfection, but must become successful—indeed already is successful—as consolation. This is the fatality of existence. Not being familiar with the concepts of the human intellect, mythology cannot describe pessimism, which is dependent on metaphysical sadness, but is naively content with optimism, the joy of being so enthusiastically celebrated by Asouzu in his complementary reflection.

The seemingly opposite concepts of creation and evolution are reconcilable at the point where it becomes apparent to the most honest intellectual observer of life and emotional participant in this same life that creationism already assumes a radical abiogenesis, in the same way that evolution already assumes *ab initio* this radical abiogenesis, in which life is seen as proceeding directly from non-life or, rather, dormant life. A moderate conception of abiogenesis may tell us that organic life developed from some inorganic substance already contained in the elements necessary for the emergence of simple life-forms and the commencement of active evolution. But may this inorganic life-causing substance not fall backwards into a condition totally inauspicious to the production of life? The theory of abiogenesis stands accused of wearing the mask of panpsychism, proclaiming that all things are alive and that all is in all. Why should all things be alive, as mechanistic evolutionism silently assumes, if there is no principle of life immanent in the world? I ask in defense of creationism. How can the life of the world (mind and finally matter) be assumed in perpetuity, be posited as an eternal phenomenon, without there being a living force coordinating and contemplating this phenomenon? If we say this phenomenon is completely meaningless and without reason, the directionality of evolution which is evidential for rationality laughs at us in the face. Evolution tells us that there is reason in the world, which is what the system of Aristotle, Bergson, Hegel, and other philosophers of nature sought to reveal in non-scientific language. Evolution is not sufficiently a mechanical process given the complexity of life and the physical world. Is reason not at work here? It is, but the reason at work is not a perfect reason, not the reason that produces or is intimate with Hegelian and neo-Hegelian Absolutes. The reason operative here is the *mood* of the universe. The nature of mood is to yearn. From *mood* intelligence develops towards its goal which is consolation, that which is already embraced in the light of the impossibility of the fond dream of the human intellect which is called freedom. This freedom is regarded in the ethical domain as happiness, eternal peace.

If we are to dogmatically regard evolution as sufficient in itself to explain all worldly phenomena and if this evolution is the eternal swirl of life it is not ridiculous to submit that at some point in the distant past, or even in the very beginning of all eternity, a Being evolved which is power and glory, to which the continuing evolution of the physical universe and human evolution owes its beginning. It is proper for us to hypothesize that a Being uncaused as a principle of eternity had reached the summit of evolution at a distant point in time which became its own consolation and won for itself the right to be called the Self-Sufficient. This Being emerging in eternity as a mere yearning impersonal principle evolved in time as a personal principle of the universe. Such a Being is called the Self-Sufficient because it won for itself freedom from the limitation of *mood*, the cosmic imperfection stamped on universal existence and most obvious in the appearance of physical and moral evil. Such a Self-Sufficient Being does not need the titles "Omniscient" and "Omnipotent" which would make Him responsible for the cosmic evil in the universe. For He is already benovelent, as yearning. The title of the Self-Sufficient is a profound enough honor for this majestic Being. Self-sufficiency entails the possession of power and glory. The point we are making is that evolutionism points at creationism and the latter refers us to the Eternal Mood conceived in its creative phase as God. God refers Himself to the Eternal Mood as the principle of fatalism beyond which there is nothing to be known. Let us simplify for the sake of clarity in the form of a chain of short questions and snappy answers. Is evolution creative? *The evidence from science says yes.* If evolution is creative is there any way we can avoid the idea of mind? *There seems to be no way of escaping this idea. We must always hypothesize chance if we embrace bare mechanicism.* If life comes from non-life is panpsychism not plausible? *Panpsychism sure is plausible because non-life becomes a form of life.* Is it possible that this primordial mind we have identified is God? *Very possible.* If chance must be reified for God to take its place, who created God? *There is no answer to this question beyond fatalism.* And the unraveling of a philosophy that seeks the explication of fatalism has been the supreme struggle of our African synthesis.

If fatalism rightly considered means the inevitability of mind arising in the affairs of the universe, a mind we have located outside space and time but in eternity as the Eternal Mood of melancholy, then fatalism as a doctrine does not overlook human actions relative to consequences. Its denial of freedom is simultaneously its affirmation of freedom as an impossible aspiration. The only being which can be said to be free is that Being which having removed from itself the tension of despair arising from the opposition of sadness and joy is worthy to be called the Self-Sufficient. The difficulty for many in coming to terms with an emotive universe defined in terms of cosmic joy and sadness lies in the tendency to regard objective nature as carrying no value whatsoever, as something simply vast and lifeless. Confronted by the terror of a fatalistic universe, we desire a gratuitous world from which we will depart into nothingness. Yet I have shown that this nothing is the cosmic reduction of silence, the sadness-state of existence denied the consciousness to recognize the fatality of its condition, its perpetual existence as nothing more than yearning. Human beings have not conquered the despair in their nature. When one tries to confront his despair, one appeals to the Being he thinks has won this cosmic victory. This conquest must have been achieved by some being infinitely stronger than humanity. Without this conquest there can be no creation and directional evolution. The recognition of the vast superiority of the *Other* (to borrow a term from Western philosophy) translates to one's recognition of how far one is from freedom and the happiness which belongs to God by virtue of His conquest of despair. An unbounded freedom such as the one Sartre celebrated is a nihilist freedom. Sartre's ontology of terror (terror because the in-itself exists without any additional capacity while the for-itself strives to become the in-itself in the unconscious quest for the annihilation state celebrated in Hindu and Buddhist thought as earthly and other-worldly nirvana) failed to become a metaphysics of terror and therefore lacked a certain depth. If Sartre had gone beyond ontology to metaphysics, beyond the situation to the reason, he would have abandoned the notion of an absolute freedom rooted in our ontological structure as a being in a world of valuelessness who paradoxically creates value. The nothingness behind us, in front of us, on all sides of us, which the masterpiece *Being and Nothingness* highlighted, is not greater than silence. Nothingness cannot dissipate the thinnest of existents which we call the silence of *mood*. Sadness is not only the denizen of the human mind but also reposes as silence in objective nature. Any monistic philosophy seeking the reconciliation of mind and nature cannot escape the necessity of projecting human emotions into the vast external world. Thus projected, these human emotions are transformed into cosmic emotions operative as energies, motions, and laws of nature. We doubt the objectivity of those cosmic impulses called laws of nature precisely for this reason, for their emotionality. The bogey of indeterminism is one great indication of the emotional character of these laws and impulses. The great difference between humanity and nature is that humans have found consciousness while nature still yearns for it. If nature never finds it, nothing is gained. If it finds consciousness, it will behave like humanity. The laws of nature will become full-fledged feelings. The nothing is not out there in the external world. What subsists in the external world is the silence of *mood*. The nothing is truly the outpouring of human despair gradually taken out of its subjective context. The nothing is the postulate of the nihilist, the unhappy person, or what Hegel will call the unhappy consciousness.

The nothing as inhering in mind remains significant because its mental subsistence identifies it with the silence of *mood* in the eternal context. Nature carries the nothing as silence and human consciousness confronts it as sadness. The nothing is not absolute non-existence but a grief rooted in *mood*. It is correctly noted that we talk of nothingness when our expectations or hopes or desires have not been met. Thus the pull of disappointment, a kind of grief, takes the place of expectation and we forget that we actually found "something" although we did not desire this "something" that was found. The insistence of analytical philosophers to see in the term "nothing" a mere quantifier is an over-simplification of the anti-reification perspective. The term "nothing" is rightly threatening. And why should it not threaten when the universe itself is a threatening universe not able to grant humans freedom? To simply dismiss this notion as metaphysically insignificant is to fall victim to the false grandeur of the human intellect, to pretend that all is well with existence when the evidence before our eyes clearly shows that all is not well. The nothing reveals to us that all is not well with life. The attitude of the logician with regard to this heavily pregnant term is one of "live, enjoy yourself, and die, for death is the natural consequence of life: so all is well." The evidence of evil contradicts this naive feel-good optimism. Existence is fundamentally a capacity for terror in objective nature and in the human mind.

In demoting freedom to the level of an aspiration which may never be realized, we do not intend to glorify determinism. We have shown that "determinism" as a demand of reason is another term for "freedom." For determinism calls for the rigid rationality of the universe, therefore a perfect structuring that terminates in freedom or absolute perfection. Since freedom is only an aspiration determinism is never complete. Determinism is incapable of thoroughly illuminating the very profound problem of causation. Determinism is a wish that all is well with, at least, the order of nature and perhaps humainty. Yet all cannot be well with a complex universe which throws up natural and man-made evil even in the eternal context which is a yearning context.

Fatalism and the Dialectic of Mood

The uniformity of nature often invoked in defense of rigid determinism is not the uniformity of a rational universe. The continuity of an emotional universe which we propose is serrated, jagged in its closure, is such that the principle we have called the Eternal Mood is outside nature and yet in solidarity with nature as the inspiration of nature, which is therefore a fragment of *mood*. Even non-living matter is potentially alive, but what is not yet alive is sleeping in profound silence. This is incipient panpsychism even if not universal panpsychism. It will be untrue that the inert matter has mind already, that all things have mind. That all things may come to have mind is a possibility since there is no "nothing" beyond "silence." On the evolutionary ladder sadness follows silence and joy follows sadness, the joy of being—that which is present everywhere but seems to be substantially absent everywhere. A man previously sitting on a chair, who gets up and observes the same chair under a powerful electron microscope will wonder whether he has been sitting on nothing because visible matter has reduced itself to sub-atomic particles. The joy of an elusive being vanishes just as it is about to materialize. From optimism to pessimism and from pessimism to optimism: thus moves the intellect in the circle of emotion in which it subsists. That which comes to pass must be, but the coming to be of things is neither the decree of determinism nor the act of freedom. Existence is the operation of the creative impulse of the Eternal Mood as consolation in the world. The Eternal Mood is principle, movement, and creativity. As an impersonal principle, philosophers have dared to regard it as an unconscious imagination midway between life and non-life. Conceived as a totality of existents, conscious and unconscious, it is an Absolute. As a personal creator it is regarded as God. This God lives in the life of emotion. As emotion, it is a mythopoeic dream and consolation. God is consolation because we cannot help not positing Him in our transcendental appeal just as we cannot know why He exists. The eternity that cancels out nothingness is a consolation because it is a compensation for the impossibility of nothingness understood in the perspective of eternal peace. This is fatalism. The emotive interpretation of anxiety by Kierkegaard and Heidegger must be seen, in the light of our hypothesis, as revealing one of the deepest insights in philosophy, anxiety as a stage in the dialectic of *mood* transforming despair into intellectual love, pessimism into optimism in the joy-state of existence. I will discuss this matter in some detail in Part Four of this work which will deal with comparative philosophy.

Yearning is the basis of mechanism. In yearning the possibilities of mind and matter are already presupposed. The more we come to grips with the complexity of the phenomenon of matter the more it strikes us that the elusiveness of substantial being is truly worrisome. We become shallow fatalists comforting ourselves with the assertion that what is simply *is* if we follow the scientific faith of mechanicism blindly. In going beyond mechanicism to seek grounds of explanation in a superior intelligence outside the world but in eternity we become profound fatalists. The doctrines of evolution and creation are both fatalistic doctrines, but the latter is a deeper fatalism than the former because it posits a God behind mechanism whose existence cannot be explained beyond the assertion that He is and beyond the suspicion or conviction that He is the Eternal Mood of melancholy.

Greek metaphysics sings: *being is, non-being is not*. For us a 21st century dialectic of being and non-being will be worthwhile only if we have a definitive understanding of the origin of the universe, the permanence or non-permanence of matter, and the utter insignificance of the "nothing." Matter is supposedly more solid than mind; yet it becomes almost as elusive as mind when we try to comprehend it. The intellect seeks to know but cannot know enough. Relative knowledge has not been transformed into absolute knowledge just as God has not been seen by a man with his naked eyes, for which reason he wonders whether there really is a God. Being is present everywhere, but nowhere is it substantial. Pessimism in all forms, even as the nihilism of the intellect, triumphs therefore.

The consciousness of sadness is pessimism. The emergence of reason deepens pessimism because this emergence enables humans to become aware of the tragedy of existence and the supreme reign of fatalism. When we are talking about human rationality (which is essentially the possession of reason) the following elements qualifies it, namely: (a) the knowledge of fatalism (b) the recognition of cosmic pessimism, and (c) the striving for the realization of the meaning of existence which is already outlined in the optimism of *mood*, satisfaction with consolation. Paradoxically, in reason, emotion has come under the burden of fatalism. Thus reason loses its apparent freedom, the seeming spontaneity of its emergence as the consciousness of cosmic tragedy. The tendency of human reason to nobility, calm, contemplation, and patience follows from the acknowledgment of the impossibility of freedom and the recognition of consolation as the only realizable goal of existence. Thus Kant says men should make themselves worthy of happiness before hankering after it.[12] The tendency to talk about human rationality as if it is independent of emotion is ridiculous. Reason is a feeling as much as emotion. Reason and emotion are one and the same thing in different phases. Emotion (spontaneous reason) is said to be blind not because it is reasonless but because it is the very foundation of reason, the power of pessimism below consciousness and therefore in the meantime delivered from the burden of existence (fatality) which it carries. We may regard the emotion as instinctual, yet it is more than instinct. Emotion is pessimism lightened by optimism, sadness relieved by joy. Sadness and joy are the basic emotions of developed consciousness. Whatever is now unconscious but later rises to consciousness and becomes capable of thinking automatically recognizes melancholy (the sadness-joy unity) as its constitution. While the intellect is the profound realization of the tragedy of existence, the foundation of being in sadness, the primal emotion is the very sadness and joy of existence. This proposition is easily confirmed when we observe people laughing or crying. Pain is a feeling of sadness, more or less; yet the person who cries because of some pain, physical or emotional, loses his pessimism or rather fails to come to terms with the full force of pessimism. The falling tears, the act of crying, bring relief. His pessimism has been diluted by optimism, the renewal of hope that things will get better since they are already as bad as they can be. He who cries does not cry because he is hopeless but because he seeks relief. He seeks consolation. The dialectic of *mood* is operative here.

If the same person were under the influence of reason he would not cry or would stop crying and become resigned. This resignation does not have to involve passivity; on the contrary, it is the spur to action. The need of consolation which emotion demands like a baby the intellect pursues with great determination in the knowledge that in the absence of happiness in existence consolation has been granted us and the universe. We are activists. The laughing human knows less pain and experiences a purer pleasure, a feeling of joy. The laughing person is not hopeless, but is trying to be hopeful. The pleasure one feels indicates consolation. Reason is actively involved in the sadness that brings tears and the joy that brings pleasure.

Some critics may want to dismiss our endeavor as a philosophy of emotion. Fundamentally, all philosophies are doctrines of emotion. The three greatest achievements of the human intellect, the conceptualization of determinism, freedom, and teleology, are all emotional demands of human existence. To our critics we respond, without apology, that the structure of rationality carries the content of emotionality. Here we have an unlikely ally in Herbert Spencer. Spencer saw the impossibility of a violent separation of cognition from emotion. He realized that a dialectic plays out between the emotive and the cognitive. While not developing his dialectic in any profound manner but still seeking a common evolutionary basis for the emergence of complex psychical phenomena in the organic existence, Spencer notes:

> When more complex and frequent correspondences come to be effected, the internal actions effecting them becomes less automatic; as, in ceasing to be automatic, they necessitate a previous representation of the motion about to be performed and the impressions about to be experienced, and thus involve at once both Memory and Reason; so in this same previous representation, they simultaneously involve the germ of what we call Feelings ... in the beginning, Memory, Reason, and Feeling are different sides of the same psychical phenomenon ... they never cease to stand in the same fundamental relation.[13]

For Spencer rationality emerges when physical changes cease to be automatic and become more complex as the interaction between mind and environment gets more complicated. At least he recognized the solidarity between intellect and emotion, for both are brothers constantly watched over by the external environment in benevolence or in malevolence but not in indifference. The evil inherent in the external world is complemented by the evil inherent in the human mind. The general evil inheres in the *mood* of the world. Spencer did not quite venture to extend his dialectic to nature; yet this extension is already implied in his definition of life as the "continuous adjustment of internal relations to external relations."[14] With this grand assertion, Spencer hoped he had avoided the fundamental problem of the conflict between biogenesis and abiogenesis. He thought he would not, thereafter, need to declare that nature mirrors mind and vice versa. To say nature and mind are in solidarity is to say both are in some way alive, a position vulnerable to the charge of idealism.

Yet we have noted how difficult it is to avoid moderate panpsychism, whether we are evolutionists or creationists. To posit biogenesis is to be painfully reminded that even the Bible asserts the creation of the living from non-living matter (dust) and therefore that it is not absurd to propose a hypothesis of the origin of life from non-living matter at the instance of chance. It is difficult for the mechanicist not to see elements of truth in a certain tenuous panpsychism if it must be held at all that non-living matter can yield living matter. Intelligence must already be operative in the world for evolution to be true. Nature must have been already programmed to produce mind because it is itself dormant mind. If intelligence is eternal, what is its organizing principle? Ultimately, the awful question "Who created God?" is less urgent than the less terrible question "Who created life?"

Our digression was necessary to bring out a dilemma Spencer must have faced as he struggled to clarify his brilliant insight, the same dilemma that will confront us throughout this book. This dilemma is actually the problem of reconciling mind with matter in a monistic universe. In confronting this dilemma we have come up with the idea of fatalism in a non-superstitious perspective. In elucidating our concept of fatalism we will not merely analyze the mind as a psychic phenomenon with different faculties but we will go ahead to bring mind closer to the world.

Rationality and Emotionality: The Human Mood and the Mood of the World

The question of rationality is glaringly the question of morality. It is only secondarily a logical question. In fact, the very term "rationality" can be substituted with the term "morality." We say a statement or conduct is rational if such a statement or conduct is coherent or makes sense. For a statement or conduct to make sense to us it must fall within the context of our moral experience. We must be able to suppose that such a statement or conduct is open to moral justification, one way or the other. We say a suicide bomber acts irrationally not because his action is meaningless or without reason but because the reason for his action is not grounded in morality. Again, someone coming from a cultural background that respects marital fidelity will be horrified to hear that there are "primitive" cultures that endorse the morality of the practice of men giving their wives to highly esteemed guests as a mark of hospitality. The person who experiences the culture shock is inclined to dismiss the cultural practice of giving wives to esteemed guests as bizarre and irrational. He is actually saying the practice is immoral. On the other hand, the feminist may condemn this practice as militating against women's rights. She may tone down the immorality dimension, but in fact she is also making the morality noise. From whatever angle the reason-emotion opposition is viewed, our point is that the rationality question is fundamentally a morality question. As a morality question, a preference is expressed. This expression of a preference does not mean that morality is purely relative. The very presence of inclination indicates the universality of morality. All is yearning. The intellect no less than the emotion is yearning. To be rational is to be moral and to be moral is to desire the good. This good is conditioned by one's experience and social approval. But it exists fundamentally as the yearning of *mood*. To desire is to yearn, and this yearning dissolves into the elements of *mood*.

It is from the analysis of rationality as a psychological phenomenon intimate with morality that we extract its various aspects of logic, aesthetics, etc. Logical rationality which claims superiority and in fact appropriates rationality merely seeks to detach itself from its origin, a struggle never successful. Pleasure accompanies the highest logic from the beginning of its operation to the end. This satisfaction derived from the exercise of mental powers is the same fundamental intensity of *mood* that makes a lottery winner break into dance or the bereaved to weep. The pride of logical rationality can be compared to the pride of a king who finds it difficult to believe he was once a helpless baby. The fear of being labeled sentimental should not stop us from acknowledging a very obvious truth. All creatures in which mind has emerged are given to sentimentality. Without sentimentality rationality cannot emerge. Sartre even goes as far as saying that human beings are passion, and useless passion for that matter.[15] We agree with Sartre that we are mere passion but disagree that passion is useless, since passion or emotion is already ethically implicated in the question of being which we have substituted with *mood*. The ethical worth of *mood* will gradually be unravelled in the course of the development of our 21st century African synthesis. If we pick out philosophy and science as the highest cerebral levels yet attained by the human intellect, if we accept these highly logical fields of human endeavor as occupying the summit of rationality, we are faced with the facts that for philosophers their thoughts are outbursts of their visions of existence conferred with coherence by some form of systematicity. These intellectual visions express preferences. Here the moral question is unavoidable given the fact that philosophers have disputed aggressively over fundamental questions. Scientists as more practically inclined thinkers are expected to fare better. Their disputes are usually over facts. In reality they quarrel just as much as philosophers because the facts they investigate can only be justified in their metaphysical dimensions. Two theories may clash because scientists range behind the one or the other although both adequately explain an empirical fact. This difference may arise based on divergent metaphysical preferences. In any case, scientism is not sacrosanct as findings in quantum physics seem to show. The best theories explaining a particular phenomenon have been known to be incompatible with theories that explain a wider range of phenomena. For instance, general relativity is incompatible with the more successful quantum field theory even though general relativity is the best available theory of gravitation. While some scientists prefer the Big Bang theory of the origin of the universe, a theory that states that the universe expanded from a singularity of infinite density, others are more comfortable with the steady state theory which endorses the eternity of the universe in accordance with the law of conservation of matter.[16]

We now know that intellect and feeling are capacities of the mind and that rationality is merely a refinement of the emotion and cannot possibly be without emotionality. But how is the one a refinement of the other? Rationality becomes a refinement of the basic emotion in the higher concentration of this basic emotion which enables it to see problems and seek solutions. Emotion is considered "unintelligent" when it is not concentrated enough to come to the recognition of its nature, of its fatality which, not only defying an ultimate explanation, introduces fear into the world as the announcer of good and evil. The emotion remains spontaneous and so unable to grasp the fatality of its existence. But once emotion loses its spontaneity by achieving a higher concentration the intellect emerges and with it arrives rationality. The intellect is therefore a perpetual seeking after the ultimate understanding of its fatal origin without ever attaining this supreme knowledge. We speculate that this tension is resolved in the Eternal Mood at the knowledge end of the ignorance-knowledge riddle, such that the creative principle of the Eternal Mood becomes qualified to be called the Being of glory and power. While the functional peculiarity of the intellect is pessimism arising from awareness of the riddle of the world, the functional peculiarity of the raw emotion is optimism arising initially from non-awareness of the fatality of its existence. Emotion can be compared to the blissful drunk who declares life to be ideal beauty because he has temporarily lost touch with reality while the intellect can be compared to this same drunk in his moment of sobriety. The creed of the emotion is this: *all is well.* Its expectation is: *all will be well.* Emotion is at the root of fatalism, blocking the penetrating light of the intellect. Emotion is the form of the mythopoeic dream of existence. On the other hand, the intellect has no expectation initially favorable to optimism or joy in its pessimistic phase which is truly its dominant phase. Its outburst is constantly a lamentation: *all is not well*. Mercifully, *mood* is engaged with itself in a perpetual dialectic that structures emotion and reason or intellect. Raw emotion invades the territory of the intellect such that what men usually call reason is an emotional reason. A pure reason which the mighty Kant isolated and criticized is an idle and powerless emotion. Indeed, it ceases to be an emotion and becomes a non-existent "thought," the Form of Plato and the Reason of Aristotle and the Eleatic philosophers of ancient Greece, a transcendent principle of perfection.

A pure reason is applicable neither to God nor to humanity, for it is nothing. Without the emotion there is no mind and without mind there is no life. The state of pessimism indicates a suppression of the creative imagination. The human intellect being an emotion is a creative intellect. Senghor was right after all. His inspiration was on a sound footing. When Bergson tells us in his masterpiece *Creative Evolution* that the intellect is anti-life he actually means that it has a functional peculiarity of pessimism. He means that the intellect is given to pessimism due to its higher concentration of self-conscious emotion which confronts the futility of existence in knowledge. He does not mean that the intellect is not an emotion like instinct, for the intellect is no longer what it is if it is not fundamentally an emotion. Then we contend with an artificial dualism. All the same, Bergson should have granted more dignity to the human intellect because more than the raw emotion the human intellect stands witness to *liberty*. The intellect announces rationality as a dimension of morality and morality as a dimension of intelligence. The raw emotion makes this declaration unconsciously or spontaneously which is the same as making no announcement at all. Hence, we assume erroneously that there is no value, no life, and no feeling in nature whereas mind and matter are in solidarity.

The more the intellect is exercised the finer it becomes in concentration and the farther it moves from its emotional origin so that we may now talk of a faculty of reason. The more the intellect distinguishes itself from the basic emotion the more inactive and pessimistic it becomes. The intellect denies life in its nihilist extremity. This nihilist intellectualism which comes out clearly in all radical ideologies ranging from radical feminism to Islamic fundamentalism and rigid communism is an outpouring of despair regardless of the bold face exponents present. The extremity of the intellect is therefore anti-life. Since happiness is not the goal of universal existence and since neither in the order of matter nor in the order of mind is freedom to be met the intellect in its extremity of knowledge seeks oblivion in the "nothing" which ironically is non-existent.

And so the pessimist says the worst is death. This last outburst of pessimism is paradoxically the ultimate surrender to the raw power of emotion which seeks and will always seek joy, driven by sadness to yearn. The intellect that begins its life subservient to emotion ends its life subservient to the same basic emotion. It returns to its mother. In falling into the nothing we have identified as an irreducible silence the intellect returns to the primal *mood*, the mood of the world from whence it sprang. Given this insight we are not surprised that questions about the existence of the external world, the existence of the other (my Brother), and the problem of other minds should feature prominently in Western metaphysics. The African philosopher who decides that these skeptical currents are baseless decides too hastily. The skepticism that infuriates the practical person in the street is a function of the pessimistic inclination of the intellect. The higher the intellect advances the more skeptical it is under the burden of a sadness driven by despair, which is decoded as pessimism. Even when theistic philosophers are discussing the fundamental questions of God and immortality it happens that these concepts become increasingly tenuous as the theistic thinkers engage them (the concepts), such that the theist becomes something of an agnostic.

It is no accident that Kant demoted the God of pure reason in the First Critique and promoted the God of emotion in the Second Critique. The two Gods are one God, the God of reason, the reason of emotion. It is not true, as some may think, that the more intellectual one is the less need he has for God, that the advanced intellect is an atheistic consciousness, and that civilization is an undermining of religion. We only need to refer to thinkers like Plato, Aristotle, Spinoza, Kant, Isaac Newton, Albert Einstein, Leo Tolstoy, Fyodor Dostoyevsky, Erwin Schrödinger, and Gabriel Oyibo to realize that in reality the finest intellects the world has seen delighted in the idea of God as the most beautiful inspiration of the intellect. And when we find fine intellects like Sartre embracing atheism we immediately see them lamenting what they consider the tragic absence of God in the universe. This phenomenon can easily be accounted for by our theory of reason. The healthiest and most robust stage of the human intellect is the stage of intellectual love. At this stage the intellect combines the best of involved feeling and detached thought. At this stage it rises above ordinariness and struggles to attain genius. Below this stage mind contends with emotional demagogy and mediocrity; below this stage mind contends with the bitter cynicism of intellectual despair. Those who live the mental life chiefly in the stage of intellectual love are more likely to embrace the notion of the reality of God in one form or the other. Reason needs faith to be optimistic enough to proclaim *liberty* as morality. Faith is drawn from emotion. The intellect in its advancement has lost this capacity for spontaneity. This original impulse of emotion (faith) was recognized by Spencer in his *Principles of Psychology* as the universal datum of belief.[17] The force of this optimistic reason is the *will*. This will is not free, but it is able to direct the act of *liberty* under the guidance of intellectual love. Will is tied to *mood* and cannot escape fatalism. The will carries the existential burden of a reality programmed to fail in attaining its supreme goal by virtue of its very nature as yearning. Precisely because of the unfreedom of the will it carries an ethical obligation. The will as the force of emotional reason witnesses to *liberty*.

Chapter 4

CONSOLATIONIST METAPHYSICS AND EPISTEMOLOGY

The Vertical Analysis of Cosmic Emotion in the Consolationist Perspective

The mighty question of being considered from the perspective of a limited consciousness such as that possessed by humans, the creatures privileged to observe nature, must always yield a tragic vision of things. Change characterizes existence, but the universal motion is not one towards apotheosis. A dialectic is ongoing not only in the human mind but also in the external world. Nothing can escape this tension which exists. Aristotle the deistic rationalist dreamed up a God who is pure form and the absolutely "real" by virtue of being pure thought or the "thought of thought." Aristotle's doctrine of God makes Him a non-existent thing since he asserts in *Metaphysics* that form without matter cannot exist. We are not satisfied with the Greek doctrine of God. The fear of extending motion to God and diluting the purity of His form is unfounded. The God which Aristotle paints is simply an impersonal principle that cannot create anything, that cannot be the basis of the universe even while remaining contemporaneous with this selfsame universe. It is easy for us to say all contingent things are in a way illusory. But the universe as a whole suffers from contingency. I prefer the term imperfection. It is possible for a thing to have existed differently before a beginning, but this thing having become reality could not have occurred differently than it did. Motion is indicative of the yearning impulse and must therefore be extended to God. Illusion is reality. Its character of unreality is only the appearing to human consciousness of the mythopoeic dream of existence. This is primal emotion. It infects everything in existence. All things exist for the purpose of consolation. Humans in particular exist as beings of joy and sadness. In these elements he finds all values, defines evil, and propagates morality. The violence of a volcanic eruption is at the same metaphysical level as the rage of a suicide bomber who murders hundreds in one violent act of bombing. While we convict the suicide bomber of murder we simply resign ourselves to the rage of the volcanic mountain, claiming the latter to be a necessary act of nature. The mountain not possessing a mind does not absolve itself of guilt. The mountain is guilty by virtue of its existence in the way that it exists which makes it to pour out murderous lava. The necessity of its pouring out the murderous lava is its interest in the matter of its eruption just as the interest of the suicide bomber is the wrong belief that he is fighting the cause of God.

In our resolve to assure ourselves that all is well we have proposed the alluring concepts of freedom, determinism, and teleology as definitive answers to the question of the origin and destiny of *mood*. In proposing these concepts we think we have arrived at a rational and uniformly structured universe; yet freedom, determinism, and teleology are emotional outbursts of the human intellect in its optimistic phase of thought. All three concepts are positive and affirmative of a future state of perfection. The non-thinking thing lies in the region of ignorance, not oblivion, since it is not conscious enough to know that it can feel joy and sadness. Were the volcanic mountain, whose eruptions destroyed towns, a thinking thing it would definitely be roundly condemned as a terrorist. But then it is already a natural terrorist. The non-living thing, as unconscious as it is, has its own role to play. It obeys natural laws. The piece of stone which scientific investigation reduces to force-fields struggling towards the reward of consciousness that it may never attain will come to humanity's very conclusion if it ever succeeds in its titanic endeavor. It will conclude that reality is a failure. This is the verdict of the despairing intellect. Reality fails because the impulse of creation could not have left the will of the Eternal Mood in its purity and develop perfectly outside the Eternal Mood of melancholy. Cosmic joy as the primal emotion which infects everything with the illusory character of the mythopoeic dream of existence pushes the frontiers of vision and consciousness ever forward towards the limit on all sides of eternity, turning the silence of cosmic space into the sadness of the consciousness that contemplates this seemingly lifeless space. Cosmic joy moulds cosmic sadness into its own nature. In the first place, it emerges out of cosmic sadness. This dialectic is as eternal as the universe is eternal. It presents reality as illusion because it is a mythopoeic dream. Thus illusion is the truth of *mood*.

When we contemplate the beauty of nature we not only feel a sense of awe but also a sense of sadness at the impossibility of this beauty becoming wholly ours in the face of a reality that fails us partly because humanity itself failed. Contemplation helps consciousness to understand the dialectic going on outside the yearning of *mood* which fits well with the internal dialectic. Joy gives to the intellect its faith in creation, such that reason becomes creative reason, emotive reason—the love of the intellect. Fear broods over the universe. Fear is the leftover of *mood*. Evil springs directly from it. Joy turns this fear away from evil towards good while sadness turns fear away from good towards evil. I will steadily illuminate this point as the treatise develops.

In this section we have made a number of points, that the universe is a totality of expressed cosmic emotion, that the world is an expression of cosmic emotion, that the human *mood* connects with the external world, exemplified in the contemplation of the beauty of nature. I will now attempt a demonstration of the existence of God to supplement the treatment of the problem of God's existence already provided in Section 6 of Chapter One.

The Existence of God

The traditional ontological and cosmological arguments for the existence of God—the one based on the concept of perfection and the other on the idea of alteration—have not fared well in Western metaphysics. Yet the argument from design (teleological argument) incorporates features of the ontological and cosmological arguments. When we say that there must exist a Supreme Being who is the mastermind of the marvellous design we read into the structure of the world, when metaphysics arrests aesthetics as we contemplate the order and beauty in the world, when the teleological argument emerges in its incipient form, the ontological and cosmological arguments are automatically co-implicated. In presenting the claim of teleology the claims of the ontological and cosmological arguments arise, namely:

a. That the notion of a designer underlines the necessity of a perfect Being who is the embodiment of ultimate greatness, such that a greater Being cannot be imagined. Here the ontological argument is implicated in the teleological argument.

b. That the notion of a designer introduces the idea of dependence and necessity since the designer must be all-sufficient and therefore subsist as a necessary being relative to the designed. Here the cosmological argument is implicated in the teleological argument.

Underlying the famous triadic arguments is the problematic issue of causality, the effect-cause regression that seems unstoppable once the cause of any effect in the world has been identified. The three arguments are in fact versions of one main argument struggling to deal with one main problem, that is, the problem of infinite regress. Who made the world? God. Who made God? Blank. Faced with this problem unbelieving thinkers comfort themselves with the cunning assertion that if God must necessarily exist, then the world could just as well have existed necessarily. At this stage Western metaphysics ceases to throw light on the question of God's existence. So we return to the consolationist synthesis.

We have seen that the main problem in the way of a proof of God's existence is the question of causality. A First Cause is presumed to be a necessary being which is omniscient and omnipotent. Religions like Christianity and Islam make this First Cause a benevolent Being as well. But the actual picture of the world is one of both beauty and terror. It is not a perfect world. In this world there are good and bad men, good thoughts and awful thoughts. There is plenty and there is lack on this planet we inhabit. There is health and disease. There is order and disorder. There is natural evil, as when a volcanic mountain erupts and obliterates a whole town, and there is man-made or moral evil as when a suicide bomber throws an improvised explosive device (IED) into a market teeming with buyers and sellers. We may emphasize man-made evil, but this emphasis does not reduce the ferocity of natural evil. When a hurricane levels a whole town questions must be asked. Merely resigning ourselves to eventualities of nature in its hostile moments with the unconvincing murmur of all being well in accordance with the formula of rigid determinism does not resolve the problem of evil. So we are confronted with the causality of an unstoppable regression and the causality of impotence.

The causality of an unstoppable regression gives us the impression that the chain of causes will never come to rest. What is the justification for stopping with God when the regression can jolly well continue beyond God? If we resolve this problem by positing the eternity of God we are still faced with the causality of impotence, the limitation of God. For if God is omniscient and omnipotent He should have designed a perfect universe, one which is not in a process, a world-in-progress, but a completed work. In this context the world should exist without evil and without blemish. This demand may appear puerile to the category of philosophers William James will call tough empiricists or realists; yet it is a legitimate demand. It gives rise to philosophy and religion and sustains the quest of science. It is not difficult to see why many men and women refuse to believe in the existence of God as a result of the indubitable evil in the world. We may wonder like Albert Camus in his *The Myth of Sisyphus* why human beings in their helplessness make an appeal for empathy and are answered with the silence of the world. Why should an all-powerful God not intervene if we assume that He is all-knowing? Or is He not benevolent, or perhaps benevolent but not all-powerful? However, the problem before us now is not the problem of evil, although we will not hesitate to refer to it in this section if the need arises. We are concerned here with the demonstration of the existence of God.

Having put aside the categories of omniscience and omnipotence as inapplicable to a God of a universe of yearning, we must have recourse to the categories of power and glory while leaving the category of benevolence intact. Humans exists as beings of emotion. The meaning of our life is joy and sadness. All our knowledge is temporalized in optimism and pessimism. In transcending ourselves, we acquire a knowledge no different from the knowledge we have of ourselves, the awareness of pessimism and optimism. The physical world outside us is not perfectly expressed, just like we are not perfectly expressed. Lower life shows the aspect of yearning, of seeking. Intelligent activities drop as the lower forms of life are reached, until the lowest life is seen to languish in a profound state of ignorance of the dialectic of *mood* in which it is involved. Even at the level of the lowest life movement is still discernible. There is still a struggle, a yearning. When we regard things supposedly lifeless, for example, a planetary body or a piece of rock, we see that the dead thing unconsciously obeys natural laws. The dead thing acts in a predictable way. Clearly the yearning that is the meaning of human life mirrors a similar process active in lower forms and things at an unconscious level. A connection is effected between humanity and lower life-forms and between humanity, lower life-forms, and "lifeless" nature. Everything therefore is in solidarity by virtue of a common origin, life and non-life. In which case abiogenesis, even a more radical variant of the theory, is a plausible theory of the origin of life.

For us abiogenesis is the theory that life or the lower life-forms emerged from non-living matter under favorable physico-chemical conditions. To endorse abiogenesis is to endorse mechanicism. It is the same as saying that natural physico-chemical processes announced life to the world. Therefore these physico-chemical processes constitute a cause. Yet the world "natural" is deceptive since it oversimplifies the complex idea of causality. The complexity of the universe is reflected in its finetuning; the complexity of the simplest cell and the human mind indicates clearly that natural causality cannot account for the eternity of the universe and the evolution of mind and matter. If we grant that physical evolution and biological evolution follow purely mechanical directionality we import teleology through the back door. If we are to fall back on chance the word "nature" becomes pseudonymous for chance and must be treated as a thing, a creative unconscious will. By granting unconscious powers of creation to chance we personify it as a living principle and imbue it with mind. In which case, chance is no longer accidental but purposeful. Chance becomes what we call God, an intelligent designer.

We can also justify the existence of God somewhat differently. Let us suppose that mechanical processes produced life and that these processes are eternal and do not require a master engineer and strategist. The problem of pan-psychism rears its ugly head and gibbers at us. How can non-life produce life if the germ of life is not already present in non-life? The point I want to make is that not only does abiogenesis lead to a belief in the eternity of matter but also, more spectacularly, in the eternity of mind or intelligence. It does not seem to us adequate that non-living matter should transform itself into living matter under certain physico-chemical conditions if the non-living matter did not already carry within itself the germ of life, not potentially but actually. That is to say, for a blind evolution to be valid or correct the idea of non-living matter in the world must be discarded and replaced by the idea that all matter is actually alive. Then the evolution of the universe is simply the development of life in many forms and in varying degrees of intensity and sophistication. And yet the evolution of life from life nullifies the radical formulation of abiogenesis. Non-life is no longer posited and we arrive at idealism. Life is related to mind. Mind is either the principle of life and therefore prior to life or mind and life are one and the same thing or mind follows life as a consequence of life. If mind comes before life as its principle we can argue for a God who is precisely this principle. If life and mind are contemporaneous and therefore one we can argue for a God who is co-existent with the eternally existing universe. If mind follows life we can still argue for a God who evolved as a consequence of life and therefore younger than the universe. I call this primordial mind the Eternal Mood.

All three results justify the existence of God. The first result yields a God who is the maker of the universe as its master-mind. For the universe is assumed to be not only dynamic but also *living*. The second result gives us a God who as life is the supreme giver of life, releasing life out of its own reserve. The third result gives us a relatively impotent God not infinitely higher than humanity. This God is higher than humanity only by virtue of his ancient age, having evolved long after the universe came into being. Such a God cannot be the supreme principle of fatalism and may create mischief in the exercise of his power. This God is not responsible for evolution but is actually subject to evolution. This God may be a vital God but a severely limited God, all the same. He never rises to the level of power and glory. This third God is the suffering God of Miguel de Unamuno. Let us briefly listen to the Spanish thinker: "For God is revealed to us because He suffers and because we suffer; because He suffers He demands our love; and because we suffer He gives us His love, and He covers our anguish with the eternal and infinite anguish."[1] The God our third result yields is a problematic God, for he is essentially idle. He is not equal to chance but less than chance. Being neither principle of life nor organizer of life, he cannot account for the complexity of the universe and the complexity of the human mind that incubates and breeds good and evil. We either eliminate this God or go beyond him since he is not only impotent but is also less than chance. Yet reify chance we must, and the reification throws up Mind or Intelligence. Pure mechanicism affirms panpsychism. Everything is mind and alive in varying degrees. If chance is a living principle with a mind it is God, the principle and master-mind of life whose eternity is at once the eternity of the universe. To reject our conclusion due to an aversion for idealism is tantamount to rejecting evolution and embracing a literal interpretation of the Book of Genesis now generally regarded as an allegory by Christians, as truth veiled by mythology. Physics and biology will be put to shame if evolution is denounced in favor of naive creationism. The logical terminus of a clinical analysis of mechanicism or evolutionary naturalism is the postulate of (1) a God who is eternal and prior to the universe or (2) a God who is eternal but co-existent with an eternal universe as its organizing principle and inspiration, its consolation. Both Gods are beings of power and glory, sentient without having to suffer as Unamuno conjectures by virtue of their conquest of the denizen of all living consciousnesses: despair. Despair is essential for *mood* as a product of yearning. I have argued all along that everything in a yearning universe is subject to the dialectic of *mood* and that there is a difference in the Eternal Mood of the universe which divides into impersonality and personality.

Without emotion there can be no universe, definitely not the universe as we know it today. No God can arise as a pure thought and subsist thus. As the primal principle, as the Eternal Mood, God is an active emotion, a mythopoeic dream. As the self-consciousness of the Eternal Mood, God is the personal principle highlighted by the monotheistic religions of the world. The unreachable God of African polytheistic religions and Hindu religion is the Eternal Mood in its phase of impersonality. If humanity can conquer the despair that recrudesce in nihilist acts without having to make recourse to an idea or symbol of consolation outside itself, without having to make the transcendental appeal, humanity will become a god in its own right. This conquest is what is impossible. For it will involve the capacity to resolve the subjectivity-objectivity conflict of mind and nature beyond what is given in a universe of mind and matter. To resolve this conflict humanity has to become God, a Being of power and glory, a maker or inspirer who can say to the illusion that we call nothingness (silence): *Come O Silence if you are good*. As a matter of fact, the great Kant used an argument rooted in our insight to prove God's existence in his *Critique of Practical Reason*. Kant's God is a Being who can command nature and bring it into harmony with the just demand of the Moral Law. For any being to command nature and make it obey the ethical demand of mind by harmonizing natural causality with moral reason it must itself be happy or blessed. If it is not a happy being it cannot reward human beings with happiness. To be happy this being must have conquered its own despair without help from outside. This being is not a cold logic created by the philosopher admiring the beauty of his thought in his emotional demand for a perfect God. This being exists as *mood* independent of humanity.

While the evolution of the universe as life in diverse forms supports the idea that these forms include the idle God of our third result, perhaps other lesser gods, the galaxies, planets, human beings, lower life-forms on earth, and "inert" matter, the evolutionary mechanism cannot account for the complexity a close study of these life-forms reveals. The human mind alone carries the complexity of the universe in its foundation in good and evil. Since the highest life-form, the God of our third result, is less than chance, we are compelled to push mechanism farther. A necessary reification process reveals chance as the God atheists seek to deny. But the victory won for theism is not an easy victory. We are still pursued by the devastating skepticism of the unbeliever. Why stop the regress now that you have found the God you desire? Yes, the theist's desire is a strong emotion. But so is the denial of the atheist. If God is eternal, sneers the atheist, chance too is eternal. We have already shown that the thingification, de-spatialization, and detensing of chance is inevitable if we are to faithfully follow the line of natural causality that we may continue to trust the conjectures of physico-chemical evolution and biological evolution. To ask us not to reify chance and be content with a bare mechanicism is to embrace an extremist dogma and push for the registration of a cult of dogmatists. It is an oversimplification of the riddle of existence based on an ideology that asserts foolishly that all is well with universal existence. We took note of the complexity of causality and rightly called our vertical analysis a metaphysics of terror. The only alternative is to embrace the unfairly denigrated Genesis account in its most raw form. The Genesis account incorporates elements of radical abiogenesis, asserting that the living human matter arose out of dust, the difference between this account and scientific account being the positing of an actively creative God. We have justified precisely this position without presenting the raw Genesis data. Between God and chance we have no choice. They are one and the same thing. Preferring the one to the other may comfort us. No argument can prove that God does not exist. It is the nature of an existent God that cannot be proved. Hence we have diverse conceptions of God in the theistic, deistic, pantheistic, panentheistic, and agnostic perspectives.

The preference for the term "chance" by non-believing thinkers may be due to the desire to have an impersonal principle of the world which has no ethical interest in the world. Whether the God whose existence we have established punishes with fire and brimstone we cannot tell since we are not mystics but metaphysicians enunciating a vision of the universe sustained by purely intellectual effort of a non-dogmatic character. Yet running away from a God with an ethical interest does not help us solve the problem of the objectivity of morality nor does it alter the truth that the slightest tension in impersonality transforms it to personality. The ethical question dovetails into the metaphysical question of existence. Morality is an objective phenomenon of *mood*. It is primarily a phenomenon of *mood* and only secondarily a phenomenon of society and social organization. That is to say, human beings do not create morality but realize it as something intimate with the *moodiness* or furniture of the universe. Not even God can decree the amoralization of the universe as Plato seems to suggest in dialogues like *Timaeus* with respect to the Good and the eternal moral order it animates. The morality of *mood* makes for the rationality of the universe. The ethical question is a metaphysical question.

We return now to the problem of regress. If chance is reified and personified as God and mind is posited as prior to the revealed universe, where is God coming from? This is the awful question only fatalism can answer. Confronted with this question, the outstanding British philosopher Richard Swinburne confesses: "It is very unlikely that a universe would exist uncaused, but rather more likely that God would exist uncaused."[2] Swinburne appealed to fatalism. We will be appealing to fatalism but not exactly in the analytical tradition of Anglo-American philosophy. Fatalism as we conceive it is not the superstitious notion that fate or God has already decreed what will happen to individuals in minute details, such that their actions are ethically superfluous. What will happen will happen indeed, but what happens comes to be as inevitability and not because details have been worked out from a given beginning. A supremely intelligent being can indeed predict future occurrences, and predict with perfect accuracy down to minute details in a perfectly rational universe. Ours is not such a universe. Since rationality is a consequence of emotionality the God we have established need not determine the future in such a way that there is no room for *liberty* (freedom is not an appropriate term in our emotional universe) and novelty. Physicists have already announced that the universe is still expanding. Of course it is expanding within a totality and therefore is not actually expanding. It simply yearns. The intelligence inherent in the world is a yearning intelligence. Human actions may not be free, but they have implications for obligation. We have to partly agree with Anicius Severinus Boethius who asserted in the impressive and most profound fifth book of his *The Consolation of Philosophy* that God foresees without predetermining since His context is always an eternal context, thereby ingeniously bringing human "freedom" within the ambit of divine knowledge and eliminating any rigid determinism. What we are trying to say here is that our notion of fatalism, while rejecting freedom, allows room for morality and human responsibility. Whether we are convinced that an action occurs in a determined or spontaneous manner, the fact remains that the action has already taken place. Its occurrence is the *fatal* occurrence. It could not have been otherwise after its occurrence although it could have been otherwise before its occurrence. The ultimate cause of a thing may be obscure, but an event did occur all the same, yielding significant consequences for humanity in the capacity to generate joy or grief. The question of human freedom is set aside for discussion in the third part of this book.

Returning to the question of origin, it is obvious that something existed uncaused. If we say this thing is the famous "nothing" we mock ourselves with ill humor. The nothing means nil. Its very definition as nothing nullifies it. Mercifully, Heidegger has told us in *Being and Time* that the nothing is the veil of being, not a nil. It is a something human anxiety symbolizes. We have identified the nothing with silence and this silence has been isolated as the thinnest form of *mood*, as the unconscious existent devoid of the knowledge of the fatality of its very existence. Thus a piece of stone exists in the silent state. Space is silent. That which exists without knowledge of its existence subsists in tragedy already. The hope of nirvana is therefore not an escape from the tragic life the Buddha reacted to with such philosophical fineness and which Schopenhauer moulded into one of philosophy's magnificent intellectual edifices. The pathway of consciousness is from silence to sadness and over to joy. Silence then is the eternal nothing or the eternal something, space and time implicated in eternity. An eternally existing being embracing this silence was needed to overcome silence and force joy out of sadness in an awesome cosmic show of power and creativity. Creation is an optimistic outburst of *mood*, an expression of primal joy. The overcoming of the eternal silence involves the conquest of despair which stands between the condition of pessimism and the condition of optimism. The being which called forth creation out of its own silence, thereby animating the uncaused is the Being we have called God. As unanimated silence it is an impersonal principle—the Eternal Mood. As animated existence upon which the world depends for its inspiration this Being is personality—the Eternal Mood of melancholy. This is fatalism in operation. The uncaused exists as a cause of causes. Why the uncaused exists defies intellectual scrutiny. As we keep saying, fatalism is the terminus of thought. To reject our explanation as fantastic is to return to the wholly uninspiring naturalism of bare mechanicism which is in itself a refusal to confront cosmic terror, a feel-good ideology that ignores a proximate danger. Naturalism follows from an emotional craving to believe that all is well and that all troubles and pleasures ends for men on earth and that the universe is ethics-neutral. Yet all is not well with life and the world as the problem of evil clearly indicates.

Our serrated monism answers the question of whether God is outside the world or is part of it. By replacing a dualistic conception of the universe with a monistic conception we eliminated the problem associated with showing how empirical phenomena can lead us to an eternal transcendental Being. There is no need for us to look for the point of a radical break between immanence and transcendence since time and space are implicated in the silence of eternity. Our time is the same flow of eternity which plays out in the dialectic of *mood*. The problem of an infinite temporal regress and an actual infinite is thus clarified, although not resolved. The universe of God is eternal, but we do not know why it should be uncaused. Time is no illusion of immanent phenomenon. If it seems so, it is because eternity itself is a mythopoeic dream, the structure and evolution of cosmic emotion. The idea of a creation out of nothing is still plausible, but we fail to fathom its possibility. Our position is not much different from the position the African philosopher Kwasi Wiredu promoted as the Akan understanding of the relation of God with the world. Wiredu writes: "God is the creator of the world, but He is not apart from the universe. He together with the world constitutes the spatio-temporal 'totality' of existence ... The notion of creation out of nothing does not even make sense in the Akan language."[3]

On the Categories of Power and Glory

We have demonstrated or rather justified the existence of God on the turf of the naturalist by appealing not to dogma but to a high probability. We saw that the probable truth of atheism is inferior to the probable truth of theism or deism since the ultimate logical consequence of mechanicism is panpsychism and the strict affirmation that life begets life. Now we will attempt a more existential proof (or rather justification) of God's existence, still within the ambit of probability. For us probability is not skepticism but a degree of absolutism. What is known is known and the unknown is either soon to be known or may never be known because no one can know it although it exists.

To be human is basically to have consciousness. This consciousness is the totality of reason and feelings, and knowledge of oneself and his external environment. Human feeling is the emotion of joy and sadness. Reason is the refinement of this emotion. The silence of one's contemplation is a longing for what we should call eternal peace. It is a terrible longing for death, yet for something even greater—the longing for the impossible nothing substituted for freedom in the face of the failure of reality. Yet happiness is not granted to *mood* which is a fatality. Therefore in our earthly life we realize joy as our only consolation. We cannot have enough of this consolation without referring to an idea outside ourselves as the source of consolation. This is the transcendental appeal. The inspiration that comes from *within* actually sneaks in from *without*. Our belief that a world exists is based on a common sense that assures us this given world is independent of us and greater than us. Human life once energized moves from sadness to joy through the temporary conquest of fear and the sublimation of anxiety. By fear I mean the unknown as it looms before human consciousness. Fear is the immensity of things unknown and the infinity of things never to be known. The validity of cosmic fear follows from the status of fatalism as the terminus of knowledge, the plain fact that the limitations of the human intellect prevent one from having adequate knowledge of the working of fatalism. Yet one goes around fear in resignation in the determined push towards the consolation joy offers.

From a fear not conquered but overlooked *mood* stands alone as anxiety. This anxiety not only points back to humanity's origin in tragedy but it also becomes a sign of our coming apotheosis, the foundation of our peace. Just as contemplation has indicated perfect peace without realizing it, so does activity desire our apotheosis without possessing the powers to realize it. Anxiety is the highest and most sublime awareness attainable by human despair. At this level despair can either descend to sadness and towards evil or ascend to joy towards the affirmation of goodness in the intellectual love (the most complete emotion) of all things. But all things exist as consolation. You may ask why their mode of existence is consolatory. The existent thing is a consolation because it exists by reason of its nature as a yearning entity. Human consciousness yearns, but its consolation is an appeal to something external—the contemplation of something outer—family, love, philosophy, science, food, sex, money, etc. These outer things are not sufficiently sentient to promise us eternal peace in a state of eternal happiness. There must, therefore, exist the ultimate principle of consolation, a sentient creative Being who is powerful, glorious, and benevolent and who is the full consolation itself. This Being is the consolation of the universe—God. Thus the human *mood* carries one to the *mood* of the world. Because emotion is not alien to the Eternal Mood, which is a fatalistic principle and a personal God, one looks up to a Being in solidarity with humanity, a Being not outside the world but inside the world as the inspiration of the world itself. What distinguishes God from humanity spectacularly is that God is power and glory by virtue of His conquest of fear while humans can only pretend that fear does not exist even though their ethics is built on this terror. This is a radical distinction.

By God's conquest of fear I mean His realization of his priority to fear, His knowledge that fear is only the development of a creative tension in His mind as impersonality transforms into personality. He overcomes fear knowing that no sentient thing is greater than Him. The overcoming of fear is the overcoming of despair. The overcoming of despair is the acquisition of the power to create a universe. Glory is the knowledge of this power. This God is benevolent, powerful, and glorious but not omniscient and omnipotent. Let us be more daring still and push probability forward to advance speculation. In the silence of eternal solitude the fatalistic principle became activity, the creative agency, in the exercise of powers resulting from the conquest of despair. Fear became love in creation, the animation of the out-going idea, the externalizing wish out of a will now optimistic. But since this optimism has pessimism at its foundation, the unity of the out-going will as a consequence of action (as optimism and pessimism), the world outside the fatalistic principle, is a poor copy of the conception which is pure optimism. The world God creates is an imperfect world by the very fact that it is a mythopoeic dream, a *moody* existence that must deal with the silence of eternity and the sadness of the existent thing that attains awareness. That which exists for no reason or whose existence cannot be explained beyond fatalism is a tragic existence, at least from the standpoint of the human intellect, which is in solidarity with the *mood* of the world. Such is the existence of God, human beings, and every inferior form. God is not the same entity as the world although He inspires it into being and is linked to this same world by intellectual love. This love also connects humans to God. We take this position in opposition to materialistic pantheism. God is distinct and superior to the universe. Since the world is eternal we do not have to travel in a straight line towards God and encounter an infinite regress. Everything takes place in a circle. God is already this circle. The world issues out of this circle as a mirror of this circle. God is eternal, accounting for time and space in the silence of His mind which is also the silence of eternity.

Because God is *mood* He is in solidarity with the universe which is also *mood*. Thus we correctly say that God is immanent in the universe. The universe is a yearning creation linked in perpetuity to its inspiring principle. There will be no void anywhere since cosmic joy will always make adjustments to fill up any void silence creates. The emotions are in motion. The main objection to our probabilistic defense of theism will no doubt be that we are guilty of anthropomorphism. This is a hypocritical objection because the only alternative to "anthropomorphism" is bare mechanicism. I have shown that bare mechanicism is no consolation for the non-believing thinker as it leads us back to the God-concept. The great argument in the philosophy of religion should be the degree of power God wields and not the question of the existence of God.

What is objectionable is not anthropomorphism itself but its extreme expression. The moment we try to understand the nature of the tiniest subatomic particle and speculate on its origin by appealing to the Big Bang theory, the steady state theory, or the oscillating model, we are thinking anthropomorphically. As an observer of the universe, one reads meanings into what is so much greater than oneself. The meanings we impose on the world outside of us are objective only because we ourselves are a fragment of this world. Humanity is in solidarity with the immense nature it is privileged to observe for a while. Asking a person not to think anthropomorphically is asking him not to think at all but to simply delude himself that all is well. If all is not well with Planet Earth, how can all be well with the entire universe? The charge of projecting human feelings, hopes and desires, into a supposedly inert and value-neutral universe, arises from a rigidly dualistic conception of the universe. If human beings have an origin, as they surely must, does this origin not also account for the developed emotions? In vain we try to deceive ourselves that we are anything more than emotion. Our perspective of the world will always be anthropomorphic chiefly because we are egocentric and significantly because we are in solidarity with the universe as coming from a common source. The dualism just mentioned is not tenable because the human *mood* connects with the *mood* of the world. The *mood* of the world only has to rise sufficiently to the level of consciousness for us to see the transparent connection of humanity with the world, of thought with matter. Teleology may be a subjective demand considered from the human angle, an emotional outburst of human reason, but when we consider all fragments of reality as pieces or parts of a whole we strongly suspect and even become convinced that what appears limited and subjective is in fact universal and objective, that our fears and hopes are also the fears and hopes of the universe. If the universe is an expression of *mood*, then it is not value-neutral. If humans create value, then the universe itself is not value-neutral. If the universe is not value-neutral, then good and evil exist as absolute facts, not as relative facts. If this is the case, then metaphysics is another term for the ethics of existence. In which case, humans are justified to read into nature a purpose at work. This purpose I call *consolation*, the realization of the fuller meanings of existence in the joy of being, the realization of greater joy or the struggle towards this realization in the knowledge of the impossibility of happiness which is the perfection of freedom, the cosmic movement towards a perfection which realizes beauty in the objective universe even as the attainment of this perfection is impossible. To denounce anthropomorphism—the very mode of human response to a moral universe—is to succumb to the pessimism of the intellect when uninspired by the emotion of joy. It is to cease to think beyond oneself, analogous to being unable to look beyond one's nose.

Chapter 5

THE PROBLEM OF EVIL IN THE WORLD

Preparatory Exposition of Consolationist Theodicy and the Response to the Logical and Evidential Problem of Evil

Fatalism is clarified to human consciousness by the futility of human life. Futility is the awareness of pronounced human limitations in a universe we have not created, whose explanation loses all intelligibility beyond fatalism. I will do fuller justice to the question of the futility of human life in Part Three of this work. But it has been noted that futility clarifies the fatalism reigning in the universe. As existence is not in its essence concept but emotion and cannot qualify for perfection, either from the beginning or in the end, futility clarifies fatalism. Concepts illuminate, but emotion blurs. Since the concept is a further development of emotion, it is better than emotion but not superior to it. The perfection attributed to God over which skeptical thinkers have found the grounds of atheism given the inconsistency of this claim of perfection with the reality of evil, this perfection turns out to be a mere intellectual wish that freedom should be real and determinism supreme. God is limited by Himself but not by the world He inspires. The majesty of God follows from His overcoming of the principle that limits Him in Himself.

In rendering the categories of omniscience and omnipotence inapplicable to God who remains supreme as the conqueror of cosmic fear, the God-concept ceases to be a static concept, a logical perfection. God becomes a creative principle. In creating God realizes. The idea of realization carries the notion of continuous creation, of an actuality not yet complete but still in the process of completion. This indicates a future completion that is possible but not certain and therefore not necessary. If completion is a possibility which, even when finally realized, cannot surpass consolation, then the universe is not determined by God to its minutest details. God is perpetually completing His creation. Thus in the place of God's supposed omniscience, we see glory, His knowledge of His conquest of despair, without which He cannot be the principle of the universe. Without this conquest creation would have been impossible and only God Himself would have existed as an entity without self-knowledge, the fatalistic principle which some thinkers have called *chance*. I also replace the category of omnipotence with the category of power, which is the force of creation itself. God is good because as creator He conquers despair within Himself after coming to self-knowledge through the dialectic of *mood*. Despair is the agent of cosmic sadness, and therefore evil, in all thinking things. This cosmic conquest results in the willing of a universe for good. If evil exists in the world—and the evidence indicates it does exist—God is not to blame. God labored under the existential burden of fear and the despair that arises from it. The very act of creation is the titanic battle to defeat this principle of fatalism within God. Creation is the very expression of this conquest. Creation could not have been perfect. If it were perfect there would be no personal God, no world with people and things, only the silence of eternity which is God in his impersonality. A world born as an expression of victory over cosmic fear cannot be a perfect world. Fear is the origin of good and evil. The fear is consciousness of the fatality of the universe, its perpetual existence in the mind of God, and God as a mere impersonal principle. God is the Supreme Being who overcame cosmic despair. Not to triumph is not to create. So the creation of the universe was a necessary act of God. He could not have helped not creating the world, since self-knowledge is dependent on His transformation from impersonal principle to personal principle. Fatalism means both to be and to become. To become is to fall into the stream of the dialectic of *mood*. This dialectic produced the triumph of God. If we are to agree that evil is necessary we must add that it is a necessary tragedy. A fatalistic existence is already a tragedy. Yet the notion of progress is real in a yearning universe, for yearning is the essence of morality. A God who creates the world as a necessary consequence of His fatalistic existence and who desires its completion is benevolent.

Preliminary Solution to the Problem of the Relation of God with the World

It is not absurd to say the past and the future live in the present. An absolute past with no link to the present seems impossible since the past is the passing away of a present which can still be summoned in memory. The future is anticipated by the present. This does not mean that only the present exists. The present cannot be absolute because it is the perception of time at the most active phase of consciousness. The present is not the totality but time is. The present is a component of time, and time is eternity adequate to human consciousness. Time is not distinctly phenomenal; as possessing the character of the *mythopoeic* it flows into eternity. Time is eternity. We posit a time that is eternal, but this is not a static eternity. This eternity is vibrant motion. It is yearning. Time is indeed a moving image as Plato says in the *Timaeus*, but so is eternity. The future and the past complete the present. Eternity, then, is not to be considered a petrified present, a perfect stillness. Eternity is what it is because it is a totality of past, present, and future, of all events occurring, all expansions and contractions. The expansions and contractions take place within a constant whole, the constancy of which makes the expansions and contractions illusory. The universe is eternal because it cannot exhaust itself. It is its own limitlessness. This is possibly what Zeno means when he asserted that there is no motion in the universe, falling back on the famous paradoxes for proofs. That which is existence and essence is *mood*. This is the universal *mood* of melancholy—joy and sadness—realized in developed consciousness or latent in unconscious nature.

Change is the desire of *mood*. Without change there can be no dream of perfection. Yet change merely realizes consolation. Time measures the change *mood* desires, which change shapes existence. The contemporaneity of the past with the present and with the future is the creation of the imagination. This contemporaneity which argues for an eternal present is one of the many fond hopes of human thought and an intellect in search of eternal peace. Time flows, linking the terms of its flow with one another. The absoluteness of the present is not what is striking—this feature has no objective foundation anyway. What is striking about the phenomenon of time is its illusion. Time past, time present, and time future are illusory. By illusion I do not mean the unreality of time contrasted with a real eternity as J.M.E. McTaggart has argued in his seminal essay, "The Unreality of Time." The illusion of time is its mythopoeic essence which is also the nature of universal existence. For time is real, as real as eternity, since it is eternity itself. Time is neither an object nor an empty thought. Time is the yearning of existence, itself inseparable from *mood*. The past-present-future asymmetry merely characterizes a mobile eternity for the benefit of human consciousness. The existent thing without developed consciousness cannot perceive time as eternity; for the condition of the unconscious existent thing is the eternal condition of silence, the barest minimum of consciousness.

To say time and existence are illusions is the same as saying they constitute one eternal *mood*. The suspicion that time is unreal is the suspicion that existence is unreal. The suspicion that both time and existence are unreal is the suspicion that the universe exists gratuitously. The question that follows is a grim question. "Is the universe pointless?" Again this: "Can it be that the more we reflect on existence the more it seems aimless?" The answer has to be a cheerless yes. Ironically, on deeper reflection, we come to realize that existence can only be aimless if it has no meaning and therefore possesses no basic values. I propose that the meaning of existence is *futility*. God is the consolation of human beings in the face of this futility. Since futility demands consolation existence cannot be aimless. Futility, fatalism, and consolation are concepts that serve as tools for combating the nihilism that leaps out of the abundance of the despair of the human intellect which is advanced enough to know itself and the world, to know, and in the process of knowing, desire the future human apotheosis and the internal peace possible only as eternal melancholy. Futility points at fatalism by revealing consciousness as the beauty, and yet the burden, of life. Our powerlessness, ultimately, in our struggle to realize joy in the world drives us into either activism or quietism. Both activism and quietism are expressions of resignation. The philosophical foundation of this resignation is fatalism. Futility characterizes *mood*. Therefore existence is consolation, and being precisely this, existence is not meaningless. A pointless universe would not exist, let alone exist as yearning.

The question of origin and destiny is the greatest torment of the intellect, puzzling philosophers, scientists, theologians, and in fact all humanity. It is tremendous because the attempt to solve it illuminates the sister question of the existence of evil in the world. These two questions nurture two essential human attitudes, the religious attitude divisible into theism and atheism and the irreligious attitude which is basically agnostic. The passion that goes into the atheistic stance makes it a species of religion. Now what are the known scientific facts about the origin of the world? Among the models suggested by scientists to explain the world's origin the Big Bang model seems the most widely accepted. It is also interesting to theists because of its apparent support for the doctrine of a creation out of nothing (*creatio ex nihilo*). The problem that comes with the acceptance of the Big Bang model and the idea of a creation out of nothing is the problem of fatalism. How can something come out of nothing? One may reply that there was always a something prior to the nothing, which is to be filled. One may say this something is God. Yet the problem of fatalism does not disappear with the postulation of God at the base of existence. Where is God coming from? How did He spring into being? The issue of the creation of the world out of nothing dissolves in the question of the possibility of nothingness and the seeming impossibility of a beginningless existence. The idea of eternity does not rule out the question of a beginning. It is not absurd to wonder where and how eternity started. This is the terrible question that torments the human intellect, for which torment fatalism provides only consolation. Thus God is the consolation of the universe and, as consolation, supplies a better basis for the explanation of the phenomena of the world than bare mechanicism. An eternal God who is at once impersonal principle and personal creator better accounts for the existence of the world than a blind evolutionary force or chance.

If we now accept that God exists or that argument tilts in favor of His existence, we still have to wonder how He can be the cause of the world and remain outside it. If He is part of the world which is imperfect He cannot be omnipotent and omniscient. If He is not part of the world He cannot know it. Dualism fails us here. The distinction between the God-world or the world of things-in-themselves and our phenomenal world is unnecessary. If the aim of dualism is to preserve God's omnipotence and omniscience, His divine perfection, then dualism fails completely. The God dualistic theories present cannot escape the charge of being either severely limited or non-benevolent for creating a world in which evil is real. The defense often put forward for the dualistic conception of reality is that it is impossible for contingency to carry us to necessity or for empirical causes to lift us to transcendental causes. It is feared that a monistic universe is value-neutral, that in such a universe there can be no objective basis for morality. "No ethics can be won from the knowledge of the universe," writes Albert Schweitzer. "Nor can ethics be brought in harmony with what we know of the universe."[1] In other words, naturalism is in eternal conflict with morality. But it has already been shown that morality has an objective basis in existence. Our consolationist philosophy has enabled us to see *naturalism* as a synonym for *moralism*. What is nature but that which yearns? If nature is yearning, then it is all-embracing. God becomes a part of nature as nature itself, such that universal yearning is the progress towards perfection. That this perfection is favored and is yet impossible does not vitiate the moral essence of nature. In the absence of perfection nature already claims consolation. Consolation recommends ethics. The human mind does not create value but rather realizes value. For value is the yearning of existence. Life at all stages and in all forms realizes this cosmic value. The struggle for survival so vicious at the organic level of existence may give the impression of value-neutrality, but the strength of the impulse of preservation never loses its ethical character. A hungry wild animal becomes calm and harmless when its stomach is full. Hunger is a natural need all right, but nature has decreed that this need can be met. After the need has been met desperation—a state of ethical turmoil—gives way to calm, a condition of ethical restoration. Wherever there is desire satisfaction is possible. Wherever satisfaction is a reality or wherever it remains a possibility as desire morality is indicated. Desire is an ethical phenomenon.

I return to the problem of causality. Has the universe a cause? Can we really jettison the steady state model in favor of the Big Bang theory? The notion of the eternity of the world itself is unsatisfactory because of our insight into philosophical fatalism. This same fatalism renders the Big Bang theory doubly unsatisfactory. What seems to us to be more certain is the fact that the mind contemplating the scientific evidence of the complexity of the universe and organic existence from physics and biology will be inclined to believe in a supreme principle of the universe. It is all very well to say space and time and everything in it came into existence at the occurrence of the great cosmic bang. But could something not have caused the explosion? Obviously, the steady state model of the universe has its strength from the philosophical point of view. As part of an eternal universe God is consolation. Time is then conceived as timelessness. Empirical conditions carry us to the plane of the seemingly supernatural. If we appear incapable of penetrating the thick fog of the mythopoeic dream shielding God from human eyes it is because we are not powerful enough, not because the phenomenal is all that there is or can be.

Philosophical fatalism suggests the possibility of the reconciliation of dualism with monism, rationalism with empiricism, analysis with synthesis, subjectivity with objectivity, biogenesis with abiogenesis. Intellect has been reconciled with emotion by showing that these two elements are engaged in a dialectic. The intellect is understood either as the faculty of reason or the capacity to think, to logically structure our beliefs. The intellect thus indicates rationality. Rationality has the dominant aspects of ethics and logic. A proposition is said to be rational if it satisfies a basic human demand of seemliness or if it satisfies conditions that warrant its being approved of. For a proposition to be rational it must first and fundamentally satisfy the demand that it be good or logically appealing. Here metaphysics and logic meet in the primal emotion of life. The intellect or rationality or logic is the refinement of this basic emotion in a state of awareness. Joy recognized as optimism belongs roughly to the emotion while grief recognized as pessimism belongs roughly to the intellect. These are rough approximations because a dialectic is on, such that emotion energizes intellect while intellect enlightens emotion. Thus the energization of intellect produces the noblest impulse attainable by consciousness—inspired reason, creative intelligence, the love of the intellect. These notions throw light on our attempt to understand the relation of a God who is the consolation of the universe with this selfsame universe that He inspires into being out of the abundance of His power, which universe necessarily is expressed imperfectly because it is yearning.

Solution to the Problem of the Existence of Evil in the World

The problem of the existence of evil in the world is indisputably the greatest problem of human existence and the most fundamental question of philosophy. Not only are humans mortal: truly their mortality is dogged by physical and emotional pain all the way, culminating in death which is yet another evil. Death is an evil because it is the loss of consciousness without an immediate compensation in the world and without a sure guarantee of any compensation in another world. The loss that death symbolizes is not balanced in the world of experienced reality by the possibility called "dreamless sleep" or "eternal peace." But just as evil exists so does good exist in the world. The evil is terror and the good is beauty. Death snatches worldly beauty from us.

The pointlessness of the universe is only seeming. The very fact that its seeming gratuitous existence resolves itself in the meaning of consolation makes the absurdity dimension only seeming. It is from the perspective of the despairing intellect that the universe is absurd. Human despair connects with the problem of evil. Yet the meaning of existence is consolation. Human hope connects with the reality of goodness. We talk of consolation because of the undeniable beauty in the world, the beauty in the sphere of human existence that underlines human joy and the beauty of the physical universe that deepens human joy, as when we appreciate the beautiful scenes of nature. This beauty opposes the terror of existence. The universe can be pointless only for one insisting on an absolute perfection nowhere to be found in the scheme of things, who conveniently forgets that he is part of the problem of evil, the very reason for the existence of evil by virtue of his status as an existent thing. A universe whose meaning is yearning cannot give us perfection. Resignation to this truth animates the love of the intellect.

While physicists rhapsodize over the complexity and orderliness of the physical world, ethicists and metaphysicians wonder at what I may label the mystery of iniquity, the phenomenon of moral evil, chiefly. Both the orderliness of the cosmos and the phenomenon of evil are marvels of complexities. Both marvels supply grounds for belief in God's existence. While the physical complexity of moving planets and the laws guiding their motions takes the mind over to the idea of intelligent design, the ethical complexity of the evil act confronts consciousness with its profound discontent. The discontent of the impulse of evil undergoes successive transformation in consciousness, from sadness to despair. The conquest of this evil impulse sees despair passing through the phase of anxiety and becoming the love of the intellect under the influence of human joy. When the evil impulse finds consolation it also finds God. Goodness is so positive that it speaks for itself. I call goodness positive morality. The evil act arises because of a failure of reality, the failure of despair to find consolation in the love of the intellect. Since good and evil have a common origin in pessimism or the sadness of *mood* and since I have shown that our universe is moral, the products of will (good and evil) are moral outcomes. While goodness is a positive morality, evil is a negative morality. In fact we will be guilty of impatience to proceed quickly to label the evil act amoral, as if the evil act does not know morality or is opposed to morality. The problem of evil is the problem of the failure of reality. To the extent that the seed of evil has been sowed in the grief-component of the sadness-joy constitution of *mood* (the Eternal Mood of God, the human mood, and the mood of nature) the existence of evil in the world is a necessity. Evil happens inevitably. But because the conscious being, for example, a human being, cannot help not knowing that evil arises as a failure of reality, because of this clear knowledge, consciousness stands guilty of orchestrating evil. Necessity is affirmed but responsibility is not denied because evil is a negative morality. It is not an absence of good or simply a minus but the incompletion of good.

Consciousness stands accused of evil as it knows that the wish of the evil impulse carrying the burden of sadness is to reach goodness through despair and anxiety. Humans are guilty of evil because it is in their power to understand the relation between sadness and joy, to recognize that evil results from the abortion of anxiety, hence the non-completion of the moral act commenced by the evil impulse in the state of sadness as anchored by despair, the denizen of thought. It is in the human power to sustain the morality of the evil impulse of *mood* and terminate it in the joyful or optimistic act of good instead of the immorality of the full-blown evil act. Perhaps it will be said that the necessity inherent in the dialectic of *mood* nurtures a rigid determinism that shields the offending individual from moral responsibility. This is merely begging the question. What must be must be not as a fixed rule but simply by reason of its inevitability. The necessity of the dialectic is a moral necessity. The failure of reality is an indictment of the whole of existence—God, humanity, and non-thinking nature. All are guilty, as Heidegger, Sartre, Kierkegaard, and even Leibniz have brilliantly noted when discussing what we may call metaphysical evil. While humans have not been able to overcome despair to attain power over evil, God has achieved this victory and is called the supreme power in the universe. It is obvious that men strive towards the status of God and are called good or righteous. Yet men have not attained this divine excellence and can never attain it. Hence, power and glory belong to God alone.

What applies to man-made evil (the so-called moral evil) also applies to physical or natural evil. If we are inclined to be less bothered with nature-induced evil than we are with man-made evil, it is simply because we know that the consciousness of nature is so undeveloped as to be non-existent. This position is not entirely true. If it is true that nature is completely devoid of consciousness life will not be possible on earth. Life itself is the product of an evolutionary process that took its long path through a gestation period in which it was identified with inorganic existence. Both science and religion attest to this. Like human beings, nature stands guilty of harbouring evil in its principle. Nature is as guilty of the charge of terrorism as the Muslim Kanuri suicide bomber in Northern Nigeria. The erupting volcano if confronted with its immorality, the destruction it inflicts on living things, will imitate the suicide bomber, provided it has attained consciousness. Like the suicide bomber, the volcano will assert boldly that it is fighting God's fight. Its justification for taking this incorrect position is that its rage will have some positive consequences for the continuing evolution of the physical universe. The erupting volcano will point to the fact that its activities are partly responsible for the origin and development of oceans and the continents now inhabited by men through geological time. This is the same as saying it is doing the work of God. This mentality of the erupting volcano is the mentality of the terrorist. What stops us from boldly admitting this to be true is the fact that the erupting volcano cannot stand trial before a court of justice. Metaphysically, the erupting volcano bears the burden of guilt. While it is plausible that a man can be the instrument of God in his witnessing to *liberty*, it is not correct for a man to presume to fight God's fight. God has fought against the evil in His principle and triumphed without human help. The divine victory made possible the appearance of the world.

I will not subsume evil under necessity and pretend it is simply a consequence of this necessity, that all is well. Necessity of occurrence cannot mitigate the tragedy of existence which the inevitability of evil symbolizes. The appearance of evil is the clearest indication of the imperfectability of the world which is the fate of *mood*, all that yearns. Natural evil is less condemnable than moral evil, but it exists nevertheless and should be deplored. How do we absolve God of blame in the appearance of evil in a world He inspires? If He is benevolent He cannot be the creator of evil. We say God is benevolent because He is not the author of evil although He inspires the world into being. It is more appropriate to say God inspires the world into being than that He creates the world because the world has existed eternally in His mind as a coming inevitability, as something that cannot be averted. God is contemporaneous with the universe. Evil is an existential burden of *mood*. Evil emerges from the fear that broods over the fatality of the universe. The overcoming of fear is the conquest of evil. God is almighty precisely because He has conquered evil in His principle. As a benevolent creator, God wills a perfect creation, having conquered despair in Himself, thus qualifying to be called a Being of power and glory. The demand for an omnipotent and omniscient God who did not have to score a victory against the fatality of His own existence is a demand of a human reason in search of nothingness, a nothingness conceived as eternal peace. If God has scored a victory without help from any other being, then He is everything that power and glory can command. With these categories we acknowledge the existence of evil in the world without the imputation of wickedness or indifference to God. With these categories we have a God who is almighty in the sense of possessing power but not omnipotent in the sense of possessing all powers.

Human beings cannot blame God for the reality of evil. The correct reading of the state of affairs is that humans have not done enough to tame the evil in their own nature. They cannot conquer evil—such a conquest will make them God. But a human can grow morally towards one's consolation by becoming better. If one chooses not to be better, God cannot be blamed. One stubborn question may stick in the mind? Why did God create the world, knowing that it was not going to be perfect? Since the creation of the world is a fatalistic inevitability, that is, a necessary appearance in an imperfect form of yearning, this question is best answered with a rhetorical question. Would it have been better if all that existed was the silence of the Eternal Mood, an approximation of nothingness? The pessimist will probably answer yes since he is disillusioned and sad. The optimist may answer no since he still looks forward to joyful moments on earth. Let us put our rhetorical question more simply: "Is it better never to have been born than to have been born?" We already know what the pessimist and the optimist are going to say. Unfortunately, the pessimist is right to the extent that not having been born is a condition that spares the human mind the torture of having to confront pain and terror. Fortunately, the optimist triumphs because it is impossible for one who has been born not to have been born. To theorize on the nothingness of the individual is merely to wish. Against fatalism, one recognizes one's impotence, a powerlessness that goads the embrace of a nihilism which, ironically, is rooted in the ethical phenomenon of existence. Given that fatalism reigns and demands resignation from advanced consciousness, must the consolation which one finds in the beauty of one's agonizing soul and in the beauty of a broken world not be enough for a human being?

Of the Origin of the Evil in the World (Continued)

We saw in the previous section that the existence of evil cannot be wished away in the manner of Spinoza, Hegel, Bradley, and other thinkers in the Western tradition. They told us that all was well and would be well. Our analysis of *mood* brought us to the conclusion that all was not well but might still be well. Neither the famous free-will defense theodicy nor its soul-making theory variant nor the appeal to a rigid determinism searching for a perfection alien to its character can wish away the problem of evil. This fundamental problem tells us that the eruption of evil in the world is not an accident but the logical or, better still, the *fatal* consequence of the development of *mood*. Our African synthesis has shown that it is only when we take this position that we can begin to explicate a more honest and true theodicy. It is true that our theodicy takes away a logical necessity of perfection from the God-concept, but then we have shown that the categories of omnipotence and omniscience are not applicable to a principle which is not only reason but is fundamentally emotion. The demand for omnipotence and omniscience is not a justifiable demand. A glorious and powerful God is adequate for reason and faith. By revealing the inapplicability of the categories of omnipotence and omniscience we neatly sliced through the problem of how an omnipotent and omniscient God fails to create a perfect world.

Let us briefly consider the practical evidence for physical and moral evil. Let us dwell on volcanic eruptions as supplying an example of physical or natural evil. The damage that volcanic eruptions have done to men, animals, and towns throughout history can hardly be quantified. We only have to remember the catastrophic eruptions recorded in history to wonder at the mystery of evil. As an example we have the super-eruption of Lake Toba on Sumatra Island in Indonesia some 69,000 to 77,000 years ago speculated as having killed a large percentage of humanity.[2] Among the benefits of volcanic eruptions we find the creation of new islands and the availability of rich soils for agricultural activities, the sight of colorful sunsets due to the injection of aerosols into the atmosphere. The beautiful side of volcanoes seeks to balance, but never succeeds in balancing, the good-evil equation of this phenomenon. A determinist appeal to the necessity of this occurrence fails because we have already shown that determinism is only a superimposition on fatalism. The evil determinism desires to wish away ("people can't help behaving the way they do" and "things happen necessarily according to eternally fixed laws" mantras) is already accounted for by fatalism which is the law of all eternity. Determinism does not explain the evil in the world; rather evil partly animates it.

Volcanoes erupt in places where tectonic plates are divergent or convergent, pulling apart or coming together. They also form where there is stretching and thinning of the earth's crust. The stretching and the thinning, the convergence and the divergence, imply the yearning of unanimated existence. This state seeks the higher state of life and consciousness. If the so-called non-living nature were utterly dead and not simply unconscious there would be no movement to cause the kind of destructive (and beneficial) disturbance we have classified under natural evil, as in the case of volcanoes. In this natural disturbance a yearning is discriminated, the yearning of the lowest form of consciousness, sadness emerging out of silence, yet unable to complete the dialectic in joy, without which intelligence cannot create. Precisely because of this cosmic yearning of the earth or the elements of which the earth is composed, value is already indicated independent of the advanced consciousness of human beings. This objective value of the inanimate provides the justification for anthropomorphism. Humans create value. Spectacular as this creation is, it merely fulfills a law of nature which states that nature is value-laden and that the more value is realized the higher the concentration of consciousness. The realization of value entails the emasculation of the evil impulse of consciousness by the suppression of pessimism and the deepening of good by the expansion of optimism. A volcanic eruption is a development that falls under the classification of natural "evil," not only because molten magma destroys life but also, fundamentally, because evil is a principle of yearning; yearning in its own turn is the character of existence.

Moral evil refers to those destructive acts traceable to the exercise of the human will. Moral evil is all the more condemnable because it is the deliberate act of a witness to *liberty*—the human knowledge of the difference between good and evil. Let us take the example of a Hausa suicide bomber. This bomber tells us that killing innocent people and getting himself killed is a pious act, a way of fighting for God. We saw in the previous section that this is a delusion of a humanity refusing to accept that intelligence fails itself, just as reality fails outside God's mind, when evil surges out of the sadness of *mood* or in the pessimistic phase of *otu*. The excuse of the Hausa suicide bomber is exactly the excuse the erupting volcanoes, earthquakes, and hurricanes will make if the latter class of entities could talk and justify the yearning of *mood*. To say one is fighting the battle of God (or Allah) is another way of saying one is fighting one's own war, fighting to conquer the evil that fear determines before consciousness out of the stuff of consciousness itself. God has already fought and won His battle. He does not need humans to fight a war He has already won, although He can help them fight their own ongoing war by becoming a moral and spiritual ideal for them. It is in this sense that Unamuno is right when he says in his *Tragic Sense of Life* that God suffers with us that He may lift the weight of the brute matter suffocating divinity and mortality. Like most Western philosophers who have struggled to explain how evil came into the world, Unamuno appealed to matter for the illumination of the problem. But matter and mind are in solidarity, they are elements of *mood*. Both matter and mind carry the principle of evil. Indeed, mind is reckoned more evil than matter because of the former's higher state of consciousness. The origin of evil is to be sought not in matter and not in mind but in the *mood* of eternity of which mind and matter are fragments. This takes us back to the African synthesis, the doctrine of *mood*. We must not be weary of the metaphysical argument, for there is no other way going forward. And forward we must go.

If it were possible for the universe to have been nothing at one time, this nothing must have been a profound cosmic indifference. Since the human intellect just cannot grasp the idea of nothingness without being tempted towards its reification, our starting point is the fatalistic principle—that which was, which is, and which becomes. If the fatalistic principle *is*, a cosmic indifference is indicated which is not as profound as the indifference of nothingness. This fatalistic principle is Aristotle's God. It is indifferent to the world and therefore cannot constitute the logical grounds of the world's existence. For it to support the world necessarily it must first be the sufficient condition of the world's existence. Indifference protects its own inaccessible majesty. In which case, the world exists in a condition of absolute independence of the fatalistic principle. Such an absence of connection between the world and the fatalistic principle seems to be impossible, for it amounts to denying intelligence as a force operating in the universe and favoring chance. The inconsistency of this mechanistic standpoint is the inevitable vitalization of mechanism and the compulsory reification of chance, which leads us back to theism or deism. Therefore I hypothesize that the indifference of the fatalistic principle is benevolent rather than absolute. Thus it has always been as yearning. Because of this yearning it becomes. Here we are simply saying that the fatalistic principle is in a process of dialectical change. As personality it is privileged to contemplate eternity. Pierre Teilhard de Chardin tried to clarify this point through the elucidation of a speculative scientific evolutionism when he mentioned again and again, in his supreme masterpiece *The Phenomenon of Man,* the impossibility of man realizing progress without positing personality as the evolution of impersonality.[3]

What we call moral and physical evils have their roots in the yearning of *mood*. Cosmic sadness, adequate to human consciousness as pessimism, accounts for the evil in the world, although this evil is only latent in the Eternal Mood. The dialectic of *mood* moves from silence to creation. Between silence and creation sadness and joy evolve. From the silence of impersonality arises the sadness of personality. But the goal of *mood* which is consolation is not yet reached. Pessimism recognizes fear, despair, and anxiety as the elements of cosmic grief. The fear element connects impersonality with personality. With fear comes the recognition that impersonality is rooted in fatalism, the inevitability of existence; one which finds no meaning or justification outside consolation. Overwhelmed by its knowledge, cosmic fear can either return to the impersonality of the Eternal Mood or pass into the personality of this same Eternal Mood.

The passing of fear into personality marks the defeat of despair and the elevation of anxiety to the level of love in God. This transition automatically translates to creation and the distinction between God as the Eternal Mood and the world. For this reason I say that God has fought and won His war and has become power and glory. He is not responsible for the evil in the world. He has carried an existential burden and triumphed. The appearance of the world which pre-existed as the plan of *mood* is the consequence of this triumph. Since the character of *mood* passes into creation evil enters the world. This virulence of evil in the world is the failure of mind and matter to achieve victory over fear. The yearning of humans and lesser life-forms is a lamentation of the powerlessness of mortality. Yet God has not abandoned His creation, for He has become an ideal for humans, who carry in their minds the concept of God and the wish to become like God. Since this ambition cannot be realized humans are content to regard God as their consolation.

By labeling the universe "objective" most people mean that it is dead and purposeless. How do we know that the universe is dead and without any purpose? This hasty conclusion is as objectionable as the most extravagant anthropomorphic mythologizing. Indeed, the hypothesis of a purposeless universe is another example of anthropomorphism. The structure of the world, which is monistic, presents itself to our anthropomorphic fancies. This is no mystery that the universe is an emotional phenomenon. Scientists must accept its vitality. Philosophers must not be slow in acknowledging the vitality of the universe simply because they are so pessimistic as to wish everything in the enigmatic universe were pointless.

The intimacy of fear with mind yields what we call moral evil in humans. The intimacy of fear with matter yields what passes as natural evil. Fear is the universal consciousness of the fatality of existence. Fatalism defines existence as inevitability. Fatalism says simply that a thing is because this thing not existing is impossible. And the only justification fatalism finds for the existence of this thing is the consolation this thing seeks as that which is constituted by yearning. It finds no perfection. Fatalism finds emotion masquerading as reason. This is tragic. Our reverence for God consists in this: He is the only Being who overcomes fear. But in His overcoming of fear and despair the world comes into being compulsorily as an entity separate from His inspiration and lacking in power and glory. The fear that produces evil on the side of pessimism and sadness is also the father of good on the side of optimism and joy. To overcome fear is to overcome the impulse of evil. To overcome evil is to become benevolent. God is benevolent. Nature outside the Eternal Mood has not overcome evil and cannot achieve this victory because it is not God. Nevertheless, nature, and I mean objective nature rather than nature as the totality of existence (which is actually the Eternal Mood), yearns because it is the expression of *mood*. Because it yearns without rising to an adequate level of consciousness nature is not benevolent, although it manifests the aspects of beauty. Nature yearns for benevolence like everything fatalistically existing, but in the absence of an adequate consciousness it cannot attain benevolence. Its yearning manifests mostly in the destructive eruptions we call natural evil. Yet it is not all malevolence on the part of nature. If it is true that it cannot rise to benevolence it is equally true that it yearns unconsciously for benevolence; hence the nurturing aspects of nature for which nature is honored with the title *Mother Nature*.

Humanity itself is not benevolent without further qualification. The peculiarity of humanity is that whereas it is capable of benevolence it willfully chooses to be malevolent. The yearning of humanity has morality at its base. Human wickedness is a species of morality. Moral evil is projected towards the completion of morality in the optimistic act, but it fails and remains within the sphere of pessimism and despair.

Chapter 6

RECAPITULATION, PROBABILITY, AND SUMMARY

On the Silence of the World as Arguing for the Supposition of a Missing God and Finally the Impossibility of God's Existence

I have limited my effort to demonstrating the necessity of God's existence as the sufficient condition of the existence of the universe without attempting to read the mind of God, an endeavor beyond philosophy. However, I did not merely provide a negative perspective on this topic but also attempted to show the interplay of impersonality and personality in the dialectic of *mood* as it relates to God and the universe He inspires into being. Our insight is an intellectual insight into the nature of fatalism rather than mystic intuition. This is an insight which must grapple with the substantiality of the silence of the world or the non-materialization of God who may be justly designated a "hidden God" (*Deus Absconditus*) indeed. But humanity cries out for a sign of the coming human apotheosis, which event will be the same as the revelation of the face of God. The natural world is silent about the direct purpose of God in nature and the human desires the direct intervention of God to halt the evil ravaging the world. All too soon we conclude pessimistically that the natural world is dead and that the utter transcendence of God means His eternal inaccessibility or even His non-existence.

The pessimistic viewpoint starts as the search for God, but, failing to activate optimism under the psychological burden of the demand for tangible proofs, the human mind ends up finding Sartre's missing God which is another way of expressing the new religion of atheism. "God, show face," the closet Nigerian atheist cries out imperiously in Pidgin, demanding for a miracle that must improve his earthly condition. He is so proud of his piety, but this is a piety not supported by the thoughtfulness which nurtures abiding faith in the unseen God. Hence, he easily violates the sanctity of morality which is the greatest manifestation of divinity, a sign of the coming apotheosis of humanity. This apotheosis may well be impossible, but it is indicated and remains future-bound. It is always indicated as the revelation of the divine.

The non-appearance of God is to be regretted. Yet morality is enough consolation for this non-appearance. The universe is God. Everything existing has a share in divinity. This universe is profoundly moral, whether one is talking about its material or non-material dimensions. If morality is not missing, then God is not missing, though we may desire to pinpoint His exact location. This desire is understandable since the universe itself expresses yearning. Still, the insistence on seeing God is presumptuous because it supposes that the intellect can see beyond fatalism. Rebellion against the resignation fatalism imposes on us leads us easily to the state of profound sadness and its condition of awareness, pessimism. This pessimistic state of mind convinces us to embrace atheism. What is obvious here is that the human stands between the devil and the deep blue sea. One has a choice to believe in God and be consoled by knowledge of the moral foundation of the universe, given the non-materialization of the God of this universe for reasons beyond us. Going with this choice entails being optimistic or having a religious hope. The second choice is pessimism, which translates to the denial of God. This is a hasty conclusion because the analysis of pessimism takes us to the necessity of positing the existence of God, as I will soon demonstrate. The inaccessibility of God should not be an insurmountable problem if accessibility implies conviction of the reality of divinity. The hiddeness lamented as His inaccessibility will be accounted for as part of a cosmic plan beyond human understanding once it is established that accessibility is not altogether dissociated from conviction of the reality of divinity. This amounts to saying that the philosophical demonstration of the existence of God—like the demonstration of the existence of the external world, other humans and minds—is in fact the justification of a conviction realizable by the strength of the probability seeking this realization. I will return to this same issue of the impossibility of a "proof" of the existence of God later in this chapter, for to find a proof is to recreate that which is to be proved, to utterly eliminate probability.

Now, is the argument of pessimism really an argument for the non-existence of God? Atheism is not in itself a rebellion against God. It is basically a pessimistic attitude emboldened by the conviction that no god has yet arisen. Let us here return to our analysis of cosmic pessimism as presented in previous chapters. Pessimism is an awareness of a basic feeling which we call sadness. Pessimism is the response of the intellect to the failure of reality, of which sadness is the lamentation. *Mood* seeks perfection, but by reason of its constitution it cannot attain perfection. Consolation, which is the very meaning of existence itself, realized in varying degrees, must be enough for *mood*. The atheistic attitude, although a consolation, is far from being the terminus of pessimism. Indeed, the pessimism that does not or cannot go beyond itself is an arrested optimism. Optimism is the terminus of pessimism, where despair is completed as the love of the intellect and cosmic fear dissolved in the cosmic resignation of fatalism. In the absence of the purpose of optimism as the final goal of pessimism, the latter loses all its validity and becomes an idle concept. In this regard pessimism existentially equates the silence of pre-creation. Yet pessimism, in this case human pessimism, is no idle concept. It is knowledge of a condition of life corresponding to the feeling of sadness, the disappointment that comes to an intellect fired up with the expectation of finding a perfectly rational world after conveniently forgetting that its expectation is in the first place conditioned by its emotive constitution.

Thus the optimism rejected as a delusion by the despairing intellect is affirmed as a consolation by the creative intellect. That is to say, the pessimistic phase of thought dissolves into the optimistic phase of thought when the mind has thoroughly contemplated its own pessimism to arrive at the conclusion that *mood* must proceed from pessimism to optimism. Optimism may degenerate to pessimism, but from pessimism the only possible movement is one upwards to optimism. Reality is a failure. But this failure of reality establishes consolation as the purpose of the universe, the reason for existence taking the form that it now assumes. God is not the mastermind of this failure of reality. He is reality itself and therefore carries the essence of this failure. In triumphing over fear and in overcoming despair He moves from being the principle of the universe to the consolation of the universe. The vertical analysis of human pessimism points to God. The belief in the existence of God is the highest form of optimism.

The early tendency of philosophy towards skepticism, agnosticism, and atheism is due mainly to the fact that the intellect is hyper-active in its pessimistic phase in the absence of a *sign* from God Himself proclaiming His existence. Philosophy too easily prefers to focus attention on the mind of God which is in fact the silence of eternity. This cosmic mind is regarded simply as a principle, an impersonal entity. Philosophy that has not yet been illuminated by the ultimate necessity (fatalism) ignores the necessity of the engagement of this cosmic principle in a dialectic with itself. The dialectic of *mood* transforms cosmic principle into cosmic consolation. Thus the impersonal First Cause becomes a personal

God. The mystical demonstration of this transformation in the decidedly complex Christian notion of the Trinity is one of the beauties of the Christian religion. The determination noticeable in some religions to purge the God-concept completely of difference and tension is a negative exertion. If the concept of God must leave the human intellect to become a living God in reality, as our analysis of *mood* has shown, then God returns to us as an eternal principle of life carrying in itself the tension of *mood* out of which arises a universe. That is, for God to exist in reality He must be a fatalistic being. The universe of God is the "something" which the "nothing" cannot displace.

The intuition that proceeds to conceptualize God partly in human terms is itself a gift of the objective universe. This intuition turns its face towards its origin when it uses subjective terms to describe a God supposedly hidden forever from us. Subjectivity may after all be nothing more than the participation of developed consciousness in everything objective.

The Demonstration of the Existence of God as Merely the Justification of a Belief in God Masquerading as Proof of God's Existence

The temptation is always strong to regard our demonstration of the existence of God as a *proof.* A proof implies the absence of probability, the creation or recreation of that which is to be proved. While a mathematical proposition can be proved or confirmed as a logical certitude, being a mere logical construction, nothing that lives can be proved to exist. The demand for a proof that a living thing exists is highly presumptuous. The living thing can only be *justified* as existing on the basis of a prior and immediate belief in the existence of this living thing. This immediacy is conditioned by both the senses and the mind. There is always an element of probability in the demonstration of the existence of a living thing because of the limitation of the human intellect which is prone to despair and pessimism. This pessimism is the knowledge of the inferiority of the power of human beings relative to the immensity of the universe. The existence of a day-old rat cannot be proved by human reason. This proof will demand that we recreate the rat, an impossibility. For the rat is a living thing, a dignified and objective existent in the world.

The existence of God cannot be proved since we cannot make God or re-create Him. Before the most daring intellect attempts to prove God's existence this intellect must first assume God's existence. The assumption is a belief.

Both the theist and the atheist have taken emotional decisions to believe or not to believe. The argument for and against announces the late arrival of reason. Reason is always a latecomer to fundamental controversies. What we later call a proof is a justification of a fundamental belief, a primary conviction. Since conviction comes before rational compulsion the proof of God's existence backdates itself as emotion seeking reason. Once again we see how dependent reason is on emotion and the existential priority of emotion to reason. The demonstration of God's existence is the justification of belief in God. Just as the existence of God cannot be proved, so is it impossible for the existence of the external world to be proved, and with this latter proof the attendant demand for the proof of other human beings and minds.

Every demonstration of God's existence carries the element of probability, from the classical Western ontological, cosmological, and teleological arguments to our own consolationist argument. The highlight of the ontological argument is the proclamation of a Being who embodies all perfection and is therefore a Being of infinite greatness. The low point of the argument is our realization that logical grandeur does not have to correspond to an existential grandeur. In other words, a God conceived as perfect in thought need not exist outside the mind with all the perfection bestowed by the mind intact even though it is plausible to assert that a Being may well truly exist, a greater than which nothing can be conceived. Here the mind is unable to escape probability. The argument declared as a proof is now shown to be a mere justification of the conviction or belief in the existence of a Supreme Being.

Neither the cosmological nor the teleological arguments fare better. The triadic arguments themselves are collapsible into one and the same argument which carries the justification of the existence of God. The cosmological argument has the inadequate observable world as its starting point and works its way up to a Being who must necessarily exist if the phenomena of the world must have any semblance of uniformity and rationality at all. This argument confronts the big problem of the relation of God with the world. The skeptic wonders why the observable world should not exist necessarily if it must be insisted upon that God exists necessarily. In proposing intelligence as the principle behind the semblance of design we perceive in the observable world, the teleological argument scores a big victory for common sense. Yet cosmic finetuning upon which this victory rests must contend with the element of chance and show that a blind chance cannot be the active principle behind the finetuning of the universe. Here again we do not escape probability. Our solution to the problem of the existence of God also does not escape probability. While our speculation can come to the help of the cosmological argument and adequately explain the relation of the world with God in a monistic solidarity, it tries from moment to moment to dodge the accusation of anthropomorphism.

Yet it is not only the consolationist doctrine of God which is haunted by the charge of anthropomorphism. The classical ontological, cosmological, and teleological arguments all stand accused. For it is the human mind that goes out in search of an idea. The existence of God is first a belief. The argument for God's existence follows as a justification of this prior belief. Those who look out perpetually for the anthropomorphic elements in the thoughts of philosophers fail to realize that the mind that goes out into the objective world in search of its precious idea must have had this idea suggested to it by the objective world. As part of the structure of the human being, the human mind is already objective. If it differs from what we call "nature" it is simply because of its higher level of consciousness and the attendant capacity to individualize humans to their very depth in reason and emotion. The demand for the elimination of the anthropomorphic character from the human way of viewing the world, from our thought-structure, is a call for us to stop thinking. The passive indignation felt by skeptics when a philosopher thinks anthropomorphically indicates unbelief. The person who does not believe in God sees no reason for anyone to attempt the justification of God's existence. He demands for a perpetual suspension of belief, an intellectual operation that ultimately leads to nihilism.

The search for divinity cannot be halted for the very reason that God is the consolation of the universe. Humans cannot stop thinking, and thinking will always project its own nature into the external world because this external world is of the same furniture as the human mind. The ontological, cosmological, and teleological arguments on the one hand and our vertical analysis of *mood* on the other hand defend the notion of a God who is sufficiently perfect. Perfection is an invention of the human mind which we project into nature and extend to divinity. Neither nature nor God need be perfect as we have shown already. Yearning does not demand perfection but consolation. Perfection is a concept meaningful in the context of progress, since we have not reached this selfsame perfection. We invent the concept of perfection because in ourselves we see the emptiness which perfection ought to have filled. What gives us the right to think that God—if He exists—is a Being in no way related to us? A close observation of animal behavior shows that some animals react to stimuli and process information like men, although at a far less sophisticated level. For instance, animals like dogs are capable of boredom, of losing interest in something that has previously held their attention after prolonged exposure to stimuli. The human-animal comparison can be validly made at a low level of analogy. God may not be a Being completely unrelated to humans in a monistic universe. He may just as well be a Being infinitely better than humans, whose consciousness retains a connection to their consciousness in spite of its excellence. We say God is humanity's consolation. If He is humanity's consolation He cannot be a human invention. Rather, the human is an invention of God.

However, probability does not exclude certainty, ultimately. The universe is already given as a fact, doubt as the solipsist may. The illusion of the universe as it occurs to the human mind in its pessimistic phase is the imperfection of the universe. Probability is the other side of certainty. Probability measures certainty before a limited consciousness. To say that the demonstration of God's existence lies within the sphere of probability means that we cannot recreate God because He is far too mighty for us to recreate Him. To fall back on probability means the admission of the fact that we do not have the details about the universal sway of fatalism to construct a precise justification of a God who exists as the principle of fatalism. We do not know why there had to be a beginning of things or no beginning, why "something" is instead of "nothing." We must, then, agree with the Italian philosopher Giambattista Vico who asserted that the true knower is the one who comprehends his own creation even though we disagree with his dualism, the elongation of the distance between conscious and unconscious existence and the refusal to regard anthropomorphism as a necessary and therefore valid mode of thinking. Vico had insisted that the true (*verum*) and the made (*factum*) are convertible.[1] Consequent upon the assertion that truth is what has been made, "we cannot demonstrate physics *per caussas* because the elements which compose nature are outside us."[2] Vico's admirable insight unfortunately led him to skepticism with regard to our knowledge of God and external nature, thus downgrading the idea of probability which he, no doubt, had in mind. "Those who try to prove that God exists *a priori*," thunders Vico, "are guilty of impious curiosity. For to do that is tantamount to making oneself the god of God, thereby denying the God one seeks."[3]

It is true that it takes some audacity of "impious curiosity" to walk the golden road to the Samarkand of philosophy; yet this audacity is not impiety, for God is human consolation, and a man will not be deterred from seeking out his consolation within himself and outside himself. The *a priori* argument has not ruled out probability, whatever its dogmatic claims may be. The *a priori* argument is a justification of the belief in God's existence and is as valid as any *a posteriori* argument. To silence the theoretical craving, to seek to stop a human from taking the golden road to Samarkand in the search for knowledge, is the same as asking a person to stop posing fundamental questions and become content with skepticism, and finally find solace in unbelief. This, of course, is not possible since physics will always turn its face, even if whimsically, from the gate of Baghdad towards the golden road to Samarkand. The unbelief to which skepticism ultimately leads us has scientism as its pillar. Ironically, this same scientism has as its foundation the metaphysics denied as mere fantasy. Yet the universe itself is a fantasy or, better put, an illusion, as we have seen in previous chapters. When we settle for atheism, an extreme skepticism, we contend with the dialectic of *mood* which throws up the analysis of pessimism and shows that the pessimism that yields skepticism and atheism cannot support atheism. I have already discussed this issue in Section 1 of this chapter. The *a priori* argument, as operative within the sphere of probability, is a valid justification of the existence of God. It loses its validity only if it boasts of being a "proof" and thus makes the prover "the god of God."

Probability does not pander to skepticism. It does not merely glorify a reality I have asserted a failure. Probability is a doubt beyond doubt. It is the conformity of certainty to human consciousness. According to the probabilistic theory, neither the *a priori* argument nor the *a posterior* argument equates proof of the existence of God, the external world, other humans and other minds, and even a blade of grass. Although not alive in the sense that a house rat is alive, the world external to mind cannot be proved to exist because it houses living things and is not mind-dependent as far as practice goes. The entities mentioned exist outside us, as Vico noted. As existing outside us, they cannot be created or re-created. Humans create machines and can prove their existence, but they cannot prove the existence of a house rat.

Probability in the Perspective of Our Consolation Philosophy

Consolation is an absolute in an essentially emotive universe that evolves rationality as the basic character of morality. God who is both imaginary and real is the Consolation. As the impersonal principle of eternity He is imaginary; as the personal principle of creation He is real. Humans are the consolation with the small "c" because it is in their activities relative to the God-ideal that they realize consolation. In other words, humanity needs God to absolutize its consolation. Truth is empirical fact enriched in thought by the possibility of the ideal. No empirical fact is ever complete because no such fact standing independent of the ideal can actualize man's consolation. The human phenomenon is a *melancholy being*, the grief-stricken mortal, who has to believe in something outside himself to realize any comfort in himself as big or bigger than his despair. Let us illustrate our point by direct reference to the human condition which is undoubtedly so much pathos.

A man has just heard that his house has been destroyed by government officials who hope to construct a major road that will be of great benefit to millions. Of course "fact" does not bring joy to this man. The fact, that which is true, is a negative fact in the case under study. This same man hears that he is to receive a compensation package of fifteen million naira. Here we encounter another fact, albeit a positive fact. Both the negative and positive facts are empirical situations subtracting from or adding to human consolation. This man proceeds to diligently invest his fifteen million naira so that in the course of time he becomes a rich man. Yet his good fortune can only be fully or more fully understood in the context of his whole life and the many relations this life bears with the world and what the world consists of. For these facts to become fundamental they must be evaluated in the context of the whole life. Probability comes as the limitation of uncertainty, as an indication of eternal truths towards which empirical truths move. Thus the rich man notes that his neighbors have become envious of him because of his good fortune which was preceded by a misfortune. He realizes the he has become the target of armed robbers who dimly apprehend the idea that everyone's wealth belongs to the world as resources of the universe. He realizes that his status as a rich man does not stop him from falling or succumbing occasionally to ennui. Before long he realizes that he has to write a will and leave all the wealth he has accumulated behind. Empirical truth fails him and he turns to faith to find solace in a belief as great as, or greater than, his despair. The purely empirical phenomenon, which had at one time seemed sufficient, now seeks unity with the transcendental factor through the transcendental appeal of humanity. The rich man—now the universal man—seeks his consolation in God who is yet hidden from his direct gaze. He is tempted to declare Him only a missing God, never found even in the beginning. Yet this is a temptation he keeps repudiating, for his despair stems from pessimism, and the analysis of pessimism nullifies the audacious claims of bare mechanicism and frustrates the atheistic creed. The atheistic creed itself thrives on the theistic manifesto. Atheism is the denial of theism. And so the world which is given as a certainty, a metaphysical absolute, is suggested to consciousness as a probable thing. The probability measures the degree of the failure of reality, the imperfection of the very nature of *mood* which sustains the illusion of existence, and the tragic reach of fatality. Consequently, I highlight the following epistemological points:

1. The empirical truth is not the eternal truth although it acknowledges the eternal truth.

2. Eternal truths do not escape probability.

3. Truth is ultimately absolute.

4. God has not been seen but is justified as a consolation.

5. No testimony is error-proof.

6. Faith is an emotive rationality taking the bite of cynicism out of every probability so that relativism, skepticism, agnosticism, etc., collapse into a belief system in search of justification.

The imaginable is possible and the possible is either real or realizable through faith—and faith as the justification of the operation of fatalism. That which is imagined is real or realizable to the extent that the thing imagined is emotionally and intellectually related to the Consolation, the hidden God who is the ultimate object of the transcendental appeal of humans. The imagination, after all, represents a longing, a wish, a purity which has been found only in the concept of God, His love for the world, and His conquest of fear. Once again the anthropomorphic charge fails. If God is a living principle He must think, and if He thinks cosmic fear remains to be overcome since God's existence is a fatality. One person says there is a place called Heaven while another does not believe there is such a place. Neither is right nor wrong. The validity of the conflicting assertions will depend on the intellectual and emotional intensity of their individual yearning for purity completed in joy and sadness. For it is either there is such a place or there is no such place. Every wish is a yearning validity by reason of its consolatory value. The wish may seem superstitious, but then superstition is truth travestied, not bare falsehood. No possibility is to be ignored on the excuse that the "thing-in-itself" is unknowable. Respect for probability would rather teach us that it is the given absolute that makes perception possible at the purely phenomenal level. Perception measures the absolute as probability. And the absolute that perception measures is an imperfect or fatalistic absolute. Perception measures yearning and, being itself a phenomenon of yearning, becomes a part of the yearning absolute. Probability gives to human consciousness the probable thing as the revelation of the absolute. The universe exists absolutely, but we probabilify it. An extreme form of idealism such as Fichte's may even dare to suggest that the human mind creates what it finds outside itself whereas mind only probabilifies absolutes. But, then, this tendency is due to the fact that mind goes out seeking not an emotive universe that evolves rationality (which is really the case) but a perfectly rational universe, strictly determined, and for good only. Our dialectic of *mood*, favored over the dialectic of being, has struggled to show what is really the case.

The thing-in-itself is a mystery not because it cannot be known or intuited but because its essence, roughly yearning, does not open itself to intellectual scrutiny and emotional demystification. The thing-in-itself is problematized within the sphere of probability because it has been intuited. Yet this intuition seeks justification within the totality of an absolute conferred with meaning by fatalism. Therefore we can divide the thing-in-itself into two categories: the "probable" thing which we know so well and can validate or falsify and which is the face of the absolute turned towards consciousness, and then the "absolute" thing which completes the probable thing beyond the world humans dominate. Things people create and the statements made about these things are probable phenomena. The absolute thing is the Consolation. Since probable things are parts of the unity held together by God as eternal principle and personal creator they already participate in consolatory existence. The probable thing, therefore, seeks completion in the absolute thing, a completion strained by the burden of *mood*—fatalism.

The thing-in-itself is already known to us fully in the probable thing and has been partially revealed to us in the absolute thing as the Consolation of the universe which must be justified by reason after its acceptance as a demand of emotion, the logic of life. If I have gone into a rhapsody of the God-ideal like so many philosophers before me it is because of the sheer impossibility of a rationalistic denial of God's existence. Our African synthesis recognizes this scenario only too well. The absolute thing is the Consolation, the fatalistic principle, a possible *a priori* existent, immanent *a posterior* (that is, eternal and intimate with the world), the Eternal Mood of melancholy transformed through the supreme conquest of cosmic terror into power and glory. The emotional and intellectual character of the Consolation is reflected in the human mind and in the objective universe. Mind and matter are outputs of *mood*. The absolute is knowable in a universe where emotion is prior to reason, one in which emotion and reason are involved in a dialectic that realizes consolation and is born in consolation. To denigrate emotion in order to find a pure rationality is an absurdity. If God did not exist, human beings who are anthropomorphic thinkers would invent Him. If human beings invent God at all, then God exists as the ground of the world that opens itself to humans to be observed.

On the External World and the Demand for a Proof of Its Existence

The fallibility of the testimony of the senses encourages skepticism. But if the senses do often fail to yield reliable knowledge of the external world it is no less true that the intellect is fallible. The intellect may be more precise than the senses, but it too is fallible because it purports to create that which is outside it. The demand for certainty or even a much higher probability than what the senses offer runs the risk of isolating the human mind in a logical cocoon, which isolation creates a kingdom of intellectual fantasy that may rival the extravagances of the senses. In which case the triumph of the excited intellect is seen for what it is: premature optimism. Consolationist dialectic has shown that for optimism to be valid it must refer to its foundation in pessimism. Subjectivity cannot dominate the universe since the objective is a given absolute. Subjectivity merely enjoys the privilege of measuring the objective, a task it never achieves accurately since it is itself a part of an objective absolute. My point here is that probability follows human consciousness all the way, from sensation to intellection and the final incomplete knowledge. Skepticism is no denial of the possibility of knowledge but an acknowledgment of the primacy of faith in the mental construction of what is outside *otu*. For why must it not strike us that the universe exists by faith rather than by accident?

With his great originality the Western philosopher David Hume outlined a metaphysics of terror when his brand of skepticism led him to doubt the reality of objects in the world and their knowability *a priori*.[4] Hume was not trying to isolate the mind from the world but was rather trying to link the mind with the world by introducing the faith-element as a mediator. It is significant that Hume respected the role of emotion in the affairs of men and women. The world is already there, whether mind perceives it or not. Once mind, itself an objective mode of existence, turns towards the external world the process of perception becomes primarily an operation of faith. An objective phenomenon has been encountered, a mode of existence governed by laws accounted for by fatalism. Mind which is primarily yearning meets something other than it which is also primarily yearning. The recognition is bare intuition, the opening up of emotional reason. To then believe that a world exists based on the combined testimony of the senses and the intellect is to cherish a high degree of probability. Not to believe the testimony of the senses and the intellect is to descend into skepticism. The state of skepticism reflects the emotional attitude of a mind wishing that the totality of existence was something far more precise and refined than yearning. The impulse of skepticism desires a rational universe but finds only an emotive universe that evolves rationality. Instead of freedom and happiness mind finds fatalism and consolation. What emotional awareness accepts as an indisputable fact reason justifies as probable.

For Kant this situation, the appeal to faith as the grounds of our knowledge of the external world, is a philosophical scandal.[5] His search for a "proof" of the reality of the external world led him to an idealist solution which suggests time as the foundation of space, thus imbuing the mind with the powers of representation and even of constituting the external world. Moore's skepticism about the idealist solution led him back to the realist position, one suggested by common sense.[6] Common sense intuition is not a bare explanation: every sophisticated proof of the external world rests on this basic intuition or faith. The external thing is already given as an absolute. It is already a thing-in-itself. The adequacy of the absolute thing to human consciousness throws up the probable thing. I may dare to say that Kant's noumenon is already given to human consciousness in the phenomenon just as time is already one with eternity. I do not deny the noumenon but propose that this noumenon is already familiar to consciousness as the phenomenon. If mind has not demystified the noumenon it is because mind has not penetrated the fog of existence, what for lack of an appropriate logical term I have called the mythopoeic dream of existence. The dynamism of reality renders a radical dualism untenable while obscuring the monistic perspective of existence. The probable thing presents itself immediately to the mind and must be endorsed as a true testimony by faith, an operation always executed in the mind's optimistic phase and is therefore related to the love of the intellect. The fog of existence or the mythopoeic element of fatalism comes between mind and the external world. Knowledge is further burdened by the fact that the fog of existence that separates humans from the external world is already implicated in the constitution of mind and matter. That is to say, mind and matter carry the stuff of illusion even as this illusion distorts the solidarity of mind and matter. Thus it is famously asserted in Western philosophy that all relations involve difference and sameness simultaneously. The comprehension of probability involves a dialectical apprehension of reality. The apparent mystery of existence is the incompleteness that yearning assumes in the name of the absolute. To dismiss the absolute as incompatible with reality while embracing the probable as all that is possible or real is to underestimate the complexity of *mood* which determines existence. Such perfunctory attention to the great question of being shows that skepticism has not returned to its foundation in pessimism.

As impossible as it is for us to prove the existence of the external world, it is nevertheless true that a justification of the belief that the external world exists yields theoretical knowledge. This theoretical knowledge is not a proof. It is rather our addition to a reality possessing its own dignity for the sake of comprehension. When someone turns his head to look upwards into the sky and declares that the sun is no bigger than a football he has acquired theoretical knowledge, which knowledge comes in the process of justifying the fundamental belief in the existence of the external world. The person who asserts that the sun is infinitely bigger than the earth also acquires theoretical knowledge of the external world. Proof which is impossible is replaced by justification which provides theoretical knowledge. Thus faith is carried over into probability by the sheer power of reason. Reason itself is not superior to faith, but it supports faith by clarifying faith's immediacy. Standing with intuition, faith gathers around itself the fog of existence which we say arises in the yearning character of existence, in the emotive constitution of *mood*.

From the foregoing the philosophical problem of the proof of the external world has come into a clearer perspective. The claim that there is a concrete proof of the existence of the external world is nothing more than the justification of what is met outside the realm of mind as the given fatality. The appeal to the concrete, the practical, is already an operation of faith. Here the realist triumphs. All the same, mind adds to what it finds (the external world) in the process of representing it. Now the idealist looks at the realist victoriously. The issue of mental representation cannot be overlooked for the very reason that justification involves knowledge. One cannot prove what one believes to be the case, in particular when the case and its history are outside one. This belief, being a bare intuition, does not generate knowledge in its immediacy. Belief does not have to yield absolute truth. Apart from not being knowledge of the absolute, belief nevertheless makes contact with the *mythopoeic*, that whose dynamism is yearning. Belief is not the thing itself but the intuition of the thing. In creating the world God has already proved its existence. All humans can do is to justify the existence of the world, to speculate about it like the metaphysician or to describe it like the physicist. It is not the impossibility of a proof that informed the radical skepticism of the intriguing Greek philosopher Pyrrho but the conviction on Pyrrho's part that an adequate justification of the existence of the external world is lacking, ultimately the conviction that God may not be the consolation of the world. Skepticism is the cause of the demand for proofs. Skepticism makes this demand on realism and idealism and returns to the refuge of probability. The failure of reality exemplified by the evil in the world nurtures skepticism. Now can we scrutinize the attitude of mind called skepticism in our resolve to understand why the existence of the external world should be doubted in the first place?

An Anatomy of Skepticism According with the Doctrine of *Mood*

The African philosopher impatient with what may seem to him the problematization of an apparently simple matter by Western philosophers will be tempted to brusquely dismiss the demand for a proof of the external world. Before he is tempted into a hasty denunciation of the skepticism that necessitates the attempt at a proof let us remind him that it is not only philosophers who doubt the external world or nurse misgivings about its substantiality at certain moments. It is instructive to note that the moments of doubt, when the external world appears an illusion, come during the pessimistic phase of *otu*. In this phase of thought the seeming illusory character of the world is sometimes considered a projection of epistemic sadness or pessimism into the objective order of nature. Yet we may ask: is this all there is to the matter? The dialectical perspective of reality always seeks a bridge to connect mind with matter. Connection may not mean identity since both mind and matter are fragments of *mood*, yet it implies solidarity. Once the connection has been effected dualism gives way to a serrated monism.

If the monistic conception of reality is triumphant, then the attitude of mind (skepticism) that prods the mind to prove the reality of the external world is already latent in the world. That is to say, the illusion of the mind is diffused already in the world. Matter is already an illusion, like mind. All that is required for the illusion of the world to forcefully strike the mind is the presence of the existential conditions that turn the mind towards the contemplation of fatalism. Here is the source of what Unamuno will call the tragic vision of life, the fatality of existence that has thrown humans into an imperfect world in which they have to make the transcendental appeal.

The existential conditions favoring skepticism include practical evidence of evil, sadness, fear, despair, and anxiety. Because of the primordiality of sadness it is sometimes considered a negative emotion that avails little. Its more overt expression is even regarded as sentimental and irrational. Ironically, nothing can be more rational than sadness, for here is the very foundation of rationality. Under the tutelage of the will—which is in fact the intellect resigned to fatalism and active as an expression of an evolving rationality—primordial grief becomes anxiety in the advanced consciousness, a less elemental grief. There are two focal points of anxiety, namely, despair and intellectual love. If the focal point of intellectual love is realized despair pales into insignificance and the illusion of *mood*, the veil of primordial emotionality, assumes the solidity of concrete existence before human consciousness in its optimistic phase, that optimism which calls forth the joy of consolation as marking the final evolution of rationality and the liberty of the will. The reverse case imposes a burden of doubt on human consciousness. The highlighting of the focal point of despair emboldens the outline of the illusion of *mood* so that what had seemed substantial previously begins to appear unreal. In this situation the concrete individual wonders to himself whether he is dreaming. Let us note that those who doubt the existence of the external world are people who are unhappy or dissatisfied with their condition of life at a particular time. This human unhappiness may be caused by illness, poverty, encounter with the numerous forms of evil, and other negative conditions of humanity. No healthy person in his joyful moment doubts the existence of the world. Here we have found the origin of the skeptical attitude.

The philosopher who doubts the reality of the external world theoretically rarely doubts this reality when he is in the midst of humanity. Even while he is at work in his study he only concretely doubts the reality of the world when he is in his pessimistic phase of thought or when he is particularly fatigued. Physical weariness, which is a mild form of evil, can initiate this doubt. It is also possible that the philosopher who doubts the reality of the external world is carrying over an existential doubt felt in everyday life into the theoretical realm. Wherever the cause of skepticism is to be found a philosophical problem arises. This problem of uncertainty generates the two prominent questions that directly inspired consolation philosophy, namely: 1. Is the universe purposeless? 2. Is human life futile? The consolationist thinker is eminently placed to answer these questions as the student of the illusory character of the universe and the investigator of the dimensions of skepticism. The exploration of the outskirts of doubt over the reality of the external world is a fit task for 21st century African philosophy.

If the demand of skepticism is understandable but impossible, skepticism as an attitude of mind must fall back and find consolation in faith. The attitude of faith tells us that illusion is not identical with falsehood, that illusion is not the impossibility of the absolute but its very possibility in the probable. Illusion does not mean an absence imagined as a presence; rather illusion signifies the non-completion of a presence whose essence is yearning and whose goal is consolation. Thus we accept probable reality by faith. By the affirmation of faith we validate that which exists fatalistically. The fatalistic existence is the complete existence, the unity of the probable thing and the absolute thing. While the probable thing is a perfect fit with the structure of the human mind the absolute thing is not, although the probable thing already indicates it. To penetrate the probable thing and illuminate the absolute thing consciousness must completely overcome the despair intimate with its nature. Such a penetration will illuminate mysticism by throwing light on what is called revelation even as the foundation of science will lose its metaphysical essence and become transparent to empirical investigation. Materialists will then cease to antagonize mystics just as scientists will finally comprehend prophets. Revelation as a form of knowledge of the elusive absolute is possible in the universe we are describing. Imagination is the truth of illusion. Its symbols are adequate to yearning, although the intellect alone can clarify the image of reality presented by the imagination.

Even if it is possible for everything to be taken out of the world to create room for the "nothing" there will remain in this "nothing" a latent absolute which I have called silence, out of which sadness as a primordial life-form evolves. The external world has to exist and has always existed. If chance leads us to the concept of necessity and the latter itself proves unintelligible beyond fatalism, then we must find solace in faith and assume the eternity of the world as an accomplishment of faith. Faith absolutizes or seeks to absolutize probability but never succeeds in this endeavor since it is not greater than yearning. Yet since faith seeks to absolutize probability the unknown becomes knowable, if not already known. All forms of knowledge, then, are faith-forms. Philosophy is animated by philosophical faith, religion by religious faith, science by scientific faith. The combined faith of all forms of knowledge leads the sentient being to the complete knowledge of the Consolation which is God. Outside faith there is neither probability nor certainty, for probability is the face of certainty. The total sway of faith does not have to embarrass us since the universe itself exists by faith.

We know things by using our senses, by imagining, by thinking, and then by believing. Having believed we will things to be because they have already been willed into existence by faith. Our willing is the affirmation of faith. We do not create anything in the world by willing; rather in willing we validate. Faith is the animation of necessity by the force of latent intelligence inherent in the eternal *mood* of sadness which is destined for development in mind. The understanding of faith renders the theory of evolution plausible not simply in terms of mechanical and biochemical processes but also in terms of a more complex process involving a kind of inescapable intelligence, one which is *a priori* impersonal and *a posteriori* personal. This complex process embraces the perpetual creation Bergson celebrates in his works, a perpetual creation in the power of intellectual love, in which one stage of consciousness takes its cue from an older and more complete but latent intelligence: more precisely put, the fatalistic unfolding of what is often casually referred to as intelligent design.

In the pessimistic phase of *otu* probable reality is considered a failure even as pessimism breeds skepticism. In the phase of *otu* dominated by optimism this failure hides behind the mask of hope. What in one phase is seen as a failure in a different phase is considered passable success. But let us maintain our grasp of the situation. Pessimism inspires skepticism. It underlines our belief that reality has failed. He who doubts the existence of the external world *ipso facto* doubts the existence of God. Ultimately, the reality of God is the target of all doubts. When we doubt we ask ourselves: Is the Consolation possible? Usually we assert an empirical state of affairs to be true since it enjoys a high probability. For instance, if we mix hydrogen and chlorine it is true that hydrogen chloride results. But hydrogen chloride is not the truth. The truth the human phenomenon seeks is the completeness of consolation. The *truth* is the consolation latent in the *true* as an idea. The truth is happiness or freedom. But this is beyond humanity, who must make a transcendental appeal to God, conceived as a Being who is the Consolation. Skepticism is a demand for God to unveil Himself. The unveiling has not happened.

The person who uncritically accepts the reality of others and other minds by faith and therefore the external world may shake his head and wonder why the philosopher has to be worried about the reality of the external world when his very presence attests to the fact that there is a world which he observes. Yet consolationist analysis has shown that doubt about the external world is an everyday reaction of men and women in the face of the difficulties life throws up again and again. The demand of the skeptic is an impossible demand. It is the demand not only that God should reveal Himself but also that the world should be perfectly expressed. In the absence of optimism faith is suspended and skepticism takes over, diminishing consolation. And it is joy that conduces to human optimism, because joy comes to us in a world in which evil is real sadness confronts joy.

Illusion is projected from within the thinking being. The greater the illusion bottled up within, and allied with sadness, the greater the suspicion that the "nothing" is possible and the easier it is to suppress the audacity of the imagination. Disillusion follows despair surely and doubt dilutes the strength of faith. In fatalism, which animates faith, chance and necessity dissolve into design. As pessimism yearns for optimism and as it gradually gets transformed under the influence of intellectual love the fantastic becomes reasonable and the shadow of life becomes life. Fantasy and superstition begin to approximate truth. The unreal becomes real and faith affirms this reality. Indeed the universe itself is a dream affirmed real by faith. A more complete picture of reality must combine pessimistic insight with optimistic insight. This may all seem forceful and even bewildering to practically minded men and women, but the basic truth of our submission is driven home when one tries to encompass the question of the origin and destiny of the universe in which we are puny observers. The concept of determinism which seems to give us very clear ideas is soon discovered to have no foundation in itself and therefore must fail to account for the origin of the world. Scientism is shown to be another system of faith in the probable thing. When one tries to pretend that only the phenomenal which is perceived is real the bogey of indeterminism arises to challenge determinism. It is for this reason that I have favored the philosophy of *mood* ahead of the philosophy of being. In consolation philosophy fatalism supports determinism and claims itself as the mother of all necessities. With the doctrine of *mood*, therefore, we cease to hide our heads in the sand and begin to unravel the metaphysics of terror.

The despairing solipsist may say that he alone exists or that he does not know or he is not sure that other selves exist beside him or that the world exists independent of his mind. Yet he has not convinced himself that he hangs in space. His stance, though misguided, is understandable to the extent that pessimism is valid. All the same, existence is the unity of the two in one, terror and beauty. Certainly, pessimism alone cannot complete the picture. The solipsism pessimism inspires is easily displaced by optimism. I have argued quite trenchantly that pessimism points over itself to optimism. In human pessimism subsists the totality of what one was in the beginning, what one is now, and what one will always be. In this pessimism subsists the ancient emotion and the complete intellect in their readiness to unfold. Pessimism is a perpetual yearning for the Consolation. While God remains hidden in His glory, pessimism is able to find a lesser god called optimism. Intellectual love effects this transformation from the condition of despair to the state of joy. Pessimism is *ab initio* a movement towards optimism. Sadness becomes joy, and the joyful person has no problem affirming the existence of the external world on the basis of common sense conviction, knowing that a proof is both unnecessary and impossible.

Conclusion to the Second Part of the African Philosophical Synthesis

The apparent paradox of the determinacy of solid matter at the level of sense experience and its seeming indeterminacy at the sub-atomic level has given a stimulus to the otherwise ambiguous project of the dematerialization of matter and the dementalization of mind. Yet the seeming indeterminacy of reality at the sub-atomic level does not justify indeterminism, although it may well provide another perspective of the very difficult problem of causality. Even if indeterminism reveals another picture of causality it is not descriptive of a lawless or chaotic state of affairs. The idea of chaos must then remain suspect. How can we show that the very moment of the emergence of chaos at levels too fine for sense perception did implicate or register order as a necessity, already developed or ready to develop? It is true that Aristotle did philosophy a world of good by suggesting that the attainment of reason or form is the goal of the universe, something Plato hinted at before him with his idealist notion of Forms which he gave the powers of constituting the world of phenomena.[7] However, this success is eternally postponed in the Aristotelian universe, thus qualifying the world as eternal. The idea is that matter will seek to attain form without ever succeeding. We will return to this matter in the section of Part Four of this work devoted to comparative philosophy.

Yet we are not satisfied with the Aristotelian view which sees the potentiality of matter indicating the impossible. Our African synthesis seeks to understand mind and matter in terms of the possible, comprehensively. This comprehensiveness is still within the sphere of probability. While Aristotle says perfection (for such is the meaning of "form") is impossible for humans and the world (except God) we see the possibility of consolation. The possibility of consolation gradually realizes all things such that the category of perfection is inapplicable to our world and the God who inspires the world into being. While for Aristotle God is without existence yet with utmost reality—being perfect form or reason—for us God exists and is real as the consolation of the universe. By downplaying the demand for perfection which is already recognized as unrealizable and concentrating on consolation which is already realized and is continually realizable we accentuate the fatality of existence and in the process kill and resurrect idealism. For at the base of life we place terror or sadness (and its unconscious state of silence) instead of non-being, not-being, or even becoming. Opposing sadness in the primordial stuff called *mood* is joy, the joy of existence. Consolation philosophy destroys idealism to the extent that it insists on consolation as the goal of the universe and founds this consolation on terror. It resurrects idealism yet to the extent that it asserts the primitivity of *mood*, therefore intelligence, the priority of purpose over bare mechanicism.

Having adopted this position it becomes easy for us to show that the first moment of the emergence of chaos in the universe was simultaneously the birth of order already developed or ready to be developed. We have argued along this line throughout the second part of this treatise. The vertical analysis of *mood* yielded being as the joy of life, thus confirming the validity of the philosophy of Asouzu. Simultaneously this analysis canceled out the possibility of nothingness by re-presenting the famous not-being of Plato and other Western philosophers as the sadness of existence. Consolation philosophy makes a unique contribution to philosophy because only with the instrument of the doctrine of *mood* that it supplies can it be shown that the despair of the human intellect traces a path of terror through nature and on to God. Only consolation philosophy has radically attempted a metaphysical construction on the foundation of the much misunderstood epistemology of Senghor. For the first time the basis of panpsychism is being illuminated, thereby confirming the validity of the monistic perspective and the ideas that flow through the philosophies of great Western philosophers like Spinoza, Bergson, Hume, de Chardin, Spencer, Bradley, Heidegger, and even Russell in his more metaphysical aspect.

From the standpoint of God all may be well. But from the human standpoint all is not well. The tragedy arises for human consciousness because while the intellect cannot comprehend a beginning from nothing, the notion of a "timelessness" prior to time (eternity) remains insistent as an alternative explanation of the riddle of existence. The chaos of the beginning was already the form of order. Every kind of chaos registers yearning. Chaos is an expansion, a contraction, a swelling in the heart of being, a movement towards purpose. If purpose is already indicated in chaos as the satisfaction called consolation, then chaos is in fact purpose in motion. If chaos is purpose in motion we can insist that chance was never there in the beginning. We must hold that intelligence was at work all the time, even though we are unable to show how intelligence made its first appearance. Something different from chance happened in the very beginning. For this reason it is easy to say that unconsciousness lies at the base of all that is.

Hence I prepared the way for the demonstration of the existence of God as the justification of a prior belief in the impossibility of God not existing. The vertical analysis of *mood* came in handy. Working from the premise of the determinism-indeterminism paradox and the other premise of the human *mood* we arrived at a conclusion that upheld God as the consolation of the world. The 21st century African synthesis failed to lead us to atheism through the analysis of pessimism, the epistemic state of mind constituting immanent justification for skepticism and ultimately atheism. This issue was dealt with in some detail in Sections 1 to 4 of Chapter Four. The quasi-phenomenological demonstration of God's existence was supported by an appeal to science. This is true since we tacitly accepted the theory of evolution and the hypothesis of abiogenesis and showed how the reification of chance is inevitable in physics and metaphysics. This reification frees chance from the blind or capricious mechanism it is supposed to be tied with. Chance becomes the shadow of intelligence or design just as chaos takes on the character of purpose. Given this scenario one is forced to ask how sheer unconsciousness can be and remain at the base of things. Even if the substratum of things is unconsciousness it is undeniable that consciousness emerges. Where is this consciousness really coming from? Is it from that which is like itself or unlike itself? The riddle of existence overwhelms us still, although we can show that there is a God. I think that intelligence is prior to bare mechanism rather than the other way round, that mind and matter detached themselves from a primordial intelligence which I have called the Eternal Mood.

EXISTENCE AND CONSOLATION

PART THREE

The Doctrine of Human Existence

Chapter 7

THE HUMAN PHENOMENON

The Scientific Vision of Humanity

It is fitting that our doctrine of human existence should come after our doctrine of God and nature. For God and nature are ontologically prior to humans. It is true that humans are observers of nature, but we are not persuaded that is the measure of all things. Indeed, the doctrine of *mood* has revealed the fundamental status of pessimism in phenomenology. Man may be a measure, but not the measure of all things. We are convinced that we exist. We need no proof of our existence. But, we are not fully convinced that God exists. Like our own existence, we need no proof of the existence of God. Although not wholly convinced that God exists, our reference is always beyond ourselves and towards God. The transcendence we look forward to is not a condition we can bring about. The idea of self-transcendence is an appeal to God. Even when intellectual rebellion leads us to agnostic and atheistic conclusions, the knowledge remains to the effect that the basis of agnosticism and atheism is pessimism. "If there is a God we cannot know anything about him." Or this: "There is no God." The outburst of despair announces the failure of optimism before the time of optimism. So we are left with the *mood* of melancholy. We are left with pessimism. Yet this pessimism, under analysis, leads us back to God, as truly as the mechanistic conception of the universe terminates in a teleological vision of the world. In other words, both philosophy and science point humankind towards God. But what has science got to say about the human being? We will briefly consider the scientific opinion before moving to the philosophical opinion ahead of the continuation of our effort to clarify our consolationist synthesis.

Science has accounted for our current situation as a complex living being with the theory of evolution. The theory traces human origin from lower life-forms, although silent on the origin of life itself. Humans are matter, an aggregation of the elements oxygen, carbon, hydrogen, and nitrogen, a physical collection of atomic and sub-atomic particles. They are complex machines run by chemicals secreted by the various bodily organs with the brain as the engine house. The body a person possesses can be divided into cells. In every cell is to be found the life phenomenon, the deoxyribonucleic acid (DNA). Battista Mondin writes with great respect thus:

> The molecules of this acid accumulate in the relevant number in all the cells of all living beings ... in man, every cell has enough DNA to form a cord about two metres long. If, then, we take the molecules of DNA of all the cells of our body, they would reach a length comparable to the diameter of the solar system.... The coffers which contain the interminable files of deoxyribonucleic acid molecules are the nuclear chromosomes. They form a chain whose links are constituted by genes—that is, by the molecules which function as depositories of hereditary characteristics, whether of the individual or of the species. DNA and genes, therefore, mark the stable confines between the various species of living beings, and between the living and non living-beings.[1]

While the plausibility of evolution is not in doubt, the knotty question of life's origin remains. It is a question which science has not answered and may never answer. The best science has done towards the resolution of this mighty question that ensures the perpetual involvement of human beings with the fundamental question of God has been to find a nexus between life and the physical universe of matter and energy, between the biological evolution of life and the physical evolution of the universe, in the overall context of anthropic coincidence. This idea that the physical evolution of the universe was from the very beginning a preparation for the emergence of life has expectedly divided scientists. This is so because the idea is intimate with the teleological argument for the existence of God. The anthropic coincidence hypothesis itself arose out of the overwhelming evidence for design unearthed by scientific research. It is the evidence of the fine-tuning of the universe that made the scientist George Wald strongly suspect that "mind, rather than emerging as a late outgrowth in the evolution of life, has existed always as the matrix, the source and condition of physical reality ... It is mind that has composed a physical universe that breeds life, and so eventually evolves creatures that know and create: science-, art-, and technology-making creatures."[2]

The metaphysical distance between mind and life is negligible. Therefore mind is life. If mind is prior to life, then our argument is an argument from life to life. This will automatically vindicate biogenesis. But the biogenesis pathway is not a simple hypothesis. The opposing notion of abiogenesis is always around the corner to find some fault somewhere in the argument. Biogenesis easily makes the mistake in divorcing mechanicism from purpose. Even when the biogenesis theory tries to make mechanicism the instrument of purpose it is still suspicious of the independence-seeking goal of mechanicism. For the notion of mind preceding life and matter (we broadly endorse this position) the difficulty lies in accounting for the very first occurrence—this phenomenon must be taken as an event or occurrence, for it is time itself emerging—the very first beginning or beginninglessness, which is called Mind or God. What conjured up the mind-stuff? How did it come to be? Can that which is the beginning or the non-beginning explain itself without reference to chance? If it must refer itself to chance it becomes unnecessary to dismiss the abiogenesis theory, the mechanistic conception of life. This is so since chance will lie at the base of evolution. That is, if chance cannot directly account for the emergence of life, in particular, human life, it indirectly accounts for the phenomenon because chance refers itself beyond God. On the other hand, we may assume that God is the ultimate, the being beyond which there can be no reference. In both cases the mystery of being, apology to Gabriel Marcel, remains and the human intellect finds itself exhausted before a creeping fatalism.

Yet we are compelled to fall back on Wald's position once the enormity of life's proportion and the complexity of our physical universe hit us. The evidence of complexity and enormity has already been thrown up by scientific researches in the fields of cell biology, astrophysics, and quantum physics. We think that we can claim to be on the road to the solution of the puzzle of existence by reifying chance and instantly finding a place for a mind-stuff prior to the human mind, and matter too. This solution will incorporate bare mechanism into the working of mind. This is Bergson's solution, the assertion that evolution is creative. It is also our consolationist solution which defines existence as the yearning of eternity. Thus we have struggled so far for the clarification of the dialectic of *mood*. If in the finetuning of the universe we find the conditions necessary for the emergence and the sustenance of life, then life and non-life meet in the design of nature. The hypothesis of abiogenesis becomes plausible as one that throws light on the instrumentality of design. The triumph of idealism becomes a belief in a certain kind of panpsychism, the belief that everything is alive in varying degrees since life is primordial in mind. This is especially so if the universe is conceived monistically and dualism in all its forms is regarded as a serration of a given whole or the division of a unity by the human mind for the sake of better comprehension.

How else can the belief that life emerged from non-life be sustained in the face of the apparent discrediting of bare mechanicism by scientific research? A black box theory of the universe which desires to stop at the description of the universe and its working through physical laws will not do here because of the bogey of chance. On the one hand, chance befriends bare mechanicism and on the other hand it suggests its hidden principles as the totality of purpose. What is this obscure totality? Schopenhauer calls it a blind will in his supreme masterpiece *The World as Will and Idea*. We call it yearning. Precisely because it is yearning it cannot be blind. It is primordial intelligence. John Leslie invites us to consider the initial condition of the universe following the Big Bang. Slight alterations in the rate of expansion of the Big Bang, very slight additions to the initial disorder, small revisions in the strength of the strong nuclear force, the weak nuclear force, electromagnetism, or gravitation or in various particle masses, would have made the emergence of life impossible.[3]

The evidence is on the good side of probability. To think that the process of the Big Bang was purposeless because of the sound of the "bang" is to be unduly influenced by the onomatopoeic. The bang could not have been a senseless explosion. The birth of chance was simultaneously the yearning of purpose.

It is the destiny of human beings, the phenomenon under consideration, to bow continually to the temptation of unraveling the puzzle of existence in their religion, philosophy, science, and art. Who designed the world? Chance cannot be the answer because chance is purpose made concrete as yearning. Yearning gradually reveals all hidden principles. If the world is not an accident (since an accident is in itself a yearning) how did God come to be? If God emerged by chance, then the claims of bare mechanicism are weighty. But if God existed uncaused as the truly free being, then He is the primordial mood, the yearning of eternity, the ultimate unity of the differences of impersonality (chance) and personality (purpose). As the creation of God, the phenomenon of human life is a piece of yearning. The phenomenon is the *melancholy being*. Having highlighted the problem and identified the limitation of the "almighty" science, we now pass into philosophy where we feel more comfortable.

The Philosophical Vision of the Human Being

Philosophy is distinguished from science not only because the former lacks the emphatic empiricism of science but also because of its speculative boldness.

While biology the scientific study of living things will not dare go beyond evolutionary human history, philosophy goes much farther back into the pre-history of biological and physical evolution to ponder the possibility of a creative evolution. Philosophy bypasses bare mechanicism to contemplate the abstruse subject of purpose. As philosophy often or always comes unstuck here, it is understandable when a Protagoras proclaims the human phenomenon a *homo mensura*, the ultimate measure of all things. Yet a Plato is never slow to insist that God, and not man, is the measure of all things. Even if we create a godless universe in which men have to worship science, a supreme atheist like Sartre will not hesitate to propose a philosophy of despair that demotes human beings from their Protagorean height of blessedness to the lowly status of useless passion. The philosophy of optimism encounters the philosophy of despair here, but human beings remain a puzzle since they yearn, and yearn completely, such that this life which they have met becomes a truly grave affair.

It is not right for science to sneer at the seriousness with which humans live, just as it is not all right for Sartre to dismiss human essence as useless passion. Passion we are indeed, but not a useless passion, for passion cannot be useless. It is the spark of yearning, and all that yearns seeks consolation. A fundamental tragedy is already indicated by human passion. This tragedy is no mystery because it is existence itself, the existence that deprives its negation of any right to positivity from the beginning. The question whether there is anything like the beginning compounds the tragedy of existence.

Bearing in mind the usefulness of passion (or the tragedy of yearning) consolation philosophy must turn to its root to throw more light on the human phenomenon. The abiding African view of human beings is in many ways a compromise between the optimistic and pessimistic views, although the optimistic view appears to have been favored by African philosophical scholars, in particular the celebrated ethno-philosophers like Senghor, Nyerere, Wiredu, Gbadegesin, Gyekye, the outstanding Asouzu, and the brilliant Chimakonam. These African thinkers were discussed in some detail in the first part of this book. If these thinkers have generally favored a radically positive view of the African community and a decidedly optimistic vision of humans as material and spiritual beings destined for immortality, it is because their thought-systems never really converged as constructive intellectual edifices. These men saw themselves more as scholars than thinkers. Our constructive alternative program, which traces its inspiration to the African community of the ethno-philosophers, insists on going deeper into the matter.

Dissatisfied with the one-sided optimism of the ethno-philosophers, consolation philosophy seeks to locate the tragic undercurrent of the African optimistic view of humanity. It is this fundamental tragedy that confers necessity on consolation and stops human passion from becoming a useless passion.

The centripetal social force that unites people in community expresses the optimistic spirit of human beings. The centrifugal social force of radical individualism underrates humanity and supports pessimism and nihilism. A superficial observation of African traditional life will seem to endorse optimistic communalism. This optimism is often contrasted with the rights-obsessed atomism of modern Western life. Yet the perceived African preference for communal progress ahead of individual glory is not an alien tendency in the Western social setting. No society can move forward if its parts gain ascendency over the whole this same society represents. The optimistic African socialist model celebrated by Senghor, Nyerere, and Obafemi Awolowo cannot withstand the scrutiny of a deeper metaphysical analysis. The optimism which upholds this African socialist model must wither under intense analysis. The progress of African society in the past came at the cost of the destruction of the feeble individual. We do not say the "individual" but rather the "feeble individual" to underline the injustice that prevailed in pre-colonial Africa and continues to prevail in 21st century Africa. The collective good is in reality the great success of a powerful minority.

Political philosophy will refer to this privileged group benefitting immensely from the ruthless domination of the feeble individual, thereby replacing optimism with greed, as an oligarchy. We will go further in our constructive analysis and undermine this perception of African social optimism preparatory to unearthing the theme of Afro-pessimism and ultimately unveiling the *melancholy being* as the universal man and woman. If undiluted African communal optimism was indeed a doctrine supported by practice or the evidence of everyday life, the seemingly intractable social and political problems confronting African today (problems of war, greed, corruption, poverty, etc., which characterize the human condition) would not exist in their current virulent mode. In which case, there would be no talk about Africa being a failed continent, one in which nothing good could occur. So far the failure of African communalism indicates the shallowness of the African optimistic vision of humanity and life in general. We do not declare its invalidity but asserts its incompleteness. When Asouzu talks triumphantly about the *joy of being*, the consolationist thinker at once realizes that something is missing. The joy of being of course reminds us that being must never be divorced from yearning. But this intoxicating concept of the African monist fails to tell us that the comprehensive demand of a state of being characterized as yearning is consolation. Without this demand being is nothing more than that impotent positivity, that bare presence Sartre dubbed the in-itself in his magnum opus *Being and Nothingness*. The universality of the black person is his status as a *melancholy being*, one capable of both good and evil and subject to both joy and sadness. This being the case, the optimistic African philosophical vision of humanity cannot be absolute.

The demand of consolation rests on the foundation of pessimism. Joy as a metaphysical condition of beauty and a constituent of yearning is never to be isolated from sadness. Any construction of a philosophy of optimism must follow from the bare definition of existence as tragedy. Such a construction is justified and labelled "optimistic" only because it fulfils the demand of *mood* for consolation. The demand for consolation is a sprinting away from the sway of tragedy. Since this escape can never be complete in a universe under the sway of fatalism, human beings talk about struggle and conflict. It is because humans must always talk about struggle and conflict that we entertain the idea of Afro-pessimism in the first place. The concept is all the more fashionable because of the relative absence of justice in the African social environment and the abundance of moral evil. If we have undermined the idea of the optimistic African worldview and entertained Afro-pessimism it stands to reason that the African vision of humanity must pass into the consolationist vision of humanity. While the traditional African view uncritically endorses the notion of communalism as adding up to a just system and overlooks the inherent pessimism in the system, the consolationist vision seeks the reconciliation of optimism and pessimism in the idea of the *melancholy being*. I want to show that it is only in becoming the *melancholy being* that the African becomes human. As *melancholy being* the African enjoys all the privileges due humanity. He is the equal of the white and the yellow man. The skin color of the *melancholy being* is irrelevant. What matters is that this universal person is the creature of *mood* who makes the transcendental appeal to a God who remains hidden from his direct gaze.

On the Necessity of the Transcendental Appeal in the Face of a Consolation-seeking Practice

The tendency in humans that lead them to appeal to higher authorities is so stubborn and persistent that it passes as a necessity. And, indeed, it is a necessity because the only alternative to it is uncritical fatalism. I distinguish this uncritical fatalism from my own philosophical fatalism, the latter being an attempt to find the grounds of the necessity of universal existence in the sufficiency of the universe. Uncritical fatalism is a bare kind of *amor fati*, bare in the sense of consciously or unconsciously excluding what Albert Camus calls *revolt* in his *The Myth of Sisyphus*. This revolt is of course an ethical struggle as radical as the futility that informs it. Yet the stubbornness of the transcendental appeal is such that the most noble and quiescent stoicism is itself a protest against a prevailing unfavorable state of affairs. The baby in the crib cries out angrily to its mother when it is hungry. A man who is wronged goes to court to seek redress. Political activists pile pressure on the state to meet their demands. These are all instances of the transcendental appeal. The most striking instance, however, is the appeal to God in human religious and spiritual practices. The invisibility of that which a human calls God has not deterred humans from believing and appealing to this Being in the face of a reality that fails again and again. Atheists may refuse to complete the transcendental appeal to God in the face of the failure of reality, but they certainly do begin the appeal, phenomenologically. An atheist may go to court to demand justice from what he considers a higher authority even as he will sternly refuse to mutter the words *as the Lord willeth* in the ultimate appeal to the symbol of supreme authority. Yet this anti-God stance may not prevent the atheist from being superstitious, from having a fear of dark places or cemeteries or from venerating science.

Everyday practice obviously fails to contain human passion. The failure of reality, existence as a tragedy, makes every practice and every thought the search for consolation. This search is transcendence, achieved or unachieved, achievable or unachievable. Ultimately, it is to God that transcendental appeals are made. The difficulty here lies in the non-materialization of God. The problem of evil in the world is not the real difficulty. I showed in the second part of this work that it is more appropriate to talk about the power and glory of God in a universe of consolation than the omnipotence and omniscience of God, the latter categories only applicable in a world where reality has not failed by reason of its status as tragedy. The God who is at the summit of a world of consolation as the personification of consolation cannot be complicit in the emergence of evil, as I demonstrated in Chapter Three of the second part of this work. If God has not appeared in the world, why has humanity overwhelmingly believed in Him across cultures, in the developed and developing world, in the most backward and the most advanced regions of the world, among the dullest men and the brightest, from generation to generation?

The answer is simple. The first demand of the living consciousness is the demand that God should exist. This is an absolute existential wish that a Being sit at the summit of existence to hear human appeals and realize their consolation. Truly, the mere concept of God as entrenched in the human phenomenon is able to cause actions that work for the realization of human consolation. For instance, the pure thought of God can be related to the thought of what is good so that this thought achieves many goods in the moral sphere. There can be no doubt about this; yet we are afraid of the silence our appeals to God often encounter. Thus we begin to doubt the existence of God. Whether we doubt or believe we are not the supreme masters of our own destinies in view of our finitude. Yet the demand that God should exist is intimate with the very structure of consciousness which endorses the transcendental appeal as a necessary appeal.

The human mind is not to be isolated from the wider life that produced it, the wider life characterized as yearning. Because the human mind is not cold but warm the logic of the intellect sustains an existential traffic with the logic of life itself. The logic of the intellect has been dubbed "reason" while the logic of life has been celebrated or denigrated as "emotion." Reason emerges out of emotion. On this account of the emotional coloration of reason there can be no pure logic. Even on the paper in front of the mathematician logic is not pure as logic still generates arguments and dissension. When I say that the demand that God should exist is a conceptual necessity I mean that the intellect will always remember its origin in emotion, and, in remembering, it will desire the Being that sits at the summit of existence as the consolation of the universe. How closely our notion of conceptual necessity relates with the Western notion of innate ideas does not bother us here. What is important is that the African synthesis must proceed. In proceeding I embrace a practice that cannot divorce itself from a higher theory, an ontology that must seek a transcendental metaphysics to legitimize itself.

The Question of Human Rationality

That which possesses reason is said to be rational. That which yields itself to impartial or dispassionate consideration amplifies rationality. Intelligence is a major component of rationality because for reason to be confident at all it must not only boast of a reliable degree of explanatory power but must also be perceived as being on the side of *right*. Reason then goes beyond the issue of knowledge (a big issue indeed) to encompass right thinking. But then the introduction of the element of right which is only a step away from the spiritual expression of righteousness complicates the question of rationality. Clearly, rationality does not refer only to intellectual firepower—after all, a villain can possess extraordinary intelligence and still commit crimes that shock everyone and then coldly seek to justify his crime in court. Obviously, rationality emerges from the interaction of the human intellect with the human community of other minds. This means that community values and customs will have an impact on the development of rationality. The social content cannot be ignored. This is not an admission that reason is a social construct. Reason itself is rooted in *mood* and is therefore objective. All the same, culture shapes rationality. This is aptly demonstrated by the opposing viewpoints of Africa and the West on the sensitive question of gay practices. While the majority of Africans consider homosexuality irrational the majority of Europeans and Americans do not consider homosexuality irrational behavior. The disagreement goes beyond the rightness or wrongness of the behavior in question to immerse itself in the matter of cultural acceptability.

We have identified the moral and cultural dimensions of rationality to go with its core logical component. The cultural components may be sub-divided into the aesthetic and religious components. We are mostly concerned with the major components of logic, morality, and culture. Better still, the logical and moral components holds us spell-bound. Yet logic has two senses, the sense of cold or dispassionate analysis (the sphere of Senghor's analytical reason) and the sense of involved thinking (the sphere of Senghor's sympathetic reason). One without the other leads to monstrosity. Both borrow from each other. The logic of cold thinking and the logic of warm thinking sustain their separate identities if and only if the degree the one borrows from the other is insignificant. The language of logic is called reason. The reason of the intellect is usually held to be synonymous with logic. If the reason of the intellect is to be called logic, the reason of the emotion is to be known as psycho-logic. Logic goes with cold thinking, the conscious attempt to ignore involved thinking. By involved thinking I refer of course to psycho-logic. The clearest indication that logic never succeeds in completely isolating itself from the imperious psycho-logic is the indisputable fact that logic engenders disagreement and debate right in its own sphere.

Any thinking process violently opposed to the finer aspect of psycho-logic, which is in league with common sense, is almost always unacceptable to the whole person. A mass murderer who argues brilliantly that he has to kill his victims because society will be better off without the victims arouses our outrage and condemnation rather than our admiration. This is not surprising because the cold thinking or logic of the mass murderer has fallen short of rationality. In other words, the moral component of rationality is missing. Logic has violently opposed psycho-logic, and the latter must triumph because it sustains the former as a substratum. It is a line of argument similar to ours that David Hume pursues in his masterpiece *Treatise of Human Nature* when he famously declared that reason is the slave of the passions in the second book of the third part of that great work. Logic may claim reason for itself, but psycho-logic will mock logic and asserts that in an interconnected universe it takes precedence over logic. Logic, then, cannot appropriate reason. There is the reason of the intellect and the reason of the emotion. Logic evolves out of psycho-logic. The reason of the intellect is subservient to the reason of emotion not because the one is wholly independent of the other but because the former evolves out of the latter as the latter's refinement. In simple language, we say the reason of the intellect (which is usually called reason) is the faculty of the human mind that structures thinking. Since the structuralization of thinking is a process connected with the morality rooted in psycho-logic, reason is a guide to action. It is because reason regulates behavior that we can talk of anything like rationality. Thus emotion infects reason. Emotion itself is psycho-logic. It is the reason that can only be understood in the context of fatalism. *Mood* (we prefer this term to "being," which seems too Greek, too Western, for our comfort) *is* because it is yearning. Its existence is fatalistic. It is what Hindu thought and Buddhist philosophy recognize as desire. As yearning *mood* cannot apologize for its existence. The inevitability here is final and awful.

It is on account of the priority of psycho-logic to logic in human consciousness that the first demand of reason is the demand that God should exist. The fundamentality of this demand gives us an idea of the emotionality of reason. Skepticism, cynicism, and nihilism arise only after this demand has been put into question by the non-appearance of God and the seeming sufficiency of the mechanical explanation of the evolution of the physical universe and the origin of life on earth. Yet this conceptual sufficiency of mechanicism lacks profundity as evolution presupposes creativity, even as chance presents an outline of purpose. Reason must always contend with the stubborn demand that God should exist, the transcendental appeal of a person in the face of human limitation, and the despair of reason at not being able to adequately reconcile chance with purpose, leading to nihilist thought-forms like skepticism, cynicism, despair, agnosticism and atheism. All these thought-forms constitute an emotional reaction of the human intellect to the first fundamental of reason: the demand that God should exist.

If we have been able to locate reason in emotion, if we have succeeded too in adequately isolating reason from emotion by presenting reason as the refinement of the emotion, how do we relate these mental categories and phenomena to the metaphysical notions of joy and sadness? Now, emotion is always optimistic, hence its perpetual striving. The bare existence of the universe is a tragedy. But its value-laden existence as the striving of *mood* is optimistic affirmation. The demand that God should exist is an optimistic demand, going with the joy-component of existence. The failure of reason to convince itself that God exists and satisfy the first fundamental leads the mind to pessimism, which goes with the sadness-component of existence. The tragedy of human consciousness is the questioning character of reason, its imperious insistence on the materialization of a hidden God right in the place where emotion takes the existence of this God for granted. Although the African philosophical thinker Senghor never dwelled on the negative dimension of consciousness and existence in general, he nevertheless obliquely arrived at a theory of human rationality fundamentally in agreement with the submission of consolation philosophy. Our submission is of course the thesis that reason is effectively the refinement of the emotion and that emotion itself is the logic of existence. We accuse Senghor of obliqueness because he woefully failed to universalize his epistemology and embarrassed Africa by presenting his grossly incomplete but luminous epistemology as a uniquely African theory of knowledge. Senghor declared psycho-logic the reason the African knows and logic the reason of the European.

With the clarification of our theory of reason, we have been able to identify Senghor's error. In the process of identifying his error, we not only rehabilitated him but we also found the basis for the construction of the philosophy of consolation. Consolationist anthropology has now thrown up the *melancholy being*. This is the human being of the 21st century, the universal person. It is in understanding this *melancholy being* that we can truly grasp such socio-political problems of our century as international terrorism, the upsurge of religious fervor in the developing world and the rise of agnosticism in the West, racism, tribalism, and ideological factionalization in the West and in Africa, the phenomenon of techno-emotivism and the disturbing issue of sexual anarchy and addiction. In the most technologically advanced age in human history, in which reason is expected to have so matured that it is able to suppress emotion for the emergence of Nietzsche's superman, we see emotion dictating comprehensively to science, technology, and the human intellect in general outside the scientist's laboratory and the thinker's study. The industrial workplace has not been spared by the fearful tide of emotion, for industrial unrest—such as the fatal mine workers' strike of 2012 in South Africa—continues to sweep through factories as employees poke angry fingers in the faces of their employers. The *melancholy being* is just as completely incarnated in the dominant political actors of modern society, actors like politicians who exploit the anxieties of the excitable electorate, the electorate itself that is prone to mass hysteria over the state of the economy and alarming power struggles, the indefatigable and sometimes iconoclastic human rights activists, power-crazy dictators and ebullient rebels raising the flag of revolution (as in Syria, Egypt, and other Arab nations). The *melancholy being* dominates the 21st century. It is the duty of the metaphysician to study the ways of this quaint phenomenon and help the political and social philosopher find a profound basis for the upsurge of emotion in a technologically advanced century.

We have taken note of the philosophical methods dominant in the West today, the Anglo-American analytical method and the existentialist-phenomenological method of continental Europe. While we think there is real merit in the two methods, it is obvious to us that mere philosophical analysis lacks the power, depth, and urgency to unravel a philosophy of human existence. We have also looked on the existentialist-phenomenological method with some suspicion on account of its postmodernist nihilist tendencies, which oppose the optimistic African vision of human life. While we recognize the priority of emotion over logic, we are not prepared to give up reason and discard the notion of the meaningfulness of the concept of rationality. The sheer vastness of the emotional life does not intimidate the rational life. As the refinement of emotion, reason is superior to emotion. Reason is already the custodian of goodness as our moral guide.

Consequently, our method of investigation claims to be an African rationalism, the consolationist method.

Chapter 8

THE HUMAN COMMUNITY

The Existence of the Other as My Brother

The unsympathetic African philosopher may be tempted to dismiss the problem of the existence of the other (and the other mind) as a pseudo-problem and fall back on the kind of bare realism G.E. Moore embraced while proving the existence of the external world, and, by implication, the existence of the other.[1] What gives one the courage to dismiss the problem as a pseudo-problem is the conviction that the other exists as truly as one exists. The conviction that the other exists as a unique identity is already an attempt to justify the other's existence by first destroying the nihilist grounds of solipsism. Affirmative statements such as "I exist", "you are Pauline", and "she exists because I can see her" are justificatory.

They cannot amount to proofs of one's existence and the existence of the other. Indeed, a proof of the other's existence is impossible. For such a proof must thoroughly confound probability. Absolute metaphysical certainty is beyond the capacity of the human intellect. It is no surprise that the problem has lingered in Western philosophical thought.

The mythopoeic character of existence confers an illusory essence on mind and matter. While we tend to be able to analyze matter and reduce it forever to the tiniest component, at least theoretically, mind suffers from illusion, a feeling of unreality most profound in the mind's pessimistic phase of thought. The optimistic phase of thought is characterized by joyfulness. In this phase no one plays around with solipsism or entertains doubt about the reality of his neighbor's existence. The pessimistic phase of the mind sees despair in full play. The neighbor previously considered as an indubitable manifestation is now set before a question mark. The man previously embraced as a brother, a fellow human being, becomes inconsequential. He becomes a non-person. The problem of the other's existence which is the same as the problem of other minds is one allied with nihilism. A healthy mind does not demand for a proof of the existence of other minds. It is enough that we seek to justify our own existence and the existence of others by creating positive values that unite the human community in which every neighbor is a brother and sister.

Yet I have kept repeating that existence is a tragedy. Since human beings must struggle in a losing war against their environment, since they possess an intellect deeply conscious of the mythopoeic character of existence, the healthy optimistic phase of thought frequently passes into the unhealthy pessimistic phase characterized by questioning. It is in this phase that humans experience nihilistic stirrings, questioning the reality of the world before them, the existence of God, whether they know themselves well, not to mention their neighbors.

The problem of the existence of the other is not just a philosophical problem blown out of proportion by eccentric philosophers. It is an existentially valid problem with roots in everyday pessimistic behavior. Philosophers have not merely imported it from another world into their books and journals. As a real problem, African philosophy should not ignore it. I am going to take a look at the problem from the consolationist perspective and determine whether a proof of the other's existence is possible and whether it is enough to seek only the justification of the existence of the other, a project that presupposes the giveness of the other which must be grasped with or without knowledge of this other.

The Existence of My Brother as the Justification of My Own Existence and the Affirmation of Faith in the Reality of the External World

Kant's hope for a proof of the external world as existing objectively is a forlorn hope. It is not possible and it is not necessary for philosophy to prove that the external world exists, although attempting a proof can help the cause of philosophical speculation and further underline the courage of the human intellect so convincingly on display in the field of philosophy. The presumptuous stance of the human intellect desiring a proof of the existence of the external world and the other (henceforth referred to as my Brother) indicates the idealist's lack of respect for nature which as a given is a totalizing whole just like mind, which is already embracing mind and is being embraced by mind. Therefore we are sympathetic to Jean-Paul Sartre who insists that the person-to-person relation is one of being-to-being rather than one of knowledge-to-knowledge.

Yet we are not comfortable with the Sartrean assertion that the demonstration of my Brother's existence on the basis of his communal giveness (which is nothing more than a justification of the obvious) does not involve knowledge, that the problem of mental representation and, consequently, solipsism is surmounted by the existentialist solution.[2] The *look*, according to the great French thinker, pushes immanence into transcendence, such that under the gaze, originally hostile, of one man to another is objectified and transcended. The factual necessity of my Brother's existence makes him a being-for-others. He is the condition for the existence of the one who stares at him and it is on account of the existence of the *looked* that we are immediately convinced that the looker is another mind. Sartre's existentialist solution is ingenious. But, like the solutions of Kant, Moore, J.S. Mill and the Anglo-American analytic philosophers, the phenomenological proof Sartre provides is only a justification of what we already believe to be the case. Philosophical exuberance must be put in its place when it presumes to do the absurd. Moore's near-comical realism is a response to the intellectual brinkmanship of the philosophers who want to prove the existence of the living Brother without being able to create him.

It is in the process of justifying his Brother's existence that Oche can justify his own existence and endorse the reality of the external world. The behavior of my Brother which Oche publicly observes, the inferences arising from this observation, my Brother's ability to communicate with Oche in a particular language, do not constitute proofs of my Brother's existence but rather indicate that my Brother's existence is already given in space and time (in the human community). Thus trying to prove my Brother's existence is superfluous. All Oche can do is to go with the evidence of common sense and the immediacy of the truth of an objective world outside him in which the community of humanity subsists and try to understand why doubt about the existence of my Brother and my Brother's possession of a mind should loom large.

It is doubt that leads to the search for a proof and the demand for a justification. While the search for a proof is impossible and unnecessary, the demand for a justification is realizable and necessary. The proof seeks certainty. The justification of my Brother's existence is subject to probability for a number of reasons. We identify the following reasons:

1. The impossibility of a proof which carries exactness.

2. The fallibility of the senses.

3. The obliteration of personal identity through death or serious illness.

4. The illusory character of the mind and the world highlighted in the mind's pessimistic phase of thought.

Justification is all that consciousness can achieve in the community of humanity. Not only is the external world doubted but the doubter's own mind is called upon to show that it is real. The doubt of the reality, not existence *per se*, of the self follows from the individual's encounter with a traumatic fact of a world that already exists. The existence of the world is not doubted in the midst of harrowing experiences which switches the human mind into its pessimistic phase, as truly as the existence of the self is not doubted in this despairing phase of the world that is put into question. What is doubted is the *reality* of the world and other minds. A given existent at any point of its existing is bare and irreducible. It is what Western philosophers will call a brute fact. Existence is basic. Reality is the evolution of value out of bare existence. While existence is bare reality it is either value-laden or able to add value to existence. Neither one is separate from the other, although one is bare and the other relatively more complete.

A human community is already given. The philosopher who insists on doubting the existence of the external world and the possession of mind by my Brother is pursuing a pseudo-problem. However, the reality of the given world and my Brother can be doubted in Oche's pessimistic phase of thought. Oche can fall sick and fail to recognize my Brother as a human being. Oche can lose his memory and live on at a vegetative level. Oche can receive terrible news and suddenly perceive the transparent mid-day sun as a red ball in the sky in a state of shock. In the pessimistic phase of Oche's thought the value of the world and the self is diminished by nihilistic currents. The questioning of the reality of my Brother is the acknowledgment of the insignificance of my Brother's existence. For Oche to wonder whether my Brother has a mind like his own Oche must have first encountered moments when he questioned the reality of his own mind and his status as a human being. In other words, Oche is seeking consolation when he puts the reality of the external world and my Brother (together with the mind he surely possesses) into question. The process of justifying his own existence and the existence of the external world—which is really the process of creating value, of adding value to bare existence—will gradually realize Oche's consolation and restore his mind to the healthy optimistic phase of thought.

In the optimistic phase of thought the existence of the external world is embraced without doubt by an act of *amor fati*. The optimistic phase of *otu* is dominated by joy. There is no place for doubt here. The abundance of joy renders the despair that inhabits the human intellect powerless. To say the external world exists, to say my Brother exists, is simply to affirm faith in that which consciousness did not create but which is not isolated from consciousness as part of universal existence. The philosophical problem of the reality of the external world and other minds is ultimately not a pseudo-problem. Whether we give the problem the kind of abstract, trivial, and dry formulation one sees in the works of some analytic philosophers of the West or we approach it more concretely like the Western existentialists, the fact is that we have revealed the source of the problem in the conceptual nihilism of the consolation-seeking intellect.

It is as a communal being distinguished from lesser living creatures and other possible beings with minds by the language endowment that my Brother's existence is to be justified. The justification has solid humanistic implications, for my Brother not only exists as a value but he also lays claim to the full dignity due his person as a member of the human community at the same level as the doubter. In the process of justifying the existence of my Brother, we will seek answers to the following questions:

1. Can there really be a conceptual or non-conceptual proof of my Brother's existence?

2. Is it possible to justify the existence of my Brother non-conceptually without involving theoretical speculation and without arriving at any theoretical knowledge of my Brother as Sartre suggested?

3. If justification involves knowledge that bows to probability, how should one comprehend the nihilism that cynically demands proofs where they cannot be found?

Human Capacity for Inter-personal Communication as Fundamental to the Justification of the Existence of My Brother

Arising from the arguments above, we assert that there can be no conceptual or non-conceptual proof of the existence of my Brother. The demonstration provided by Western philosophers are justifications. These demonstrations, whether in the idealistic tradition or the realistic tradition, whether existential or analytic, are explanations of a phenomenon rooted in human consciousness as a reality. To prove my Brother's existence I must first obliterate the human community. I must then create him newly in the process of proving his existence.

The consolationist approach may be termed non-conceptual to the extent that it insists that the reality of my Brother is already given to consciousness immediately in the human community, which therefore requires no proof. In the first place, justification is necessitated by the nihilism of *otu* in its pessimistic phase of thought, when the faith strongest in the phase of joy gives way to despair strongest in the phase of sadness. Yet, our approach is analytic since there can be no philosophy without analysis.

Language developed in the human community because members of the community had to establish a point of contact. This contact is one of mind to mind, not just body to body. Body-to-body contact can be established as a physical necessity (e.g. in the mating act of animals). Mind-to-mind contact can only be established by creatures who are not only similar but are also capable of developing a language, mastering it, and communicating with it as a means of revealing thoughts and feelings of joy and of sadness, of everything that makes a bare existence real. If A can learn and communicate effectively in a language in use in a particular community, A must be deemed to have a mind and to exist independent of any other entity in the same community. A does not have to be a human being, but in the human community A is a human being. As a human being he is a brother to every other human. He is a separate identity with a mind like other separate identities because he is capable of pouring out the despair of his mind or its joy, depending on the phase of his thought.

The desire for communication, the ability to communicate in a language, not only shows that my Brother exists and is not me, although linked to me as a member of the community, but also reveals my Brother as a *melancholy being* like myself, as a being seeking consolation. The conscious seeker of consolation is a human being. I am a conscious seeker of consolation in my acts. My search for consolation I make into a history by verbalizing my triumphs and failures. Verbalization involves thinking and writing. While a primitive kind of thinking may well have been possible at the pre-linguistic age, writing is impossible without the full development of language. My Brother too exists as a thinking being seeking value in existence. My Brother and I, and all melancholy beings, rejoice when value is added to existence and mourn when value is subtracted from existence or when it seems value has not been found. We are the melancholy men and women who roam the world seeking consolation in the face of a reality whose failure is the imperfection of a universe that is yearning and has nothing but yearning.

Of course communication as providing the grounds for the determination of the existence of myself and my Brother is subject to probability. Therefore knowledge is involved. The knowledge involved in the justification is probable knowledge. It is built on faith in the existence of the external world. Consciousness cannot help not having faith in the testimony of common sense in its joy-phase. Optimism is strongest in this joy-phase. Yet this simple faith in the given seeks the help of the intellect to attain to a certain probable knowledge because of the need for the justification of the existence of the external world, the existence of the self, and my Brother's or Sister's existence. The justification becomes necessary as the mischief of the mind in its pessimistic phase of thought is its nihilistic power to query its own existence and the existence of everything outside it. Given this power of doubt rooted in the despair of the intellect, the intellectual justification of that which seems so indubitable, which was accepted as true on the basis of faith, becomes the process of the acquisition of knowledge. The grounds of doubt must be attacked, despair must be challenged, and consolation found. This process is not merely concrete; it is also speculative. The knowledge acquired is the probable knowledge that a being like me exists now, or has existed before now, exists by reason of possessing the capacity to communicate, although tomorrow he may be dead or may be transformed beyond recognition through plastic surgery or may lose his power of thinking through some illness or brain damage. However, this probable knowledge of my Brother's existence is highly reliable. The probability comes into play because of the justificatory sway of the intellect made possible by its involvement in the combating of nihilism.

One may ask how friendly communication, rather than hostile communication, is the original relation of person to person in the human community, upon which the existence of my Brother or Sister is to be justified in this human community, and consequently the resolution of the problem of other minds.

Friendly Communication as the Fundamental Condition for the Justification of My Brother's Existence and the Original Relations of Minds

Having discarded the conceit of philosophers who made an elaborate show of proving the existence of the external world and my Brother and having shown with much sympathy that the problem of other minds is not a pseudo-problem, it is fitting for us to call upon consolationist metaphysics to help us construct an optimistic philosophy of inter-subjective interaction where Sartre was only able to produce a profoundly pessimistic ontology. To be sure, we are not denying the evil in the world, nor are we trying to make excuses for a humanity that is undoubtedly fascinated by evil. At the heart of this communication is a friendly intent. This friendly intent presupposes the existence of separate identities with minds. To rule out the initial friendly intention is to eliminate the joy-sadness unity in humans, to insist that a person's life has immanent meanings outside human joy and human sadness. To reject the *melancholy being* in favor of the *rational being* will amount to the discrediting of consolation philosophy. Happily, consolation philosophy stands as a compelling hypothesis because I have shown through vertical and horizontal analyses that human rationality is grounded in the emotionality of the *melancholy being*, thanks to the inspiration of L.S. Senghor. We are dealing with conscious beings, not laboratory-made robots.

There is no longer any doubt over communication being the grounds for the justification of the existence of my Brother. The question now is whether this communication is originally hostile as Sartre asserted in his complicated solution to the problem of my Brother's existence or whether it is originally friendly in intent. Our doctrine of *mood* has given us a yearning universe. Mind encounters a universe which it grasps as a totality of matter and energy, an eternal moving circle working towards an eternal stability. Terror is real for the mind which grasps the existence of the universe as having no other purpose than the realization of consolation at diverse levels. In the absence of perfection, an impossibility, humans and the world find striving. This striving is consolation, for it realizes beauty in its advance.

Now if a man who is made for consolation finds himself thrown into a community of like minds the first push toward the acquisition of language is the need to avoid conflict, the desire of *mood* to express its fears and convey its hopes. The expression of fears and hopes, typically representative of metaphysical sadness and joy, is a friendly communication between minds. While this friendly exchange immediately and non-conceptually asserts the existence of my Brother in time and space (the human community), the intellect is called upon to justify my Brother's existence or the basis of this friendly intercourse. Hence knowledge is involved in the process of justification, leading to the mind representing my Brother as an object of knowledge. True, my Brother becomes an object in my mind and therefore an idea, but this idea has a basis in a reality outside my mind, the authenticity of which my communal existence triumphantly confirms as a non-theoretical fact. First, the given in the human community is embraced as true by the affirmation of faith in this given. So far knowledge is not involved. Second, this given has to be justified as truly existing because of my capacity to doubt my Brother's existence, to doubt that Oche is really Oche under certain circumstances. Justification gives the mind the right to objectify my Brother. The process of determining my Brother's existence comes before the justification of his existence. The first process is fundamental and concrete while the second process is secondary and conceptual.

Fear already subsists in the world as an element of *mood*, as mind's realization of the fatality of the universe. This terror, arising from the inability of one to solve the puzzle of existence and drive purpose through consolation on to perfection, is a primitive thought in human consciousness preceding the developed thinking which philosophers cause to be dependent on language. At a less intense level this evidential terror is the despair of the human intellect. And how can despair express itself eloquently if not in language? The possibility and actuality of the terror felt by consciousness is the transcendental appeal of one person to another and to a God whose existence consciousness simply demands. For while humans have appeared in the world and have been seen by fellow humans in the human community, God remains hidden. Thus the demand of consciousness is that He should exist. One person has seen another and discovered that his fellow man is not a god but one puny and miserable creature. Consequently, the friendly intention of communication is transformed into hostile engagement, into the conflict of moral equals competitively seeking advantages.

A human is a being whose consolation consists of joy and sadness and all things that add value to these emotions or take away value from them. Proximity of one person to another follows the need of mind for transcendence. This transcendence is immediately directed to one from another as a way of deepening consolation, of weakening fears, and strengthening hopes. The potent instrument for the realization of this consolation, following the failure of sexual intercourse to establish effective communication outside the evolutionary imperative of the continuity of the species, is language. But before the development of language in the beginning humans possessed primitive thought-forms. This is yearning, the yearning for consolation and the fear of the world. I hypothesize that language was born as the mind's outpouring of the despair inhering in the intellect. The emergence of language announced a friendly intention of one to the other. Language was a transcendental appeal of one person to a fellow human being. Friendly communication was prior to hostile communication. The latter triumphed in the end because of the failure of the transcendental appeal of human to human. Since my Brother is not a god and since he cannot do much for me, cannot make me perfect and liberate me from the tyranny of mortality, I underrate him and then underrate humanity as a whole. Conflict naturally arises.

Jean-Paul Sartre has said something similar to what we have said in the monumental *Being and Nothingness*. While Sartre opted for a Heideggerian obscurantism in the elucidation of his thought, we prefer a clear style of elucidation. While Sartre was content constructing an ontology of terror, we have gone further to construct a metaphysics of terror and a morality of consolation. Consequently, we were able to present a more optimistic vision of the human community with regard to what Western philosophers identified as the problem of the existence of the other but which we prefer to label the problem of the justification of the existence of my Brother.

How do we comprehend the nihilism that cynically demands for a proof of my Brother's existence when such is impossible? We may go further yet to try encompassing the nihilism that seeks this proof. Skepticism is not only directed at the external world and the things in this world but also often directed inwards at the self. The doubter is sometimes compelled by traumatic experience to see purposelessness in the activities of the mind. He is tempted to dismiss the mind as a mere bundle of ideas and feelings as David Hume and the Buddha did. He cannot see how mind can claim substantiality and immortality. Even in the optimistic phase of his thought the idea of immortality is nothing more than the hope that humanity will endure, that somehow his transcendental appeal to God will succeed and he will be liberated from the bondage of mortality. If the mind doubts itself it is no mystery that it should desire to hide under the convoluted hypothesis of solipsism to bracket the external world. But then the true solipsist is rare if not non-existent. The philosophical solipsists are sophists. The true solipsist is he who, while still living, has lost all his mental powers and no longer experiences joy and sadness. Someone whose brain no longer functions but who is still alive may be called the true solipsist. Joy and sadness, the constituents of psycho-logic which also constitute the foundation of logic, are the focus of an introspective life validated on the basis of its commerce with the external world. Optimism and pessimism as states of the mind look outwards. Since solipsism has no case in the court of philosophy, whatever is valuable in it passes into nihilism, the intellectual tendency to question, scorn, and reject

Nihilism is very much an intellectual phenomenon. We have confirmed that the very first demand of consciousness is the demand that God should exist. This demand encompasses the wish that everything should be perfect for us. Given the impossibility of this perfection, we despair. Since our reason is an emotional reason, despair emerges as the impish denizen of thought. The despairing intellect goes into rebellion, challenges and ultimately renounces the first demand of consciousness. Having failed to convince common-sense perception and advanced thinking that it is on solid conceptual ground, solipsism takes refuge inside nihilism. The discredited claim that the mind is utterly cut off from an objective external world, that probable knowledge is no knowledge, is transformed into the claim that probable knowledge is highly unreliable. In embracing nihilism, solipsism makes the claim that the absence of certainty is a licence to undermine all foundations of belief. The nihilist seeks consolation too like the believer. The condition of not believing or of remaining unconvinced is a balm to the despairing nihilist intellect.

Western philosophy is lucky to have produced so original a philosopher as Sartre. He missed elucidating a metaphysics of terror but successfully expressed an ontology of terror with the notions of being-in-itself and being-for-itself, the one inert positivity and the other a restless questioning consciousness. The terror lies in the impossibility of the in-itself founding itself and the for-itself becoming its own foundation. Sartre does not guarantee that the annihilating power of the reflective consciousness will somehow succeed in uncovering the being of the phenomenon. Since the being of the phenomenon is not a Kantian thing-in-itself but the condition of the revelation of the phenomenon there is nothing behind the phenomenon. Sartre's ontological pessimism terminates here, and with this early—if not hasty—termination he shuts the door of one's house to God, and the Westerner is cut off from God. Unlike Sartre, we have investigated pessimism further and taken ontological pessimism to the level of metaphysical pessimism by showing that the reality behind the phenomenon does not have to be a perfect reality but rather a consolatory reality, that human freedom is not unlimited but circumscribed by the universal sway of fatalism. While agreeing that God has not appeared in all His majesty, we showed that belief in God is a conceptual necessity, with the human intellect endorsing the idea of God as the consolation of the universe. Sartre provided a very interesting solution to the problem of the other and other minds. He might have regarded it as a proof, although it is basically a justification of the declaration of common sense. His notion of being-for-others is nothing more than "communal being," just like Heidegger's *mitsein* (being-with). This makes his severe criticism of Heidegger, an equally compelling and indisputably more original thinker, unconvincing. While Sartre's existentialism started with pessimism and ended with pessimism our consolationist perspective started with pessimism and ended with optimism. This was possible for us because we pushed pessimism through immanent ontology to transcendental metaphysics. Tragedy is a reality and so pessimism is justified. But such a reality too is consolation. Thanks to the reality of consolation, optimism makes its appearance as a consequence of the dialectic of *mood*, the passage of cosmic fear in the mind from the sadness of the intellect (despair) to the joy of the intellect (love). Therefore the discrediting of solipsism and the justification of the existence of my Brother in the human community (in time and space) is an affirmation of faith in a life which is at once tragic and consolatory. I will return to Sartre and Heidegger in the section on comparative philosophy in Part Four of this work.

The Individual and the Community

It is true that the individual is prior to the community. Yet the community is superior to the individual. The existential priority of the individual does not stop him from acknowledging the need for community without which tragedy is ever magnified. The great social and political philosophers of the world all recognized the indispensability of society, from Plato to Isaiah Berlin. It is possible to imagine a hermit who has lived in the forest all his life and feels no urgent need for human company. However, his contempt for the general humanity of which he is a part fails since his individual humanity which he cannot alienate is constantly validated by a community that deputizes for humanity, the community of birds, trees, flowing streams—his general environment. The peace he desires is not to be found in solitude, the breeding ground of solipsism, but in the pure thought of what is good. The thought of the good cannot hold up humanity as a mere abstraction but as a concrete universal consisting of its particular details—human beings.

The individual who comes into the world first discovers a great need for the community if his individuality is to have any meaning. His individuality is already a world. But without a population to build ethical, legal, and other socio-juridical structures, the world of individuality is a useless world. The individual is an appeal transcended by the community. It is the community, being constituted of many individuals and therefore greater than the individual, that will sit over the appeal of the individual. The individual's case, we say, is an appeal for consolation to lessen the impact of the horror of solitude and the tragedy of existence. If social freedom is predicated on individuality, as proponents of the atomization of society claim, why does the same individual appeal to the community to help in the realization of his joy by way of being born and bred within the family—the beginning of the community, by way of cultivating rewarding friendship, getting married, etc?

The individual appeals to the community because his freedom is an illusion, as we will discover in the next chapter. The agency of the individual is a moral agency. Morality, which is already alive in the individual, presupposes the community. For it is the community that must decide on the merit or demerit of the individual's appeal.

If in the course of his interaction with the community the individual feels an intense need to detach himself from the larger community, this is likely due to the injustice the community increasingly tolerates as it learns to take the individual for granted. Tyranny is a tendency in human nature. The individual carries this tendency too, although it is the community that realizes it at an impersonal and therefore horrifying level. Yet, the individual detaching himself from the larger community (the public sphere) has his first stop in the smaller community (the private sphere of the family). He is unable to escape the community altogether because he himself is an appeal which the community must sit over. If nihilist obsession gets the better of the individual, he not only turns his back on the larger community but also on the smaller community and retreats into his introspective world like the solipsist engaged in a game of self-deceit, claiming to have knowledge only of his own mental experience while using a language others use and understand.

We see, then, that the exaggerated claims of individualism arise as a response to the injustice of the larger community and its institution at all levels, most exemplified by the totalitarian state. The individual finds himself a world without a meaning. Finding himself isolated, he affirms faith in the existence of an external world and the presence of my brother as the other. He embraces the community of brothers in an act of joy and optimism. The optimism is the hope that consolation will be more fully realized in the community than in the isolated world of the individual. To his dismay, however, he finds a very unjust community, a thoroughly corrupt society. He refuses to accept the fact that the failure of the community is first and foremost the scandalous failure of the individual. For, if individuals are just, the community will dispense justice to the individual who appeals directly to it. The individual becomes an anarchist and proclaims individualism a creed to be embraced.

A more realistic response to the injustice of the community is ethical individualism (sometimes called moral rearmament) on the one hand and collective activism on the other hand. Ethical individualism, having thoroughly analyzed the problem of individualism, comes to the conclusion that the individual is the real culprit rather than the more abstract community. In his state of awareness, the individual finds a solution in moral activism beginning at the level of the individual life, what Albert Camus calls *revolt* in his *The Rebel* and *The Myth of Sisyphus*. Ethical individualism starts with the cleaning out of the Augean stable at the level of the individual. With the house of the individual put in order it is expected that the individual will become value added to the community, thus improving the latter. Collective activism is of two kinds, the religious and the secular. Collective activism is very effective in bringing about social change rapidly but hardly has any profound effect on people's ethical lives. The religious kind proclaims one religion or the other as its inspiration while the secular kind claims that the cause of social justice inspires its activities. Both have proved very effective in many countries. Where religion is strong as in Africa, Arabia, and parts of Asia and Latin America, religious social activists dominate the scene of public morality. Where the religious sense is weak, as in Europe and North America, secular social activists dominate. As discontented individuals come together to form ideological groups to fight what they perceive as communal or state injustice, particular philosophies (analogous to ethno-philosophy) transform the emergent groups into interest groups in search of a universal philosophy (e.g. consolation philosophy) which they may never find regardless of the grandstanding about pursuing universal human rights and values. In this way society is factionalized. In Africa this factionalization is a hard partitioning, the division into tribal and other interest groups jostling for power and imposing themselves on weaker factions. In the West the partitioning is a soft one, consisting of the divisions of political party affiliations (e.g. conservatives versus liberals in America), religious and secular organizations, and other factions within the state. In this way the individual initially threatened by the community becomes a threat to the community.

The failure of solipsism demands the reconciliation of the sphere of the individual with the sphere of the community (the public). Indeed the failure of solipsism underlines the importance of the community. The community is either equal to the individual on the scale of importance or greater than the individual.

Being composed of more than one individual, the community cannot be less than the individual. The freedom of the individual is no more important than the stability of the community. While the community is under obligation to mentor the individual and even pander to some of the more moderate eccentricities of this same individual, there is the other obligation of the individual to the community, which is to contribute to the social good. If necessary the individual must be ready to sacrifice his joy for the joy of the community.

Pessimism and Optimism

The word pessimism (derived from the Latin *pessimus*—meaning worst) has not been accorded the respect it deserves as a basic ingredient of human consciousness and the conceptual correlate of cosmic terror which is the metaphysical building block of the universe. We positively detest the word, look upon it as the harbinger of ill luck, and oppose it to optimism. Pessimism is the gloomy perspective on life and human affairs. Pessimism runs the gamut of culture, politics, economy, ethics, etc. It reveals itself in a bleak view of future development and in a certain tame resignation to unfavorable circumstances. As a response to a true state of affairs, pessimism arises as a yearning for the consolation that optimism represents. It is not a last stop. It dissolves into optimism as soon as the circumstances that inspire it are removed. Standing as optimism, pessimism will yet assert itself as the yearning negative the moment life-negating circumstances are restored. Pessimism is the grief of existence.

Our approach to the study of pessimism differs from the psychologist's approach, although we agree with the psychologist that painful experience and a terrible state of affairs in the world can engender the pessimistic attitude. We also agree with the psychologist that anxiety cannot be divorced from pessimism. Nevertheless, our philosophical analysis goes beyond the unfavorable state of the affairs of the world that engenders pessimism and seeks to establish pessimism as a *mood* of the universe. This is so because there is already a cosmic state of affairs that is unfavorable, precisely the fatality of existence. Pessimism is not only an empirical fact of human existence, but it is also metaphysically grounded. Pessimism is the passage that leads one to optimism and God as the consolation of the universe. The *melancholy being* wishes he was never born when he witnesses the brutal wars in the Middle East, the collapse of the world's economy, state sponsorship of violence, political treachery, mindless exploitation of the poor by the rich and of the poor by the poor, natural disasters of fearful magnitudes, the ravages of diseases, and the necessary ritual of dying.

But if pessimism is a yearning for a better state of living, can it become a force against one's difficult march to a better state of existence? Can it claim the mystique of a faith in itself by going on about its being better not to have been born? I do not quite endorse this. To start with, a state of oblivion, the nothing, is impossible. Consciousness can only sleep in the beginning. It does not cease to exist. While a particular man as an instance of consciousness coming out of its cosmic slumber might never have existed in the world, consciousness in general always was, making it possible that a particular consciousness would come into being in the world at some time. The perpetual yearning of the general consciousness imperils the wish of the particular consciousness that it was never born. Bringing the analysis down to a more horizontal level, it is obvious that if oblivion is the condition of the unborn human, nothing is lost if we are born into the world and return to the oblivion whence we sprang. The pain we experience is for a certain duration. Apart from pain, we experience a lot of pleasure. We should consider ourselves blessed for having had the honor of feasting our eyes on the magnificence of the natural environment and felt the intensity of joy. If the world had no value, most people would commit suicide. The reality is that human beings have a great fear of death. They will not hesitate to believe in spiritual immortality and explore the technological possibilities of physical immortality. It is certainly better to have been born than not to have been born, much better to have emerged out of oblivion to enjoy and suffer before returning to our silent origin than to have remained an eternal silence in the state of oblivion.

The absolute pessimism of Arthur Schopenhauer must, therefore, be challenged. Pessimism is not the terminus, although one may well live and die grieving. Human existence is not worthless. Consolation remains the greatest meaning of futility in the face of the impossibility of perfection. Consolation confers objective worth on human existence. Thus the absolute pessimism of Schopenhauer passes into the untried and anarchic optimism of Friedrich Nietzsche who is so wildly optimistic that he celebrates the future arrival of his *übermensch* (the superman). This same Nietzsche poignantly confesses: "It has gradually become clear to me what every great philosophy up till now has consisted of—namely, the confession of its originator, and a species of involuntary and unconscious autobiography...."[3] His optimism, therefore, does not quite arrive, for the superman is never coming. We cannot appeal to this superman. A human appeal is a transcendental appeal. The shaky optimism of Nietzsche passes into the theistic pessimism of Kierkegaard. Here pessimism boldly points to optimism. This is not the kind of optimism that says all will be well. All will only be well if the coming wellness has already been guaranteed. Rather, the optimism that follows from pessimism calmly asserts that *all will be well that must be well.* This prepares us for inevitability which may be good or bad but which will not disturb our *amor fati* beyond a temporary turbulence of joy and sadness.

An absolute pessimism would be valid if solipsism could be true. For we would then have isolated consciousnesses, each consciousness a law unto itself, outside the community, able to commit great atrocities on the assumption that there is no humanity and that if there is any humanity at all it is an overrated humanity. In such a solipsist world there will be no desire to actively realize human consolation. The community is already out of existence or has been atomized to look more like cells, individual spheres of influence. Since solipsism is false the community is real. The reality of the community pushes the consolation of the individual towards greater completion. It is definitely true that this is not an ideal community, but it is a community of human beings all the same. The failure of the community truly engenders pessimism. Even as pessimism subsists in the unjust community the cry of the individual (who must be indicted as being complicit in the failure of justice) is the cry for consolation. We see that while pessimism is basic optimism is the next terminus.

Chapter 9

THE SECOND WITNESS TO LIBERTY

On the Enduring Question of Freedom

God is the first witness to liberty as the supreme consciousness of the universe. Human beings are the second witness to liberty. By the term *liberty* I mean the possibility of morality where freedom is denied. The idea of freedom is an illusion, not falsehood *per se*. Freedom is as much an ideal, an illusion, as the notion of perfection. If one was destined for perfection he could validly talk about being a free agent. Indeed, when people say they are free what they really mean is that they are at liberty to do certain things that please them. The notion of freedom still has a place in consolation philosophy, but only the place of an ideal that indicates what one may gain if his destiny is in his hands. As things stand, freedom is a vanishing phenomenon. It vanishes beyond the reason Kant rated so highly, leaving behind only the real, the trace of liberty which is, in fact, what Kant struggled to find in his metaphysical and ethical works. The notion of freedom asserts that a person necessitates his own actions as a rational (or emotional) being, who consciously chooses his goals and works towards their realization. Yet the shallowest analysis clearly shows that necessity is a burden a human carries, that one makes choices under necessity and struggle, often grimly, to realize these choices. Sometimes one gives up the struggle in frustration, as circumstances beyond control manipulate the law of necessity. One encounters reasons for one's actions that come from the external environment, physical, social, cultural, and even biological reasons. Yet we may apply the label *freedom* to the mere knowledge that we are able to choose at all under constraint, the awareness of intentionality. Mere awareness is impotent in causation. Impediments shape human actions.

For every effect there is a cause. If the cause is given the effect follows unfailingly. This is the rule of causality which even chance bows to. For chance is directional as a part of a yearning whole. The only phenomena that defy this rule are God and the universe conceived as eternal. But then the existence of a First Cause lies outside the grounds of necessity and within the limits of sufficiency.

Necessity is entailed by sufficiency. That which is necessary is what it is because it is founded on grounds of sufficiency. It is either sufficient in itself or it answers to another condition for its sufficiency. Thus Leibniz famously asserted his doctrine of sufficient reason. The sufficiency of God's existence is a fatality. It is to be understood not in terms of cause and effect but in terms of the inevitability of a yearning essence contemporaneous with the universe as its principle. But homo sapiens is a young creature, having made his appearance in the world relatively recently. Whether we attribute this emergence directly to God's creative will or directly to chance (paradoxically, a *purposive* chance), the mystery of human emergence is lightened by the law of causality.

Truly, the rigid rule of causality that governs the physical world cannot be wholly applied to the human sphere of thought, of deliberation, and action. All the same, there is a similarity in natural causality and causality in the mental realm. The rule of causality holds sway in both realms, rigidly in the physical realm and non-rigidly in the mental realm. In the physical realm causation is essentially mechanical, significantly predictable. In the mental realm causation is more flexible. Here causation is about the making of decisions dictated by external and even extraneous circumstances. Although decision-making is a victory for the will, this same will hesitates to proclaim itself free on account of the struggle ahead of it, the overcoming of impediments that should not exist if one is truly free. The concept of freedom is existentially a bold concept. It assumes that one is happy. It is a concept that at once asserts that human beings are permanent agents whose spontaneous acts of creation lie outside external influences as well as beings who, to borrow a term from Kant, *command nature* by willing and enforcing their own happiness. Human acts are barely spontaneous. I decide to marry because I see most adults embarking on the journey of marriage or because marriage fulfils the goals of evolution by sustaining the human race, providing a conducive environment for child-bearing and child-rearing. While it is true that I cannot predict a future divorce on the day I decide to marry, I can look back to the past and trace the causes of the divorce. It will then come to light that I have struggled to overcome impediments along the way, finally giving up the struggle. How can I be free if I cannot sustain my action in the face of external impediments, if I have to struggle with external impediments all my life in pursuit of a happiness that I cannot find? Given this reality of perpetual struggle, that unique capacity for decisionmaking, of being aware of a direction to take, is neutralized by the necessitated or constrained circumstances of the struggle to realize the goals chosen by the human mind.

Freedom is indicated but not granted. Mind indicates it, reality denies it. Mind wishes it, reality declares it impossible. If freedom is an illusion, can a man or woman hope for any consolation? Mercifully, the answer is an emphatic yes. One's consolation is liberty. In the absence of freedom, one stands witness to liberty. The concept of liberty is not as ambitious as the notion of freedom which is a vanishing phenomenon. As a concept freedom is not false since the mind indicates it. Its non-applicability arises from its impossibility. Instead of contemplating a perfect and rational universe that might be or might have been we ponder a consolatory universe that already is, whose rationality follows from its emotionality that constitutes the grounds of its sufficiency. Thus we are reluctant to apply the category of happiness to human beings. We choose to regard humans as beings of consolation.

With the notion of liberty the conflict between determinism and freedom is finally resolved in the more complete idea of fatalism. We have already seen that fatalism is cosmic inevitability, not the postulation of the primitive understanding which asserts that a definite state of affairs *must* follow from an initial condition which takes an unbranching route from the beginning to the end. Theological, biological, and physical determinism may well be true, but these forms of necessity cannot stop people from being witnesses to liberty. A human being, like the objective universe, is value-laden. One enters the world as a moral being, and grows into a more robust moral being from the beginning of existence as an undeveloped moral being, the baby crying for food in the maternity ward, surrounded by a small human community. This community does not bestow any new moral nature on the individual consciousness. The community serves only to guide the moral consciousness, to improve it or to pervert it. What is the root of this morality? I answer that it is in fatalism, the inevitability of *mood* as the outburst of emotion. If being is composed of the elements of joy and sadness it is already a value, already a moral essence. If *mood* remains silent as matter the value it carries as a function of its basic emotionality is not active. When *mood* becomes active as mind, consciousness recognizes itself as value. Where there is neither joy nor sadness, nor the primordial form of *mood* (silence), there can be no value. If for a moment the anthropomorphic charge should prevail against our African idealism, our theory may lose objective universal application. Still, it will remain valid for human beings whose emotionality cannot be refuted. The very attempt to refute our theory validates it because in refutation, in questioning, the emotional intellect returns to its emotional base. That is to say, psycho-logic overwhelms logic.

So fatalism seeks the reconciliation of freedom with determinism by undermining both concepts. By entailing necessity fatalism undermines determinism. By declaring freedom an illusion, a mere wish and hope of intellectual love, fatalism undermines freedom. In positing *consolation* fatalism reconciles freedom with determinism. The principal ethical thesis of consolation philosophy is that all things happen, and as they happen they are well if they must be well. If a state of affairs is unfavorable, one has the power to protest, to make the transcendental appeal, whether this appeal brings any succour or not. And humans do appeal. They are creatures of *mood,* of joy and sadness, recognizing good and the evil; rejoicing with the good and lamenting and condemning the evil.

The Problem of Freedom in Perspective

So much work has been done on the problem of freedom by Western philosophers. It even begins to appear that the problem has been exhausted. Indeed, one suspects that the current, almost purely analytical works on freedom are desperate attempts to enliven a theme that has already been dissected from all angles. Nevertheless, the problem of freedom continues to be an interesting one. In ancient Greece, primitive fatalism had solidified into scientific determinism in the thoughts of Democritus. Plato and Aristotle did not quite highlight the problem of freedom although both thinkers paid serious attention to the question of morality. While the Platonic approach to the morality issue is rationalistic the approach of Aristotle is broadly practical. We find Platonic ethics particularly interesting not only as the prototype of Kant's Christianity-enhanced ethics but also for positing an ethical absolutism that seems to ground morality in existence itself. Plato the philosopher and "spectator of all time and all existence" propounded the idea of an eternally fixed moral order, in *Timaeus* and *The Laws* in particular.

For a fuller comprehension of the problem of evil and in the pursuit of obscure theological problems, Christian philosophers of the medieval era developed the notion of free will—which was beginning to become a weighty question in Greco-Roman philosophy, in particular Stoic ethics—far beyond anything Greek philosophy dreamed of. Man was the *imago Dei* and therefore was endowed with free will. The Catholic dominance in philosophy and the favorable disposition to the notion of freedom of the will did not stop rebel thinkers like Martin Luther from standing firm on theological determinism and insisting on the bondage of the will.[1] Benedict Spinoza who was just as God-intoxicated as the church fathers and doctors went closer to Luther than St. Augustine and St. Thomas Aquinas. He sternly rejected the idea of free will in his masterpiece *Ethics*. The following quotation from Spinoza's Letter 62 is instructive. The most thoroughgoing determinist in philosophy writes:

> I do not place freedom in *free decision* [my own italics] but in *free necessity* [my italics]. However, let us descend to created things, which are all determined by external causes to exist and operate in a given determinate manner. For instance, a stone receives from the impulsion of an external cause a certain quantity of motion, by virtue of which it continues to move after the impulsion given by the external cause has ceased. The permanence of the stone's motion is *constrained* [my italics], because it must be defined by the impulsion of an external cause.[2]

For Spinoza intentionality does not provide any strong support for the belief in freedom, the will itself being nothing above the mind which is a succession of ideas and a fixed mode of thinking. Spinoza is willing to grant God only the right to be free, a God operative both as thought and extension. This gives us a pantheistic doctrine, one that already presupposes panpsychism. In refusing to be convinced by the argument of intentionality, Spinoza is insisting on a transcendental basis for the belief in human freedom. David Hume in his *Treatise of Human Nature* thought the question of freedom as metaphysically posed is a pseudo-problem, preferring to regard freedom simply as the absence of coercion. Hume's over-simplification of the matter is understandable since he was unsympathetic towards metaphysics. Since Hume had declared necessity indispensable to causality, the elimination of which would lead to the emergence of chance as a real creative force—a new dimension that would entail seeing chance in the light of teleology, we can safely conclude that Hume was a determinist.

Coming after Hume, the great Immanuel Kant faced a dilemma. Is the question of human freedom as posed by metaphysics to mean the absence of necessity or at least physical necessity a pseudo-problem? How do we tame the bogey of necessity if we are to uphold freedom and insist that transcendental freedom is what we really mean when we talk about freedom, such that in the absence of transcendental freedom there can be nothing like freedom? Realizing that there was no way the idea of necessity could be put aside, that immortal thinker went round the philosophical bogey of necessity, examined it from the rear, and came up with his masterstroke. A cause can be material in the natural world and spontaneous in the rational world. What we call freedom is the creation of reason, resting on no physical foundation. Freedom is informed by rational necessity. To bridge the chasm created by the isolation of rational necessity from natural necessity, Kant turned to the concept of morality which he first introduced in *Critique of Pure Reason* and fully developed in the second and third critiques and the ethical works. With Kant the problem of freedom came into sharper focus. Underneath the supreme psychology and the philosophical architectonics of this mighty thinker lay the naked fact of the impossibility of freedom. Democritus was right. Spinoza was correct.

Yet the unbranching view of the affairs and the circumstances of human history and cosmic history must leave one doubting the plausibility of rigid determinism. The great American philosopher and psychologist William James, the link between modern and contemporary Western philosophy, recommended soft determinism. With this approach James forcefully reconciled freedom with determinism and made freedom the senior partner in this difficult relationship.[3] The existentialist philosophers generally favored the reality of human freedom. Jean-Paul Sartre was so enamoured of freedom that he absolutized it for human consciousness and bizarrely deduced the grounds of pessimism and atheism from this unlimited freedom. This is in stark contrast to the consolationist thesis that in a world where freedom is real there can be no alternative to optimism. What the contemporary analytical philosophers in the West lack in originality and profundity of thought, they more than make up in intellectual sophistication. Today these scholars talk about complex compatibilist and incompatibilist theories, indeterminism, etc.[4]

The balance of probability has tilted towards determinism, at least a diluted or soft determinism. The ethno-philosophical research of African scholars like M.A. Makinde and Segun Gbadegesin show that determinism holds sway in African traditional thought.[5] External influences always threaten human freedom. God is at the pinnacle of causal processes, as it is the case in Spinoza's pantheistic system. Lesser gods, forces, and even ancestors participate in the causal processes. Natural causality is not denied, but there is a constant readiness to attribute a person's fortune to benevolent forces and misfortune to malevolent forces like evil medicine men, witches and wizards, enemies, etc. This sounds superstitious. But superstition is actually a travesty of truth. Superstition is invoked to support natural causality where a sense of mystery persists. And there is mystery in the world that reveals the character of the *mythopoeic*.

Yet African ethno-philosophy clearly highlights the importance and potency of human agency. Analysing the Yoruba concept of *ori* (the term means head but is truly a symbol of the human mind), Makinde distinguishes between primitive fatalism and the Yoruba understanding of *ori*. Fatalism is identified with the strong sense of destiny while the concept of *ori* is interpreted to indicate a weak determinism. Makinde believes the Yoruba conception of destiny indicates a soft determinist position. *Olorun* (God) is the ultimate cause of everything that happens in the world. Gbadegesin sees this Yoruba conception as problematic because it seems both rigidly deterministic and moderately libertarian. The findings of Yoruba ethno-philosophy is, in my opinion, representative of African ethno-philosophy in general. It is noteworthy that the investigations of Gbadegesin and Makinde are ethno-philosophical. These investigations have not risen to the full dignity of philosophy. Unfortunately, there is hardly any African philosophical scholar who has put forward an original theory of freedom. The scholars who have done some work in this area have had to work in the shadows of Western philosophy, with Western philosophical concepts regularly invoked for the purpose of clarification.

For philosophy anywhere to rise to full dignity it must address humanity with an eloquent voice. It must become universal. If Greek philosophy addresses only the people of Greece it remains what it is: Greek philosophy. If Indian philosophy addresses Indians only it is merely Indian philosophy. If modern and contemporary Western philosophy addresses itself to the West alone we reject its universalist claims. We must then pronounce it Western ethno-philosophy, no matter the level of general intellectual sophistication it has attained. Our post-postmodern consolation philosophy must now advance the cause of the African ethno-philosophers by ceasing to speak for the African tribe and commencing the 21st century address to human being—the *melancholy being*.

The Vanishing Ideality

When we bring freedom under the heading of ideality we are saying that it is an illusion. The illusive is truly elusive. It provides traces of its possible existence in human consciousness and in the external field of human activity but dissolves into a mere wish as soon as it is to be tested for substantiality. Libertarians are no fools. While it is true that the libertarian position ultimately fails to account for the human as an integral component of nature and therefore subject to natural laws, our analyses of the human as a *melancholy being* and the whole of nature as a yearning expression of *mood* are already taking us towards fuller comprehension of humankind's enduring fascination with the word "freedom" which presupposes a "free will." To dismiss the libertarian concern brusquely by the invocation of nature and its laws is to unduly pander to scientism at the foot of a science that needs metaphysics to dare to understand its own foundation. What is a law of nature in the first place? Laws of nature are patterns of occurrences in the world with which we have become so familiar as to rule out the possibility of miraculous intervention. While we favor a relatively objective or realistic interpretation of the identified laws of nature, we must not forget the prominent role the mind plays in convincing us about the truth of necessity. Is necessity sacrosanct? This is doubtful. The universe has a right to exist but presents no reason for existing adequate to human consciousness except what we intuit. In our case, we have intuited *yearning* and have consequently tried to explicate the doctrine of *mood*.

Intuition comes into play as the primary way of connecting with reality. The role of knowledge is justificatory and secondary. To undermine the intuitive element and be content with a bare knowledge that merely serves practical purposes of believing by faith that a world truly exists is to play the ostrich. This is scandalous. The insistence of scientists on the investigation of the questions of human origin, the world's origin, and the destiny of the universe is a rejection of this scandalous quietism. This is true since the impossibility of acquiring exact knowledge of how the universe came into existence does not deter scientists from asking questions.

Positing a monism that connects one thing (for example, a human being) with everything (the universe) does not really score a victory for determinism. The determinist doctrine has as its principal bulwark the concept of necessity. But necessity merely asserts that there is an operative law of cause and effect, that when the cause is given the effect *must* follow. We make this assertion only after we have observed regularities in nature over a long period of time. Yet the operation of necessity in the universe is not sacrosanct. Necessity is usually indicted in every case of the disappearance of freedom under the microscope of analysis. But this bogey itself does not escape probability. Necessity is postulated by the human intellect which needs the support of intuition to make a direct connection with reality. It is a perception rooted in nature, yes, but a perception all the same. As a perception it suffers distortion at the hands of the intellect which (sadly for necessitarians) perpetually seeks a path to complete joy through despair. The human intellect, being an emotional intellect, need not be antagonistic towards intuition. Possessing the form of emotion, the human intellect will always be prone to error. Before it stands something greater than it, the *mythopoeic*, the yearning density of the universe.

If we connect all the phenomena in the universe and thoroughly discredit dualism, the concept of freedom itself cannot be discarded still, although it vanishes under intellectual scrutiny. Freedom will not cease to fascinate humanity because the nihilism of the intellect indicates it as that which can adequately comfort the despairing intellect. It is this discernible hope of the intellect that informs teleology, the belief in a purposive universe that has evolved and continues to evolve towards completion. As a matter of fact, the enigmatic German philosopher G.W.F. Hegel reminds us again and again in his metaphysical and ethical works that freedom is the goal of the universe or Spirit. Another worthy Western philosopher, Sartre, sternly rejects the determinist thesis in a manner that may appear careless and anarchic. Yet Sartre's dissolution of rigid determinism in his analysis of the human act, a type of agent-causation theory, is justified by our realization of the emotionality of the intellect, its wish to be free in a rational world, a perfect universe. *The tragedy of reason is the impossibility of this freedom which is already indicated as highly desirable.* The desirability of freedom and the human capacity to struggle in the ethical space of existence makes freedom an ideality. Intentionality and everyday ethical striving reassure us that necessity can be resisted and that humans are, however constrained, agents. The form of freedom thus makes its appearance before the human intellect. But as soon as the intellect that desires this freedom tries to test its substantiality (what Kant will call empirical reality) it reveals itself as mere ideality, a wish of consciousness. Nevertheless, this is no idle wish because it enlivens intentional processes.

Not only does the human intellect aspire to the realization of freedom (conceived as happiness), it also projects the same destiny into the objective universe. Since we can regard humans as beings destined for happiness in a state of perfection either in this world or in another world, it is likely that the universe of which we are a part is moving towards a state of perfection guided either by God or some impersonal principle of the universe. This hope of the human intellect should not be taken lightly. The existence of the universe is a greater absurdity then the hope of Heaven, the realization of freedom. The universe is a great absurdity, yet it exists. Happiness or perfection in this world or in another system of things is an absurdity too. A thing being absurd is no reason for its not existing. Once a monistic conception of the universe trumps dualism, the notions of freedom and determinism become capable of switching places. In an attempt to reconcile freedom with determinism, we have sought the grounds of the existence of the universe in sufficiency, thereby subordinating necessity to the notion of sufficiency. In doing this we had to find a theory of reason that traces rationality to emotionality and expresses the universe as *mood*. This metaphysical language is not radically different from the "physical" language of energy and matter. Quantum physics has shown that matter is a vanishing phenomenon, reducible to atoms, electrons, neutrons, quarks, etc., and even a state of indeterminacy that gives the theory of chance a foothold.

If chance were to be considered real it would no longer underlie chaos. Chance would cease to be chance and switch places with purpose in much the same way as an electron would switch roles, behaving like a wave now and the next moment like a particle, as the two-slit experiment has demonstrated. Chance as the condition of indeterminacy becomes purposive directionality and therefore teleological determinacy. This line of thinking will tend to lend support to the Einstein-Podolski-Rosen thought experiment which concludes that the quantum mechanical theory of a real underlying indeterminacy lacks completeness. We are not venturing into a scientific field in which we lack competence. Here we have appealed to scientific findings in quantum physics to help clarify the inter-relationship between freedom, determinism, and the spoiler-notion of indeterminism. If freedom and determinism switch places in a monistic system and if the postulation of the reality of chance transforms it into a kind of teleology, the resultant indeterminacy in the system must be regarded as an incomplete picture of the ongoing complex processes. The chance element casts a slur on the integrity of determinism and freedom. If chance is real, freedom is meaningless and determinism is absurd. To complicate the matter, if chance is real it is automatically transformed into directionality. Chance becomes a goal-driven force, a principle seeking self-recognition. However, this hypothesis must be substantiated. To give it flesh we must appeal to consolation philosophy, the doctrine of *mood* (refer to the last chapter of Part Two).

Freedom is already a vanishing phenomenon. The reification of chance helps speed up its disappearance. On the other hand, determinism, in all its forms, stands on firmer grounds and is not about to surrender to chance which it recognizes as the incomplete form of teleology. That the idea of freedom has to stubbornly resist the notion of determinism and persist in human consciousness requires the invocation of the doctrine of *mood* to give us something in the place of this impossible freedom as a consolation. The consolation which is granted us is called *liberty*. Indeed, when men talk about freedom they are actually referring to liberty. While freedom is an ideality, an illusion, liberty is real. The concept of liberty follows from human moral nature, the capability of decision-making in the face of necessity and ability to answer for the actions one takes. If freedom is removed from the scene of reality human responsibility will remain side by side with the notion of determinism. To be responsible for one's action is not to be a free agent but to be simply a moral agent. To be responsible is to have the capacity to make choices under the weight of causality and then struggle towards the realization of these choices. Freedom implies making a choice and not facing any hindrance on the way to the realization of this choice. To be at liberty means to be able to make a choice and pursue its realization in the face of impediments. To be at liberty one's goals do not have to be realized in the end since determinism has already been embraced. To be at liberty means to be able to engage in ethical struggle.

Moral responsibility arises not from the bare consciousness of an impossible freedom but from the reality of ethical struggle. There is struggle because the universe is not perfect. One aspect of the universe's imperfection is the reality of evil which no thinker has been able to philosophize into oblivion. Evil is a testament to reality. If one truly struggles in the world, one learns to distinguish between the good and the bad. If a man knows the good and contrasts it with the bad, he is morally responsible for his constrained actions. If a man is morally responsible he is a witness to liberty, the theory that man is a moral being who desires to complete his experience of joy in the world by the maximization of goodness.

Liberty

The demand for freedom is a radical demand. Freedom is the reality of perfection in nature and happiness for humankind. The question of freedom is posed transcendentally. If transcendental freedom is not possible, if philosophers must view the problem of transcendental freedom as a pseudo-problem, then there is no reason for us to continue talking about freedom. The notion is already a mirage, an illusion. So radical is this primal demand that J.J. Rousseau famously declared at the beginning of his *The Social Contract* that one is born *free* but suddenly finds oneself in chains. The chains of freedom are not only political but, more profoundly, metaphysical. Political freedom is dependent on metaphysical or transcendental freedom. Transcendental freedom projects freedom as an absolute good in the world, independent of natural necessity, spontaneous without any connection with chance. Under analysis, however, transcendental freedom wilts and disappears until all the traces of it that we can find is liberty. Indeed, liberty compensates for the ideality of freedom. The optimism of *mood* terminating in the projection of freedom encounters freedom's ideality and it becomes pessimism. Joy is turned to sadness. Transcendental freedom is an illusion. But it is in the nature of that which yearns that it will keep striving until something is found to comfort it. And *mood* does find its consolation. We call this consolation liberty. It is the joy of the human spirit in its capacity for goodness. This existential joy is intimate with the indubitable knowledge of one's goodness. As tiny as this individual goodness is in the ocean of human wickedness, it validates the moral worth of the human phenomenon and proclaims humans a witness to liberty. God, if conceived of as a conscious spirit, is the first witness to liberty. Humans, the conscious but limited beings, are the second witness to liberty.

In Part Two of this work we enunciated a restricted panpsychism that granted the potentiality for the attainment of mind to all things in the universe without asserting that all things are alive. This is the case because universal existence clearly manifests the character of yearning. Human yearning is expressed in conscious joy and sadness. The joy-phase of *mood* is the phase of liberty. Even if a good action does not bring rewards or it leads to misfortune, the contemplation of the goodness of the action adds to human joy by completing it in sadness. This contemplation will produce moral elation in the disappointed good person. The elation is his liberty. He is a witness. In the joy-phase of existence characterized by the witnessing to liberty the capacity for evil is diminished in most men and eliminated in a few called saints. In this joy-phase no one thinks of doing evil, of hurting nature and life. The pure thought of the good has lifted the weight of despair from the intellect, such that the despair of the intellect is transformed into the love of the intellect. This is a movement from pessimism to optimism mediated by human joy.

Even if a satisfactory state of affairs is absent, it is enough for the intellect to witness to liberty once it is able to contemplate the good, to ponder over its capacity for goodness. Human suffering does not have to shut out joy. This feeling itself is an emotion expressive of faith in life as it should be. Life as it should be embraces the reality of freedom. This freedom is not given in a universe that exists fatalistically, that is value-laden only because it expresses *mood* and therefore yields both good and evil. In the state of suffering the human mind rises to the optimistic phase of intellectual love once despair passes into anxiety. The transformation from despair to intellectual love is effected by the pure thought of the good. In this phase it is easy to believe in God and believe too that humanity cannot be overrated. We acknowledge that there is sadness in the world. In this acknowledgment, however, we assure ourselves that this is one vast sadness that will be complete in a vast joy. This joy comes as the affirmation of life in moral deeds, in the witnessing to liberty. In the joy-phase the moral person who is truly the *melancholy being* distances himself from evil and deplores evil in his fellow men and women. If he is powerless in reducing the evil in the world, he is burdened by sadness. This sadness he completes in joy so that he is able to recognize his sadness as a sacrifice, his resignation to circumstances beyond his control. He is still a witness to liberty. Yet he is something else or something more now. He has become a lover of fate, a believer in ethical fatalism. His motto has truly become *I believe in fate*.

This *amor fati* arises from ethical fatalism. *Amor fati* is the recognition of the anonymity of sacrifice, the human truth of being born to struggle and suffer because of the evil in the world, the making of which the human is complicit as a creature of *mood* capable of good and evil. Sacrifice means accepting the suffering in the joy-phase of existence, in the witnessing stage when the human mind proclaims itself morally responsible although not free. Its anonymity means its commonplaceness. Sacrifice must be consigned to ordinariness because the abundance of moral evil demands that we keep regretting and deploring the countless instances of nihilistic outbursts of the evil in the human *mood*. But if sacrifice is anonymous because it is everywhere required, it is also great because it furthers the case of human witnessing to liberty. To carry the burden of sacrifice is to deplore evil in oneself and in others. To deplore evil means to oppose it with goodness. Therefore the resignation of the believer in fate is a call to moral activism. The person who carries the burden of sacrifice, which is anonymous, is a moral activist. We are not saying he has to mount the soapbox and shout himself hoarse about human rights. Moral activism is simply witnessing to liberty. The hermit who abandons society because of its tolerance of evil is a moral activist. The political activist who campaigns against corrupt practices in Nigeria is a moral activist. Whatever action is taken in pursuit of the goals of morality is ethical and he who takes this action is a witness to liberty.

Unlike the concept of freedom which vanishes into ideality under attack from necessity, our concept of liberty is not shaken one bit by the threat of determinism. Liberty thrives best where necessity reigns. The concept of liberty co-exists comfortably with necessity. Our consolation philosophy has already submitted the thesis that fatalism provides the sufficient conditions for universal existence and therefore supersedes physical necessity. Liberty as an ethical phenomenon born in the struggle of consciousness to comprehend and neutralize the evil it recognizes in itself is no stranger to the dialectic of *mood*, the evolution of cosmic fear into good and evil and the struggle of good against evil. Liberty is defined by the ethical struggle to overcome impediments thrown on its path by circumstances of the determined state. Freedom requires an impossible spontaneity while liberty insists on ethical struggle in the knowledge that evil is real and determinism operative throughout the universe. Liberty itself is a necessity; it is a moral necessity, the compulsory ethical impulse that advances the cause of freedom (which vanishes before the determined state).

In the phenomena of human joy and sadness liberty is fully accounted for. There is a solid abundance of evil in the world and in human nature. The condition of amorality is not possible. We can have only morality and immorality. Since immorality is conceptually dependent on the prior notion of morality, the former is a species of morality. The evil person truly believes he is serving the cause of good, if not his own good, then a wider good. The pedophile, for instance, is pursuing his own carnal pleasure which to him is very important. The good he seeks, however, is a corrupted good, and therefore counts as evil. Morality is aborted by the action of the pedophile. The moral consciousness, possessing all the moral facts of the matter, including the grave harm done to innocence, pronounces the pedophiles act immoral. The act is immoral because it has failed to satisfy the conditions of morality which demands that a human act starts and ends with the pursuit of good, that from the beginning to the end the human act must help the human witness to liberty. An act is called immoral because it begins with the pursuit of good (yearning for something conceived as beneficial) and ends in the service of evil.

Any act which releases joy when complete is moral. Joy is said to have been released if:

1. The moral consciousness approves of the act after its completion.

2. Having been approved by the moral consciousness, the act turns out to lead to sadness because sacrifice has been incurred.

In the first case, the joy that follows the act is an eloquent testimony to the completion of the moral act. In the second case, the sadness that follows the completion of the moral act will turn out to have been completed in the joy that intellectual love bestows on sacrifice. Human moral consciousness will contemplate the act of sacrifice and approve it for the love of the intellect to pronounce it an ethical victory worthy of celebration. Then sadness will be complete in joy. The act of sacrifice is a harder and loftier victory. Let us consider an example. A building has just collapsed, trapping men, women, and children. A woman digs her way through the rubble to rescue a child. She rescues the child but suffers a severe injury when a metal rod falls on her foot. Later the foot is amputated. Although this woman has completed a difficult moral act, she is nevertheless likely to spend her remaining days in bitter regret. She will be a sad woman. All the same, on those occasions when she is able to contemplate a heroic act she will recognize the approval of the moral consciousness and rejoice. Despair will pass into anxiety and be transformed into intellectual love which is the closest thing to purity the human phenomenon is capable of. For this woman, her sadness is complete in joy. She is a witness to liberty.

The proclamation of liberty is the outstanding achievement of human rationality. With the notion of liberty monism gathers up its integrity before a dualism that cannot succeed, such that the human mind acknowledges its primordial kinship with everything outside it. The concept of liberty does not deny necessity. Rather, it embraces necessity through the act of *amor fati*. This love as an emotion endorsed by human rationality does not consist in quietism, the passive surrender to necessity, but struggle, and not struggle simply but ethical struggle. Struggle that is not ethical will cease to conform to *amor fati*: such striving does not follow from the keen awareness of the abundant evil in the world. Intellectual love cannot sanction this struggle. A typical example of such a struggle is a situation that throws up a man fighting with all his might to become a millionaire so that he can be able to beat his chest and shout: "I'm the richest man in town!"

The entity that yearns is certain to find something. What it finds may or may not satisfy its yearning essence. The concept of liberty cannot be allocated fundamentally to "reason" which must fail to account for freedom. Emotion is life and mind. Reason is its refinement. Life and death are necessities which liberty embraces. To be born is to be prepared to suffer under one adverse necessity or the other. Liberty accepts the challenge of birth and stands firm on the side of good. To die is to have the active life of consciousness terminated. It is not clear whether consciousness will return to the silence from which it sprang, but liberty still stands firm on the side of good. Liberty gives one the right to die clinging, to struggle ethically to the very end. It is in this ethical struggle that liberty is reconciled with necessity, for the struggle at once implies opposition, overcoming, and moral progress. Transcendental freedom is ignored in the struggle while the notion of moral responsibility is retained. Decision-making as embracing intentionality and choosing from a set of options open to the agent reaches beyond necessity into the territory of moral triumph. *The notion of cause must not be divorced from the reality of evil.* Physical necessity often follows an evil path just as psychological necessity expresses an evil intention in the human mind. The moral character of the world and everything in it is striking. It is not for nothing that Plato philosophized under the impression that there is an eternal moral order that reigns supreme. This is the fatality of the universe. Morality conforms to this pattern while immorality perverts it.

It is not necessary for one to possess the capacity to have acted differently than he did in a particular situation since freedom is not real. One cannot act differently than he did. This sticky point in Western philosophy is a philosopher's luxury. In real life what we have is regret. The person who performs an act with negative consequences suffers the pangs of regret precisely because it strikes him that he did something that *should* have been done differently but which was not done differently because it *could not* have been done differently. Men must accept that their deeds are fatalistic. They are inevitable. Once they are inevitable they become irreversible. Thinking that one could have acted differently is an emotional reaction sunk in grief and therefore worthy of human sympathy. Judgments of regrets merely endorse the role of necessity. Yet freedom is not falsehood. Even as it is indicated by the human mind it is simultaneously recognized as an unrealizable. Thus there is a sadness in the world which the human phenomenon feels keenly. In the absence of freedom, however, we stand, and will always stand, witness to liberty.

Fatalism, Determinism, and Indeterminism

It is a great irony that the notion of fatalism is so easily dismissed as primitive and tied to the whims of unstable gods while we pay great respect to determinism as the scientific theory of physical causality. Throughout this work I have endeavored to explode this myth. Fatalism is the master of determinism.

Determinism is posterior to fatalism. Our philosophical understanding of the notion of fatalism has taken it out of the prevailing malicious context of superstition and primitivity.

Determinism itself is essentially the theory that the rule of causality governs the interaction of physical phenomena, precisely the theory that for every event there is a cause. This theory seems sound enough. It is not threatened by quantum physics and the indeterminacy the latter seems to suggest (see Section 3 of the current chapter). Indeterminist impulses operate within a determinist framework. In a closed system a fundamental cause has already been given. If at certain moments the system behaves oddly we are not to conclude that there has been a new beginning, that the system in question has been obliterated and a new system has come into being uncaused. Quantum indeterminacy as part of a state of an existing world is already subject to the law of causality.

The only radical achievement of the idea of sub-atomic indeterminacy is to cast a slur on classical determinism and show that the much talked about determinism is overrated. If we agree that quantum indeterminacy or sub-atomic uncertainty provides a complete picture of reality at the micro level we certainly must contend with the element of chance since it will appear that certain events have no cause. But the acceptance of chance as a real force will not only lead to its reification but will also grant it causal powers, in which case chance will cease to be chance and will become a potent cause. If this is true, determinism is not threatened by indeterminism.

If determinism bows to the rule of causality, fatalism overrules this rule by absorbing it and thus becoming its source. The essential submission of fatalism is that a thing happens because it is inevitable. Before a thing happens, however, it does not have to be rigidly conditioned. There is no necessity of a decree fixed from eternity or from a given initial condition operating through intermediate causes up to its final effect, inexorably. Fatalism simply means the inevitability of an event. An event, having occurred, could not have occurred differently than it did. This is the direct thesis of fatalism, a thesis deserving great respect because fatalism succeeds in accounting for an ultimate beginning or, at least, vigorously pursues this objective while determinism always commences with this beginning.

To say there was never a beginning of the universe is to over-simplify the matter of origin. It is to pretend out of intellectual laziness or psychological fear that there is no problem here. Why should the universe exist if it has no cause? I think I hear you asking why something should exist before the universe as its cause. You are right. But what the riposte achieves is to show that determinism is not sacrosanct. This is also the achievement of quantum indeterminacy. That which has always been must account for itself. God was and is. The universe was and is. This is the eternity of God and the universe. Yet before God there was no God and before the universe there was no universe. That which has always been must account for itself, I repeat. The idea of a beginning which is spontaneous is no more threatening than the idea of the eternity of the universe. There must have been a free beginning, the outburst of nothingness, if we are to grasp the idea of eternity. This spontaneous beginning called forth the rule of causality. Determinism animates a universe that has existed always but cannot account for the existence of this universe. Fatalism succeeds by submitting that the notion of eternity is an over-simplified approach to the question of nothingness. Fatalism submits that the occurrence of the universe is an inevitability, a coming into being of the universe, and therefore a beginning that gave power to the rule of causality. Our consolation philosophy has enabled us to assert that the universe came into being as an emotional outburst of the Eternal Mood. This *mood* is eternal because of its ancientness, not because it has always been. Its coming into being was a spontaneous outburst of yearning.

Thus fatalism provides the sufficient conditions of the existence of the universe while determinism provides the necessary conditions. The sufficient conditions entail the necessary conditions. It is necessary for the rule of causality to reign supreme if the world is to seem rational to us. Yet the rule of causality is not sufficient because this rule is not sacrosanct and cannot account for the existence of an eternal universe. Hence, indeterminism puts determinism into question.

Fatalism expresses the attitude that is intimate with the realization that something happened and became a first cause, itself spontaneous or uncaused. Fatalism insists that because of this primal occurrence other events were realized with the activation of the rule of causality operating through laws of nature (which nevertheless have a yearning character), are being realized, and will continue to be realized. The necessity linking subsequent occurrences to the primal occurrence is not a rigid necessity but an instance merely of causal dependence. The link of a rigid necessity would be possible only if the springing into being of the primal occurrence was preeminently an act of rationality. If it were fundamentally a rational act we would have a perfect universe and free human beings. Freedom in this case would mean happiness and the absence of moral evil. Perfection in the universe would mean absolute beauty and the absence of physical evil. Clearly, the world we are born into is neither perfect nor full of happiness. It is a world that, yet, offers advanced consciousness consolation. The inferiority of determinism to fatalism is most obvious here. A consolatory universe could have sprung into being through a primal emotive act of a yearning essence, which, having been, gave potency to the rule of causality. The primal occurrence was born in emotion. Thus existence manifests a mythopoeic quality that presents being everywhere but makes it nowhere eternally substantial, the crux of very interesting arguments of Bradley in *Appearance and Reality* (see the relevant section of Part Four of this work) and also of quantum indeterminacy. The emotive act of *mood* in the beginning and the mythopoeic character of existence make it difficult, if not impossible, for us to reconstruct the beginning.

If the universe emerged as an expression of rationality principally, absolute necessity would reign. From the very moment of the emergence of the universe all events subsequent upon this emergence would have been rigidly determined, such that there would be no place for novelty and error. Existence would unfold, in Hegel's term, as a *rational necessity*, as a perfect expression of being. It is mere academic exercise to dwell on this perfect and rational universe because *it is not* and could not have been. This is the fatality of our emotive universe. Its inevitability is a tragic inevitability because it expressed consolation rather than freedom or perfection. However, we are in no way saying the universe is pointless, that its existence is a gratuitous existence. Rationality clearly emerges out of emotionality. The human phenomenon, for instance, has a reason that is conditioned by feelings. Yearning is the reason for the existence of the universe. Freedom is certainly indicated but cannot be realized. Therefore, consolation is the most the universe can achieve. For one to achieve freedom a Being who is all-mighty is required. This is the hope of religion. Where philosophy stops religion begins.

The fate of a thing is its happening the way it happened. Its occurrence is its fate. Fate is not predetermined destiny *per se*, but the very phenomenon of destiny. Rigid determinism is not necessary here. Since fatalism is prior to determinism, the latter is only a conceptual necessity sought by the human intellect for the practical purpose of comprehending everyday events without reference to the mother of all necessities—fatalism. Necessity itself is a term for existential yearning. Fatalism is the yearning to be and become. The goal of this process of yearning is an impossible freedom. Hence, the mighty cosmic quest of being terminates with consolation. If necessity is basically an emotional demand of the human intellect, then emotion is prior to reason and what we call rationality is in fact emotional intelligence. Properly speaking, a human being is a creature of emotion. If fatalism is the yearning to be and become, then in both animate and inanimate existence we see the elements of cosmic joy and sadness (beauty and terror) operating through determinism to realize consolation for humanity and the universe. Since it is in the human phenomenon that yearning has reached its highest level of self-knowledge any solution to the problem of freedom must take into account the two elements of *mood*—joy and sadness—which are first of all advanced human emotions. They are resources of the universe.

Human agency accounts for the persistence of the freedom illusion. This agency finds its bearings in the environment of *mood* whose division yields the primal elements of joy and sadness. No conscious human action is neutral in relation to the primal elements. Human actions either directly or indirectly decrease pain or directly and indirectly increase pain. The decrease of pain increases human joy and reduces human sadness. Even the ascetic state is not neutral. It is ethical and therefore stands in a direct relation with the primal elements. Joy and sadness are conditions which answer to fatalism for their existence. The ability to act under these conditions is not freedom but liberty. As we keep repeating, liberty means acting in the service of goodness. This goodness is also morality. To be free one must be transcendently free. One must become so perfect that he is able to master himself and nature. Man must become God. Perhaps not even the promise of Heaven can realize human freedom. To be free a person must be able to choose only one particular course in every situation, without any alternative, which always turns out the ideal choice that does not lead to regret and sadness. Simply put: *freedom implies the strictest determinism*. The free person is a perfect person who has become a god. You may say: "But it is not necessary that humans should become a master of nature. All that is required for freedom to be asserted is that a man who acts in a particular situation should have a concrete sense of alternative possibilities." This is a lame objection. This requirement simply means conscious choosing. To this objection we restate that the demand of freedom is a radical demand. Conscious choice out of available options is already a determined choice. It terminates in joyful or sorrowful consequences. There is always a reason and a desire for the course one takes. This course has positive or negative consequences. It matters much if these consequences fly out of control so that one finds oneself in dire circumstances. What is decisive in the argument against freedom is that the choices we make unfold in the field of ethical struggle.

Let us consider the following example. **A** wishes to go to the beach on a particular day. He also wants to attend a community meeting. After weighing the relative importance of these two needs he chooses the latter. Even at this early stage determinism is already operative. **A** is acting under a mild pressure. The pressure intensifies on his way to the place of meeting. He is involved in a motor accident, sustains serious injuries, and is then condemned to an entire year of inactivity. While he recovers he goes through a soul-searching experience that also involves the development of character. Learning to cope with pain is a process of existential struggle, the coming to grips with impediments. Determinism accounts for the reasons for **A** wishing to go to the meeting. Deciding against the competing desire to go to the beach is making a conscious choice that may lead to negative consequences, thus revealing **A** as an agent responsible for his actions. Suffering injuries in the car accident and struggling against regret and bitterness in the state of confinement declares **A** to be a witness to liberty. While determinism can tell us that **A** is not free it is fatalism that provides insight into the meaning of this absence of freedom and shows liberty to be the consolation for the impossibility of the illusion of freedom.

Every choice a person makes shuts out other choices even as the preferred choice may yield consequences worse than the forgone alternatives. The very fact that a person makes a choice at all in an environment of profound evil is itself problematic. The choices one makes will sooner or later reveal their ability to irritate *mood*, to yield ugly consequences either predicted and predictable or unpredicted and unpredictable. Liberty has already reconciled itself to necessity. But this radical demand called freedom, this vanishing ideality, is a different thing. Since the question of freedom cannot be transcendently posed, we are compelled to turn our back on this idea and give the nod to the concept of liberty. The tenacity of the concept of freedom in the human mind we attributed earlier to the love of happiness. For this reason freedom is an illusion but not a delusion. It is a beautiful concept. As an illusion the notion of freedom is intimate with the truth of a universal desire for a happiness which is unrealizable beyond the deepening of joy. Yet this is a joy threatened and diminished by cosmic sadness. The reality of joy drives human morality. The human phenomenon is fit for joy but not destined for happiness. To leave the problem of evil at a highly abstract level, at the level of a contest between free will and determinism and the challenge of a reconciliation philosophy, as is largely the case in Western philosophy, is to do great injustice to the person in the street. The person in the street suffers and struggles under the weight of evil. Indeed, the problem of freedom is compulsorily carried into the other problem of evil. The isolation of the freedom question from the question of evil in the world closes the door to liberty.

The will which is the faculty of choice cannot be free if the human phenomenon as a whole exists fatalistically. The fatalistic existence is the compounding of basic emotional elements that are prior to rationality. However sophisticated the human intellect, however advanced the achievements of this mighty intellect may be, one is nothing more than yearning. Sartre did well to acknowledge this fact, although only pessimistically. Obviously, *we are condemned to be sad*. Human choices are assailed on all sides by existential fatalities that irritate and frustrate *mood*, enriching and deflating human joy, refining and embittering human sadness. The trinity of deliberation, judgment, and election (terms signifying intentionality) deployed by medieval Christian philosophers like St. Aquinas to defend free will cannot guarantee freedom. To deliberate is to contemplate, to judge is to decide, and to elect is to choose. These mental processes are dimensions of liberty rather than freedom. They play out in the field of ethical struggle. They encounter internal impediments in their search for freedom even as the same processes encounter impediments external to them.

The human will is structured along emotive impulses. The will cannot be free as a result of its emotive constitution but it certainly enables us to proclaim ourselves witnesses to liberty. Determinism says that every event has an antecedent cause and necessity adds that a law of nature will be broken if this rule is violated. Yet the meaning of human existence is futility. It is our comprehension of futility that leads us finally to fatalism, the supreme necessity. A universe in which evil is real, which indicates perfection but has not realized and cannot realize it, exists for futility. The futility of existence is most striking in the case of one whose intellect directly encounters this futility and suffers the pain of despair and nihilism. Determinism is not sacrosanct as it cannot account for futility. Indeterminism puts determinism in question. On the other hand, freedom can be dispensed with because it is idle in a fatalistic universe such as ours. It is ideal, a vanishing phenomenon. The human consolation is liberty, the constant affirmation of faith in life as the evolutionary movement towards fuller joy. All things ethical have implications for only two concepts: joy and sadness.

Our solution to the problem of freedom is a horizontal solution. We have not invoked the authority of religion. It is not for nothing that the enigmatic Hegel famously declared the realization of freedom the goal of cosmic history.

We too agree. However, we assert its impossibility and hasten to replace freedom with liberty. How can the *mood* of humanity realize the radical demand of freedom without help from a God who is powerful enough to grant one freedom? Yet when one becomes free one transforms into a god in one's own right. This means that a wise God will ensure that a person never attains freedom. It will therefore appear that freedom is impossible. In the absence of freedom, however, liberty has been granted to humans. They should be content with this compensation which confers on them the privilege of being *witnesses*.

Emotional Being

The person we seek to research is the *melancholy being* who this moment is fighting in Syria and Mali, defying bullets in Egypt for the love of revolution, gnashing his teeth at poverty and bad governance in Nigeria, pushing the frontiers of minority rights activism in Europe and America, etc. The *melancholy being* is everywhere. He is the drug czar, the gangster, the computer games freak, the soulful crooner, the football hooligan, the fame-seeking physicist, the pub brawler, the aging dictator, the sex addict, the single parent, etc. The *melancholy being* is everywhere as the creature of a privileged race, cursed yet with the blessing of his privileged existence. He is the mystery child of a mysterious evolution whose process of natural selection cannot guarantee the emergence of a superman. This person of joy and sadness cannot be overlooked by the philosophy of the 21st century because he dominates the century completely as the being of pessimism and optimism.

In the beginning what was a human being? A vacuum of silence outside the womb of time encompassed by eternity, a mass of hydrogen struggling to catch the light of life, an eternal *mood* in the mind of God ready to go out of the divine mind as problematic emotion and intelligence? Whichever option we take, what is not in doubt is the fact that the new being called human is a creature of emotion in an emotional universe who did not arrive by chance. In the emotional equipment of human beings can be found the nucleus of intelligence fully formed and ready to unfold one way or the other. Humanity has emerged out of the silence of a profoundly unconscious state as an inspired being out to know joy and complete his fundamental sadness in joy. One comes into the world for no other reason than to know joy. This is noteworthy. It is for this reason that the human is a witness to liberty. The joy-act is a moral act. In the consolationist phase of joy evil is completely suppressed by intellectual love. Thus in everyday life we see that those who commit evil acts do so at moments of unhappiness or rather at moments of joylessness. The joyful person is a pure spirit. He attains to purity because he ceases to despair. The route of evil passes through despair. Skepticism, cynicism, and nihilism in all its forms are consequences of despair. This existential despair, failing to be transformed into intellectual love by faith, convinces the human mind that the "nothing" is an actuality, a desirable actuality. But the intellect never finds the impossible "nothing"; so it expresses its despair in nihilistic acts ranging from "healthy" skepticism to suicide and murder.

The input of chance or blind determinism in the emergence of humankind is negated by the indestructible intelligence which is its second nature. Fatalism absorbed chance. Necessity and design took over from chance and illuminated the dark road which the human creature must take in search of his own consolation and finally God who is the consolation of the universe. The *melancholy being* is the person of emotion whose sole quest is to find consolation which he has decoded in his pessimistic constitution. Pessimism carries one over into optimism. The failure to reach optimism causes one to embrace evil. The person of emotion has arrived, not to build skyscrapers and make fighter jets, not to design weapons of mass destruction. He has arrived, not to enjoy the good things of life primarily, not merely to reproduce, nor engage in intellectual activities—these are all secondary developments. The human who is in solidarity with the universe enters the scene of universal life in search of consolation.

A basic pessimistic constitution convinces one of the futility of existence since pessimism is the awareness that human life is virtually pointless in the absence of freedom. Yet this very primordial pessimism is engaged in a dialectic with optimism. The appropriate response to the apparent aimlessness of human life is ethical resignation to the circumstances of life. Since this resignation is ethical it is not at all the quietism that leads thinkers to dismiss the theory of fatalism as primitive. Ethical resignation leads to ethical activism because in the absence of freedom (for which the human mind grieves) the consolation of liberty is granted (for which the human mind rejoices). Ethical activism is directly inspired by the imperative of liberty which is morality. If the great German thinker Schopenhauer had investigated pessimism thoroughly and traversed the length and breadth of this mental phenomenon of despair he would have discovered the philosophy of consolation and seen the will to live for what it is: the witnessing to liberty.[6] Another great German thinker Nietzsche, coming after Schopenhauer, thought he was going to reform Schopenhauer by forcefully causing the incineration of Schopenhauer's pessimism and arriving magically at a solid optimism. Only through a dialectic of *mood* can sadness be transformed to joy, pessimism to optimism. A study of the more prominent works of Nietzsche shows clearly that he was a closet pessimist all his life. The *will to power*, confirmed a metaphysical impossibility, is essentially the reincarnation of Schopenhauer's *will to live*. The superman of Nietzsche is never going to emerge, and yearning is all that one can possess.

Whereas God is his own consolation, a man cannot be his own consolation. He needs the idea of the good and therefore freedom to refer him to a bigger power (his community and, ultimately, the idea of God) in what we have called the transcendental appeal. The idea of the good unrealizable as freedom but compensated for by the consolation of liberty must always comfort the emotional human. One distills ethics out of the emotionality of existence consisting merely of the elements of joy and sadness and gradually clarifies rationality, the logic of the intellect. Thus all human intellectual striving, no matter how grandiose in the most demanding fields of science and philosophy, operates to satisfy the fundamental need for consolation. This consolation, having been anchored on earth in the reality of liberty, seeks transformation to become freedom, the impossibility of which results in sadness, pessimism, and all forms of nihilism. Let us state again that nihilism is the quest for an impossible nothing motivated by a reality that has failed. The nihilist tendency is noticeable in all aspects of life, both in the intellectual and non-intellectual life. In philosophy, for instance, Schopenhauer's pessimism and current feminist writings confirm the profound dissatisfaction with the state of affairs answering to inevitability and the nihilism that displaces joy. The brilliant physicist commits suicide after years of contemplating the problem of the sufficient condition of the eternity of the universe. The famous soccer player criticized for dwindling performance decides to hang his boots and pay greater attention to the well-being of his nuclear family. At the bottom of these nihilist tendencies is the craving for the materialization of God, the perfection of the good, and the emergence of freedom. The pathos underlying nihilism and all philosophies of despair is the perceived failure of the transcendental appeal.

The emotional being is inherently good and inherently bad. The idea that one is inherently good without further qualification is a great error of secular humanism. The emotional being is not a pure being, not wholly bad or good. He is a pessimistic creature who desires to complete his sadness in his joy, who seeks to become the being of liberty. He is afraid of life and the world because of the absence of freedom. Evil emerges out of his fear as a negated positive. The positive is his goodness which advances yearning towards freedom but finds that the only terminus reachable by immanence is consolation. The intellect which has invented freedom because existence compulsorily indicates it (and not because freedom is a delusion) is confounded. This confounding of the intellect leads to nihilism. Crime, then, can be seen as an act of nihilism.

The moral content of human ethical resignation compels this very attitude of the mind to be an active resignation. One's resignation does not consist in sitting idly in a chair, bemoaning the rot in one's external and internal environment. Action is never far away from resignation. Resignation is valid because pessimism is metaphysically grounded. Yet the emotional being is also a creature of optimism. A man himself may be evil, but his yearning is pure. Since the human is a being of optimism his contemplation is always a preparation for action. Thought itself supports action. Action provides an outlet for emotion. It is in action that one comprehensively witnesses to liberty. Passivity is an act of nihilism and deserves to be rejected. It is in witnessing to liberty that the human phenomenon actualizes the rationality latent in emotionality. Where is the rational being? The rational being is *ab initio* in the emotional being. The role of the intellect is to refine feeling and pronounce it reason.

As psycho-logic comes before logic, so does emotion precede intelligence. The being for whom the meaning of existence consists of nothing more than the full ramifications of joy and sadness is the emotional being. Emotionality draws its vitality from the pursuit of a perfect happiness indicated by the mind but confirmed outside the mind as impossible, since the very pursuit of this happiness exhausts the idea, such that what is real is joy—the witnessing to liberty. Human emotionality also consists in the acceptance of the reality of sadness which underlines the tragedy of existence. Emotionality is that basic state informed by the *mood* of the universe and the response to this same universe considered as existing as a consolation for the non-existence of an ideal universe. This is the necessity of consolation in the face of terror. Thus the human mind conceives the universe as purposeful and human life as meaningful. This optimism, however, operates within the sphere of fatalism. Human emotionality does not deny the relevance of the question of the pointlessness of the universe in the face of an encroaching indeterminism or the question of the futility of human life in the absence of happiness. It takes these supreme questions into consideration, certainly. Yet it goes further to consider that other dimension of existence that sees joy being added to sadness and optimism augmenting pessimism. This positive side is of course the realization that consolation rooted in fatalism is enough compensation for the impossibility of happiness.

It is not out of teary sentimentality that love is popularly identified with emotion. Love itself is the expression of that longing for beauty in a person which is truly the demand that happiness should belong to him. It is mostly celebrated as romantic and sexual love, but its highest expression in the universe is intellectual love. Love is fundamentally a need of the thinking and feeling being. Who is a human if not that being that actively seeks consolation where terror subsists, for whom there is no meaning beyond the ramifications of joy and sadness? Love is emphatically the outcry of the individual man and woman, an appeal for beauty in the midst of terror. If one is too reserved to express or even entertain romantic or sentimental love such as one sees on television, in movies, novels, and in gardens one can experience a quieter version, the highest emotion of intellectual love, an ethical attitude of resignation to the inevitable, and therefore reconciliation with nature in what Spinoza famously termed the context of eternity.

Intelligent Being

The emergence of mind is the most beautiful and at the same time the most dreadful thing to happen to the *melancholy being*. It is the most beautiful thing because yearning was expressed in optimism in the capacity for a higher perception. Human beings became thinking things, not just mere living things like dogs, goats, and—worse still—a lowly amoeba reproducing asexually. The dreadful thing about this occurrence is the intellect's apprehension of the profound fatality of existence. This knowledge is denied non-thinking things. With the emergence of mind the emotional being becomes aware of the dependability, and yet the gross insufficiency, of science in providing satisfactory answers to the question why there is something instead of nothing. One becomes aware of the speculative futility of philosophy and religion which, yet, supports the most concrete practice. This is the question of the relationship between sufficiency, necessity, determinism, and freedom. We have tackled this great question with some candor all through Part One, Part Two, and now Part Three of this book.

The knowledge of the severe limitation of human being in a totality that is yearning weighs heavily on the mind. All human' actions take their reference from the impossibility of freedom. Whether one shuts one's eyes to the fatal intimation of his mind and declares the pursuit of pleasure the chief goal of human life like the Greek philosopher Epicurus or he embraces the stern asceticism of the Stoic philosophers, the intellect has opened a Pandora's box. Not only have we gained knowledge of the tragedy of existence, but have been declared complicit in this tragedy as an agent of evil. The knowledge of the futility of existence is automatically the knowledge of our contribution to this futility. In the unthinking thing this dreadful knowledge is dormant. In the thinking thing the privilege of thought brings knowledge of horror.

Consequently, the intelligent being struggles to become free even while recognizing the incapacity for absolute self-sufficiency, the power to fill the void of change with the meaning of necessity and the life of design, the right to wholly comfort self and then become the consolation of the universe. This is humankind opening its eyes at last after sleeping through eternities as unconscious *mood*. It is the destiny of *mood* to aspire to active consciousness, to realize this aspiration, and contemplate the non-materialization of God who is goodness reified, the perfection of freedom. God may well be free, but humanity is not. The categories of omniscience and omnipotence applied to God deepen human disenchantment: humans who imperiously demand that God should show His face and wield His power that evil may cease to be. Our philosophical system has sought to show that the categories of power and glory are more appropriate to the understanding of God than the categories of omniscience and omnipotence.

Humans are or can be said to be good because the mind emerged as the joy of their existence. To become is to have cosmic joy liberated out of primal *mood*. The awareness of the event of becoming is called optimism. So the coming into being of a thing is an optimistic eventuality. But a thing having become reality continues to exist under the sway of fatalism, the knowledge that the joyful becoming has failed and that the meaning of its existence is nothing more than consolation. Of course, it is advanced consciousness that perceives the failure of reality and relates optimism with pessimism. Even if humankind did not exist the dialectic of *mood* would still play itself out as long as it is the same universe minus humankind. The cosmic movement would proceed with no one to comprehend it. The processes of the dialectic are objective and primal. The joy-state neutralizes the evil of the sadness-state. Humans are good for this reason that in them intelligence emerged in the joy-state to neutralize the basic emotion of sadness. The emergence of mind, however, highlights the incompleteness of pessimism, for yearning seeks consolation. In recognizing optimism as the peace of pessimism, the emotion of the intellect which is called intellectual love (see Section 4) declares humans a witness to liberty. This is the sense in which they are said to be good. Bracketing the joy-state of existence and the mind's optimistic phase of thought leaves us with a profoundly evil phenomenon. This is the evil person who cohabits with the good person and often overpowers the good person.

Pessimism inspired by the tragedy of existence is the curse of human existence while optimism inspired by the beauty of human existence is the blessing of human life. The tragedy is the fatality of existence, the impossibility of freedom. The beauty is the consolation existence offers in the form of liberty. Therefore humankind is a real value in the universe called to generate values in the world. And ethics in a proper sense is the horizontal interpretation of metaphysics. Optimism is a blessing, the joy of the intellect. Just as one sees much through the prism of pessimism, so does one see much through the prism of optimism. The philosophical contraction of pessimism throws up a Schopenhauer. On the other hand, the philosophical concentration on optimism yields a Spinoza who will struggle to convince himself that all is well or an Asouzu who will isolate the joy of existence from the sadness of this same existence or a Bradley who will unabashedly tell us that evil is only appearance (and therefore a vanishing phenomenon) with sophisticated but unconvincing arguments to buttress his point.

With the development of intelligence out of the joy-state of *mood* the beauty of existence neutralizes the terror of existence and animates the mind in its optimistic phase. Rationality is an ethico-logical phenomenon of the mind born in this optimistic phase. Thus we confirmed in a previous section that the rational is that which the intellect endorses as meeting a minimum ethical standard. Rationality is not just the ability to think or the possession of reason but the ability to think right and the possession of a right reason. Reason itself is the light of the emotion, the power and faculty of right thinking and therefore the refinement of the emotion. Reason is the life of intellectual love, the logic of the intellect which seeks reconciliation with the vast logic of life and of existence. Awareness of the fatality of existence—thanks to the intellect that penetrates determinism and reveals it to be inadequate—alerts us to the fact that the whole of existence desires consolation. This awareness made possible by the emergence of mind convinces us that our intellectual insight into the fatality of existence is the basis of empathy for and kinship first with our fellow human beings, then with all living things, then with objective nature, and finally with a personal principle of the universe or this same principle in its phase of impersonality. The truth of life and existence in general is consolation into which both appearance and reality dissolve as the yearning total. Every existent fated to never seeing the light of consciousness, every stirring of unconscious life, every movement of conscious life—everything turns blindly or consciously towards consolation, stretching the transcendental appeal to God. This God is a Being of power and glory and the absolute He commands is a yearning totality.

Human Yearning

The moment a person feels a need which, of course, must be satisfied, in that moment one's life activates the ever-present conditions of sadness. One yearns. However, intellectual love that is the capacity of the intellect to comprehend the solidarity of all existent things in the eternal context (what Asouzu calls the complementarity of missing links) is suppressed if one's yearning does not move out of the sphere of pessimism into the sphere of optimism. In the mind's pessimistic phase the totalizing impulse of intellectual love is arrested and one tries to deny the sympathetic character of the intellect, returning to the existential base of raw emotionality to work into a rage, to become bitter, violent, and even coldly indifferent. The negative triumph of pessimism is the eruption of evil inside and outside the human mind in which evil already inheres. The psychological explanation of evil which may refer us to the social environment, biochemical and genetic factors, is a secondary account of evil. The secondary and empirical account has failed to note the metaphysical status of the human person as a composition of mind and matter, which composition refers itself to *mood*. This *mood* is the fundamental element of life and the home of good and evil.

When the intellect does not expand with the love inspired by the totalization of the eternal context—a context that declares all to be well that must be well—humans unleash on their world their great potentiality for evil. Then we hear of Islamic terrorists, massacres in war-torn countries, hate speeches, shooting sprees in America, massive financial corruption in Nigeria, and sundry crimes of passion. These supposedly irrational acts are not without reason. They are backed by the reason of the emotion (psycho-logic) but are deprived of the reason of the intellect in its highest refinement which we call intellectual love. Every reason is an emotion. The reason not backed by intellectual love narrows into extremity and exclusivity. We are now solidly in the sphere of pessimism, one dominated by the despair of the intellect. The despair of the intellect is a direct passage to evil while the love of the intellect opens the road to goodness. The truly optimistic person or the person whose optimism has reached a high level of development is the person of intellect who can hardly violate liberty by committing crimes against humanity because the larger picture of existence superimposed on eternity dominates the space of his ever-expanding mind. The optimistic person indeed belongs to all humanity as a civilized being regardless of race or tribe. He is moved to sympathy not just by the tears of humanity but indeed by that psychological disposition mirroring the philosophical understanding of intellectual love as the emotion of an eternity that strives towards freedom but finds only consolation in the very fact of eternity's imperfect expression.

The optimistic person has not won a final victory over despair, yet. He contends with pessimism all his life. He is called the optimistic person because he strives to be a perpetual witness to liberty. Both the optimistic being and the pessimistic being unite in the *melancholy being*. They are different in the sense that while the optimistic person constantly seeks the realization of the love of the intellect the pessimistic person stagnates in the sphere of the despair of the intellect and plots all kinds of evils acts.

I have proposed the state of silence as the barest condition of existence beyond which there is no dialectical tension. This silence annihilates nothingness. Beyond silence there is no rest. The hope of nirvana and eternal rest cannot go beyond silence. The intelligence that contemplates it as a fatality suffers pessimism because in contemplating a condition that has annihilated nothingness or has brought about its impossibility it confronts the futility of existence. The term futility as used by the consolationist thinker does not indicate pointlessness or meaninglessness. Futility rather refers us to fatalism given the loss of explanatory power by determinism whenever the problem of the eternity of the world rears its head. A futile universe is one in which freedom is indicated as the goal of existence but which, ironically, cannot actualize this freedom by virtue of its constitution as yearning expressed fatalistically. A futile universe characterized by yearning is a universe of terror and beauty.

Despair inheres in human thought. Let us struggle with the despair of our *moody* existence and let the temporary conquest of this same despair be the euphoria that endorses liberty, the phenomenon of the moral act. This euphoria cannot refer us to freedom since human joy is a completion of sadness. The human being must live and die clinging as a witness to liberty.

Chapter 10

THE METAPHYSICS OF MORALITY

Preamble

"Ethics may refer simply to the value judgments that people have and to the beliefs that people hold—individual and collectively—about what is right or wrong, good or evil, precious or worthless, beautiful or ugly and sacred or profane."[1] This quotation is self-evident. We can go on to say that ethics is the branch of philosophy that investigates the claims and counter-claims of morality. Morality is the awareness of what is right and what is wrong. This awareness creates a standard for human behavior. Radically conceived, morality is the awareness of the existence of evil in the world. So conceived fundamentally, we will be able to show that morality is an objective phenomenon of the world and not a mere conventional standard of social behavior projected by culture. This fundamental understanding of morality as the consciousness of evil in the world that forces the right-wrong distinction out of unstructured passion and practice effectively holds up ethics as the metaphysics of morality.

Is morality absolute or relative? Is it objective or subjective? If we can show that there is no state corresponding to amorality it can be established that morality is absolute. Immorality will then be seen as a perversion of morality. That which is relative owes its existence to the absolute; it becomes parasitic when it seeks to deny the absolute that validates it. The relativization of morality is not the denial of the absolutism of morality but rather the realization of an absolute and objective morality in degrees of non-completeness. When we say a thing is relative we mean that the limited human mind has provided a perspective of an absolute. In simplifying this submission on the absolutism of morality, let us examine a seemingly odd cultural practice of Community A with regard to hospitality. Community A has a "primitive" custom that allows a man to offer his wife to an esteemed guest. Community B which prides itself as civilized denounces the practice as adultery. A feminist group in Community B overlooks the adultery charge (which is judgmental, anyway) and cries out that the rights of women in Community A are being violated. This scenario highlights the following ethical issues:

1. The absolutism of morality.

2. The relativity of morality.

3. Normative cultural relativism.

4. The persistence of prejudice and its origin in the absoluteness of morality.

The question of amorality, the absence of value or non-awareness of the value-ladeness of states of affairs in the world, is completely ruled out in the scenario above. All the parties recognize immediately and mediately that they are involved in activism either for the community or in defense of custom or for the individual and the claim of universality in the ideal of human rights. The feminist snarls at the man who gives his wife to his esteemed guest for violating the woman's fundamental human right to choose who to associate with sexually. The secular feminist who pretends not to be making a value-judgment hides behind the presumed universality of human rights to project her prejudice. This prejudice is her disdain for the cultural practice of an "unscientific" community. The feminist has a fundamental belief about the wrongness of the contentious cultural practice. Thus she self-righteously pronounces it as inhuman. A commitment is here made underlining the belief in an absolute moral standard with the phenomenon of pleasure as its point of departure. The analysis of pleasure yields the concept of justice which in turn points to the notion of happiness as the goal of the good life.

To escape the accusation of inhumanity and incivility brought by the feminist and Community B against Community A, members of community A will plead normative cultural relativism. They will tell the feminist and Community B that goals (the attainment of justice and, ultimately, happiness) may be the same for everyone but means to their realization are different. This cheeky plea cunningly introduces the issue of cultural relativism. Indeed, Community A is far from being amoral. What Community B regards as immorality and the feminist as inhumanity carries the dignity of morality because it is a people's perspective of an absolute moral imperative. This absolute moral imperative is the collectivist claim of equal importance of the individual and the community if not the outright superiority of the latter, the culture-specific call to the individual to stand by his neighbor and help realize his happiness through the increase of his sexual pleasure. Community A is aware of the fundamental moral question of goodness and justice as much as the feminist and Community B. Community

A pretends that values are culture-specific because it comprehends an absolute moral demand through the prism of culture. Morality is objective and absolute. The validity of Community A's relativization of this absolute morality is traceable to limited knowledge of human practices. Community A is said to suffer a certain degree of ignorance. Hence, with enlightenment Community A may declare its wife-sharing custom obsolete in the continued commitment to justice and goodness. The feminist who may condone wife-swapping in order not to be "judgmental" relativizes an absolute morality and seeks grounds of justification in gynocentrism which is a prejudice. A prejudice laying claims to rationality validates the feminist's relativization of the absolute morality which everyone can trace in the demand for justice and goodness.

Whatever yearns realizes a morality absolutized in its very essence. Humanity has appeared on the scene of the universe as an absolute value desiring completeness as the mind endeavors to comprehend our seeming gratuitous existence. Society does not create morality. To fall back on a "social contract" theory of the origin of morality is to oversimplify the very grave problem of evil. Recognizing the shortcoming of a purely social naturalism in accounting for this profound phenomenon called morality, Udo Etuk has found it necessary to appeal to God as the giver of morality.[2] He does not show how this is possible. In this chapter I will discuss the origin of morality and see if I can find any path that can lead us to Etuk's conclusion. I will try to show that while morality is in many situations truly relativistic, this relativization is true only because morality as a phenomenon of consciousness is an absolute. If moral institutions are established based on social conventions, then moral relativism is a sign of the coming human apotheosis, the foundation of human peace. Human activism in the private and public spheres seeks this apotheosis, happiness as the final release from yearning. In this chapter I will try to show that moral absolutism trumps moral skepticism. If evil truly exists in the world, moral skepticism will be shown to have its place in the philosophy of despair.

Is Human Life Pointless?

A pointless universe would be an amoral universe, one in which struggle avails nothing, a universe in which one strives in vain. The greatest pessimist in philosophy, Schopenhauer, thought our universe is a pointless universe, yet he recommended a quiescent surrender, a kind of intelligent resignation to calm the will which he considered tyrannical. While Kant found refuge in the epistemological skepticism of the impossibility of knowledge of the thing-in-itself (which holds the key to the illumination of the mystery of the origin of the universe), Schopenhauer asserted that will is the thing-in-itself, a universal blind agency defined by its insatiable quest for life that perpetually animates the will to live, the inner nature of things manifested in the non-living realm as low-grade objectification of its ceaseless drive, demonstrated in the whole of objective nature as force and in human beings as action.[3] Schopenhauer's inspiration bears a similarity with our consolation philosophy, for we have also submitted that there is a yearning essence in things. While Schopenhauer had no insight into the dialectic of *mood*, we were able to move from a philosophy of pessimism to a philosophy of optimism, thanks to insight into the dialectic. With this dialectic we have been able to justify the evidence of common sense, the reality of beauty cohabiting with terror. If pessimism is absolute there will be no value in the world, no morality. The reaction of the man who receives a nasty slap from me, unprovoked, is always predictable. He will either retaliate directly or, if he is too powerless to stop me, cast an evil eye on me or, if he is absolutely powerless, defy me in his heart and even curse me. The vehement reaction of this man who has been slapped for no reason arises from the fact that he is an absolute value, the vehicle of an absolute morality which seeks for man a path to his moral apotheosis, a state of perfect happiness.

The will Schopenhauer demonizes as the source of a futile and entirely bleak existence is, ironically, an intelligent core. This will manifests itself outside itself in various grades of objectification in the world, ranging from unconscious things to living conscious things. This is a metaphysical account of an evolutionary universe. Can such a universe characterized by directionality be pointless? Can a world in which rationality is a reality be gratuitous? Can human life which indisputably manifests an aspect of beauty be absurd? We have sought in the course of this work to answer these weighty questions in the negative. In the light of our rebuttal of absolute pessimism, we insist that Schopenhauer and other philosophers who romanticized despair philosophized chiefly in their pessimistic phase of thought, heavily influenced by the emotion of sadness. Pessimism is the knowledge of a terrible state of affairs and the fear that this state of affairs will persist. Consequently, pessimism is properly the hope of better things to come, a preparation for optimism (see Section 6 of Chapter Two, Part Two).

Beauty exists side by side with ugliness. Terror cohabits with evil. Just as the evil in the world demands explanation, so does the beauty in the world. To say there is no beauty in the world is to deny the reality of joy, an intellectual operation no one can successfully complete. So goodness must be allowed to exist as much as evil. The vicious armed robber who murders his victim and escapes with the victim's money is the same man we encounter as a loving husband on the morning after his ugly deed, giving his wife part of the money snatched from his victim to buy baby milk and clothes for their five-month-old baby. This murderer would be the saddest man on the earth if someone were to murder his baby; yet he could will himself to callously deny life to someone not close to him, refusing to recognize his value in the value of the other, my Brother. His act of murder is an absolutely immoral act even though it may lead to some good consequences, such as sustaining his baby's life. Those who suffer from the act of the robber are creatures of *mood*, which insists on the emotional satisfaction called joy. The demand for joy is absolute, whether realized or not. Morality demands joy as that state of *mood* in which the human witnesses to liberty. In denying a person the right to live, the armed robber has thwarted the joy of one person capable of witnessing to liberty. Immoral acts are deeds of evil. If men and women disagree on what constitutes immorality it is not because morality is not fundamental but because men and women recognize that there are degrees of evil deeds and that some evil deeds are tolerable while others are not.

The evil act itself arises out of the failure to complete the moral act. Since every act is expected to either increase or reduce human joy, it is by that very reason already a moral act. Whatever brings one pleasure or pain looks back to morality. Let us go back to the armed robber. His evil impulse prods him to go out and violently assault unarmed people. His good impulse desires money for personal upkeep and for the sustenance of his family. The desire to sustain himself and his family begins the moral act. This act can become complete if money for self-preservation is obtained in a way or ways that take away nothing from the joy of others. In this particular case of the armed robber, the moral act fails because this man allows selfish consideration to dissipate the idea of the *anonymity of sacrifice*. The anonymity of sacrifice makes it known that one is born to struggle and suffer in a world one did not create, one in which fatalism is clarified as futility. Self-centeredness which is primal in the self-preservation instinct, having commenced the moral act, can only become complete if it bows to the anonymity of sacrifice. Unless the self-centered will bends to the dictates of sacrifice, extremism is born and one cannot be a witness to liberty. He thwarts the joy of being, which is a reality in human capacity for liberty, by refusing to complete the moral act. The armed robber is responsible for this non-completion. He knows that the joy of his victims would be thwarted by the extremity of his selfish act. Determinism in this context is accounted for by the psychology of self-preservation and self-centredness. Determinism does not nullify obligation here because there is another necessity of witnessing to liberty. The moral act begins its life as the need for self-preservation (selfishness) and completes itself in the knowledge of the anonymity of sacrifice (altruism).

We can no longer doubt that good is as necessary as evil is necessary in human nature. The necessity lies in the structure of *mood*. As yearning the human mood throws up joy and sadness. The joy-state affirms the beauty of life and urges one to act in defense of liberty. The sadness-state is dominated by the despair of the intellect as truly as the joy-state is dominated by intellectual love. The sadness-state which is given to nihilism perversely denies the beauty of life. The great German thinker Schopenhauer philosophized in the sadness-state. So do contemporary abortionists, radical feminists, misandrists, misogynists, misanthropists, Islamic terrorists, and other extremist groups and movements.

I ask again: Is human life pointless?

Human life can only be pointless if pessimism is absolute. The absoluteness of pessimism will be dependent on the absence of joy. It is true that pessimism is fundamental, yet it is only an aspect of a reality involved in a dialectic with itself in order to be creative. To embrace pessimism is to assert that life is futile. If life on earth is futile, then futility demands to be analyzed. The analysis of futility characterizes it as yearning that cannot be satisfied, as the totality of joy and sadness, beauty and terror. What is the meaning of futility if not the affirmation of the sway of fatalism? A state of affairs in the world is said to be futile if it is necessary, such that the condition of necessity makes it impossible for anyone to improve this state of affairs or substantially improve it. This is the ordinary understanding of futility. Consolation philosophy asserts that futility is also positive. The joyful event that comes to be is a futile event. It will not endure. Futility is the failure to achieve and sustain freedom. If a terrible state of affairs cannot be improved to such an extent that a difference becomes noticeable futility reigns. If a loved one dies awful necessity is encountered; the situation is futile because no one can bring the dead back to life. Nevertheless, it is possible, and in fact desirable, to explore the phenomenon of futility to show that pessimism can never be absolute. While it is impossible to restore a loved one who has died to life, it is within one's capacity to revisit the past in which the dead lived and invoke memories whose reality lessens the pains of bereavement. What is more, one can comfort oneself over the loss of a loved one.

Futility is not denied, but it is being understood in the context of fatalism as the inevitability of a state of affairs that burdens the intellect. Profound sadness is the worst emotion that futility can engender in humanity. The sad person can carry out certain shocking acts such as self-violence and suicide, but he cannot feel any emotion worse than sadness. This sadness is a fatalistic state, just like joy. Suicide sends one back to the unconscious existential state of silence, a condition of sadness not apprehended by mind. So sadness is basic as a fatalistic state, as an emotion that necessarily follows a terrible occurrence. The sad person is down on his back with grief. He has two options to complete his sadness in joy, picking himself up or committing suicide. The first option is reasonable and pro-life as the ethical embrace of *amor fati*. This response is a moral revolt. The second option is anti-life. It is an immoral revolt. It does not escape fatalism because the dead returns to the profoundest state of sadness. Thus human life is not pointless in spite of its futility. The pessimistic philosophy is far from completion because it cannot account for the good in the world. Pessimism shuts its eyes to the good in the world while opening the same eyes wide on encountering evil. The pessimist who declares life to be pointless because of the undeniable evidence of evil all too soon forgets that he is part of the cosmic problem, that he, like everything else in existence, is complicit in the reality of evil. Everything that yearns is already evil in nature because out of fear comes the impulse of evil.

The determination of human life as fatalistic rather than pointless brings us back to the main problem before us. We are trying to illuminate the problem of morality, beginning with the objectivity and relativism of morality. The foregoing analysis has clearly shown that there is no place for amorality in the metaphysics of morality because of the intensity of joy and sadness which characterizes human existence. As the constituents of *mood*, and therefore yearning, joy, and sadness are in fact ethical states. The person enjoying his joy-state believes life is good and cannot knowingly commit evil acts. An act is evil if it is going to diminish someone's joy and thwart the witnessing to liberty, no matter the good consequence it yields for one or one's friends or even strangers. An evil act is intrinsically evil but can be measured in degrees of severity. The evil act is that which begins as a moral act but is never completed because egoistic consideration disallows the will to bend towards the anonymity of sacrifice. What is evil is evil, regardless of where evil occurs. Its relativization is a secondary process that takes into consideration factors such as culture, degree of gravity, popular opinions, etc. The evil act which begins its life as a moral act is absolute.

The Objectivity of Morality

Morality is the value that measures right behavior. It is more than a standard; it is the value of right conduct. That which is immoral deviates from the path of morality. Immoral behavior is not antithetical to moral behavior strictly speaking, since immorality has its root in morality. A conduct is said to be immoral if it does not pass through the stage of sacrifice. Conduct, we have shown, begins its life as a moral impulse. For conduct to succeed as moral the stage of sacrifice must be encountered and negotiated. When sacrifice is not encountered its anonymity is not acknowledged, thus rousing egoism and extreme views of nihilism such as solipsism. Without the conscious acknowledgment of the anonymity of sacrifice no conscious act can claim to have completed the moral act.

Therefore morality is an emotion. Still, it is more than an emotion: it is the emotion of reason. Morality is rationality, the refinement of the emotion. How can emotion be equal to morality? When someone performs an act we consider good we are moved to ascribe morality to this act. The *moving* is an emotional reaction of the person of *mood*. This emotion of approbation is pleasure. Yet it is something more fundamental than mere delight. We are here dealing with the fundamental emotion of joy. Joy indicates the passage of despair into hope and hope into the love of the intellect. The moral person is joyful, though he may be tormented by misfortune again and again. The joy of the moral person must not always express itself noisily in delirious shouts and vigorous dance. The moral person is joyful as soon as hope has come to stay in his mind, the moment he abandons the despair of the intellect and accepts that a step is being taken towards the full realization of happiness for all, not just for himself but indeed for all. We can now expand our definition of morality to mean the *value of joy attached to human conduct*. Because morality is the value of joy in the eternal context of one's yearning for happiness, this selfsame morality and goodness are synonymous. Both are emotions, and therefore existents, carrying the sanction of reason.

As an emotion the objectivity of morality is guaranteed. Human reality and reality in general is organized feelings. The first knowledge of that which yearns is the knowledge of the fatality of the universe. Before we are able to attain depth of thought the fatality of the universe convinces us about the purposelessness of the universe. It takes much deeper thinking for us to be persuaded that the pointlessness of the universe is an over-simplified perspective. Knowledge of the fatality of the universe arouses fear of the immense unknown, one that may never be known. The ideas of God, the permanence of the self, immortality, and freedom are all born in this fear. Morality, which has been identified with goodness, is rooted in this fear. The thinking mind contemplates this cosmic fear and reacts by believing or not believing in God and the other ideas. The decision to be a theist or an atheist is therefore an emotional decision.

Let us repeat again that evil acts are performed under the influence of the despair of the intellect while good acts are performed under the direction of the love of the intellect. Despair is always allied with the mental states of sadness, discontent, and rebellion. On the other hand, the states of joy, contentment, and resignation are always allied with love. Sadness and denial go together. The affirmation of intellectual love suppresses the fear of the universe while its denial (the despair of the intellect) magnifies this fear. The critical reaction to cosmic fear is usually in the form of skepticism, cynicism, and discontent. This critical reaction is anti-God, anti-nature, anti-man, and anti-value, in spite of its being value already. In this nihilism evil has its inspiration; thus we are able to confirm our position once again that evil is rooted in the human mood, which itself is a fragment of the *mood* of the universe. The evil act does not begin its life as evil but as the thinking thing's consciousness of the fatality of the universe, the awareness that fear broods over the universe. Fear is inherent in *mood* as long as *mood* is characterized by yearning. This cosmic fear is also the inspiration of goodness. One's guilt lies in existing as a yearning being, and therefore as a being that affirms and denies what is good and evil. Inclination towards God and life, solidarity with nature, and solidarity with humanity diminish the threat the thinking mind reads into the absence of a satisfactory explanation of the origin of the universe. The acts that follow from these diminished states of fear are acts of reason, emotional reason. Love is this emotional reason in the context of yearning. This is the "sympathetic reason" Senghor thought was an African peculiarity. In this treatise I announce it a heritage of humanity.

By proceeding from fear and representing the value of joy, morality is objective. As the incomplete moral act the phenomenon called immorality is also objectively rooted. There is no other way that moral realism can be justified. We may half-heartedly ascribe mathematical truth to moral acts and impose on them mathematical objectivity. This solution is mere logical sophistry. It is far-fetched and unconvincing, remote from the experience it needs for its validity. We may also appeal to human nature, a better approach indeed. Yet this second approach cannot be complete without reference to the emotion. The most this second solution can achieve is the invocation of human reason as commanding one to behave in certain ways in accordance with conscience. But we have discredited the rigid theory of knowledge which exaggerates the powers of reason by showing that reason is in fact an emotion and rationality refers itself to emotionality for a better understanding of itself. While according great respect to reason, we have not hesitated to puncture its claim to superiority over the emotion. Our approach to the vindication of moral realism combines the human nature perspective with our own insight, the doctrine of *mood*.

As the emotion of goodness, morality has found an objective foundation in the essence of yearning shared by every existent thing, whether sentient or not. The possibility, indeed reality, of non-sentient things participating in the vaster life of yearning did not elude the pessimistic Schopenhauer, since he saw the operation of the indomitable will in non-living nature as force. The remarkable thing about beings that have become sentient, and human beings in particular, is that they grasp self-knowledge within themselves and in the operation of nature. Human beings are beings who think, even though at bottom they are a mere fragment of *mood*. Humans are able to come to the conclusion that they are complicit in the reality of evil and that it is unjust for them to blame God for the evil in the world, as I have shown. Just as the universe exists necessarily as an imperfect expression of *mood*, so do humans exist necessarily as an imperfect expression of *mood*. There are times when we are even inclined to extend the guilt of existence to inanimate objects. While such tendency may appear anthropomorphic, it nevertheless underlines our point that all existent things are fundamentally evil. The greedy dog that grabs a chunk of roasted mutton and scampers behind his owner's house to enjoy its loot is guilty. The plastic chair that causes one to stumble and receives a furious kick for the unsolicited "favor" is guilty. The hurricanes that torment the United States of America are guilty. Indeed, these violent outbursts of nature are routinely dignified with fancy human names like Nancy, Katerina, etc. God is guilty by virtue of His reality. But the existence of God is a remarkable reality because He fought against and conquered the evil in His principle and became the powerful and glorious Being worthy of adoration.

We are not here saying that objects like stones are morally accountable or even animate. These objects are only potentially alive. They yearn at a subconscious level, without knowing that they yearn. Since the fatalistic threshold of animation has not been crossed by objects such as stones we can conveniently pretend they are not even potentially alive. However, the caveat is to remember that we pretend.

The Relativization of Morality

If the foundation of morality had not been laid already by *mood* it would be impossible for us to talk glibly about concepts like moral realism, ethical constructivism, normative cultural relativism, etc. The quest of nihilism, as we keep discovering, is the search for the oblivion which the nothing supposedly promises. But this nothing is actually the silence of eternity, a cosmic state of unawareness of the fatality of existence and therefore the saddest possible state. The moral foundation of the world has been laid and represented as the value of emotion in the world. Since an objective foundation has been laid, subsequent relativization of morality arises from divergent perspectives of absolute morality. All the people on Planet Earth possess emotion and can speak personally about "universal" human rights. The example of the aggrieved individual who receives a nasty slap for no just reason is significant here. This man will vehemently protest his innocence wherever he finds himself and regardless of his cultural loyalties. He protests vehemently that he has been wronged because he is not guilty of any crime and has caused no offence. His being wronged is a violation of an absolute morality that looks up towards the fullest realization of freedom, an absolute morality which, in yearning for freedom, finds the discovery of freedom an impossibility and settles for the consolation of liberty in the joy-state of existence.

It is possible for this primal morality to be relativized by positive legal consideration in a court of law. It is possible for the judge handling the case of the man who was slapped to determine that the offender is mentally ill, a psychopath, a paranoid, etc. It is possible for the judge to insist that the mentally ill offender is not responsible for his action. That the offender is mentally disturbed does not take anything away from the fact that he has violated an absolute moral law stamped on the human mood as the value of joy in the universe. Absolute morality is recognized in popular language usage by the insistence that everyone has a right to be happy by pursuing goals that work for their happiness as long as their activities do not restrict the rights of others. But one can only be happy if one is free. One's euphoria is soon assailed by necessary impediments and dissolved into illusion. Everyone seeks the right to be happy. But what they actually find is the right to strive after goodness in the witnessing to liberty. Morality comes before happiness. In the absence of happiness morality finds consolation in joy. To fulfill the condition imposed by morality one does not have to be happy. All that is required is that one be a witness to liberty. It is therefore not true that morality cannot be grasped in its absoluteness. Absolute morality is not comprehended in the clouds, in abstract thought; rather it is grasped in everyday life and intellectually justified as the value of the emotion of joy in one's optimistic phase of thought in which the love of the intellect dominates.

The relativization of morality is actually the perspectivization of an absolute given in the human yearning for happiness. The innocent person who receives a nasty slap remains aggrieved because he thinks an absolute moral law has been violated, even if by a madman. The judge who declares that the mentally disturbed offender is not responsible for his action relativizes an absolute morality for the sake of humanity.

Alisdair MacIntyre has suggested that rational justifications are products of history and culture.[4] The idea of historical determinism dovetails into ethical constructivism over a period of time. Normative cultural relativism completes this picture with the claim that values are not universal but culture-bound. It is fitting for us to make it clear from the beginning that moral relations enjoy logical and real validity. But this validity is possible because of a prior moral absoluteness. To show how historical and cultural determinism can be subordinated to moral absolutism let us refer to the Africa cultural practice of polygyny which is not shared by the Western world, in principle at least. The African believer in polygyny sees nothing immoral in having many wives. He may refer to utilitarian determinants like needing a large family to help out in the fields to justify the cultural practice of polygyny. The Western monogamist, under the influence of Christianity, may insist that there is something wrong in the cultural practice. If the Westerner in question has become secular he may appeal to women's rights to prove the wrongness of polygyny. However hard he tries to appear non-judgmental, he is already passing judgment on the African. He has put himself in opposition to polygyny because he has made a moral judgment. The status of this judgment is absolute as the fundamental demand of a happiness ably represented by human joy. The position of the monogamist that a woman who has to compete with other women for the attention of her husband in a "harem" cannot be happy is a judgment rooted in the absoluteness of morality, the awareness of which is the object of morality.

That the concern of the Westerner is primarily moral and only secondarily cultural comes out clearly in the willingness of the Westerner to break the rules of strict monogamy and indulge in variants of polyandry and polygyny such as keeping multiple partners while in the condition of marriage, the tendency to dissolve a first marriage and subsequently contract multiple marriages, engaging in the liberal practice of swinging and spouse-swapping. The Westerner, having liberalized his environment, will no longer accuse the African of immorality. He will now adopt a liberal attitude towards unconventional conduct in the name of the pursuit of happiness. This Western monogamist turned liberal anarchist will now decide that if a woman is happy in an Africa harem he has no problem with the practice.

On the other hand, the African believer may dismiss the concern of his Western antagonist and declare African values independent of Western moral standards. He announces that his wives are happy because he takes good care of them, overlooking the issues of competition, jealousy, and hatred that assail the typical extended African family. He announces that having many wives and children makes him feel powerful and happy. Once again we are contending with a basic question of morality. The question of happiness is a moral question, not a cultural issue *per se*.

While we do not deny the validity of normative cultural relativism, we insist that this phenomenon is consumed by the objectivity and universality of morality. The validity of relative morality is rooted in the absolute morality of the demand of liberty. Culture itself is a set of values. A value may be tangible (for example a Cadillac) or intangible (for example, belief in God). Whether we are dealing with tangible or intangible cultural aspects, for value to be represented as real, the tangible and intangible must become emotion or have implications for human emotionality. It is the psychological interpretation of emotion that subjectivizes it. The metaphysics of terror which we have announced and elucidated in this work declares emotions objective states of the mind. Emotions exist, as truly as human beings exist. If they appear to succeed one another it is because a dialectic of *mood* is at work whose laws emotions obey. They are not mere appearance. In any case, an appearance is not something unreal but rather an illusion. The illusive is real. We tend to regard it as not permanent because it is expressed as the mythopoeic veil of existence. All values unfold out of the human mind in the context of what Western philosophy calls the *summum bonum*, the perfect good—freedom or happiness. This is the goal of cosmic yearning. This goal is humanly unattainable. Yet no void is left gaping in human life because joy fills up the space reserved for this desirable but unrealizable happiness. Culture itself is universal as a symbol attached to values unfolding out of the human mind. Culture can only be shown to be primarily relative if it is not instrumental for the pursuit of the perfect good, either for the humanity of the individual or the humanity of the collective (community). The individual and the community are already dependent on each other. Service to the individual is service to the community and service to both is service to humanity. We can juggle the three concepts of individuality, community, and humanity and reverse the order of dependability and still achieve a result of mutual moral benefit.

As long as culture unfolds on the horizon of yearning for the perfect good it is universal. What emboldens normative cultural relativism is the impossibility of the attainment of the perfect good, which compels multiplicity to find refuge in normative cultural perspectivization to grasp the profound problem of morality from easily accessible particular points of view. These points of view may stand alone, isolated one from the other, but they cannot detach themselves still from the universal standpoint of the yearning for the perfect good, an absolute value realizable in the state of freedom. Human joy is the consolation granted to one for the impossibility of freedom. The projection of the demand of this consolation into the demand of culture and its sundry particularist expressions makes culture primarily a universal phenomenon. The relativism of culture follows from the perspectivization of the demand of consolation.

Why do we ever think a deed is evil? Is it because one particular culture denounces it? If this is the case, why does another culture approve it? Whatever is evil remains evil, regardless of clashes of cultures. The evil deeds are immoral. Yet immoral deeds have their varying degrees of gravity. Cultural disagreement over the morality of polygyny, for example, is not as grave as cultural disagreement over the morality of the ancient African practice of the destruction of twins. Fortunately, most cultural disagreements are of the order of the clash between African polygyny and Western monogamy, in which case the objectivity of morality remains sacrosanct while the relativity of morality stands valid as the perspectivization of an absolute morality.

God and Morality

How can God be the giver of morality, the supreme lawgiver of the world? Our work is truly progressing with what has been achieved on the theme of consolationist theodicy in the relevant sections of the third chapter of Part Two. Our thought on humanity, God, and nature continues to unfold organically. We have made morality intimate with the furniture of the universe. This translates to making morality intimate with the structure of *mood*. With regard to the question of the origin of morality, we may either agree that morality exists independently of God or that He is the giver of morality. The objectivity of morality, which the analysis of *mood* has just justified, rules out a constructivist conception of morality. Neither the individual nor the society creates morality. The moral phenomenon is far too profound to be trivialized by the reference to society as the inventor of the moral code. To say the society creates morality is the same as saying a person constructs his own DNA and breathes reason into complex coded information systems within the DNA.

We endorse the two options before us. They combine well to explain the origin of morality, a phenomenon most remarkable in its manifestation as good and evil. Morality is intimate with the structure of *mood* and is given to objective nature by God who inspires the universe into being. The independence of morality is the cosmic history of its fatality and its contemporaneity with God. There could have been no God without morality just as there could be no morality without God. What are we saying? We have seen that determinism must fail to account for the existence of God and the existence of the universe. In the search for the sufficient grounds of the universe we must have recourse to fatalism, the inevitability of events, and not merely the inevitability of events but indeed this inevitability as a cosmic process of the unfolding of the dialectic of *mood*. The universe has been shown to exist necessarily and eternally, first in the eternity whose principle God is and then as the unfolding of creation out of the mind of God when God becomes power and glory with His conquest of the fear inherent in *mood*. Thus the contemporaneity of morality with God hollows out morality's own sphere of influence, the independence of morality. This indicates that God is not above morality. His coming into being caused the rising of morality. Neither is He inferior to morality. Without His emergence there would be no morality.

Yet the concept of morality is dependent on the concept of God. While it is true that morality is eternal, it is God who animates morality by first comprehending it in the act of self-knowledge which sees Him ceasing to be an impersonal fatalistic principle of the universe and becoming a personal principle. If the world God inspires is a necessary world it is because the processes of the dialectic of *mood* are necessary. These processes produce an imperfect world because they are grounded in emotion, fundamentally, rather than reason. This is why I say the universe is a fatality. It is not the necessity of its existence that is so compelling but the dialectic of *mood*, the emotional origin of things. God existed in eternity as a reason-seeking emotion. This emotion by its very nature is value. Morality lies in this value. God became self-knowledge as the reason of emotion. Without this first emergence of reason morality would not have become the object of knowledge. Fear would brood without knowing it carried good and evil within itself. In this regard it is true to assert that God is the author of morality. Without His transformation from impersonal principle of fatalism (the Eternal Mood) to the personal God of consolation there would be no consciousness of morality in the world, as truly as there would be no world and no one to contemplate nature and speculate about the awesome processes of the dialectic of *mood* which brought the world into the state of animated existence.

Why then would one wish to separate morality from religion or declare that morality did not, and still does not, need God? One may out of religious fanaticism elevate religion above morality. One may seek justification in revelation. Yet the goal of revelation is to throw light on the God-concept in a way that reason—so easily given to despair and nihilism—cannot do. Revelation does not invent God; it sheds light on the nature of God which reason cannot access as it is no longer bare emotion. The God whose nature revelation seeks to illuminate emerged with morality. If morality is contemporaneous with God, then there can be no religion without morality. This implies that ceremony, including miraculous events, cannot dethrone morality from its privileged position in the territory of religion. The contemporaneity of God with morality accounts for God's holiness and the popular saying that God is just where humans embrace injustice.

The tendency to magnify morality in its own right and diminish God and religion (as if God, morality, and religion are separable) is the outcome of the secularization of knowledge. This is an atheistic trend, and one that must be seen as a parasite feeding on the blood of religion. The opposite of religion is agnosticism, not atheism. The absence of belief in God is not atheism. The declaration that God does not exist is not of the same kind as the declaration that one does not know whether God exists. It is significant that atheists are more passionate about the question of God than agnostics. The atheist cannot be indifferent to the God question in the way that the agnostic can. In his disdain for, and hatred of, religion and God, the atheist espouses a new faith and consciously or unconsciously projects what we may call the religion of humanity. Indeed, Auguste

Comte went as far as weaving this "secular religion" around a secular priesthood, with its system of prayers, sacraments, and a calendar system that deified figures who had rendered great service to humanity.[5] It is the fate of atheism not to be able to stand alone. Its passion is derived entirely from the unlimited energy of theism or deism. Atheism is a proposition that follows the contemplation of theism and expresses itself as nihilism. Atheism is for this reason of dependency less threatening to the theist than agnosticism. The position of agnosticism is a most pathetic and ethically threatening position, for it craves a condition of anomie, an amorality that does not fit into the profoundly moral structure of the universe. Atheism must remain an appendage of religion, however loud the noise it makes, since it is completely lacking in originality. When religion says there is a God, atheism says there is no God. When religion says God is the author of morality, atheism declares that morality is independent of God without demonstrating how this is the case beyond asserting that morality is the creation of society, an assertion we have shown to be false with empirical and metaphysical arguments. The humanism atheism seeks to elevate to the status of a religion is itself the invention of religion, in particular the Christian religion with its emphasis on man as a being created in God's image, the emphasis on freedom and the radical moral equality of all human beings.

When we put the secularist narrative in its proper place, at a position of the appendage of religion, we can better appreciate the place of morality in religion, how the one enriches the other for the benefit of humanity. The inseparability of religion from morality mirrors the inseparability of the God-concept and the concept of morality, ultimately the contemporaneity of God and morality. The rejection of the existence of God does not free us from the burden of questioning a bare naturalistic account of morality. The adjective "naturalistic" is derived from the noun "nature." Nature is conceived as the totality of things and forces outside the human mind. When secularists refer to the noun "nature" they actually mean a blind nature, the aimless working of things and forces which now and again succeeds in realizing rationality. The testimony of common sense will convince the observer of nature that the very second one uses the noun "nature" one is already referring to God, or some living principle, a First Cause, etc. Avoiding the term "God" for whatever reason does not alter the situation.

So we find ourselves taking over from the puzzled observer of nature. We find ourselves asking whether a blind nature can sustain its power in the intensely emotional universe we have described in this book. We realize once again the impossibility of reifying nature without personalizing it and arriving at the idea of God. In fact, this exercise, symptomatic of the profoundly anthropomorphic tendency of the human mind, has been started and completed quite unconsciously the moment we commence the contemplation of nature. The contemplation of nature leads us to the same reification of chance, and the same conclusion arrived at while we discussed mechanicism in relation to the evolutionary universe and the emergence and development of life-forms. Naturalism loses out even in its own territory. To stubbornly stick with the naturalist account of morality is to put faith in the most superficial empiricism, a way of refusing to look beyond one's nose for fear of perceiving things that shatter one's illusions. Whether we believe in God or in nature, what cannot be doubted is that we have here forcefully attempted to provide a credible argument for the objectivity of morality in the consolationist perspective by appealing directly to indisputable facts of human life, the facts of joy and sadness.

Chapter Eleven

ANATOMY OF THE MELANCHOLY BEING

The Melancholy Being

The *melancholy being* is not a crying philosopher. He is not a weak-willed pessimist who crumbles in the face of existential obstacles and retreats into the solitude of his mind. We have promoted the *melancholy being* as the universal man. We have defined the *melancholy being* as the creature of joy and sadness, the human phenomenon whose entire life is the struggle to reconcile pessimism with optimism in fidelity to the enduring law of a universe expressed both as beauty and terror. While we are convinced that the great Senghor caught a philosophical glimpse of the *melancholy being*, we note that he could not proceed to make him a universal man. Whatever profound insight he gained with regard to the term *melancholy* could not have surpassed its psychological connotation of grief. But to equate this philosophically significant term with mere grief is to celebrate the ridiculous. Asouzu went further philosophically by underlining the joy element of *melancholy*, asserting that humankind was moving progressively towards the realization of a greater state of the joy of being in humanity's future referentiality.

However, Asouzu moved too sharply to the side of optimism and kept losing the *melancholy being*. Hence, he did not quite succeed in giving African philosophy a constructive alternative program to ethno-philosophy after surpassing Senghor. We have now stepped in to put the inspiration of Senghor in proper philosophical focus. The *melancholy being* is black, white, brown, yellow, red, etc. He is in Europe campaigning for the elimination of all forms of control in society. He is in Africa struggling to understand a modern world in which he does not want to be the last. He is in China dreaming of world domination. The *melancholy being* is an anarchist; he is a visionary, dreaming of a better world for all. He is tyrannical, plotting wars in his mind and spreading the message of death. The *melancholy being* is in the Middle East fighting a war for God which God does not require. He is a terrorist who cannot complete the fundamental moral act and therefore turns away from embracing the concept of the anonymity of sacrifice. The *melancholy being* is in Asia pursuing economic progress. What we cannot doubt is the fact that the *melancholy being* is intensely emotional and vigorously intellectual. He lives in a techno-emotive world today and uses propaganda to promote his beliefs as he seeks to impose those beliefs on others.

He schemes perpetually and seeks advantage for himself while making a lot of fuss about being a humanist. Even as he schemes with all his might, he fights a losing war with his fellow human beings and, ultimately, with nature. Confronted by the forces of disease and death, he knows that every victory he records is a pyrrhic victory. Yet he is so brave, so optimistic, that he chooses to die clinging. He insists he will die still propagating his beliefs. The *melancholy being* is a natural activist, a witness to liberty. Whatever his shortcomings may be, his vices and foibles, he is acting from a profoundly moral standpoint. The moral task before the *melancholy being* is how to lift emotion to the level of reason through the stages of despair, anxiety, and intellectual love. He encounters and is intimidated by the task of transforming basic pessimism into optimism internalized as joy and externalized as good will to meet the yearning of intellectual love. Yet this is a task that must be accomplished if one is to successfully witness to liberty and halt one's slide into a purely emotional life in which one not only does not care to know but brutally refuses to know. This is the condition that breeds moral evil in the world. It is true that human beings are inherently good, but this picture of basic goodness is only complete if it is acknowledged that they are also inherently bad. One cannot help not being fundamentally bad. The justification of one's moral responsibility is the keen knowledge of their own badness and their capacity to be a witness to liberty.

In this chapter I will discuss practical topics such as anxiety, despair, resignation, death, and immortality in the perspective of consolation philosophy. Since the perspective established throughout this work is idealistic, in this chapter I will not regard these topics as merely existentialist themes. I prefer to regard the consolationist perspective as a "post-postmodernist" perspective from Africa. The construction and analysis in this chapter will be essentially horizontal, although we will not hesitate to return to the vertical analysis of *mood* to support our practical viewpoints.

Human Empathy and Its Philosophical Grounds

Empathy is a capacity and phenomenon of human consciousness. It is a sentiment truly but a noble sentiment all the same. Empathy features significantly in the life of the *melancholy being*. It is the same thing as sympathy. The philosophical justification of empathy is found in the nature of optimism. Optimism testifies to the correctness of empathy. To desire to understand humanity is to acknowledge one's membership of the community, to admit one's humanity, and applaud the endurance of the *melancholy being*. A person seeks to understand the other or my Brother or Sister only after overcoming nihilism and its solipsist aspect. This overcoming of nihilism convinces me that my Brother exists as an independent reality full of value in accordance with the prescription of *mood* which is itself the fullness of value. Thus to be empathetic is to be optimistic. The coldly indifferent human being does not act in the sphere of rationality; indeed, he has left the sphere of rationality and is sunk in the negative emotional state of nihilism. Under the power of despair and pessimism he has ceased to be a witness to liberty. He is already in a state in which evil thrives, the state that alarms the clinical psychologist who may suspect the onset of depression and psychosis.

We have so far constructed a universe of consolation, elevating metaphysics and again uniting it with ethics. The universe we have revealed is one in which the cosmic music of melancholy echoes the *mood* of all eternity in the condition of silence. A universe such as the one we have constructed cannot but embrace human empathy as an impulse of intellectual love—the warm engagement with humanity, the constant adoration of God as the most high, and solidarity with nature. Empathy enlivens the pure thought of God and what is good for the continuing endurance of the *melancholy being*. The first sign of human optimism is the capacity to empathize. The noble emotion of empathy which is reason emerging out of raw emotion has now become possible in one who is at this point without the slightest doubt that the external world exists and houses one's fellow human beings. Empathy is a capacity of the optimistic phase of thought in which it is impossible to dream evil.

To be empathetic then is to arrive at a conclusion, to decide that optimism is a reality in a fatalistic universe. To become empathetic is to make a decision that in spite of the obvious terror of human existence the reality of beauty cannot be denied. This decision, reflecting optimism, has gone through the mental stages of fear, despair, and anxiety. This victory of consciousness over itself denies the condition of indeterminism which the analysis of an illusive freedom threatens to throw up.

Since optimism is so important for empathy, how do we protect optimism from determinism which fills the space vacated by the illusion of freedom? The emotion of joy practically vindicates optimism and protects it from the law of cause and effect. Optimism is connected with morality. Joy can rise in the midst of an unfavorable state of affairs as long as one witnesses to liberty. What will happen will happen, but the happening of that fated to happen unfolds fatalistically in a consolatory universe. Hence the primacy of the emotion of joy and sadness. To deny optimism is to deny the reality of human joy which is impossible. The lightest laugh is always available to disturb the nihilist. A lengthy discussion of optimism is not necessary now since we have already done this in the previous chapter.

The idea that empathy is symptomatic of the weak-willed human being or that it is a form of teary sentimentalism is the unfounded luxury of meaninglessly abstract thinking. With the doctrine of *mood*, however, we have elevated emotion (psycho-logic) to the level of reason, restoring to emotion the intellectual dignity belonging rightfully to it. We have found a philosophical basis for human emotion by appealing to philosophical fatalism which is a theoretical reconstruction of the universe. In announcing a fundamentally consolatory universe, whose rationality is a consequence of a supreme emotionality, we parted ways with German idealism. While Arthur Schopenhauer described a profoundly bleak universe Leibniz intuited an optimistic universe and vainly sought to explain evil away. Schopenhauer intuited a pointless universe and vainly sought to comprehend the aspect of beauty the "pointless" universe manifests. The great pessimist failed to understand how *yearning* could hold the meaning of consolation. So he was largely satisfied with his metaphysics of terror. Even for the greatest pessimist in philosophy, the morality of consolation held its own intellectual attraction. After failing to find beauty in the world, Schopenhauer proceeded to enunciate a morality of resignation. The notion of resignation already presupposes consolation. The metaphysics of terror cannot overwhelm the morality of consolation, a clear indication that the universe is not pointless. It is only pointless for the radical determinist and the radical libertarian demanding rationality independent of emotionality, insisting naively on a perfect universe.

By enunciating a morality of consolation, Schopenhauer inadvertently questioned the insularity of his metaphysics of terror. In his masterpiece *The World as Will and Idea* he celebrated a humanistic morality. Specifically, in the famous essay "On the Suffering of the World" he enjoins us to address one another as "my fellow sufferer" rather than as "mister" or "mein herr" or "monsieur" in the name of empathy. There is nothing out of place here since we, in fact, use such terms as "brother," and "sister," and "comrade." The acknowledgment of the necessity of the morality of consolation makes him a deeper thinker than his brilliant, exuberant, and highly iconoclastic successor Nietzsche. Having lionized Schopenhauer as his "great teacher," Nietzsche proceeds to criticize his predecessor for proposing a morality of pity that he felt ended in denying life altogether in favor of a certain oriental nihilism. Nietzsche casts himself as the champion of optimism by seeking to replace the *will to live* with the *will to power*. But he never really transcended pessimism and succeeded, ironically, in radicalizing Schopenhauer's pessimism by embracing a comprehensively nihilist philosophy, thereby paving the way for the despairing doctrines and iconoclasm of postmodernist thought. About pity which is in fact different from the empathy Schopenhauer recommends, Nietzsche writes thus in *The Genealogy of Morals*:

> I had to fight this issue out almost alone with my great teacher Schopenhauer... The point at issue was the value of the non-egotistical instincts, the instincts of compassion, self-denial, and self-sacrifice, which Schopenhauer above all others had consistently gilded, glorified, "transcendentalized" until he came to see them as *absolute* values allowing him to deny life and even himself... It was here, precisely, that I sensed the greatest danger for humanity, its sublimest delusion and temptation—leading it whither? into nothingness? Here I sensed the beginning of the end, stagnation, nostalgic fatigue, a will that had turned *against* life.[1]

It must always be noted that Nietzsche's "masculine" concept of the *will to power* is fundamentally a response to the futility of human existences which I premised not merely on the reality of evil in the world but, more importantly, on the fact of the appearance of a world humans did not create and therefore cannot tame, a world whose origin one can only speculate on. Suffering is tied to this human powerlessness. Nietzsche's exuberant optimism lost itself in contradiction because he tried to pretend that all was well with the world, that necessity can explain the problem of evil. By shutting his eyes to the terror of existence which Schopenhauer saw with a clarity that blinded him, Nietzsche was never going to have the insight into a consolatory universe which softened the great pessimist enough to afford him a level of insight into the necessity of the consolation Nietzsche denounces as pity. Expectedly, Nietzsche the false optimist lost faith in the values he met and called for a reevaluation of the old values to pave the way for an illusory superman who, ironically, would remain subject to emotional perturbations, continue to feel like an ordinary human, and suffer appropriately. This superman is just a mortal anarchist who must reject God, undermine the idea of humanity, sneer at women, dismiss the notion of purpose, and seek power more abundant. This superman will have to be self-sufficient to be really super. If he has to be part of the community of human beings as only a gifted individual, then the concept of the *will to power* does not escape pessimism. Pessimism is the starting point of human knowledge of the world. Any optimism that discounts pessimism, such as Nietzsche's, will yield an extremist doctrine of man and woman, life, and the world, and get itself lost in nihilist contradictions.

Nietzsche at least admitted that all great philosophies, including his own, no doubt, are a form of confession and a kind of involuntary autobiography.[2] If we take this admission seriously, and I think we must, we may safely assume that Nietzsche is raising a lamentation for himself in the following lines while characteristically pretending to be giving us a true picture of Jesus Christ.

> It is possible that under the holy fable and travesty of the life of Jesus there is hidden one of the most painful cases of the martyrdom of *knowledge about love*: the martyrdom of the most innocent and craving heart, that never had enough of any human love, that *demanded* love, that demanded inexorably and frantically to be loved and nothing else, with terrible outbursts against those who refused him their love; the story of a poor soul insatiated and insatiable in love, that had to invent hell to send thither those who *would not* love him—and that at last, enlightened about human love, had to invent a God who is entire love, entire capacity for love.[3]

It is arguable whether Nietzsche was referring to himself or was convinced he had painted the real picture of Christ. What is beyond contest is that Nietzsche acknowledges the depth of frustration that assails the human heart and which is revealed in human behavior. This frustration is real because human life seems futile. Frustration is a response to futility. We have already clarified what this term means to us. Any philosophy that has not grappled with the question of futility can never successfully pose itself as optimistic. Nietzsche's teachings on the reevaluation of values and the superman constitute such a philosophy. The celebration of the *will to power* is a hasty response to a futility that predates celebration. As a response to that which is primal and overpowering, the celebration of the *will to power* must lose its coherence in the dissolution into discordant nihilist standpoints. This is the result Nietzsche achieves with his master-morality doctrine. The strenuous pursuit of power by force of will leads to the human attempt to replace God as the consolation of the world (something humans can never be, anyway); the *will to power* leads to the trampling on the rights of the powerless, the elimination of foundations for the emergence of a certain normlessness in social relations, precisely the wilful refusal of one to complete the moral act. This wilfulness will always yield existential tension because every human act is born in morality. This morality is not the master-morality of Nietzsche but the morality of consolation which Schopenhauer intuited but never clarified.

The following passage from Nietzsche reveals the bravado behind his conception of the *will to power*:

> Every animal, including *la bête philosophe,* strives instinctively for the optimum conditions under which it may release its powers. Every animal, instinctively and with a subtle flair that leaves reason far behind, abhors all interference that might conceivably block its path to that optimum. (The path I am speaking of does not lead to "happiness" but to power, to the most energetic activity, and in a majority of cases to actual unhappiness).[4]

Power without happiness is futility. Nietzsche's genius is not in doubt. His writing shines forth with flash after flash of brilliant insight. Yet this exciting brilliance is marked by the exaggeration of a deeply iconoclastic spirit. Nietzsche traded profundity for intellectual excitement. Philosophy, to be true, cannot deny the reality of which it is a product, not creator. This reality subsists in futility, hence the validity of pessimism. The same reality manifests beauty, hence the validity of optimism. Nevertheless, pessimism is so fundamental that optimism must find its bearing with constant reference to pessimism.

Empathy is the consequence of optimism finding its bearing with direct reference to a pessimism which arises as knowledge of life's futility, the position of human beings in the universe, whose consummation of peace is the state of oblivion Schopenhauer promoted, something which is a tragedy in itself, being truly an eternal peace in eternal melancholy. In a consolatory universe, to empathize is to be optimistic, to come out of a discredited solipsism and endorse the reality of humanity on the basis of faith in intellectual love which is the height of human sublimity, beyond which nothing better for mankind can be found. Empathy and pity are not the same. Pity is a degeneration of empathy. It is truly nihilistic, as Nietzsche noted. Pity is nihilistic because it has lost sight of optimism and withdrawn into the sphere of pessimism. Human empathy stands on solid grounds. No sane philosophical reasoning can invalidate it without obliterating the world and humanity by philosophical fiat. The skeptical philosopher in his isolated study can humor himself that the external world is unreal in his moment of intellectual grandeur, but his philosophical pronouncement will not alter the smallest detail in the fact that people are passing on the street and making a lot of noise metres away from the window of his study.

Despair

Despair is another phenomenon of consciousness that confounds logic. It is itself the logic of pessimism. As an emotion, it plays a prominent role in the dialectic of *mood*. While fear is the consequence of our awareness of the futility of life, this awareness itself has despair as its sense, its logic. Despair is the denizen of thought. As the impish denizen of thought, it is the burden of the intellect, in a similar way that consciousness is the burden of human life and is declared a disease by Unamuno in his *Tragic Sense of Life*. Despair characterizes the intellect in its pessimistic phase of thought, urging it towards the questioning of all foundations without being capable of replacing old discredited foundations with newer and reliable foundations. Thus despair has been compared by us to an imp.

Despair informs the coldness of mind a thinker is inclined to call indifference or disinterest. Our situation in the world frustrates our desires. This frustration brings on disappointments. When these disappointments linger they transform into the state of despair from which the intellect sees no escape in affirmatory existence and proposes the embrace of all or limited aspects of negatory existence. For instance, Schopenhauer says human life is worthless and that the only cure for this worthlessness is extinction or transition into oblivion, the stilling of the *will to live*. Sartre cannot find God, so he concludes that God does not exist. A man suffers heartbreak at the hands of a woman and becomes a misogynist. A woman who proclaims herself a feminist convinces herself that all men are responsible for the suffering of women and becomes a misandrist. Schopenhauer forgets that there are good things in life. Sartre forgets that others have found God through faith. The man who learns to hate women because one woman treated him badly forgets that there are women who have been treated badly by men. The rabid feminist conveniently forgets that Schopenhauer has enjoined us to address one another as "my fellow sufferer" because everyone suffers in the world.

The foregoing affords us a peep into the intensely emotional world of the human phenomenon. Where is this emotion coming from? The psychologist says it is coming from disappointment and the sense of hopelessness triggered by traumatic events in the social environment. This is not a bad explanation. The psychological explanation can be empirically confirmed. Philosophy can come to the aid of the psychologist to more intimately describe "depression." We have shown in a previous section that crime is an act of surrender to despair. The psychologist pinpoints a social or biological element that triggers the reaction that amounts to human despair and depression, but he has no stomach for ethics and metaphysics and so condemns his knowledge to a kind of bare practice. The philosopher steps in with his ideas about evil, free will, necessity and moral responsibility. After providing a deeper picture of the problem of despair with reference to the moral environment and the metaphysical foundation he assures the psychologist that there is a philosophical basis of human empathy, that the demand of love has already been endorsed by philosophy for the amelioration of the despair of the *melancholy being*.

The path to this amelioration is the path of anxiety. The *melancholy being* is a person of action. All actions are born in morality and seek completion. Since despair is inevitable in the affairs of the *melancholy being* and since the realization of intellectual love provides the standard for normality, despair must be transformed into anxiety for psychological harm to be averted. One may fight against circumstances beyond his control and protest vehemently, but must become a lover of fate by recognizing himself as a morally responsible being, one whose duty it is to complete the moral act which is in fact every human act. *Amor fati* calms despair (which goes together with depression) and carries anxiety over into intellectual love.

Anxiety

Human consciousness registers life's futility by activating the emotion we call despair. As the logic of existence emotion demands consolation which human reason endorses as the goal of existence. The course of despair takes it through the stage of anxiety. Human anxiety is distinguished from fear because the latter is fundamentally consequent upon our awareness of the fatality of existence, the inescapability of the sense of the immensity of things unknown and the infinitude of the things never to be known. The psychologist who tries to calm the neurotic individual by assuring him that there is nothing to be afraid of knows himself to be a fraud. There is so much to be afraid of even in the phenomenal world. The *melancholy being* must be afraid of loss of job, poverty, heartbreak, disease, death, disappointment, wars, failure in one endeavor or the other, and other ills too numerous to itemize. The pessimistic character of anxiety prepares us to face these disappointments. Yet anxiety, even as it is possessed of a pessimistic character—the sense of foreboding—is already turning its face towards optimism, already evolving liberty and the determination to witness to this liberty by first embracing fate and then resisting it in what is nothing more than ethical struggle. The person who throws himself into the ethical struggle of life, who witnesses to liberty, is he who is called a lover of fate. The lover of fate is not the quietist or the uncritical fatalist. The one who embraces *amor fati* is the one who witnesses to liberty. For, ultimately, anxiety is a sign of the coming apotheosis of man, the foundation of peace.

The psychologist is either too shallow or too insincere to tell the neurotic client waiting to benefit from psychoanalysis and cognitive-behavioral therapy that although this apotheosis is indicated, it is yet impossible. Thus he tells the *melancholy being* prone to anxiety disorders not to be afraid, that psychology has identified the genetic, psychological and social causes of anxiety. The psychologist tells the neurotic that if the procedures of psychoanalysis and cognitive-behavioral therapy do not succeed there is always the option of using tranquilizers like benzodiazepines and antidepressants like tricyclics, and even the desperate option of brain surgery. While it is beyond doubt that the psychologist's method does assist the anxiety-prone *melancholy being* to cope with the emotionality of his nature—after all, the non-clinical solution to anxiety derives its efficacy from the notion of empathy which we have provided philosophical support—his tendency to regard the state of anxiety as abnormal is not in order. He may defend himself by insisting that he is concerned only with anxiety as a form of mood disorder, anxiety that has overleaped the sphere of rational control. But, then, the mildest anxiety is already a *neurosis* of the *melancholy being*.

It is necessary for the psychologist to recognize that not only is anxiety a sign of the human apotheosis but also that this apotheosis is impossible, regardless of scientific intoxication with the powers of technology and obsession with the myth of the superman. In other words, the psychologist must not replace the pastor and overlook ethics in the name of secularity. Anxiety is the most remarkable fact of consciousness, the salvation of despair and the pessimism despair engenders. The God which the despairing person loses the anxious person seeks to find through anxiety. In human anxiety the love of freedom lives. Since one cannot be free, anxiety turns the despairing person in the direction of intellectual love, a state of mind in which faith is complete in the love of God, the love of humanity, and solidarity with nature, one's healthiest psychological state. The state of intellectual love cannot be attained without an encounter with anxiety and the successful resolution of the ethical crisis the state of anxiety engenders.

We discover that fear is basic as humanity's final awareness of its pathetic condition. Here is one who does not know where he is coming from and where he is going, who has only two options in life as a way of reacting to his pathetic condition, the option of believing in a God who has not materialized as the sufficient grounds of the universe and the option of embracing an atheistic view that dismisses the universe as an aimless expression of a blind chance. Here we find the philosophical grounds of fear which eludes the psychologist. Anxiety on the other hand has evolved out of fear and is no longer synonymous with despair. In anxiety the worst has been confirmed. In anxiety fear has been justified to human consciousness. While despair leads one towards nihilism, anxiety seeks a solution to the problem of despair, however imperfect this solution may be. Anxiety demands self-transcendence. For this reason we hail human anxiety as the most remarkable fact of human consciousness, a sign of an impossible apotheosis and yet the foundation of peace. Anxiety awakens the moral and pro-life impulse of optimism which despair crushes. Anxiety reminds the *melancholy being* that God and not an impossible "nil" is the foundation of his peace, the consolation of the world. The human mind is an awesome unity of elastic *mood*, for it is *mood*. Every process is linked to a preceding operation in the perpetual transformation of *mood*. There is continuity and continuum.

Anxiety is the dream of self-transcendence. Despair loses its destructive power when the vision of intellectual love comes into focus. At this stage morality becomes religion and the pure thought of what is good becomes the dream of God. Human beings are eager to see their dreams fulfilled. This vision is seen in the optimistic phase of thought, but it keeps receding as it is approached. Pessimism and optimism complete each other to dominate human life. Since anxiety itself is not intellectual love, the anxious person suffers emotionally. He visits the psychologist or the pastor in search of a faith in God that he thinks he has lost at an earlier period when he thought it was necessary for God to materialize for him to believe. The psychologist tricks the anxious person into believing that psychology is a perfect substitute for religion. In this regard the psychoanalyst is a voodoo pastor and the expert in cognitive-behavioral therapy a witch doctor.

The secular existentialist philosophers Heidegger and Sartre missed the mark by several inches, Sartre recording a wider margin of error. One cannot be condemned to a freedom that is not real. The condemnation of humanity is the condemnation to fear, despair, and anxiety. These are all elements of fatalism and not freedom. The nothingness anxiety seems to reveal as Heidegger suggested without exploring in any detail, the apparent meaninglessness of human life and universal existence in general, is the sadness of existence. The barest state of this sadness is the silence of eternity. (See the relevant sections of Chapter Three of Part Three for further illumination of the issue just mentioned).

Practical and transcendental limitations stand between human beings and their apotheosis. Let us dwell briefly on the person whose most urgent need is food. He is hungry and may not have enough money in his pocket to buy himself lunch. After overcoming this limitation, after getting lunch money by fair or foul means, he realizes that there is still life outside the restaurant. He realizes that the satisfaction of his great hunger has only solved one problem out of many. At the end of every laugh sobriety returns to mock his earlier humor. He tells himself he is a failure. Yet time is running out for him. He is not going to live forever. He earnestly desires consolation. While despair justifies atheism, anxiety is a longing for God. The song of existence that the *melancholy being* composes is a woeful song. But it is in the sadness of this great song that he sees the shape of joy which he proceeds to seize. He is by nature a lover of God. It does not matter whether he replaces God with chance, science, money, sex, etc. He is doomed to always make a transcendental appeal. Humanity has a mind that is so great that it thinks God in anthropomorphic terms, a thing probability sanctions.

The *melancholy being* is the focus of two antagonistic forces, one life-denying and the other life-affirming, one seemingly negative and the other seemingly positive, both valid and true. Pessimism versus optimism. Ultimately, anxiety is not a lamentation of nothingness or an indication of meaninglessness. Anxiety is intimate with one's hope of transcendence and the promise of self-transcendence. For anxiety to reveal nothingness there must be a degeneration to despair. Despair must trace its origin to the eternal *mood* of sadness. This basic sadness must fill the universe in its simplest form as silence. Beyond this silence of eternity, the nucleus of all that is—matter, mind, energy—there is nothing to be encountered. Silence is the foundation of *mood*.

As a preparation for the embrace of *amor fati* anxiety turns away from that which denies life. Anxiety turns away from despair towards consolation, even as consolation has not been guaranteed finally but is being realized gradually. The culmination of this consolation is the materialization of God, what Christians call the coming of God's kingdom and what Marxists predict as the age of a classless society. This would see humans reaching their moral apotheosis, for they would have completed the process of self-transcendence to enjoy an era of eternal peace.

I said earlier that eternal peace for humans is eternal melancholy. The anxious person imagines his self-transcendence. This state of anxiety is taut with tension due to the impossibility of the completion of the process of self-transcendence. It will take the intervention of a God who is benevolent, glorious, and powerful for humanity to be adequately comforted. Truly, anxiety is as full of tension as despair, but unlike despair it nurses hope and renews faith. The state of anxiety enables one to construct hopes and dreams according to the plan of self-transcendence with the thought of God either in the foreground or in the background and the thought of good ever in the foreground. Believers put the idea of God in the foreground together with the idea of goodness while non-believers think they can dispense with the idea of God. Yet the two ideas are so related that they have become inseparable. The notion of a benevolent supreme principle of the universe animates one's natural morality with living warmth and confers comforting values on the effort that moves him towards the completion of self-transcendence, which he immediately recognizes as self-expression towards self-realization shorn of all metaphysical significance at the God-man interface and later as the search for God.

If the *melancholy being* is never going to find his supreme consolation (God) he is also never going to achieve self-transcendence although transcendence is already within his reach. All he can hope to achieve is the small mundane progress within reach, such as falling in love and getting married, graduating from institutions of higher learning, having children, securing a job, finding solace in various agreeable forms of activism, having much fun, dreaming of going to the nearest paradise of his imagination (for example, the moon or Mars), etc. The elimination of the God-factor will give us the dry and bare picture of human life. The picture is also a dirty picture. With faith gone, evil will multiply on earth. Islamic terrorists may disappear, but they will be replaced by secular terrorists who will create their secular religions and fight for what they believe to bring consolation. Mercifully, elimination of the God-factor is a psychological and sociological impossibility. The *melancholy being* whose moodiness we have since explored is an incurable God-lover like Spinoza and Leibniz. For him anxiety is always a sign of his self-transcendence and the foundation of peace. He rests this hope in a Being greater than himself. This phenomenon called a human being is a being of faith that only has to affirm and be convinced even while he doubts the reality of the absolute. Consolation is the beauty of existence, creating hope where there seems to be none. The anxiety that emphasizes the terror of existence is the same phenomenon of consciousness that moves one to positive action in self-determination, self-expression, and self-realization.

Despair is an emotional evil only intellectual love can tame. The mediator between these two phenomena is the phenomenon of anxiety. Human thinking is never cold because despair inhabits thought. When one declares himself indifferent he merely attempts to protect himself from possible disappointments. The state of indifference, however, cannot help him avoid anxiety since he lives in a world which exists independent of him. The objective world will sooner or later disturb his incomplete peace. Events in the objective world will compel him to react. He either becomes resigned or he goes into rebellion against the world by embracing the claim that the reality of the external world is not certain and that he is only certain of his own existence. In other words, he finds refuge in skepticism and cynicism. Resignation is the non-violent acceptance of the fatality of life while rebellion is the nihilist response to tragedy. Indeed, indifference is a form of resignation. Ethical activism is the most valid form of resignation. In ethical activism nihilism has already been rejected so that humans consciously act as moral agents. The ethical activist has successfully negotiated the despair-laden and anxiety-laden phases of the mind and is consciously projecting himself as a witness to liberty. He has become true to transcendental humanism, no longer satisfied with moral skepticism and the constructivist conception of morality. Ethical activism affirms the intimacy of morality with human consciousness, the *mood* of the world, and everything in existence. The transcendental humanist may be religious or secular. What makes him a transcendental humanist is the fact that he has turned his back on moral anarchy and has embraced liberty.

Humanity rises to intellectual love from the state of anxiety, having come to terms finally with the fatality of the universe. What remains is ethical activism. Albert Camus called this *revolt* and Heidegger chose *resoluteness*. In intellectual love the anger of the pessimist which is often unleashed on the world as crime becomes the warmth of the optimist which is always beneficial to the world. In his pessimistic phase of thought the *melancholy being* whose intellect has embraced *amor fati* experiences sadness rather than anger. In his optimistic phase of thought he exudes joy. As a lover of faith and activist of the highest order, he pursues peace, finds it, and goes on to expand the sphere of peace to the best of his ability. The fascination of the 20th and 21st centuries with Nelson Mandela rests on the fact that more than any other African political leader of the 20th century Mandela understood the politics of "eternal democracy" which anxiety energizes. He understood politics as an activity in which an anxious set of men and women seeking dominant powers clash with a larger set of anxious men and women resistant to domination. The former comes under the category of politicians while the latter is called the people whose voice is the voice of God. Armed with this intuitive knowledge Mandela was able to calm the anxiety of white South Africa after the collapse of apartheid and pursue the project of reconciliation.

Human anxiety is integral to the affirmation of faith in life. We see no hope for humanity if we make the retrograde shift to despair by surrendering completely to this impish denizen of thought for the mere fact that God has not materialized and not the fact that anxiety remains just a sign of our possible apotheosis. The non-materialization of God must not translate to an endorsement of nihilism. Fatalism will not and cannot justify nihilism. The objectivity of morality has ensured that whether we believe in the existence of God or not we are witnesses to liberty. Neither the challenges of life, whose beauty contrasts sharply with the terror that highlights the painful plight of mankind endemic on a planetary scale, nor the uncertainties surrounding death and immortality can alter the empirical fact that the *melancholy being* is a witness to liberty.

Death and Immortality

Life is the positive affirmation of the validity of fatalistic will and the subsequent reinforcement of cosmic inspiration in direct relation to intellectual love. The unity of life reveals the complexity of existence. At one moment this complexity is simplified (for example, the moment of laughter) while at another moment the simplification becomes a complexity (for example, the moment of death).

The phenomenon of death calls for philosophical reflection, not mere analysis. We are to weigh life and death on the practical horizontal scale and the transcendental vertical scale. Death is an empirical certainty endorsed by the laws of evolution which pursue the continuity of the human race and the elongation of the line of adaptable human beings. Yet, for many, immortality is a hope. This is spiritual immortality. The plausibility of the aspiration of spiritual immortality strikes one when one considers the depth of the desire for continuity in nature and in the human soul which has found expression in the dream of biological and physical or technological immortality, the fond hope that a time would come when science would be advanced enough to eliminate death-causing diseases and put a stop to human cell senescence, when it would be possible to upload the content of human consciousness to a physical medium like a computer while retaining and sustaining some form of personal identity.[5]

Human existence is like a bottomless pit. We peer into this fearful pit and see profound darkness instead of the bottom. Shall we blame the man who throws himself in despair into this bottomless pit, thereby obliquely justifying the famous assertion of Albert Camus in *The Myth of Sisyphus* that the problem of suicide is the most serious question for philosophy?[6] This is definitely an exaggeration since suicide has its antecedent in the phenomenon of despair, indicated by moral philosophy and metaphysics as the impish denizen of thought. The theme of evil rather than suicide is philosophy's biggest question, and this is the case only because the question of death leads us to the fundamental question of the origin and destiny of humanity in particular and the universe in general. Death is the last evil one suffers on earth. This puts forward the question of God as the greatest question of philosophy. The transcendental appeal that one necessarily makes bypasses humanity and anchors firmly in the God-concept, regardless of the fact that unbelief persuades us to find a substitute for God in human beings (who, unfortunately, make the transcendental appeal), in science (which reifies chance and imbues bare mechanicism with the character of purpose), in money, sex, fame, etc.

Death refers us to the God-concept with the possibilities of extinction and survival coming between us and God. Death itself is a terror of human existence. And it is disputable whether there can be a happy ending for us. A peaceful ending is possible, but the idea of a happy ending must embrace the reality of immortality and our final apotheosis, the realization of freedom. Death is a terror, therefore a real evil—indeed, the last suffering of humanity—because it terminates a process which enables the human phenomenon to grasp the notion of beauty and consolation. The anxious person staring out of the window of his room on the thirtieth floor of an imposing skyscraper who, on an impulse of *mood* or after a long deliberation, throws himself out of the window and perishes in the street far below to the horror of passersby is declared to have killed himself. The architectural masterpiece that used to appear majestic to him in happier days as a symbol of the tenacious and audacious human spirit has suddenly been obliterated with the death of the one who used to contemplate the beautiful. But it is despair that anchors this suicide. The way backwards to *mood* magnifies fear and pessimism. The suicide has seen the night of his mind without seeing the light of his life.

Pessimism seeks to justify death as a blessing, a release from a meaningless existence. The pessimist hopes that death opens the door to the ultimate nil, the profound nothingness. But this is merely a hope, at the level of the notion of immortality. What can pessimism say if there is no nil, what can pessimism gain if there was a nil in the beginning of all beginnings, but which nil has been filled up to the extent that it can no longer be? The nil might have been filled up with cosmic sadness as one meaning of existence, but what happens to the oblivion of the pessimist if death cannot open any door to total extinction? This situation may mean that life and emotion are one and that the woes of humanity do not end with death. It may also mean the possibility of immortality and moral apotheosis. What form immortality will take is disputable. What cannot be in doubt is that for any form of survival to be possible a Being vastly superior to men or a principle acting purposefully throughout the universe must confer this privilege. Death answers no question and solves no problem. Death is a speculation on extinction and survival merely. Indeed, death is an evil which deprives one of the beauty of consolation without guaranteeing him oblivion or survival. If one survives it will be at the pleasure of a higher being or a supreme principle. Thus human apotheosis is postponed indefinitely. If it is extinction that awaits us this means passage from a state of awareness of the condition of beauty and terror to a state of non-awareness of the condition of beauty and terror, the latter being what we have called silence. In other words, oblivion cannot cancel out the tragedy of existence. The dead man continues to exist in a state of ignorance, unable to enjoy the dubious luxury of awareness.

Death is futile. It represents a loss to humanity. By now we understand what futility means. Life's futility finds solace in consolation. The futility of death animates life, invigorating morality and the lives which death has left behind. One person's death reads a lesson to the person who is still alive. The meaning of death at the horizontal level is its positive implication for the gospel of life, the ethics of life. Placed side by side with death, life outshines death and emphasizes its own aspect of beauty, as that which is a lesser evil than death and bestows the power of thought and action to us so that if there is nothing more than pain that we must encounter we are, at least, assured of the privilege of acknowledging an apparent worthlessness of life and accordingly railing at a God who has failed to create a perfect world and eulogizing the atheistic creed. Nihilists of all ages have done precisely this. Yet the nihilist creed can still lead one to the consolation that is secular humanism.

Both the pessimist and the optimist reveal themselves as lovers of fate when they deepen their moral consciousness by benefiting from the lesson of death as a tribute to life. The last suffering of the dying must highlight the beauty of life for the living. When this lesson of death is learned there is a keener appreciation of life and a greater willingness to resist despair and welcome anxiety as a sign of the coming human apotheosis, the foundation of peace.

The optimist too learns the lesson of death, just like the radical nihilist. The believing optimist has no problem expressing hope in the immortality of the soul, satisfied even in the absence of certainty that he is on the right side of Pascal's wager, whatever the ultimate truth may be of human destiny. If humanity survives, the religious optimist wins. If humankind goes into extinction, one that cannot be complete since silence cannot be annihilated, the religious optimist loses nothing. At the vertical plane there is no certainty. At the horizontal plane the religious optimist as a lover of fate sees and appreciates what the radical nihilist has also perceived: the objectivity of morality—its universal sway—and death's ultimate tribute to life in the deepening of a moral consciousness that was never constructed through man's interaction with his external environment. This is the moral awareness which is intimate with life itself and develops as mind grows and matures. The religious optimist joyfully agrees to keep the moral consciousness intimate with the God-consciousness so that his religious humanism, like the secular humanism of the radical nihilist, is a witnessing to liberty, the celebration of life as joy and sadness.

The positive meaning of life, the implication of joy, renewed in the life of the individual makes life a precious possession. Death not only energizes life by constantly pointing the hour hand of the clock of life towards the dreaded twelve midnight mark, it, more importantly, completes its own definition on the terror side of life so that the reflection on death turns the thinking person away from despair and makes him a person of action more than ever determined to pursue goodness which has finally been justified to consciousness by the necessity of human empathy. Death is the last sigh of despair. There is no special earthly destiny for anyone since death beckons to all. There is wisdom in the saying that death is the great leveller. The death of the celebrity may astound the world, but it is nothing new to human nature. And so death can be regarded as that inevitability which confirms the radical notion of equality that is Christianity's great gift to secular humanism. As the last suffering of one on earth, death discredits human pride and deals a blow to all claims of superiority. The terror of death, which is only neutralized by *amor fati*, teaches the living of the virtue of humility. Humility in this sense is an attitude of mind that arises from the possibilities of extinction and survival as weighed by the anxious mind. If it is survival that one encounters after death, a more complex case is presented to human consciousness. The question of what form survival will take and the question of whether misery will continue must also be asked.

It does not matter that death cannot be experienced before it happens. That it cannot be experienced does not mean it is not a fit topic for meditation. It may be that all is well or may be well. Yet from the standpoint of humanity and its world all is not well. Even if life cannot be fully celebrated because of the burden of anxiety, we know that it can still be celebrated as having positive implications for joy and sadness. The celebration of life, perfectly within reach of the individual, will expand the sphere of the individual so that he will come to regard the common destiny of death as the beginning rather than the end of a wider human solidarity. This way intellectual love mitigates the terror anxiety validates.

Mood accounts for everything that is and will ever be. Its fatality is that it *is* and will always be. Death challenges *mood* and *mood* mocks death by pointing at silence as the irreducible foundation which death itself cannot conquer. The tragedy of *mood* is that perfection is not its goal. Indeed, one is tempted to think that our universe is not ambitious enough. But once the supremacy of fatalism is taken into consideration it becomes clear why the universe is as imperfect as it appears to us.

Despair the immediate inspirer of evil in the conscious person prevents him from regarding life with the profound respect life demands and deserves. If death is in fact a celebration of life, how do we approach the idea of immortality? How can it be shown that immortality is an absolute certainty? If we cannot find any conceptual proof of the immorality of the soul, how can we attempt to justify the idea that there is in us a principle that survives death? We have already established the basis of the desirability of immortality as the human wish to continue to enjoy the consolatory aspect of human existence in spite of the strain of the terror aspect of human existence on life. This wish expands to cover not only an instinctive loathing of extinction but also the fear of what awaits us after death, the keen suspicion fueled by religion and mythology that after-death condition may be worse than the conditions of this life. The ideal of immortality is expressed the desire to continue to experience the joy already known while enduring familiar suffering. Since biological death is unavoidable the good person wishes to have his experiences on earth transferred to another life and suffer less there, believing he has lived on earth a life deserving reward.

Life is the burden of consciousness. As burdensome as this life is, we consider it a light burden indeed compared to the horror of extinction which is in fact a greater tragedy than the condition of a burdened consciousness. For it is a privilege to come to the knowledge of having existed and the realization that universal existence is a tragedy. It is no privilege to exist in the silent mode without knowing that your subconscious existence and universal existence in general is a tragedy. Yet if immortality is desirable, how can it be shown to be possible? Denying the possibility of a conceptual proof, Kant proclaimed over two hundred years ago after a thorough examination of the classical arguments for the simplicity, substantiality, and immortality of the soul that "the logical exposition of thought in general has been mistaken for a metaphysical determination of the object"[7] There is no reason to doubt that Kant is easily in the top three of the list of the finest intellects of all time. But the question remains and insists on a response from us. Kant pretended to seek a non-conceptual solution to the question of immortality by sidelining the "pure" reason of metaphysics so that the "pure practical" reason of ethics could accomplish the task of showing that the notion of immortality is inextricably linked to the ideal of morality in *Critique of Practical Reason*. Kant's acute genius has not deserted him in spite of the intellectual contrivance here. My problem with Kant is his invocation of "pure practical" reason. Reason is reason, a refinement of emotion, whether pure or practical. I will return to this Kantian dilemma in Part Four of this work.

Given the futility of a conceptual demonstration of the soul's immortality, the question before us is no longer "how can we show that we have an immortal soul?" but, "Can human consciousness survive death?" It is true we are still in the realm of argument. Yet we feel more comfortable with the recasting of the question. The ethno-philosophical works of African philosophers like Gyekye and Anshi (see Part One, Ch Two, Section 3, Sub-section B) clearly endorse the idea that we carry within us an immortal principle. The widespread belief in reincarnation in traditional African societies supports this position. But we are African rationalists philosophizing radically in the consolationist perspective. We have clarified what immortality means to the consolationist. May we dare to speculate on the possibility of consciousness surviving biological death?

Now we note that human being is *mood* irreducibly. We feel and think. This feeling and thinking are actualities and conditions of emotion. All the meanings of human life are compressed to constitute joy and sadness. There is strong reason to believe that human beings evolved or were created from non-living matter; therefore the *mood* of humanity is connected with the *mood* of the universe. Whatever has existence cannot be reduced to any essence beyond the silence of eternity. The *mood* of humanity, having existed, must continue to exist, at least as a silent form, lost to consciousness but existing all the same. This is a kind of immortality. It is not an active immortality since neither spatio-temporal continuity nor psychological continuity is guaranteed. For argument to sustain an active immortality concept, we must fall back on the classical metaphysical proofs for the soul's immortality. But these "proofs" have long been discredited. We may embrace empirical evidence from parapsychology or put our faith in religion. Here, again, there is no certainty. Near-death experience (NDE) stories also do not convince because there is never any proof that someone who had a near-death experience actually went into the unexplored realm beyond life. Spiritual immortality which major religions such as Christianity and Islam teach is proposed and accepted on the basis of faith. If active immortality is possible, then a Supreme Being or a supreme principle working consciously is required to guarantee this immortality. The *melancholy being* who makes the transcendental appeal is in no position of power to guarantee himself immortality although he can attain a mocking type of immortality on earth such as immortality through children, fame, and other worldly achievements.

While philosophical agnosticism over the immortality question stares us boldly in the face, we realize yet that this boldness may not be all there is to the matter. If one can spring into existence in a universe that has also willed itself into existence the final conquest of death should not be a task too difficult to be accomplished by that indomitable and unyielding principle of things. If there could be a big bang in the beginning there is no reason for another bang not to occur in the end, the miracle of resurrection. The law of cause and effect cannot account for these mighty cosmic occurrences, for we are faced with an indomitable and unyielding will asserting itself as a fatality, as that which must be and therefore is, and which having become, exerts its influence throughout a universe that grows within a stable cosmic sphere. In such a universe the mission of immortality should not be a mission impossible if immortality is desirable.

Conclusion to the Third Part of the African Philosophical Synthesis

One peculiarity of the *melancholy being* is endurance by clinging. A human being must die but dies clinging. One has to cling to life all the way to the end because one is a moral being who desires the absolute good that they, tragically, cannot realize. We endure in ourselves while yet alive and functional. We endure too when we are dead and the human race continues on earth. The endurance of humanity is the perpetuation of the individual who is the clinging man. His daily life resounds with sighs of ohhs and ahhs, hisses of rage and oaths, and the silence of defeat. He it is who insults and is insulted, humiliates and is humiliated. He is so easily moved to love, anger, irritation, and violence. He will never stop complaining. If it is not his own self (the follies of this very self) that torments him at one moment it is the "other," my brother, who irritates him. If the *melancholy being* is not complaining about the poor state of his country's economy he is raining curses at inept politicians or clamoring for war. When he is war weary he becomes anxious and calls for peace.

It is this *melancholy being* that I have pinpointed in the third part of our 21st century African synthesis, this man who will not stop complaining because he must die clinging. My doctrine of humanity develops from the investigation of this most moody creature who endures in himself and in his species. I have been compelled to dwell at some length on the enduring question of determinism and freedom in the realization that the illumination of these all-important concepts holds the key to the door of philosophical fatalism as the master-concept animating necessity. Thus I stumbled upon the doctrine of *mood* in our pursuit of the *melancholy being* and later discovered how much of a God-lover this *melancholy being* is. His walk in life is a walk with a God he has never seen but in whose existence he instinctively believes, whether he finds the intellectual conception of God a contradiction or not.

Deepening my investigation further, I saw clearly that this *melancholy being* must die clinging precisely because he is the emotional person who pretends to be rational. It was necessary for me to modify the dominant Western theory of knowledge which tends to value reason as a phenomenon distinct from emotion, and even superior to emotion. I developed my theory of reason, thanks partly to the insight of L.S. Senghor and the African intellectual environment. Consequently, it was easy for me to present a compelling analysis of pessimism and optimism, always from the African perspective but continually in solidarity with the Western perspective.

Instead of demanding proofs of the existence of God, the world, the self, immortality, and the other (my Brother), I was content seeking justifications, aware of the futility of proofs. I insisted on friendly communication as the fundamental condition for the justification of the existence of the other, my Brother. I brought the individual and the community closer while giving the thumbs down to radical individualism and collectivism. More profoundly, my analysis of pessimism and optimism revealed the very emotive and therefore immensely influential concept of freedom as a vanishing idea which must be replaced with the notion of liberty for moral responsibility to be guaranteed. The notion of liberty led me to transcendental humanism (the precursor of the so-called secular humanism). The idea of intellectual love justified empathy upon which the endurance of the *melancholy being* largely depends.

The transcendental humanist is no mystic. Rather he is the lover of God and man. While secular humanism seeks to suppress and eliminate the God-factor transcendental humanism asserts the primacy of the God-factor in the conviction that money, science, and sex cannot be the ultimate objects of men's transcendental appeal. The hollowness of the idea of man being the measure of all things has been exposed by consolation philosophy, which unveiled man as a melancholy being whose attempt at self-transcendence is nothing more than the transcendental appeal calculated to pierce the darkness separating man from God. Transcendental humanism (which may take the form of Christian humanism or Islamic humanism or Hindu and Buddhist humanism) is the strong devotion to mankind founded on, and externally animated by, the love of God. Man separated from the God concept is nothing and the God concept isolated from man is meaningless. The insignificance and meaninglessness contemplated in the proposition above translate to the impossibility of a godless humanity. Secular humanism being a denial of the necessity of the God factor is by the very fact of its denial already dependent on transcendental humanism. No one familiar with the progress of Western liberal thought from Francis Bacon, through John Locke, Immanuel Kant, Isaiah Berlin to the contemporary ultra-liberal secularists of Europe and America, can deny that Western secularism is an attempt to subvert Christianity and take away the right of this religion to be regarded as the inspiration of universal humanism. The moral philosophy of Kant must be seen to have surpassed the moral philosophy of both Aristotle and Plato precisely because of Kant's Christian influences.

In vain do we try to divorce God from morality in the name of a humanism that is ironically God illuminated as the recognition of man's need for God conceived as the consolation of the universe. The word "goodness" charms us because the God concept lurks in it. The only way we can suppress the God concept that animates that magical term is to welcome the vilest nihilism by declaring the overrating of humanity and proclaiming an era of moral anomie, such that everything becomes permissible. This moral anomie is what humanity cannot bear since it will mean the final crushing of the *melancholy being* who is already broken. The human being who takes a gun and goes on a shooting spree and the Islamic terrorist are fine examples of the godless man who decides that humanity is overrated and follows up on this anti-God illogicality with the proclamation of the era of moral anomie.

The appeal to reason cannot claim to know enough to deny God who is man's consolation. The appeal to reason is less immense than the transcendental appeal which has the unveiling of God as its intimate goal. The appeal to reason is an appeal to intellectual love, which has already been reached by the phenomenon of human anxiety. Ultimately, humanism, whether it is Western individualism or African communalism, is the vocalized music of melancholy, at once a lamentation and celebration of human existence. Humanism is not a nihilist cry of agony but an elevated doctrine of man. The elevation of man towards his apotheosis involves the God-concept. The chief error of secular humanism, which transcendental humanism corrects, is its uncritical claim of man's inherent goodness. I need not dwell on the issue of man's basic goodness because I have determined that the principle of evil in man perpetually threatens to overwhelm the principle of goodness. I replace the supposition that man is basically good with the assertion that man is fundamentally *moral*. For the evil of man, and his goodness, are rooted in his moral essence. The manifesto of the transcendental humanist can be summarized thus:

1. A great unhappiness broods over the earth on which men live.
2. Chance and necessity argue for a supreme principle of the universe.
3. Life is an affirmation of *mood*.
4. Everything is *mood* in various stages of realization.
5. Immortality is a hope.
6. This hope mystifies.
7. Man loves God indirectly with all his might.

8. Man loves himself with immediacy and directly with all his might.

9. Man must die,

10. But he dies clinging.

It is joy that shields man from the ontological nudity, the tragic dimension of existence. This joy becomes more substantial in our optimistic phase of thought as we increasingly link liberty with morality. That which is called morally good is the value which recognizes that selfishness or self-centeredness is the starting point of morality. It is sacrifice that elevates selfishness to the level of selflessness, the magnitude of the selfless act being directly proportional to the sacrifice involved in that act. Every man loves himself, but love demands that the moral act begun in selfishness be completed in selflessness.

The consolationist doctrine of man is the presentation of the philosophical anatomy of the *melancholy being*. I showed in Part Two of this work that the universe was expressed as a consolation from the very beginning of its decidedly mysterious springing into existence. Man being a fragment of the universe is in solidarity with the universe. His *mood* is a fragment of the *mood* of the world. Consequently, I justified a universal idealism shielding a certain degree of panpsychism. Concentrating my effort on man, I freed the human phenomenon from raw nature by making man a witness to liberty, man as the being endowed with a fully developed moral consciousness, that knows this to be the case precisely by virtue of this being's capacity to feel pain and pleasure, to experience joy and sadness and contemplate these as optimism and pessimism.

PART FOUR

COMPARATIVE PHILOSOPHY

Chapter Twelve

THE FUNDAMENTAL HARMONY OF CONSOLATION PHILOSOPHY WITH THE BASIC WESTERN PHILOSOPHICAL IMAGINATION

Preamble

In the first part of this work we were at pains to show that consolation philosophy is African philosophy. We anchored our demonstration on the originality of our inspiration and traced this selfsame inspiration to the African community and the simple worldview of this community. While the ethno-philosophers regarded this worldview at its most sophisticated expression (and this in the light of Western philosophy) as substantial African philosophy, we identified it merely as the foundation of African philosophy. It is now necessary for us to justify consolation philosophy as world philosophy. The universal is what it is by virtue of the intellectual elevation of the particular that constitutes it. Before we have a world philosophy, we must first have a particular philosophy. For decades African philosophy failed to command universal respect because what was presented as African philosophy was either a particularist philosophy (as in ethno-philosophy) or polemic (as in African hermeneutics and philosophical analysis).

The philosophy of Plato is fundamentally Greek philosophy. Yet the intellectual accomplishment of Platonic philosophy makes it a world philosophy, one intelligible to both Europeans and non-Europeans. In this fourth part of my work, I will endeavor to show that the main ideas of consolation philosophy are not unknown to Western philosophy. By summarizing the main ideas of a number of the iconic thinkers in Western philosophy and comparing what I have distilled from Western thought with the main theses of consolation philosophy, I hope to highlight the areas of agreement and disagreement between the black philosophical imagination and the white philosophical imagination. The audacity of philosophy consists in the fact that it respects no boundaries and inquires into all areas of life and all disciplines, from the humanities and the social sciences to science and technology. While this is true, we must never forget that philosophy is essentially an intellectual vision of the universe. As Friedrich Waismann puts it, "from Plato to Moore and Wittgenstein, every great philosopher was led by a sense of vision."[1] This "sense of vision" driven by the search for truth that is, yet, doomed never to be more fully realized makes every speculation of man a consolation of philosophy.

Plato and Aristotle

When Dario Composta calls Plato the sovereign master[2] he is not exaggerating the centrality of this philosophical "spectator of all time and all existence" to Western philosophy. We may add that Plato is the sovereign master of idealism. His intellectualist influence on the philosopher Kant, whose greatness rivals Plato's, cannot be denied. Indeed, Plato is the father of Western philosophy, predicting developments in philosophy well in advance of his time. The pillar of Plato's philosophy, a universal idealism, is the doctrine of the Ideas. Having taken the notion of change from Heraclitus, the notion of an eternal unchangeable absolute from the Eleatic philosophers, and the truth of conceptualization from Socrates, Plato the myth-creator proceeded to unite these discordant notions into the fantastic yet compelling theory of the Ideas. For Plato the Ideas are not processes of thought but substantial, essential, and eternal realities of which the phenomenal world is a mirror. Plato was an idealist and could not resist the rationalist longing for uniformity and intelligibility in a world that patently manifests aspects of instability and non-uniformity. Like Parmenides before him and Spinoza after him, Plato constructed a perfectly rational universe where everything was determined, and perfectly so. This is the world of Ideas. Every phenomenon of the world has its Idea in the world of Forms in which it participates. The Idea of the Good is the greatest perfection. Indeed, it is at the summit of all perfection. Plato does not demonstrate how the Idea of the Good is the logical grounds of existence, nor does he explain the relation of the Idea of the Good with God whose existence he clearly asserted in the *Timaeus*.

Nevertheless, the Good is asserted as the source of being in the *Republic*, that which imparts truth to what is known, and the power of knowing to the knower.[3] Simply put, the Good is the cause of things. If being is that which is, the not-being is not simply a negative. For Plato the not-being shadows being as that which is essential for the very definition of being. For instance, the being of that which is, say light, is the not-being of what helps constitute light, which is darkness. Plato's treatment of the question of being in a highly metaphysical context was to influence Martin Heidegger in his struggle to grasp the meaning of being. His treatment of the question of being with the horizon of not-being in sight lays bare the profound question of the origin of the universe and the place of determinism in this most perplexing of questions. Is the universe eternal? If yes, was there ever a beginning of this eternity in a state of non-existence or nothingness? May this primordial nothingness not equate being itself?

Where We Agree with Plato

Now Plato's tendency to mythologize may be objectionable, but he resorts to the myth after his supreme rationalism reaches the end of its penetrative capacity with the positing of the Idea of the Good. Here Plato has come to the limit of thought. Beyond this limit even philosophical fatalism cannot go. In making the Good the cause of being and essence without explicating further, Plato simply puts his faith in an optimistic vision of the universe, the attitude that says *all is well*. This optimism agrees with one component of consolation philosophy, the optimistic component. The philosophy of the Good underlines the fact that the goal of the universe is consolation, the realization of a more complete joy. For the being which the Good brings about is the substantial meaning of the joy of existence realized in varying degrees. Thus the being of man will express joy in a far more intense way than a lower life-form like the amoeba or a non-living thing like a piece of stone. We are therefore compelled to regard the Good as corresponding to the impersonal principle of the Eternal Mood described in this work in the metaphysical language of consolation philosophy. Yet we saw that impersonality is a difference in the Eternal Mood which passes into personality in the same principle and becomes the God of Christianity, Islam, and Judaism. As a fatalistic principle, of eternity, the Good is a yearning for beauty and perfection, for absolute rationality. The Good (as the name implies) is good. Whatever is good is moral. The Good is absolute morality. This interpretation of Plato's basic philosophy agrees fundamentally with the core doctrine of consolation philosophy, a sure proof of the fact that Africa and the West can feel at home in the same theoretical universe.

Where We Disagree with Plato

Our disagreement with Plato is connected with the fault we have found with almost all the great Western rationalists—Aristotle, Leibniz, Spinoza,

Hegel and Bradley, the forceful demand for rationality and uniformity in the universe. This demand is forceful because it imposes a *wish* of man (an anthropomorphic variant) on the destiny of *mood* or the course of things. We do not doubt the consolatory value of the speculations of these great minds, but we read exaggerations into the claim that the universe is a perfect expression. For expression it must be, and yet an expression of *mood* or mind, whether we conceive *mood* in terms of first causes, unmoved movers, life-forces, intelligent designers, etc. The universe is an imperfect expression although an absolute expression. *Mood* has yearning as its basic character. Whatever yearns is not perfect *ab initio* but indicates perfection as its goal. We cannot be certain whether the cosmic goal of the realization of absolute perfection or rationality is possible or impossible, objectively. But from the standpoint of man, and arguing from immanence to transcendence, this project is impossible. The progress of the universe can only achieve fuller consolation rather than perfection.

The Good which Plato grants the power of spontaneous causation is absolute rationality and perfection, like Spinoza's Substance and Hegel's Absolute Spirit. Instead of going the Greek (and Western) way of subordinating emotion to reason I subordinated reason to emotion. The grounding of rationality in a primitive emotionality enabled me to proceed with the construction of my system on the foundation of the doctrine of *mood* rather than the Greek notion of being as being. If being is present everywhere but is nowhere eternally substantial, then it makes sense to talk of being as *mood* rather than being as being.

Aristotle

With Aristotle's replacement of the idea of non-being with the idea of potentiality, Plato's difficult theory of the Ideas gained greater coherence. The dim purposiveness of Platonic idealism metamorphosed into the supreme teleology of Aristotle's moderate idealism. The equation of matter and form figures prominently in Aristotle's metaphysics and his philosophy of evolution, although the notion of "pure" matter and form must be regarded as mere theoretical postulates of the human mind in its search for adequacy with objective nature. The metaphysics of being as it unravels within the framework of the matter-form equation or the potentiality-actuality formula does not really escape the necessity of dialectic. If Aristotle appears far more coherent than Plato it is because Aristotle largely avoids transcendental questions. Where Plato seeks insight into the impenetrable mythopoeic dream of existence by positing the Good as the supreme causal principle and ends up mythologizing, Aristotle avoids this confrontation and is content hinting at the reality of an Immovable Mover who is the logical basis of universal existence.

For Aristotle matter is that which needs form to become coherent and active. Without form the potentialities inhering in matter cannot begin their striving towards actualization. Form is self-subsistent. The goal of the universe is the attainment of pure form. However, this goal is unattainable; hence the world, and its striving, is eternal. God is the Form of Form, Thought of Thought, the pure Act. He is the most real thing but does not exist in the sense of not having matter in His constitution. He is outside the causal chain of the world and is yet the logical grounds of the universe, a teleological cause working from the end.[4] This God as Prime Mover is self-contained and simple, without contradictions. He is pure form, the self-thinking subsistent thought that is perfect happiness.[5] The God of Aristotle is benevolent, almighty, and omniscient without yet being aware of His attributes. This is true since He only knows Himself and yet is the teleological cause of the world. Since God is lovable the world is moved to love and seek Him. He does not know the world, but the world knows Him. God is the Prime Mover. That which is good is meaningful and thus attracts the knowledge seeker.[6]

Critical Perspective on Aristotle

Aristotle's teleological vision intrigues us. His submission that the world is eternal agrees with our submission on the eternity of *mood*. For Aristotle God is not *creator* but *inspirer*. He is the inspiration of a world that exists eternally, distinct from the world and immutable.[7] On the relation of God with the world He sustains, it is either God is prior to the world or He is contemporaneous with the world. In this work I showed a preference for God's contemporaneity with the world. This seems to us to be the Aristotelian formulation. Yet we fail to see how Aristotle's God can be the perpetual inspiration of the world without making contact with this world. If God's radiant all-encompassing goodness (love) is invoked to bridge the gulf separating the self-thinking God from an eternal universe that *perceives* His radiance, then a dialectic is already at work reconciling God with the world.

Aristotle dreamed up his impotent God because of the rationalist's romantic demand for perfection from a universe that is born in consolation. Like most of the great rationalists in Western philosophy, if not all of them, Aristotle overlooked the problem of evil in the world which is an aspect of the world's imperfection. If he had thought twice about the evidential problem of moral and physical evil he might have modified his religious philosophy. Besides, Aristotle felt that a God with knowledge of the world would enter the causal chain and no longer account for the world's existence but must Himself seek for a spontaneous cause beyond Himself. Thus God becomes in a way limited. Our solution to this dilemma yielded the notions of power and glory as replacements for the notions of omnipotence and omniscience. Subsequently, we argued for a God who is the consolation of the universe. This way we diluted rationalist romanticism.

Aristotelian metaphysics presents a God who is simple thought. He lacks any contradiction internally. Here we disagree with Aristotle. At this point it is instructive to note that Hegel made man the vehicle of Spirit. For Hegel, God rises to absolute self-knowledge through man's consciousness. In other words, the existence of the world is necessary for God to exist. There can be no God without the world. Shedding light on this theme, Charles Taylor writes: "Consciousness is only possible when the subject is set over against an object. But to be set over against an object is to be limited by something other, and hence to be finite. It follows that if cosmic spirit is to attain full awareness, it can only be through vehicles which are finite spirits.... The notion of a cosmic spirit which would be aware of itself directly, without the opposition to an object which is the predicament of finite subjects, is incoherent."[8] Indeed, Hegel rates dialectic highly.[9] It will even appear that Hegel considers dialectic a universal category.[10]

Like the concepts of necessity and freedom, the principle of non-contradiction (and excluded middle) is a demand of human reason for the perfect structuring of the phenomena of the world for the comprehension of the human mind. In the *Categories*, Aristotle states that: "It is impossible that something is and is not simultaneously for the same reason."[11] This, of course, amounts to saying that it is not possible to affirm and deny one and the same thing. Taken literally, the principle of non-contradiction loses touch with the real world and with life. The strict demand for the sanctity of identity must fail because the rationality of the world is not independent of the fatality of this same world, as we have labored to show in this work. Rationality corresponding to intelligibility assures us that all is well with the world and that what seems incongruous is a non-essential aspect of a necessary whole. Fatality, on the other hand, insists that rationality is born in emotionality and that the latter's character of yearning infects rationality itself so that the logical grandstanding of human reason is a wish that all should be well.

At a deeper level of understanding the principle of non-contradiction implies the incomplete nature of the world in its beginning. It is after all a wish that uniformity and intelligibility prevail in the universe. And what about a beginning? Even if the universe is posited as having no teleological cause, it must still be logically pictured as having a beginning, as referring itself to its foundation.

In this work I identified this foundation as the Eternal Mood of melancholy or the fatalistic principle. By seeking logical purity, the principle of non-contradiction recognizes the practical failure of reality and acknowledges the chaos that characterized the formative stages of the universe, the haziness of all creative combinations. When I assert that good and evil are principles of the human mind inhering in *fear* or when I assert that optimism evolves out of pessimism, the principle of non-contradiction cannot challenge my thesis. This is so because the principle cannot explain change. It is an intellectual imposition on change. It comes into operation after change has occurred. The advantage the law confers—and it is a great advantage indeed—is that it helps us streamline the illogicality the mind reads into the ways of *mood*, which illogicality is in fact the compulsion of yearning. The law does not invalidate that which precedes it, which is primeval and intimate with being itself: the universal dialectic of *mood*.

Consolationist dialectic acknowledges the dignified status of the principle of non-contradiction as a demand for intelligibility. The principle is important but not absolute. It is a demand of reason that feeds off emotion. What is true of the principle of non-contradiction is also true of the principle of excluded middle. The latter is merely a variation of the former. Aristotle himself employs dialectic when explaining his theory of purposiveness. The jump from potentiality to actuality is a dialectical jump. We must agree that while Socrates is seated, he is seated. He is not seated and at the same time standing. It is easy to see how the principle of non-contradiction applies here. But when we are talking about fundamental changes like the origin of the world, evolution, and the relation of reason to emotion, the principle is impotent. Hegel was wise to have considered dialectic a universal category. Dialectic is already implied in the Aristotelian proposition of a self-contained God (perfect identity) whose goodness attracts mortal creatures. How can that which is self-contained be perceived by things it does not know if dialectic is not already at work? Plotinus suggested the process of emanation to explain the relation of the One with the sensible world, thereby diluting Aristotelian dualism, introducing some element of dialectic, and, in his extremity, making the One a mere principle of existence.[12] Aristotle recognizes myths as stories announcing thought and morality, indicative of divine revelation.[13] The admission of the possibility of revelation will appear to compromise the awesome Eleatic dignity of Aristotle's God.

We note Aristotle's introduction of a nebulous, very tenuous, bond to explain the relation between God and the world. We may call this bond *love*, a distant echo of our notion of *intellectual love* and Spinoza's *intellectual love of God*. Aristotle's God is good, though only aware of Himself. In being good He is lovable. Therefore man desires God because He is lovable. If man can reach God through an external bond of love, a connection has been effected which must disturb the awesome unity of God as a tension in His thought. Radical separation has been diluted. If this God is good He will be in solidarity with the world that knows He exists as the summit of love and truth.

Let us attempt to reconcile our religious philosophy with Aristotle's religious philosophy. The sphere of the self-thinking God is silence. What God contemplates is more than happiness: it is the fatality of His own existence. At the bottom of God's thought lies sadness, the basic yearning in His own principle that enforced His fatalistic existence. In His state of impersonality, the condition in which He is identified with chance, this cosmic sadness is the silence of eternity. As a being of power, however, God overcomes despair in Himself and thinks His happy thoughts, which thinking is the willing of a universe outside His mind. This creative activity commences as self-thought, then proceeds to the level of creative thought which transforms into outwardly directed thought, the productive thought that makes the world. Such a willing of a universe would not amount to an act of caprice in spite of the imperfection of the willed thing relative to its perfect conception, because it is the expression of yearning. Aristotle's religious philosophy gives us an impotent God. In taking great care not to present an anthropomorphic God, the God of mythology, Aristotle ironically presents the supremely anthropomorphic God—a necessary being who is absolute perfection, the self-thinking thought, a mere wish of human reason. As the Form of Form rather than the form of matter, God is the most real thing without being an existent thing. But can a thing lacking *existence* have any abundance of *reality*?

While we easily sympathize with Aristotelian teleology, the notion that the world is not meaningless and that it strives futilely after the realization of form, while we sympathize with this majestic vision of the cosmos, we find the account of the Immovable Mover profoundly unsatisfactory. Aristotle completely ignores the problem of evil in the world. But then Aristotle is not only a supreme rationalist but also a thorough-going empiricist. He is less concerned with transcendental questions. The problem of evil is a transcendental question. Aristotle imputes a false perfection to God and enforces an extreme kind of dualism. The imputation of perfection to an impotent, even lifeless, God betrays the rationalist trivialization of the problem of evil and the subsequent effort to escape from the fact of the failure of reality. While condemning everyone for thinking anthropomorphically, the rationalists themselves become guilty of conceiving God anthropomorphically when they impute to God perfections and the excellence demanded by human reason. This weakness reveals the anthropomorphic cast of the human mind. Anthropomorphic thinking cannot even be uprooted by atheism, the belief that God does not exist. For the atheist will have to anchor his belief in the findings of science, in mechanicism. He will have to replace God with chance. I showed in Part Two of this work that mechanicism is no alternative to the religious way of seeing the world. The philosophical contemplation of chance compulsorily yields its reification and personification.

Suppose we assert that the goal of the world is not the attainment of form (perfection) right from the beginning as Aristotle indicated or of the Spirit's freedom, as Hegel would assert? If we make this assertion we will be able to conceive God as the principle of fatalism and vitalize His essence even as the evil in the world will be necessitated without its being trivialized. This is what we have done in this work.

Benedict Spinoza

The system of Benedict Spinoza represents the most thoroughgoing pantheism in Western philosophical thought. Rejecting the dualistic vision of the universe enunciated by René Descartes while retaining the religious attitude entrenched on the non-physical side of the Cartesian vision, Spinoza proposed a unified physical and non-physical realm in a totality which is also an eternal context—Substance or God. Indeed, Spinoza proudly makes God the starting point of his neutral monism. The result of his "correction" of Descartes is the expression of a system of thought that is at once compelling and ennobling, scientific and romantic, analytical and mystical. The general theory of Substance, the replacement of dualism with monism, the assertion of the correspondence of the mental and physical realms, of the order and series of ideas and things within the eternity whose essences is God, makes Spinoza one of the greatest thinkers of the West.

Spinoza identifies nature with God and goes ahead to make the latter the principle of nature, the very essence of eternity. God who encompasses the universe is the only truly necessary being, the being that possesses true freedom as the cause of all determinations. True freedom for Spinoza means free necessity.[14] Man may make free decisions but he is not a necessary being, his mind being a fixed mode of thought. So God-filled is Spinoza's philosophy that one realizes at once that he did not philosophize in the usual Western style which basically lacks intuitiveness. T.S. Gregory resolves this little puzzle by noting that Spinoza was first and last and always a Jew.[15] If God is nature as Spinoza implies, why should we not simply ignore the God-factor and be content with nature? Gregory answers:

> In fact, however, Spinoza's *Ethics* is the voice of a mystical devotion so relentless, a sanctity so pure, that such misconception of it serves only to reveal the scope of its *amor intellectualis Dei*.... But to understand the *Ethics* it is necessary first to realize that Spinoza believed in God and loved God in unperturbed singleness of life, and that this book was written not as instruction or apology but as prayer.[16]

In plainer words, Benedict Spinoza was a philosopher of consolation.

Critical Perspective on Spinozism

The God question has always been a burning question for man. In our technological age it is emotion that reigns, not reason *per se*. Religious fundamentalism among Christians, Muslims, and Hindus has taken firm root in the midst of the triumph of science, with man expressing profound indifference towards the great achievement of science and sometimes even contempt (as is the case with the Taliban Islamic fundamentalists of Afghanistan). Where religious fervor has waned, as in Europe and, increasingly, North America, men and women have put their faith in money and even sex (that human anxiety may be assuaged). Yet this optimism of the masses of Europe and North America is shown to be tenuous once the science which is the basis of Western materialism is exposed as a body of assumptions subject to the same probability that undid religion in the first place. At the highest level of science knowledge dissolves into faith in the unseen and unknown ultimate reality. At this level science is indistinguishable from religion, which puts faith in an unseen reality, and metaphysics which speculates about the nature of this reality. Ultimately, science pleads the cause of religion. If God is scorned as a delusion created by man's imagination the assertion follows in the defense of the God-concept that man merely seeks an encounter with that which is necessary and absolute and therefore cannot be simply the product of the imagination. The denial of the existence of God leads to the glorification of science and visible things like money and the human body. These visible forms coalesce in a closed system called nature. The anthropomorphic cast of the human mind desires the reification of nature. Thus the God-concept sticks firmly to human nature.

The above consideration saved Spinoza's system from bare mechanicism. It is in this light that Spinoza's celebration of a God who is the totality of nature, who can be worshiped through intellectual love, is best understood. His is a philosophy of consolation, like the philosophy of Boethius, and not a body of knowledge to be confirmed by science. Spinoza's pantheism is the result of the intellectual struggle with universal fatalism, the futility of existence which yet finds its truest interpretation in the idea of consolation. Spinoza the rationalist who casts his magnum opus *The Ethics* in a rigid geometrical format in deference to science does not neglect to define such "unscientific" terms as emotion, hope, fear, joy, despair, etc. "Hope (*spes*) is an uncertain pleasure arisen from the idea of a thing past or future, the event of which we still doubt to some extent,"[17] he announces sagely. Fear differs from hope in being a source of pain rather than pleasure.[18] He acknowledges the power of dialectic when he says there can be no hope without fear and *vice versa*, since both phenomena are interdependent. Emotion generally is a confused idea by which the mind apprehends the degree of intensity of the body's state in terms of pain and pleasure.[19]

In the preface to Part Four of *The Ethics*, Spinoza denies purpose to nature completely. Nature exists for the same reason that God exists. This existence is purposeless, without any end in view. We merely project our desires into the world outside our minds when we talk of final causes. Nature is neither perfect nor imperfect. Spinoza's motto is, *all is well.* His materialistic treatment of the idea of purpose ties teleology to human subjectivity, to desire which is at the root of human existence. Yet human desire is itself determined, as truly as the human mind is a fixed mode of thinking. Causation is best understood in the context of universal necessity, of eternity whose essence is God.

I demonstrated in this work that necessity, like the notions of freedom and teleology, are demands of human reason that all should be well with the system of things. The concept of necessity is a product of man's anthropomorphic mental cast. The concept comes through as decidedly anthropomorphic when applied to God.

Spinoza is projecting a vision of consolation and knows this to be the case, although he presents his findings dogmatically as the definitive theory of Substance. Spinoza asserts that God has an infinite number of attributes but identifies only thought and extension. Yet the attraction of the philosophy of Spinoza is essentially on account of the consolatory value of his vision of the universe, which assuages our hopes and fears. The stable logical picture of what he paints does not convince because we grapple with life and the world in all their complexity. Human life and the universe in general are not in themselves uniformly structured but are rather complex. The intelligibility we draw out of existence is the meaning—never complete—of complex organization. Existence is not granted as something stable but as a consolation. It is this consolation that yields meaning, not the necessity that asserts that all is well when the human mind is confronted by the complexity of things.

Spinoza writes, "For nothing belongs to the nature of anything except that which follows from the necessity of the nature of the effecting cause, and whatever follows from the necessity of the effecting cause, necessarily happens."[20] This is very subtle. We have exposed the term *necessity* as the biggest fraud in philosophy. Necessity as employed by philosophers equates reality or existence. To exist is simply to be. Hence all is well. This is what necessity means, especially to rationalists. The rationalists avoid discussing the question of the origin of the universe regardless of the great significance of this question in relation to the problem of evil. As far as these rationalists are concerned, it is enough that the universe *necessarily* exists.

Spinoza takes an anti-anthropomorphic position. He pursues this position in his depersonalization project. In the human sphere the project commences with the conscious destruction of anxiety—the attempt to reassure the human phenomenon that all is well when what is meant by this subterfuge is that futility is supreme—while in the non-human sphere it is expressed in the denial of purpose to nature and consciousness to God. Spinoza writes: "Therefore the more we endeavor to live under the guidance of reason, the less we endeavor to depend on hope, and the more to deliver ourselves free from fear and overcome fortune as much as possible."[21] This salutation to courage is noble indeed; yet it is an impossible ideal because emotion is the primitive prototype of reason. Carrying the project further in what I interpret as the strong pessimistic response to human despair, Spinoza asserts that the man who lives according to the dictates of reason distances himself from pity.[22] Now this position would have delighted Stalin,

Hitler, and other sociopaths. If pity is a form of suffering, a reduction of man's mental power, I assert that suffering itself is unavoidable and therefore passes as a *necessity*. Man's task is to confront suffering and endure it with dignity. For man is the being who dies clinging, suffering and still hoping. In Martin Heidegger's ponderous language, man is "concernful Being-alongside and solicitous Being-with."[23] It may be suggested that Spinoza is actually isolating pity from compassion. But the two concepts are not radically different. Pity becomes compassion when the emotion is applied to humanity as a whole.

Good things are those things which help man enjoy the intellectual life or the rational existence. Evil things deny man the enjoyment of his rational life and the chance to perfect his reason.[24] This definition of evil is convoluted and enables Spinoza to dodge the real and burning question of moral and physical evil. Reason may help prevent moral evil, but evil itself is a principle of existence. Spinoza's system has no solution to the problem of the existence of evil in the world. Therefore he invokes necessity to cover up what cannot be covered. Necessity is after all the eternal context (*sub species aeternitatis*)._

Spinoza's God is an even more severe God than Aristotle's God. The one is a monist and the other is a dualist. Both desired a God who is perfect rationality. While Aristotle's God thinks only of Himself, Spinoza's God does not think at all and therefore has no feeling of pain or pleasure.[25] It seems to me that Spinoza is here referring to what I have identified as the impersonal phase of the fatalistic principle of eternity. All Spinoza has to do is introduce a little bit of dialectic for impersonality to pass into personality. On this matter of God not having feelings, Spinoza actually contradicted himself, as we will soon see. The recognition of God as a necessary being who is the essence of eternity is described as the intellectual love of God.[26] This makes God the ultimate cause of all things material and mental, to the extent that He is conceived of as infinite or as containing everything in His mind. Foreshadowing Hegel who made man the vehicle of *Geist*, Spinoza says the intellectual love of God is the very love which God loves Himself to the extent that the human mind conceives this love in the eternal context. After all God is the cause of man's mind and body. Man's intellectual love of God is part of God's infinite love of Himself.[27]

Suddenly the cold logic of rational necessity gives way to the glorification of love. "Hence it follows that God, in so far as he loves himself, loves men, and consequently that the love of God for men and the mind's intellectual love towards God is one and the same thing."[28] Elsewhere Spinoza had noted that God has neither feelings of pain nor of pleasure. Or are we to argue that love, even if intellectual, is not an emotion of pleasure, or, at least, satisfaction? Given his monistic conception of the universe, God should have feelings like man but in a far nobler way. This apparent volte-face restores coherence to Spinoza's doctrine of the intellectual love of God. This doctrine agrees broadly with our notion of intellectual love which revolves round the constant adoration of God as the most high, the warm engagement with humanity, and solidarity with nature.

Spinoza only needed our concept of reason to make his pantheistic system less impersonal and our idea of fatalism to subvert the term *necessity*. All the same, we see elements of consolation philosophy in his great system. It seems to me that the depersonalization and anti-anthropomorphic project of Benedict Spinoza fails while leaving intact a truly magnificent vision of consolation.

From David Hume to Immanuel Kant

What the consolationist finds most intriguing in David Hume is his seeming contempt for human reason based on acute observation of human behavior and a profound insight into human nature. The Scottish genius asserts with brutal frankness that reason is so passive that its proper function is to serve the passions or emotion.[29] For Hume reason is idle and largely impotent, even in matters of morality. His conviction that human rationality cannot claim priority over human emotionality agrees with our consolationist standpoint. However, we are not ready to go so far in the denigration of reason as to insist that reason is passive, that it enjoys no privilege relative to emotion. The Humean standpoint is radical only because Hume had no interest in dialectic and could, therefore, not connect emotion with reason dialectically, something which Spinoza foreshadowed in his parallelist theory of the relation of the mind with the body within the context of his monistic system. Hegel benefitted from Spinoza's work but failed to grasp the dialectic of *mood* while enunciating a superb dialectic of reason. Our moderate position is that emotion is basic and that reason evolves out of this basic emotion as a refinement, thereby equating the logic of the intellect but still retaining the character of the emotion that is its source. The proof that reason retains the character of emotion is the tendency of the human intellect to despair, skepticism, and cynicism. Despair, skepticism, and cynicism are intellectually grounded phenomena of the human mind. Their essence is emotion.

Let us take a second look at Hume's empiricist epistemology before proceeding to Immanuel Kant's solution to the epistemological problems raised by

Hume. We have had cause to refer to the term *necessity* as the biggest fraud in philosophy, invoked by all philosophers to bail them out of philosophical *cul-de-sacs*. We have subverted this term with the idea of fatalism. Yet the term remains a stubborn motif in philosophy. Hume is aware of this status of necessity, for he writes: "Since it is not from knowledge or any scientific reasoning that we derive the opinion of the *necessity* [italics mine] of a cause to every new production, that opinion must *necessarily* [italics mine] arise from observation and experience."[30] Just as Hume is obliquely casting doubt on the term *necessity* he is guilty of falling back on the adverb *necessarily* to make his point. Having noted this comic contradiction, we can now proceed to see how Hume identified the source of necessity. He explains necessity as an inference of the mind based on custom, on the feature of the regularity of external phenomena or the constant conjunction of objects given in experience.[31] Hume's position is a justification of common sense. Yet he laments that, "We cannot penetrate into the reason of the conjunction."[32] In other words, Hume sought necessity (as a vital factor in causality) in the mind and failed to find it there. Hume is skeptical, yet magisterial. The spirit of his philosophy comes out brilliantly in the following lines:

> Thus all probable reasoning is nothing but a species of sensation. 'Tis not solely in poetry and music, we must follow our tastes and sentiment, but likewise in philosophy. When I am convinc'd of any principle, 'tis only an idea, which strikes more strongly upon me. When I give the preference to one set of arguments above another, I do nothing but decide from my feeling concerning the superiority of their influence. Objects have no discoverable connexion together.[33]

The position above agrees broadly with my position concerning the role of reason in human affairs. I have shown that reason refers itself to emotion and emotion loses itself in *mood* and that fatalism rather than determinism can account for the nature of *mood*. Having altered the direction of Western philosophy with his critical perspective, Hume left the task of the justification of common sense to an even greater genius, Immanuel Kant. The German phenomenon accomplished this task while holding fast to the elevated conception of human reason like a true rationalist.

Immanuel Kant

Kant distinguished between pure reason and practical reason. By "pure" Kant means independence of empirical conditions.[34] While pure reason drives the metaphysical enquiry into things beyond the scope of the "understanding" practical reason asserts the moral necessity of believing the ideas of reason, for example, God, freedom, and the soul's immortality. Kant's greatest work *Critique of Pure Reason* is divided into the Transcendental Aesthetic, the Transcendental Analytic, and the Transcendental Dialectic. Kant uses the term "transcendental" to underline his critical philosophy. The term is so called because the critical philosophy examines the powers and limitation of reason, how knowledge is possible *a priori* and its practical employment *a priori*.[35] The Transcendental Aesthetic deals with *a priori* knowledge of the external world or what Kant calls sensibility. He understands space and time as pure forms of intuition underlying outer and inner experience. The direct apprehension of reality is rendered intelligible in intuition. The imagination structures this knowledge which is then brought under the concepts of the understanding to become valid knowledge. Kant declares: "Consequently, all possible perceptions, and therefore everything that can come to empirical consciousness, that is, all appearances of nature, must, so far as their connection is concerned, be subject to the categories."[36] The Transcendental Analytic deals with the deduction of the categories while the Transcendental Dialectic deals with the theoretical difficulty of demonstrating the validity of the ideas of pure reason.

While it seems impossible for us to transcend phenomenal reality, metaphysics seeks to realize this impossible project. Hence Kant's criticism of the grandiose metaphysical project. But Kant the ethical thinker is sympathetic to the metaphysical quest of human reason. Reason posits the unconditioned, the spontaneous cause of the conditioned chain of naturalistic events. The idea of the unconditioned, Kant confesses, seems contradictory if we think we have direct knowledge of things-in-themselves (since our intellect cannot grasp noumenal reality). This contradiction disappears if we regard our knowledge as mirroring only the phenomenal world (appearance). Skepticism over metaphysical necessity is mitigated by certainty over moral necessity. The metaphysical arguments purely marshalled cannot prove the existence of God, the soul's immortality, and the reality of freedom. Yet morality (conduct) leads us to assume the reality of these ideas of reasons. If they are not to be conceived as constitutive truths, as accessible to the *understanding*, they are compulsorily conceived of as regulative truths by practical reason. Kant argues for freedom, and therefore God's existence, as a moral necessity, a causality of reason.[37] One obvious implication of this position which relies heavily on the all-season term *necessity* is that Kant was not justified in denigrating the ontological, cosmological, and teleological proofs of God's existence as he did in *Critique of Pure Reason*. A discussion of the matter is, however, beyond the scope of this book.

Critical Perspective on Kant

Our criticism of Kant will largely focus on his theory of reason. It is on the basis of his epistemology that he presents his metaphysics. Jonathan Bennett has noted that the Kantian architectonic clumsily rationalizes the preoccupations of the German academic philosophy of his day while pretending to tackle problems raised by the very structure of reason.[38] There is no doubt that Kant's obsession with systematicity sometimes comes across as forceful, therefore unconvincing. But then Kant was a very ambitious philosopher, the most ambitious philosopher in fact. He wanted to be thorough. In spite of exaggerations here and there, the Kantian system is most compelling. Kant's epistemology is very much psychological in essence. We can overlook the psychological nuance in his theory of reason. For he is grappling with problems far beyond the power of bare logic. Here we are in solidarity with Kant. In the main body of this work we discussed two types of logic, namely, the wider logic of existence (psycho-logic) and the logic of the intellect which is derived from the former (see Part Three, Ch 1, Section 4). While the logic of the intellect animates the Transcendental Aesthetic (the doctrine of experience) psycho-logic animates the Transcendental Dialectic and most of the Transcendental Analytic. To discard the psycho-logical aspect of Kant's philosophy will mean compromising his magnificent system and overlooking his moral doctrine. Our concept of the emotionality of reason vindicates Kant's psycho-logic. Of course, Kant the rationalist extraordinaire was never ready to concede much to emotion and preferred to talk ceaselessly about "reason." I intend to show how reason loses itself in emotion and how the ideas of pure reason, in particular freedom, are vanishing phenomena. While freedom disappears beyond reason and gets lost in emotion alongside the notion of determinism, philosophical fatalism is invoked by us to underline the existence of God as a necessity.

Freedom is a fundamental demand of *mood*; yet realizing this basic demand is what is impossible. It is indicated by the very structure of consciousness, by the primal emotion (Kant prefers "reason") but eludes man just as it is being grasped. The seeming impossibility of human freedom is not consequent upon determinism and the laws of nature, supposedly immutable, which follow from the formula of determinism. Determinism is a conception of the emotional reason, just like freedom. These laws cannot be sacrosanct to the extent that they hold sway under fatalism, the universal necessity that supersedes determinism, as we showed in the main body of this work. Fatalism is the mother of all necessities. The impossibility of human freedom, in its true and radical sense of perfect willing and therefore happiness, follows from the absence of the happiness just indicated, an absence reflected by the human intellect in its pessimistic, cynical, and skeptical tendencies.

We are interested in showing that what Kant demonstrated is not freedom but *liberty*. Freedom demands a radical, therefore transcendental, interpretation. On the other hand, liberty is tied to morality and simply means the ability to choose with the moral question either in the foreground or in the background. For Kant man cannot escape the shadow of natural necessity as a being located in space whose logical processes are time-bound. However, the logical processes of the human mind seek their ultimate grounds in conditions or a condition beyond space and time. According to Kant, the human mind assures us through reference to our moral nature that noumenal reality underlies the phenomenal reality we know so well. Reason thus allows freedom to the noumenal reality, being outside natural necessity. Now I ask, what is man free to do? He is free only to *yearn*. This obviously is no radical freedom. The capacity to decide rationally cannot satisfy this requirement. Kant's reason encompasses man's unique power of thinking, the capacity to think right and act accordingly. This reason is in fact the faculty of the mind that directs the operation of right thinking and right conduct. This reason as an appeal to morality, a call to ethical living, is constrained, "burdened by questions which, as prescribed by the very nature of itself, it is not able to ignore, but which, as transcending all its powers, it is also not able to answer."[39]

The third conflict of the transcendental ideas focuses on the claim of freedom and the counter-claim against it, the thesis and the anti-thesis. The thesis asserts that: "Causality in accordance with laws of nature is not the only causality from which the appearances of the world can one and all be derived. To explain these appearances it is necessary to assume that there is another causality, that of freedom."[40] The anti-thesis counters that: "There is no freedom; everything in the world takes place solely in accordance with laws of nature."[41] Bennett has correctly observed, in response to Kant's confession that we cannot tell how much of the empirical character of our action is due purely to freedom or to nature (determinism), that the theory of freedom is idle since we can never determine the extent of freedom's encroachment into the domain of natural causality.[42] An idle freedom is an impotent freedom. The mind yearns for an active freedom that realizes human happiness. Kant evades this problem by downplaying the happiness component of the *summum bonum* in favor of the virtue component.[43] This agrees well with the strict discipline of his own life. But freedom is not here vindicated. Not even his dilution of his rather dualistic conception of the universe, with reason bridging the gulf between the noumenal-phenomenal totality, is able to save freedom, although *liberty* is put firmly within the orbit of human rationality. Kant's intellectualist inclination leads him into the error of identifying happiness with matter and virtue with form (a moral law preceding all notions of good and evil, which law in reality corresponds to what I have described as the pure yearning of *mood* for consolation). The German thinker continues with the Greek tradition of underrating emotion, which I have argued is prior to reason or intellect, for emotion is a kind of intelligence. I stand in opposition to that mighty thinker here. Freedom as a radical demand of the human mind can be nothing more than the yearning for the reality of happiness. This happiness means perfection in a state of absolute willing of the good that does not lead to further yearning. As a radical demand freedom is either within man's capacity or it is not. I believe it is beyond man's capacity as a vanishing ideality.

It is true that, for Kant, a free will and a will that obeys moral laws are the same. Hume had noted before Kant that emotion drives morality. I have asserted that morality is fundamentally a requirement of emotion. The Kantian appeal to reason has taken us into the domain of morality, the last stronghold of freedom. Kant tries to avoid theoretical probability (in the field of metaphysics) in order to find practical certainty (in the field of ethics). Yet if the pursuit of certainty as a project is in the name of reason, then the rejection of theoretical probability automatically yields ethical uncertainty because we do not know whether our actions are motivated by freedom (autonomy of the will) or natural desires (heteronomy of the will). When probability engulfs moral freedom, this freedom itself begins to vanish. The only thing we are left with which continues to sustain the illusion of freedom is the objectivity of morality. By 'objectivity' I mean basically moral necessity in harmony with nature, not in opposition, a rationality at peace with nature. We have seen in the main body of this work that morality remains objective even after the idea of freedom has been discarded.

The unconditionality of the demand of the Moral Law has no foundation in reason. The origin of the Moral Law is lost in the depth of the human mind which is fundamentally emotional. If reason loses itself in emotion ultimately, the Moral Law must be a requirement of emotion. In which case, the rigid Kantian distinction between the matter and form of the law is an unnecessary Aristotelian subtlety serving mostly to support the Kantian architectonic. Kant stands accused of giving Greek philosophy too much respect. I believe it is possible to trace the foundation of the Moral Law to God rather than to the reason of man. Kant's account of freedom mystifies the subjective grounds of freedom. If transcendental freedom cannot be established by speculative reason, practical reason cannot fare better. Freedom, therefore, is an illusion of human consciousness. It is not a fraud perpetrated by the human mind since it is a fundamental demand of this selfsame mind which, however, cannot unravel it within itself or find it outside itself. Freedom is an illusion sustained by the concept of right and wrong, or moral responsibility. Morality ignores the conflict between freedom and determinism, being itself a supreme law of a unified nature, of the totality of existence.

If freedom for man does exist but cannot be realized within time (or even outside time), reason cannot dare claim to be its ultimate cause in the first place. Reason cannot be the last stop. The reason identified as the giver of the Moral Law lies in the region of the shadow of mystery. Hence, Kant is fond of saying in his great works that the depth of the human soul is inscrutable to man. We are aware of possessing reason, we are conscious of our rationality, only because of our capacity for goodness, a capacity always contrasted with another fundamental capacity: the capacity for evil. If man is not free and morality is objective, then there must be a real cause of morality which makes it possible for freedom not to be missed. Kant probably has this idea in his mind when he talks about the inscrutable nature of the human mind.

What, then, is left for the philosopher and the layman? Freedom vanishes into ideality and determinism gives way to fatalism, but the consolation of philosophy remains. Like Spinoza, Kant has proved himself an able philosopher of consolation. Having put a question mark before the most problematic theme in philosophy, religion, science, and even the arts—the theme of God's existence—in his critical work, he struggles to rehabilitate this theme in the constructive aspect of his works. I agree with K.C. Anyanwu who suggests that Kant's ethical work represents a spirited attempt to rescue the increasingly skeptical Western man from the determinism of science and restore his faith in the freedom required for religion to thrive.[44] Kant writes not only as a philosopher but also as a visionary. Rejoicing in the exercise of his great powers, he calls the territory of "pure understanding" the land of truth, waxing poetic: "This domain is an island, enclosed by nature itself within unalterable limits. It is the land of truth—enchanting name!—surrounded by a wide and stormy ocean, the native home of illusion."[45] His euphoria and intellectual exultation is soon checked as he confronts the problem of teleology and bare determinism, the conflict of purposiveness and mechanicism. This, of course, is one conflict that must trouble every serious thinker. Kant believes that the tension between teleology and mechanism may be resolved if we posit a thing-in-itself as underlying all phenomena. We may not recognize or comprehend this supersensible reality, yet it is the basis of nature and we belong to it as rational beings. Thus we can view nature mechanically from the perspective of the phenomenal or immanent world. We must also, at the same time, consider nature in a teleological perspective as thinking beings. Nature and its laws become a whole grounded in the supersensible. In this way Kant avoids a radical dualism in favor of what I may call a *serrated monism*. This way the mechanical and teleological views of the universe come into harmony.[46] Kant makes this concession to the idea of purpose because of the compulsory anthropomorphic tendency of the human mind, the tendency to see God in nature and to conceive Him in terms as human as possible without offending common sense and the intellect. This is the personalization project that constitutes the core of Teilhard de Chardin's speculative philosophy of evolution.

Even when we have denied God's existence, the temptation to reify and personify chance and read teleological meanings into purely mechanical processes remains strong. Kant himself admits that we cannot think of God or any other cause of the world without bringing in elements of anthropomorphism.[47] In response to the question whether there is a final purpose in the world, he says solemnly: "There remains then nothing but the value which we ourselves give our life, through what we can not only do, but do purposively in such independence of nature that the existence of nature itself can only be a purpose under this condition."[48] When Kant talks about the unconditioned and the limits of reason, we infer that he is referring to what we have called the mythopoeic dream of existence beyond which the human intellect cannot penetrate, merely stopping before it to speculate about it. Any claim of penetrating the mythopoeic dream is mystical. And mysticism presents its own problem just like atheism and a bare mechanical conception of the universe.

G.W.F. Hegel and F.H. Bradley

With the Kantian dialectic of pure reason failing to bridge the gulf between the phenomenal and noumenal planes of reality, the task of logically conceiving a monistic universe became Hegel's. Hegel's work masterfully attempts to reconcile the realm of nature with the realm of mind by positing an all-embracing Absolute who expresses nature and comes to self-knowledge through the world it posits.

In Hegel's monistic equation mind balances nature through a dialectical process of imperfect parts becoming adequate to a perfect sum, hence the seeming paradox of an absolute finite and infinite. Things in the natural world cannot be different from what they are. This is necessity. The Absolute is subjectivity, but things constitute its structure. The world is the unfolding of rational necessity, the goal of history the realization of the freedom of the Absolute. In revealing itself in nature the Absolute alienates itself. Temporal processes commence the Absolute's return to itself through its recognizing itself in nature, using such vehicles as man, the state, and man's intellectual creations (art, religion, philosophy). While Aristotle makes reason or form the unattainable goal of the world, Hegel asserts directly that this goal is the freedom of the Absolute, the world being a manifestation of the Absolute. Thus a world emerges which is both dependent on God and necessary for God to realize His radical freedom by coming to self-knowledge. Without the world there can be no God.

Mind presupposes nature. Universality is the basis of the mind's actuality. Its mode is to manifest itself. In revealing its freedom the mind creates or unfolds nature, which then becomes objective. Hegel notes:

> Mind is the infinite Idea; thus finitude here means the disproportion between the concept and the reality—but with the qualification that it is a shadow cast by the mind's own light—a show or illusion which the mind implicitly imposes as a barrier to itself, in order, by its removal, actually to realise and become conscious of freedom as its very being, ie. to be fully manifested.[49]

When mind is realized in the world we have the objective mind. The subjective mind is in its own relation to itself. The absolute mind is the unity of the mind as subjectivity and as ideality. The three stages of the (finite) mind involve discovering a world already presupposed before it, producing a world mind claims as its own, and, consequently, gaining freedom by positing itself as different and yet as the basis of objective reality. According to Hegel, at the level of the Absolute, the *show* gradually becomes the consciousness of the complete dialectic, the realization of the mind's freedom, gained from and in the world the mind presupposes. Unlike Spinoza's universe of Substance, Hegel's universe is time-bound. Hegel's universe is a perfect universe, like Spinoza's universe. The illusion of imperfection arises when parts are isolated from the whole. Every given stage in history, every proposition or state of affairs, constitutes a thesis. The thesis, being an isolated part or aspect of the Absolute, seeks completion in a new thesis that has emerged from its encounter with an anti-thesis, leading to an ever-expanding picture that attains stability in the perfection of the Absolute.

To better understand Hegel's decidedly tricky philosophy, let us summarize F.H. Bradley's absolute idealism. Throughout his masterpiece *Appearance and Reality* Bradley distinguishes between appearance and a stable reality in which bare existence and its content (form and matter?) come into harmony. Whether Bradley is analysing the ideas of time and space, mind and body, relation, quantity, truth, good, evil, etc., he identifies with great logical subtlety a process in the phenomenon under critical examination that causes a ripple which in turn produces an infinite regress that leads ultimately to the condemnation of the phenomenon to the realm of appearance, not reality. This line of reasoning is very much Hegelian. Appearance being divisible and therefore open to change is ultimately illusory. Yet it qualifies reality and leads us to it. The whole is stable, having no history and not exposed to division and change. That which is relative (appearance) is anchored in the Absolute. The Absolute is reality, the unity of existence and its content. Anything less than the Absolute—time, mind, matter, etc.— throws up an internal contradiction which proclaims it the mere appearance of reality.[50]

Where We Agree with Hegel

Hegel used the dialectical method to support his vision of the purpose and evolution of the universe. I have also used the dialectical method to show how fatalism is the mother of all necessities. While Hegel is dogmatic, we admit the strength of probability. Hegel believes that everything is in sensation (feeling), the insightful declaration that "everything that emerges in conscious intelligence and in reason has its source and origin in sensation."[51] By sensation Hegel is referring not only to sensory vibrations in the mind (body) but also the subjective essence (emotion) of these vibrations. It is satisfying to note that about two hundred years ago a major Western thinker had caught a vision of consolation philosophy. Hegel is actually putting emotion at the base of movement and life like Hume before him and the enigmatic Schopenhauer after him. However, the doctrine of *mood* is different from the Hegelian dialectic in the sense that we have put reason in its proper place as a derivative phenomenon. Instead of arriving at an absolute idealism in the German and therefore European tradition we constructed a philosophy of consolation insisting on being recognized as African philosophy.

Where We Disagree with Hegel and Bradley

Hegel appears to equate rationality with necessity. I do not deny that some kind of intelligence is required for the structuring and evolution of the universe. Indeed, I have identified the Eternal Mood as a primordial mind behind the evolution of the universe. Instead of equating rationality with necessity, however, I asserted that fatalism is the mother of all necessities, the supreme necessity which expresses reason, this very reason starting out as a yearning impulse, as emotion. This insight did not elude Hegel, for he asserted that intelligence has its root in sensation. The universe that Hegel and Bradley announces is one that cannot account for the reality of evil in the world beyond the insincere assertion that incongruity (e.g. ugliness and error) are aspects of the total, enriching and completing the larger picture of things. The Hegelian position asserts that all is well when all is not well. Our doctrine of *mood* led us to the conclusion that all is not well although all may still be well. The optimistic Hegel, understandably intoxicated by his discovery of the dialectical method as a metaphysical instrument, overlooked the urgent need for a philosophy of consolation, having not realized that the dialectical method could outsmart itself by proving white black and *vice versa*.

The glorification of a distorted rationality (certainly not a false rationality) enabled Hegel to avoid a metaphysics of terror. How can a perfect totality have good and bad aspects? What causes the completion of the bad aspect within the totality? Surely, the Absolute as the ultimate synthesis, looking inward, cannot say to itself that all is well. It may not be aware of the failure of reality if it is unconscious. If the Absolute comes to self-knowledge, then it must recognize the imperfection within and outside itself. I have argued that this awareness is actually the beginning of creation and the transformation of impersonality to personality in the idea of a personal God. Hegel seems to use the terms God, Absolute, and Spirit in the same sense. There is no doubt that Hegel goes beyond the empirical description of the world to allow for a God who sustains the world, contrary to the assertion of Stephen Houlgate that Hegel's philosophy essentially eliminates the God-factor.[52] Hegel and Bradley do not show themselves able to avoid the temptation of reifying nature as a totality and personifying it in the Absolute, more or less. Bradley keeps up the pretext of avoiding the reification better than Hegel because the former is a non-mythologizing thinker. When these eminent thinkers talk about the Absolute they refer to what I have identified as the fatalistic principle, God in His phase of impersonality. The Hegelian Absolute is the God of the pantheist. The Absolute can only be perfect existence if it is the logical creation of the anthropomorphic intellect. If the Absolute is truly involved in the awesome cosmic dialectic it must open itself to change. Hegel admits this while stubbornly holding on to the idea of the Absolute's perfect rationality. Bradley shields his Absolute from change and unwittingly gives it away as an existential impossibility.

Once doubt has been cast on the completeness of phenomenal reality the noumenal foundation is automatically exposed to human doubt and subsequent nihilism. Thus we see in real life people refusing to believe in the existence of God because of the reality of evil. Doubt is negative. Yet Bradley proudly sets out to create doubt in his masterpiece, even if this is regarded as academic doubt. Doubt is a rational deficiency of the intellect, a sure indicator of the emotionality of reason. Notwithstanding our disagreement with Hegel, Bradley, and other absolute idealists, we express admiration for the profundity of their insight. We endorse idealism in general as a perspective of the universe that seeks to dispel doubt by indicating the purposiveness of the universe and the meaningfulness of human existence. Before we move on to the greatest existentialist philosophers of the West we must pay homage to Hegel and idealism in the profound words of T.L. Sprigge:

> For we cannot conceive of an existing physical world which is unexperienced, and cannot think of anything else which might exist, once it is granted that we cannot conceive of anything as unexperienced. We may be agnostic idealists in the style of Kant, or we may be panpsychist idealists, but (if my arguments are right) there is no further alternative. And it seems to me that we should embrace the latter, at least in the sense of attempting to understand the world in terms of it, because otherwise we sit complacently behind a wall without even attempting to get over it in the only way possible.[53]

The Existentialists 1: Martin Heidegger and Jean-Paul Sartre

The foremost Western existentialists are difficult philosophers, not only because of the difficult task before them but also because of the manner they employ language, deliberately playing with words and twisting meaning. Heidegger himself is not unaware of the dangers of obscurantism, for he writes that "we must avoid uninhibited word-mysticism. Nevertheless, the ultimate business of philosophy is to preserve the *force of the most elemental words* in which Dasein expresses itself, and to keep the common understanding from levelling them off to that unintelligibility which functions in turn as a source of pseudo-problems."[54] His justification of his ponderous and bombastic choice of words on the grounds of the abstruseness of the question of Being is not convincing.[55] All the same, we have grasped the spirit of the philosophy of Heidegger and Sartre. In their thoughts we have seen reflections of some of the concerns of consolation philosophy.

Martin Heidegger and the Ontology of Care

In exhibiting the dimensions of Being, Heidegger is no doubt contemplating the question of the origin of the universe. He seems to have given up on this problem and embraced an existential phenomenology that avoids the need to reify and personify Being, which reification must yield the idea of God. Thus the promise of the unveiling of Being announced with fanfare in the beginning of the monumental *Being and Time* is lost in the phenomenological investigation of the being of man. The ontology of *care* does not tell us who throws man into the world as care, but it assures us that man is a social being (Being-with) who authenticates himself in his futurity (Being-towards-death) and therefore has temporality as the core meaning of his anxious life. Heidegger does not fail to note that as a being thrown into the world man considered from the standpoint of metaphysics is *guilty*. He is in one dimension an inauthentic being who embraces the attitude of resoluteness in the human community to authenticate his life within the community of fellow humans.[56] This state of mind which follows from our metaphysical guilt helps us to manage anxiety which brings the future near.

Heidegger distinguishes between fear and anxiety. Fear is something threatening from outside. It is himself that Dasein really fears.[57] While anxiety is an immediate fact of consciousness, fear is prior to anxiety and intimate with the structure of the world. Man lives his life in everyday averageness, pursued by the concerns and preoccupations of a world in which he is "fallen." The German thinker links fear with anxiety by saying that it is anxiety that makes fear possible.[58] He notes: "That in the face of which one has anxiety is not an entity within-the-world.... This threatening does not have the character of a definite detrimentality which reaches what is threatened, and which reaches it with definite regard to a special factical potentiality-for-Being."[59] As a state of mind anxiety discloses the world. In anxiety free choice finds its basis. Sartre would later tie man's unlimited freedom with nothingness in the capacity for anguish. However, this freedom based on anxiety is not the radical demand of the human mind, the insistence on absolute willing of the unproblematic. Dasein is only free as a seeker, not a finder, who is a denizen of the world.[60]

Man resolutely awaits death, knowing this event to be inevitable, from the moment of birth. Death has no meaning for the dead, only for the living who yet can never really grasp the loss the dying suffers. By throwing light on the life of A the death of B has a meaning for A. For B the meaning of death contemplated beforehand is the conviction of the radical individuality it brings, the very realization which awakens B to his authenticity. Besides, death gives Dasein rest. Death is necessary.[61] Just as the process of the ripening of a fruit is integral to the development of the fruit, so is death to man's development. With death man fulfils the course of his life regardless of not having realized all his dreams. Death is man's ownmost potentiality-for-Being, as his most intimate and individual event. It is as intimate as it is final, ending all active relations with the world, confirming itself as, in fact, an ontological necessity.[62] Anxiety enacts this most intimate event in the contemplation of death even prior to biological death. Death thus individualizes man, bringing him out of the group life into the solitude of his authentic self.[63] Heidegger avoids despair by allowing man the exercise of his power of resoluteness, his moral pro-life courage.

As defined by temporality man is care. Temporality is indeed the ontological meaning of care. Ordinary time conceived as the conscious experience of duration with its asymmetrical characteristics of past, present, and future arises from temporality which is an originary time. Ordinary time is reckoning and anticipation of the future, a disclosure of Dasein's concern. Ordinary time is the flow of the series of "nows."[64] Since Dasein is spiritual in the sense of being care and man is spatial only as care—not a thing in space but an entity that takes up space—Heidegger founds or attempts to found spatiality on temporality. He insists, however, that this project does not mean that space can be deduced from time.[65] His analytic is after all an existential analytic. The ecstatico-horizonality of man (the priority of the future in the unfolding of man's projects within time) makes man a historical entity. Historicity is Dasein's reckoning with time, which prioritizes the future to which Dasein journeys.[66]

Critical Perspective

Heidegger defends himself against a hypothetical accusation that his system is a philosophy of emotion when he says the concepts of care and anxiety do not directly indicate terms like melancholy, tribulation, or the cares of life and their more positive opposites. As though catching himself in the very act of lying, he confesses that care and anxiety precede the more overtly emotional events of life and constitute a logical horizon for their unfolding. No other Western philosopher has understood the phenomenon of anxiety like Heidegger. Not even Sartre has achieved Heidegger's brilliance in this area. The ontology of care is a staid intellectual music of melancholy, the bare lamentation of existence. He should not have been worried that his system might be construed as a philosophy of emotion since every philosophy is directly or indirectly a philosophy of emotion, a projection of the vision of the individual in a universe where intelligence began its mysterious life as yearning. Like consolation philosophy, Heidegger's philosophy recognizes the priority of the logic of existence over the logic of the intellect.

I am inclined to think that if Heidegger had not appealed to ancient Greece, that if he had adumbrated his ontology of care guided by the consolationist theory of reason, the title of his *magnum opus* would not have been *Being and Time* but *Joy and Time*. Instead of the seemingly mystifying "nothing" he writes about with such brilliance we would have "sadness" simply. Any philosopher who asserts that human life has a meaning beyond the horizon fixed by human joy and sadness, that the intellect realizes a world in which joy and sadness are irrelevant, perpetrates an intellectual fraud. Given our appeal to Africa and Heidegger's appeal to Greece, the results of our separate investigations are not the same although Heidegger and I attempted a philosophical description of the *melancholy being* as the universal man and woman. Heidegger's ontology of care could not go beyond man and therefore became agnostic with regard to Being in general (the reification of which throws up a personal God). My metaphysics of terror led us through the analyses of human joy and sadness to a theistic conception of God. While in Heidegger, anxiety leads man to "resoluteness" and agnosticism and finally "nothingness," this analysis of anxiety leads man to intellectual love and theism. There is no room for "nothingness" in my philosophy because I identified this condition in human affairs as the sadness rooted in the fatality of existence and which has the "silence" of existence as its barest expression, such that there is nothing beyond "silence." Like Heidegger I created a system that is a staid intellectual music of melancholy. Like Heidegger who avoided explicating a philosophy of despair using the instrument of "resoluteness" (allied with anxiety), I avoided explicating a philosophy of despair using the instrument of intellectual love (allied with anxiety).

Heidegger's thought on nothingness deserves examination. He conceives nothingness differently from Sartre. For Heidegger the nothing is the veil of being, that which hides being. "For Nothing is the negation (*Verneinung*) of the totality of what is: that which is absolutely not."[67] Anxiety reveals nothingness. Being and nothingness therefore hang together. Thus he endorses Hegel's notion of the identity of pure being and pure nothing. Heidegger asserts that, "The only thing that remains and overwhelms us whilst what is slips away, is this 'nothing'. Dread reveals nothing."[68] He confesses that nothingness is not an object or anything like an object but a condition or a necessity that enables us to relate with the fact of being human. Man carries nothingness within him as a being defined by anxiety. Man represents nothingness because he is an anxious life. Heidegger insists that man's projection into nothingness which we can be sure of on account of the fact of our anxious life is a kind of transcendence. He says this because anxiety goes together with resoluteness which is decisive for man's realization of his utmost potentiality-for-Being.

I mentioned earlier that nothingness corresponds with human sadness and the barest expression of sadness in existence is silence. Beyond this silence there is nothing (no play on words here). When existentialists like Heidegger and Sartre write about nothingness they are actually highlighting the riddle of existence, the puzzle of the origin of the universe. There are two ways of going around this puzzle. The first way says that the universe is eternal while the second way favors a beginning for the universe. Both ways are tremendously problematic. The first way pictures the universe as a circle, whether stable or expanding. The second way imagines the universe as a line with a beginning and an end or with no end. We are not sure that this line terminates somewhere. A circle can become a line if we regard it as having a center which is a dot or a point. A line too can become a circle if it is regarded as starting off as a point. What I am trying to say is that the two views of the universe involve the ideas of eternity and duration. Eternity may have a beginning which is the "nothing." Still, if nothingness is foundational for being, can it still be nothingness? The difficulty posed by this problem contributed in no small way to my preference of the doctrine of *mood* to the doctrine of being. We may be accused of circular thinking here, yet we find the doctrine of *mood* more convenient than the doctrine of being, especially as it has enabled us to think in a way independent of the Western philosophical tradition, in terms of originality.

Jean-Paul Sartre

While Heidegger set out to investigate the nature of Being in general and later became agnostic about the possibility of discovering Being and turned to the phenomenological description of the empirical man, Sartre considered this Being (the in-itself) not worth investigating, concentrating on the being of man (the for-itself).

Sartre distinguishes between being-in-itself (*être-en-soi*) and being-for-itself (*être-pour-soi*). Sartre's ontology of terror emphasizes nothingness. Man carries nothingness inside him and is faced with it outside him. For Sartre nothingness is vital for transcendence since this nothingness radically opposes what is being-in-itself and is the condition of all questioning attitudes and enquiry.[69] Existent things are phenomenal. As appearance there is nothing behind them, no Being, no Substance, no thing-in-itself, although we can rightly talk about the being of the phenomenon. Sartre contrasts this being with the phenomenon of being. This being of the phenomenon is merely the condition of all revealing. It is different from the phenomenon of the existent thing as the latter is an organized whole of the qualities of the existent thing which we perceive. Yet this appearing requires a basis. The being of the phenomenon supplies this foundation by being transphenomenal and yet uniform with the phenomenon. As the condition of the revelation of the existent thing the being of the phenomenon surpasses our knowledge of it. Consequently, Sartre downgrades the conceptual method of philosophizing, like Heidegger before him, in favor of an existential ontology. He notes: "By not considering being as the condition of revelation but rather being as the appearance which can be determined in concepts, we have understood first of all that knowledge can not by itself give an account of being."[70]

Sartre is the one existentialist philosopher convinced of man's radical freedom. According to this outstanding French thinker, freedom is not free not to be free and it is not free not to exist. The first proposition in the conjunction is the facticity of freedom while the second proposition is the contingency of freedom. Freedom is a given relation of the for-itself to the in-itself because freedom is a non-being which depends on being for its constitution, the in-itself being merely inert positivity. Being simply negation, freedom has no essence.[71] As possessing a mind which is basically negative, man is not only conscious of himself as the creature who punctures a hole in being but also as an acting being for whom freedom is the "indispensable and fundamental condition of all action."[72] Therefore man is condemned to be free.[73] For Sartre the idea of freedom supersedes, subsumes, and, in fact, nullifies determinism. As the fundamental condition of all action, freedom already presupposes obstacles and resistance to its projects which must be overcome. This point introduces Sartre's idea of transcendence, one tied to man's worldly projects. This is also Heidegger's idea of transcendence. The hostility of the environment of man does not mean the triumph of determinism but rather signifies a challenge to man's freedom. Freedom acts on its environment, modifying, changing, and triumphing over the resistance of things. He declares that the end is given in the choice which is free.[74]

Determinism is in reality merely the demand of the self for unbroken continuity of existence. Consequently, to reject freedom is to treat man as a being-in-itself, as part of nature, if nature is conceived as something lifeless and inert. Freedom is already given as the nothingness of being, yet man keeps trying to deny it. Sartre is at a loss how to regard a being which is unity but which is yet regarded as a causal system, as a chain, a series of facts determined by one another on the one hand and as a self-determining spontaneity on the other hand.[75] Still thinking of Kant, he believes that there can and should be no middle ground. If man is not completely free, he is completely determined.

On account of man's awful freedom, bounded by nothingness, moral responsibility is a commitment man cannot escape. The knowledge of the radicality of human freedom, of the impossibility of a transcendent being existing as a limitation of man's freedom, makes man suffer anxiety or anguish. The theme of anxiety is not as decisive in Sartre as it is in Heidegger, but it is still central in the phenomenological existentialism of the French thinker. Freedom is defined as nihilation. Through nihilation man recognizes himself as consciousness which creates itself by choosing its projects. This freedom to act brings man face to face with the grimness of his solitude, the fact of being ultimately answerable only to himself. Thus anguish is born. Fear is the apprehension of the transcendent as dreadful.[76] Anguish is the recognition of a possibility as being specifically one's possibility. Determinism, psychological or otherwise, is a reaction to anguish, a way of denying it. Another way of avoiding anguish is *bad faith*, hiding the truth from oneself. In the phenomenon of bad faith man exposes himself "as a being which is what it is not and which is not what it is."[77]

Unlike Heidegger, Sartre derides the idealization of death as an untenable humanization of that which is not part of the ontological structure of man. As the door to nothingness, death has no meaning for man.[78] Death comes from outside man. It has no meaning for freedom and cannot be interpreted as the resolved chord at the end of a melody. Sartre seems to consider death absurd because men do not choose it. But if death is absurd, so is life itself. For he asserts that it is absurd that we are born and absurd that we die.[79] Sartre does not see the fact of the inevitability of death as constituting finitude. Finitude rather means the necessity of choosing one possibility to the exclusion of others. Since human nature is of the kind that chooses one thing and loses other things not even immortality will save man from finitude.

The atheistic Sartre fails to see how a transcendent being can be constructed out of elements of human wishes and desires. The idea of God is contradictory and in dreaming God man merely expresses the desire to become God, to become a being-in-itself. If God must exist, then He is contingent. Not even Sartre's insistence on moral responsibility saves his philosophy from a certain pronounced pessimism. Thus I call his system an ontology of terror. He notes:

> Each human reality is at the same time a direct project to metamorphose its own For-itself into an In-itself-For-itself and a project of the appropriation of the world as a totality of being-in-itself, in the form of a fundamental quality. Every human reality is a passion in that it projects losing itself so as to found being and by the same stroke to constitute the In-itself which escapes contingency by being its own foundation, the *Ens causa sui*, which religions call God ... man loses himself as man in order that God may be born. But the idea of God is contradictory and we lose ourselves in vain. Man is a useless passion.[80]

Consequently, "The being of human reality is suffering because it could not attain the in-itself without losing itself as for-itself. Human reality therefore by nature is an unhappy consciousness with no possibility of surpassing its unhappy state."[81] Why did Sartre not simply abandon the idea of man being unboundedly free given this pronounced pessimistic vision? The eloquent lamentation above is a lamentation of the impossibility of freedom. Sartre could not give up freedom because his system is an ontology of terror rather than a metaphysics of terror. He avoided a theoretical confrontation between teleology and bare mechanicism or scientific determinism. In line with this general ontology of terror, Sartre makes hostility the original relation of men in the community of human beings as each man tries to transcend his fellow man, overrating himself and denigrating the other, my Brother, as we saw in Part Three of this treatise. The great French thinker is aware that finally only consolation remains for mankind. He notes: "We grasp one of the most fundamental tendencies of human reality—the tendency to fill. A good part of our life is passed in plugging up holes, in filling empty places, in realizing and symbolically establishing a plenitude."[83]

Sartre's philosophy is less consolatory than Heidegger's philosophy. The task of providing a morality of consolation to go together with a metaphysics of terror was not a task for Western philosophers. It is our task, and we think we have accomplished this task in this book although there is room for future improvement of this philosophical project.

Critical Perspective

Sartre's notion of absolute freedom collides with our idea of freedom. Sartre condemns man to freedom, but we declare man a fatalistic being who finds *liberty* as a consolation for the impossibility of freedom. The very fact that Sartre uses the negative word "condemn" in his declaration of man's absolute freedom is self-indicting. It reveals this supposedly absolute freedom as strange, illusory, and therefore untenable. Having provided mankind with an ontology of terror, Sartre faltered when he should have pursued his pessimistic vision to its logical conclusion. The logical conclusion of his endeavor would have been the realization of the inescapability of dialectic, which dialectic would have eliminated, or, at least, diluted the radical dualism of being-in-itself and being-for-itself. Pursuing his pessimism to its conclusion would mean encountering optimism and discovering *liberty* as the shadow of a freedom that is impossible precisely on account of man's finitude and the futility of human existence. Clearly, Sartre recognizes man's finitude and his unhappy consciousness which not only bears witness to moral evil but also perpetrates it by orchestrating it outside the human mind, in the realm of action.

If man's environment is unpredictable and full of adversity, whatever freedom he possesses is an idle freedom, an abstract freedom. Free choice, his self-creation in his specific projects, is nothing like freedom, for freedom is a radical demand for absolute rationality and perfection. I showed in the main body of this work that rationality is rooted in emotionality and that this emotionality exhibits the existential character of morality or yearning. Sartre's free choice actually refers to moral action. The concepts of anguish and moral responsibility are pivotal for his system. Determinism is no threat to free choice, as I have already shown and as Sartre seems to concur. As involving the notion of liberty, free choice pursues a moral imperative. Sartre seems to have overlooked Kant's problematization of the question of freedom and his subsequent solution while formulating his existentialist theory of freedom to fit into his ontology of terror. As sympathetic as we are to the idea of a *philosophy of consolation*, we are unable to agree with the Sartrean notion of an unbounded freedom which bows, nevertheless, to moral impulses and in fact reveals a hostile environment whose overcoming is predicted in advance in the very structure of human freedom. Human life is defined by the struggle to extract meaning out of what seems meaningless but which is truly the meaning of futility. On this question of freedom, and a monumental one indeed, we must accuse Sartre of trivializing his discourse.

Perhaps recognizing freedom as a radical demand that cannot be met, Heidegger cautiously links freedom with the transcendence of the projection of human reality into nothingness, into terror at its barest level of silence. Anxiety has to come in to move man forward in the search for the possibilities of his being. "So finite are we that we cannot of our own resolution and will, bring ourselves originally face to face with Nothing. So bottomlessly does finalization (*rendlichung*) dig into existence that our freedom's peculiar and profoundest finality fails. This projection into Nothing on the basis of hidden dread is the overcoming of what-is-in-totality: Transcendence."[84] Our reference to Heidegger brings us to the turf of transcendence. Here both Heidegger and Sartre agree that transcendence is essentially a within-the-world phenomenon. Neither of the two thinkers appeals to the God-factor which makes their phenomenological approach different from our consolationist method. It is true that both thinkers flirt with the idea of the possible reification and personification of the notions of Being and being-in-itself; yet none of them seriously entertains theistic notions of transcendence. While Heidegger is studiously agnostic, Sartre is joyously atheistic.

I was able to reach a theistic notion of transcendence because of the necessity of the transcendental appeal. This appeal is not foreign to the thought of Sartre (and Heidegger) since he conceives man as a being of possibilities regardless of his finitude and unhappiness. While Sartre and Heidegger acknowledge this appeal as a sign of a future (yet impossible) apotheosis of man, neither the one nor the other develops the startling idea that anxiety is the foundation of peace. Heidegger is preoccupied with a Schopenhauerian extinction and Sartre with a fearful freedom. The analysis of the transcendental appeal enabled me to cut a path from man to God through intellectual love.

On the question of death, we agree more with Heidegger than with Sartre.

While disagreeing with Heidegger that death is part of the ontological structure of man and announcing that death is absurd, Sartre paradoxically extends the absurdity charge to life. He asserts that it is absurd that we are born and absurd that we die. This is a philosophy of despair, a doctrine of futility. Does he pursue the notions of despair and futility to their logical conclusions? He does not. Otherwise his analysis of despair would not stop with the formulation of the question of *nausea*, conceived as the ontological basis of bodily disgust, as representing a relation of body to consciousness.[85] He would have transcended the boundary of nausea and anguish and taken a closer look at the immanent phenomena of joy and sadness instead of merely dismissing man as useless passion and death as absurd. Futility confirms the absurdity of life and death. The most thorough analysis of futility throws up joy and sadness as the very definition of human life, the focal points of religion, science, philosophy, and all artistic activities. If death has implications for human joy and sadness, then it is part of the ontological structure of man.

Death may be a bitter loss for the dead (or better still the dying); yet it holds a moral lesson for the living who learn that the futility of human existence makes it more worthwhile for man to express himself and achieve all that can be done in his lifetime with the goal of deepening human joy and reducing human sadness. The contemplation of death constantly reminds man that as a being that yearns he must die clinging, either to loved ones or the world itself as a scene of excitement, to wealth, and other worldly things. The grief which the living feel at the death of loved ones can have a genuine impact on their moral perspectives of life, their subsequent relations with fellow humans. Therefore death is not absurd. It individualizes man and enriches morality. Heidegger is right after all.

I am convinced that no system of thought, not even scientific thinking, can escape panpsychism which I discussed in Part Two in connection with the anthropomorphic cast of the human mind. I suggested that radical evolution and creationism in the biblical sense would be impossible if panpsychism were wholly objectionable. Sartre is hostile to this idea, not being ready to concede any point to metaphysics beyond his immanent ontology. Yet does his concrete phenomenology completely shield itself from the invasive concept of panpsychism? I think not. He says again and again in his masterpiece *Being and Nothingness* that being-in-itself can experience a "fall" in which it degrades to being-for-itself. Nothingness itself is a hole in being. The creature man is constantly striving to become an in-itself-for-itself. The struggle perfectly acknowledges the solidarity of nature and mind implied in advance in the nature-mind dualism. Human beings keep failing in this project of course. Yet is the very fact that we relentlessly pursue or desire this reconciliation not an indication that the possibility or impossibility of the reconciliation makes sense? Can it be that all the people of the ancient world, people in Africa, Asia, Europe, America, who worshiped God through the deification of natural objects, were utterly mistaken? Without the in-itself the for-itself cannot posit itself as negativity, as the power of questioning, doubting, and denying.

Going by Sartre's understanding of the possible, not as mere potentiality in the sense of something not yet real, but as a concrete existence capable of finding another mode of being, may we dare to presume that the absolute positivity of being-in-itself is illusory, capable of becoming the impulse of life which is yearning? With regard to Sartre this is a strong position since "trans-phenomenal" discourse irritates him. Yet if we are to find explanations for our worldly observations we must appeal beyond the immanent phenomenon. Sartre himself appeals to what he calls the "being of the phenomenon" to provide some tenuous support for the existent thing. He even thinks that man becomes an in-itself at death. Here again his radical dualism is compromised.

The Existentialists II: Sören Kierkegaard and Miguel de Unamuno

It is fitting for us to complete our exercise in comparative Western and African philosophy with a short note on the theistic existentialists as ably represented by Kierkegaard and Unamuno. Unlike the agnostic Heidegger and the atheistic Sartre, Kierkegaard and Unamuno are not systematic thinkers. Yet both made important contributions to existentialism, with Kierkegaard not only supplying Heidegger with the existential framework within which to articulate his exemplary ontology of care but also providing an early model of Christian humanism which Unamuno was later to brilliantly articulate in his philosophical masterpiece *Tragic Sense of Life*.

Sören Kierkegaard

The Christian philosophy of Kierkegaard has been dubbed a philosophy of indirect communication due to the Danish thinker's lavish use of innuendoes, the deliberate rejection of systematic thinking, and a great love of paradox and irony. Yet in his emphasis on inwardness, the meaningfulness of what seems at the surface irrational, the importance of emotion in concrete living, the conflict of the aesthetic life with the ethico-religious life, we have seen echoes of our own thought and perceived areas of solidarity between consolation philosophy and Western existentialism.

Kierkegaard's philosophy of life turns away from abstraction and embraces a concrete subjectivity because the purely logical for him is nothing but a hypothesis in relation to the concrete situation of life. Logic is indifferent to life.[86] Truth is subjective, the revelation of the content of inwardness to the self in the consciousness of the fixed relation of thought and action, the identification of the content of thought with the whole self that alone makes one live in his thought. This is concrete living. The disinterestedness and objectivity of thought are only apparent. In truth these conditions are already unstable, already merging into the involvement and intensity of reality which reaches out to the mind by insisting on responsibility. This action is inwardness. Existence itself cannot be thought of without passion. For Kierkegaard all existential problems are passionate problems. Abstract thought is thought without a thinker.

God cannot be encountered objectively because He is a subject, existing only for subjectivity. It is in the reality in the depth of the human soul, one necessitating the leap of faith, that we come to know God. The demand for God to appear to the senses is a foolish demand since God is embraced in inwardness when passion rises to the level of despair. He asserts paganism as man's immediate relation with God. There is no direct access to Him. His existence is demonstrated through worship and not proofs. When we are cut off from the ethical we experience dread or anxiety as a state of mind. In the individual dread is the inwardness of sin, that which indicates the gulf separating man from God. For Kierkegaard anxiety carries the ethical element and is a factor in man's God-relationship. Anxiety follows from the recognition of human capacity for freedom, which, though representing emancipation, is yet bound to human finiteness. He compares anxiety to dizziness. In *The Concept of Anxiety* he suggests that the phenomenon of anxiety can be interpreted positively to mean that state of mind which positions human freedom towards God and salvation by deepening our self-consciousness through the sense of guilt.

With suffering a requirement of the religious life, Kierkegaard says man must be guided by the absolute *telos*. Eternal happiness is a religious context and exists only for he who has brought himself to a state of absolute devotion to the absolute *telos*.[87] The absolute *telos* is man's real end. Other ends are relative and require only a relative relationship. Since suffering characterizes human existence, human action is essentially a manifestation of existential pathos. The relationship existing between man and his eternal happiness is expressed by his consciousness of guilt, as man comes into the world separated from his absolute *telos*. Guilt then may signify man's consciousness of this separation and his desire to fill the breach. Like Heidegger, Kierkegaard views man as a guilty being by virtue of his very existence.

Fear and Trembling examines the question of faith in relation to the Christian life and human life in general. Faith declares as possible what the intellect considers impossible. While faith does not overlook the judgment of the intellect, it nevertheless asserts, transcendently, the possibility of the impossible. Kierkegaard illustrates his point with the story of the young man who falls in love with a princess, a lady far above his social level. The situation says he can never marry her; yet he is able to believe in the impossible through completing the movement of infinite resignation, a condition of mind consisting of involvement and detachment. Infinite resignation is the last stage preceding faith and is therefore necessary for faith.[88] This echoes Heidegger's notion of resoluteness since infinite resignation consists of emotional involvement and intellectual detachment. Indeed, "he who has resigned absolutely is sufficient unto himself."[89] The absurd here is God's possibility in the face of man's impossibility. The young man resigns himself to the impossibility of marrying the princess; yet in the transcendental dimension he believes marriage is possible.

Kierkegaard calls Abraham the knight of faith. So fascinating is the story of Abraham for the Danish thinker that he finds it more profound and impenetrable than Hegel's metaphysics.[90] Abraham is ready to sacrifice his only son if God demands this of him. At the same time he believes God will not demand this of him. Abraham's mind entertains this paradoxical belief "on the strength of the absurd.... And the absurdity consisted in God's, who yet makes this demand, recalling his demand the very next moment."[91]

Miguel de Unamuno

With the Kantian critique of reason leaving reason severely exposed as a semi-potent phenomenon assuming powers it does not have, Unamuno finds existential solace (and intellectual perturbation too) in the "philosophy of flesh and bone." Consciousness is a burden and reason itself arises from instinct. Love is the instinct of preservation and philosophy becomes a drug for quieting human sorrow. The very demand for explanations, something which consumes even the exact sciences, indicates the tragic sense of life. This tragic sense of life is the fundamental standpoint of human consciousness "which carries with it a whole conception of life itself and of the universe, a whole philosophy more or less formulated, more or less conscious. And this sense may be possessed, and is possessed, not only by individual men but by whole peoples."[92] This consciousness is a disease since it causes man to suffer in the quest for an ultimate explanation that is not forthcoming in an adequate form. Unamuno invites us to participate in the concrete life, away from the false security of abstraction. In fierce and poetic language he asserts that his philosophy is aimed at shaking human faith in progress, in science, even in God, for the sake of a more enduring faith.

The longing for immortality takes centre stage in Unamuno's intense philosophical rumination. This is a longing inseparable from the longing for God. Just as man wishes to live forever, so does he long to see God who shockingly remains veiled. He considers the possibility that the second law of thermodynamics, which envisages entropy reaching equilibrium level and causing the death of everything in the world and the decay of the world itself, may mark the final victory of spirit over matter. He wonders if everything is being reduced to consciousness. If this is the case, then God will become everything, the all in all, the phenomenon of the *apocatastasis*. The dissolution of individual consciousnesses, individual souls, in the active or universal consciousness is for Unamuno the climax of cosmic tragedy. "Do not destroy time!" he cries. "Ours is a hope which is continually converting itself into memory and memory in its turn begets hope.... The eternity that is like an eternal present, without memory and without hope, is dead. Thus do ideas exist, but not thus do men live."[93] If in the end oblivion is man's end, we should not live in a manner that would make this oblivion a just fate.[94] That is, men should live morally and deserve immortality.

Unamuno's humanism is a Christian humanism that projects the Christian spirit of love, faith, perseverance, and finally victory through suffering. The commitment to humanity, that was assuming a definite shape in Kierkegaard, develops fully in Unamuno's thought. Unamuno thinks that strict atheism is impossible because for one to be strictly considered as an atheist one must believe in his "heart" that there is no God. Popular atheism will appear to follow from the conviction of the intellect. For one to be truly an atheist one must have executed a movement of true wickedness.[95] Like Hume, Unamuno suggests that Spinoza might have been an atheist given his pantheism and great faith in the human intellect. It is passion that triumphs in the world, not reason which fails to comfort man. For Unamuno all arguments skilfully organized in defense of such fundamental philosophical questions as the existence of God and the immortality of the soul are essentially emotional formulations pretending to be grounded in reason. In pushing the frontiers of critical thought, and doing so relentlessly, reason ends up as mere skepticism. "The rationalist dissolution ends in dissolving reason itself; it ends in the most absolute skepticism, in the phenomenalism of Hume or in the doctrine of absolute contingencies of Stuart Mill. The supreme triumph of reason, the analytical ... the destructive and dissolvent—faculty, is to cast doubt upon its own validity."[96] Kant is right in deflating the balloon of reason, but he is wrong in attempting to use the very reason he has degraded to prove God's existence from the perspective of morality.

Unamuno draws a radical line between feeling or emotion and reason. According to him, emotion cannot transform consolation into truth just as reason cannot transform truth into consolation. Emotion is ennobled by love which is in its turn a kind of resigned despair. Unamuno all but succumbs to despair. All human beliefs, all affirmations and negations, everything the intellect comprehends or tries to comprehend express human despair. If this is the case, as it must be, "atheists deny God from a kind of rage, rage at not being able to believe that there is a God. They have invested Nothingness with substance and personality, and their No-God is an anti-God."[97] Despair is the basis of faith. Like Kierkegaard, Unamuno is of the opinion that uncertainty prompts us to take the leap of faith. This way suffering which consciousness embraces as its own is rendered bearable. The true philosophy of life involves the compulsory personalization and subjectivization of all phenomena external to the mind. If reason asserts that everything is vanity, imagination enlightened by faith counters that everything is plenitude. Ultimately, we live the vanity of plenitude.

Reason tries in vain to prove the existence of a perfect God. Yet it is a vital God that we intuit in ourselves. It is impotent in this regard. "Every rational conception of God is in itself contradictory. Faith in God is born of love for God—we believe that God exists by force of wishing that He may exist, and it is born also, perhaps, of God's love for us."[98]

Unamuno thinks love will be an absurd thing if there is no God. The vital God of Unamuno is a suffering God who demands our love just as we demand His love. His anguish is also human anguish. With the vision of the suffering Christ before him, no doubt, he says even at the risk of sounding irreverent that, "God, the Consciousness of the Universe, is limited by the brute matter in which He lives, by the unconscious, from which He seeks to liberate Himself and to liberate us. And we, in our turn, must seek to liberate Him ... Religious anguish is but the divine suffering, the feeling that God suffers in me and I suffer in Him."[99] If God does not suffer He will be the cause of suffering, which is the barrier matter sets up against consciousness. For this reason and for the fact that consciousness directs itself towards suffering and death, this same consciousness is a disease. The impossibility of consciousness curing itself of this disease accounts for the tragic sense of life.

If death is a certainty may we hope for immortality? Spain's most eloquent philosopher insists that we may not only hope but also long most passionately for it. It is the discovery of death that opens man up to the idea of God. We lean on faith in God, believing that if "there is a Universal and Supreme Consciousness, I am an idea in it ... After I have died, God will go on remembering me, and to be remembered by God, to have my consciousness sustained by the Supreme Consciousness, is not that, perhaps, to be?"[100]

Critical Assessment

Commitment to Christian humanism links Kierkegaard to Unamuno, although the latter develops this humanism more deeply. While Heidegger hesitates to connect human anxiety to the God question and while Sartre pointedly grounds it in "nothingness," Kierkegaard clearly links anxiety with the God question by connecting the phenomenon with sin, freedom, and salvation. Kierkegaard makes of anxiety a moral phenomenon, an intellectual path already being taken by Heidegger in his idea of man being a "concernful Being-alongside and solicitous Being-with". Sartre too is on the same page with Heidegger since anguish recognizes a terrible responsibility arising from an absolute human freedom. Kierkegaard steers the existentialist discourse in a theistic direction by linking anxiety with existential guilt and making both anxiety and guilt states of mind tuned to the absolute *telos* which only God can grant. Unamuno is in agreement with his illustrious predecessor and clears a path to God through despair even though the question of immortality is all-consuming for him.

The consolationist theory of anxiety is closer to the models developed by Unamuno and Kierkegaard than those developed by Heidegger and Sartre largely because of our unapologetic theistic inclination. Armed with the doctrine of *mood*, I traced the phenomenological history of anxiety from the state of despair to the state of intellectual love, thus rehabilitating the reason which the critical intellect had twisted into an uninspiring skepticism.

There can be no doubt that the anti-rationalist project of Kierkegaard receives a truly anarchic, even if brilliant, expression in the Christian humanism of Unamuno. The great Spanish thinker dismisses reason as entirely critical and cynical and creates a gulf between reason and emotion by asserting that emotion cannot realize truth out of consolation while reason must always fail to convert truth to consolation. When Unamuno asserts the priority of emotion over reason he gets my approval. When he dismisses reason altogether as critical and skeptical, I shake my head in dissatisfaction. The dialectic of *mood* enabled us to avoid Unamuno's somewhat extreme position. We were able to rehabilitate reason after grounding it in feeling. We even declared reason the refinement of the emotion, thereby conferring superior dignity on it and making it a guide to emotion. It is contradictory for Unamuno to recognize reason as emerging from instinct and yet go on to assert that reason is not a consoling faculty.

What makes the faculty of reason different from the emotional capacity in man is not a radical dualism that isolates the two spheres of perception but rather the power of the intellect which reason appropriates. Yet emotion has a claim to ownership of the intellect since it is the foundation of reason. Because of this indirect claim we notice in real life, and even in the mental life, that the human intellect is emotional. The proof of this assertion is the destructive analysis which the intellect is capable of, a fact that does not elude Unamuno's insightful but over-romantic mind. The destructive power of the human intellect is called criticism. This criticism is not always of the honest kind since emotion infects its natural effervescence. To criticize is to harbor some form of doubt. Doubt expresses cynicism and in its turn cynicism is rooted firmly in discontent and despair. In the main body of this work I repeatedly referred to despair as the denizen of thought. If this is true, then reason is a consoling faculty in addition to being a destructive faculty. It is reason which furnishes the love of the intellect. Bare feeling, unassisted by reason, cannot throw up the concept of intellectual love.

We agree with the Spanish thinker that the classical idea of God as omnipotent and omniscient is untenable given the reality of our imperfect universe. We agree with him that the human mind personalizes and subjectivizes. The human mind is very much anthropomorphic, for which reason Kierkegaard identifies paganism as the immediate human relation with God.[101] Yet we find Unamuno's process theory of God unsatisfactory. His God is an impotent God who needs man to be who He is. This seems to us over-romantic. Unamuno's view does not agree with our own view which regards God as the Being that has conquered despair within Him and has become a personal principle of the universe, no longer the impersonal Eternal Mood of pre-creation. All the same, Unamuno has enriched existentialism and provided insights that have benefited philosophy in general.

Conclusion to the Fourth Part of the African Philosophical Synthesis

It was necessary for us to show in Part One that consolation philosophy is African philosophy. I achieved this by tracing my inspiration not to ancient Greece and Greek philosophy but to African ethno-philosophy and my general African heritage, consisting of my mother tongue, my tribe and its worldviews, and the very fact of being an African. Just as this demonstration was necessary in Part One, so also was it necessary for me to show that any system of thought which meets the strict requirement of African philosophy is automatically world philosophy. Hence, I undertook an adequate study of the fundamental ideas of some of the greatest philosophers in the Western tradition, namely, Plato, Aristotle, Spinoza, Hume, Kant, Hegel, Bradley, Heidegger, Sartre, Kierkegaard, and Unamuno. The list is not exhaustive, but it is adequate. If I have overlooked contemporary scholars of Western philosophy in the analytical and phenomenological traditions it is because I feel that the contemporary Western philosophical scene is largely devoid of original thinkers although the level of scholarship remains awesome.

The exercise in comparative philosophy showed that the basic ideas of consolation philosophy are not unknown to Western philosophy. In Plato's philosophy we saw the attempt to demonstrate the objectivity of morality and the "moralness" which resonates with our idea of the fundamental moralness of the world. We largely agreed with Aristotle's teleological vision of the universe. Spinoza's monistic universe also harmonized with ours even as we pointed out that his theory of reason collides with ours. We noted with much satisfaction that Hume declared emotion the master of reason although we were not prepared to sustain the assault on reason in the knowledge that human reason is the refinement of the emotion and therefore should not be subjected to emotion's lordship. In Kant we encountered the West's greatest philosopher, greater than even Plato and Aristotle. After paying homage to Kant and appreciating his Critical Philosophy we identified the breach in his theory of reason. Consequently, we could not accept his proof of freedom. We showed that what Kant meant by the term "freedom" is what we call "liberty"—simply, endorsement of the objectivity of morality. We saluted Hegel for discovering or rather developing the method of dialectic and identifying it as a universal category. However, we noted the failure of the Hegelian dialectic to account for the reality of evil in the world. We reconsidered Hegel in the light of Bradley and noted that both thinkers were absolute idealists.

Like us, the existentialists were struggling with the question: "Is human life futile?" The results of their investigations showed that consolation philosophy has much in common with Western existentialism. Yet world philosophy transcends the Western and African traditions. Much as we would like to attempt a comparative exercise in African and Oriental philosophy, we realized we were unprepared to throw light on the philosophical aspects of Hinduism, Buddhism, Confucianism, Jainism, Taoism, and other religio-philosophical systems of the great peoples of the Orient. Indian, Chinese, and Japanese philosophies resemble African ethno-philosophy to the extent that the former are in many ways mythological and religious in character. One may say that Oriental philosophy produced individual thinkers in the distant past while African philosophy came into existence as a written tradition only recently. But then the work of Odera Oruka in sage philosophy has shown that African communities actually produced independent thinkers.[102] The main difference here is that Oriental philosophy has existed for ages as a written tradition while African philosophy developed late as a written form. The main sources of Indian philosophy, for instance, the Upanishads, the Rig-Veda, the Baghavad-Gita, etc., are written documents. The schools of Hindu and Buddhist thought are so many that a close study of their teachings and doctrines will be required before we can attempt a comparative study of Indian philosophy, in particular, and consolation philosophy. The challenge of a close study of the highly idealistic thought of the people of India is something we hope to meet in the future.

Nevertheless, in saivism (the doctrine of a universal absolute consciousness), the union of Brahman and Atman, the four noble truths of Buddhism, the idea of nirvana, and karmic conditioning, we find echoes of our own thought. This is hardly surprising since humanity is one everywhere. Since the physical life precedes the mental life, since life is first a lived experience before being an abstract intellectual construction, the fundamental question of life, the question why there is something instead of nothing, morphed into the most intelligent question of human existence on the insistence of a philosophy of life: "Is human life futile?"

Despite the increasing number of philosophical schools that emerged in the centuries after the Buddha's death with their preoccupations with epistemological and logical questions, the fact remains that Buddhism was born as a philosophy of life tasked with finding answers to life's most intelligent and terrifying question: "Is human life futile?" The Buddhist solution is a profoundly pessimistic solution regardless of the noble heights it attained in its moral dimension. The extinction of yearning expressed in the concept of nirvana, whether in a condition of nothingness metaphysically grasped or in an unperturbed state in the world ascetically engineered, is a wish of the despairing intellect. The longing for nirvana follows from resignation. It is not for nothing that I make fatalism the mother of all necessities.

If the concept of nirvana is accounted for by fatalism, then the concept itself is still determinant for yearning, still a conditioning for yet another state of yearning rather than the overcoming of desire. Nirvana promises perfect bliss with the future realization of a condition of eternal peace. We approve of foundational Buddhism up to a point just as we approve of the philosophy of Arthur Schopenhauer up to a point, that is, the limit of pessimism. To stop at the definition of life presented by the pessimistic perspective in the search for an answer to the question of life's futility is to blur reality. This much the analysis of *mood* has shown. Thus while we agree with the basic submission of Buddhism, and should explore it further, we insist on having a more balanced picture of reality by introducing the optimistic perspective (a kind of anti-thesis) to arrive at the idea of consolation which is the direct and indirect resting place of all philosophizing, all scientific and non-scientific thinking.

Conclusion

The Metaphysics of Consolation

The second and third parts of this work contain the philosophical justification of the consolationist thesis posed in the first part. I asserted in Part One that a constructive alternative program to African ethno-philosophy is possible without this alternative program being subservient to Western philosophy, with its roots in the authentic African culture. I showed clearly how indebted my system is to ethno-philosophy. Given the fact that ethno-philosophy in itself cannot provide a sustainable challenge to world philosophy, I promoted consolation philosophy as an independent system that has attained a level of constructive and analytical sophistication adequate to challenge 21st century philosophy.

I argued in the main body of this work, precisely in the second and third parts, that the doctrine of *mood*, the emotion-intellect theory of reason, the concept of the *melancholy being* as the universal man and woman, the subordination of determinism to fatalism and the consolationist solution to the problem of evil in the world constitute an original contribution to African philosophy, speculative thought, and world philosophy. Part Four was dedicated mostly to the justification of consolation philosophy as a universally applicable philosophy.

The great question of philosophy, science, and religion is the question why there has to be a universe instead of a no-universe or nothingness, the absolute nil which the human intellect cannot comprehend because it is already familiar with the condition of existence, the universe of matter and energy. We cannot dismiss the possibility of nothingness which troubled the Western existentialists because of the possibility of an eternity in duration, a timelessness that has a beginning. Yet a nothingness that has become positive ceases to be an absolute nil. It becomes a form of existence. The question remains, therefore: What is being? I recast it thus: What is *mood*?

I identified joy and sadness as constituting all the meaning of human existence. If there is any meaning for humanity beyond these elements of the *mood* of man, then I beg to be enlightened. To lift the sphere of human subjectivity to the objective universe or what is glibly called nature (of which man is surely a part), I subordinated determinism to fatalism. I affirmed man to be a being of melancholy, thereby confirming and universalizing the great inspiration of L.S. Senghor. The Senegalese thinker, a man Africa can be proud of always, announced erroneously that the reason of the African is emotional while the reason of the European is logical and disinterested. I showed that there is only one reason for both the African and the European, indeed all races. I showed that not only is this reason moral as Kant had announced but also that it is an emotional reason. The emotional reason is not an African reason or a European reason or an Oriental reason. The emotional reason is the reason of the mind of the *melancholy being* who grapples with the question of life's futility and the seeming pointlessness of the universe. This reason is the mental life of the universal man. The *melancholy being* is the heir of humanity.

Mudimbe noted that post-colonial African philosophy consciously or unconsciously directs itself towards the West and ends up being shaped by the Western knowledge-universe. This dilemma of African philosophy arises because Africa arrived late on the intellectual scene and must therefore take Western intellectual concerns into consideration while reinventing itself. This reappraisal which Mudimbe seems to discount is legitimate and necessary. To ignore the Western experience altogether in the search for an authentic African episteme is to artificially accentuate the We-Other or Africa-Europe dichotomy and narrow the shared horizon of humanity; it will amount to canceling the project designed to supersede ethno-philosophy, whether this ethno-philosophy is the African type or the Western type which arrogates universalism to itself while losing touch with Africa. It is only in reacting confidently to the achievements and failures of the West in the knowledge that we have a past and will possess our future that we can reinvent Africa in our own image as advocated by Mudimbe and other Afrocentric authors. This is the path I have taken in this work. I believe that this path has guided me past ethno-philosophy and Western philosophy, leading me to a truly African knowledge-universe, the consolationist universe.

Scope for Further Research

While it is true that African philosophy has firmly established itself as a written tradition since it was announced by missionaries like Placide Tempels, African nationalists and freedom fighters like Senghor and Amilcar Cabral, and academic philosophers like Kwasi Wiredu and J.O. Sodipo, the tradition has largely stagnated in the form of ethno-philosophy. It is even possible to identify

African philosophy with ethno-philosophy in view of the ubiquity of the latter and its indisputably stupendous achievements. The attempt by scholars like Oruka to provide constructive alternative programs to ethno-philosophy failed because of the inability to break away radically from ethno-philosophy which has no doubt exhausted itself. With the idea of sage philosophy Oruka tried to show that traditional African communities produced critical and independent thinkers. As part of the criticism of Oruka's project, sage philosophy has been deemed guilty of ethnic chauvinism and insularity arising from the extreme glorification of what is African.[1] The weightiest indictment is the fact that these indigenous sages did not contribute much to African philosophy. The question now is: If African communities produced independent and critical thinkers in the past why did these original thinkers not advance the tradition? Hermeneutic thinkers like Okolo believe African philosophy should restrict itself to the project of liberating Africa from the suffocating aspect of both traditional society and modernity.[2] Sadly, the consequence of this kind of anti-intellectualist commitment is the absence of great metaphysical, epistemological, and logical works in African philosophy, and the super-abundance of works in the philosophy of culture and the philosophy of development which blurs the line between philosophy and such disciplines as political science, sociology, development studies, and anthropology. Inter-disciplinary cooperation is no doubt desirable, but such commitment must not come at the expense of the development of African philosophy as a unique and proud identity. At the moment this identity has not assumed a formidable aspect.

I have said much already about the revolutionary character of Prof. Asouzu's work which has inspired me in many ways. Certainly, we can continue from where he stopped and keep pushing the frontiers of innovation in African philosophy. It is fitting at this point to mention the achievement of Jonathan Chimakonam Okeke in the field of African logic, another testimony to the quality of the works of the researchers of the Calabar school which claims Asouzu as a member. Every self-respecting African philosopher will not fail to notice the stagnation of African philosophy. Taiwo raised his famous lamentation because of the striking nature of this intellectual stagnation of the black people. He found the cause of the scandalous stagnation in a subtle Western intellectual racism, forgetting that Black Africa itself has largely failed to dignify its finest minds, thus necessitating the search for intellectual validation in the West. This puts the Western intellectual "hegemony" in a position of power, which has always been abused by all who wield it. I locate the cause of the stagnation of African philosophy in the relative absence of original and innovative thinkers. The great achievement of Chimakonam is the daring he exhibited in tracing this absence of originality to the fundamental thought processes of African philosophers. He not only identifies the problem but he also proffers solution.

Chimakonam's work in African logic led him to the conclusion that African philosophers have been trying for too long to think like Westerners and coming off perpetually as second best, if not third best. Chimakonam has systematized and formalized the fundamentals of African logic. I will condense his main submissions into a paragraph here. He has formulated three laws of thought that are more or less in opposition to the Aristotelian laws of thought which the West has claimed enthusiastically. According to him, the laws of integration (*njikọka*), complementarity (*nmekọka*), and included middle (*ọnọna-etiti*) are the African equivalent of the laws of identity, non-contradiction, and excluded middle. The law of integration is an in-context law, very rigorous. A variable can be true only if it has been evaluated relative to all other variables having a bearing on it. For instance, A is true if and only if A is true with all necessary facts available. The law of complementarity underlines group strength. Individual variables lose their strong identities in the complementary state. Consequently, African logic lends dignity to inconsistency and completeness as valuable elements of African thought. This is in opposition to the consistency and incompleteness demanded by Western logic. The complementary state is a perfect and complete mode. For a variable A to be strictly determined it must move to the contextual mode. The law of integration must come into operation. According to Chimakonam, the complementary state is pre-contextual.[3] The law of included middle asserts that A is both true and false but para-contingently. Something could be what it is and something else within the complementary framework. Chimakonam's submissions are radical. He is not saying that African logic encourages lawless reasoning; he is rather telling us that Africans have a unique way of seeing the world, much like Senghor before him. Unlike Senghor, however, Chimakonam has systematized, and is still systematizing, African logic. He believes that African science and philosophy will take a big leap forward once African thinkers recognize their basic thought patterns. With this realization must follow originality and innovation, the absence of which has been much lamented in African philosophical and scientific thought.

At the height of his powers Wiredu sent out his famous call for the decolonization of African philosophy. Today Chimakonam has sent out another call. Not satisfied with merely sending out the call, he has shown us the logical structure of the black intellect. While I believe that Chimakonam's logical theory is not altogether alien to the Western intellect (being basically an endorsement of dialectic)—in the same way that the law of non-contradiction is not altogether foreign to the African intellect—I have come to see the profundity of his achievement. For consolation philosophy is the perfect demonstration of the truth of Chimakonam's submissions. The convergence of the works of three Nigerian researchers working independently is a clear indication of the ongoing reorientation of African philosophy in the direction of rationality, systematicity, and individualism. It is safe to assume that independent work is going on in other African countries; in which case the post-ethnophilosophical era has dawned in African philosophy.

This book presents the basic ideas of consolation philosophy. The ethical principles adumbrated in this work form a preliminary outline of the ethics of consolation. There is room for further research in epistemology, comparative philosophy, the philosophy of culture, Oriental philosophy, Latin American philosophy, and the further development of the metaphysics of terror. This work is in fact an introduction to consolation philosophy.

Notes

General Introduction

[1] Antony William Amo addressed the words quoted to Europe and the rest of the world. They are appended to a line from Epictetus, which he picked as his personal motto. The exact words of Epictetus are: "He who can accommodate himself to necessity is wise and has an inkling of things divine." Abraham reports that Amo appended his own thoughts on an album of a friend of his, Gottfried Achenwall, on May 5, 1740 in Jena. See William E. Abraham, "Anton Wilhelm Amo," in *A Companion to African Philosophy*, ed. Kwasi Wiredu (Oxford: Blackwell Publishing Ltd, 2004), 197.

[2] Hountondji used the term "unanimism" to indicate the tendency to hasty generalization by ethno-philosophers. Here a researcher, fully aware of his own lack of originality and therefore lacking the intellectual confidence to break out of the shadow of the tribe, will announce to the world a particular philosophical nuance of the tribe to which he belongs while, at the same time, coloring the supposedly collective philosophy with his own personal opinion. See Paulin Hountondji, "Scientific Dependence in Africa Today," *Research in African Literatures* 21.3 (1990): 5-15. See also Paulin Hountondji, "From the Ethno-sciences to Ethno-philosophy: Kwame Nkrumah's Thesis Project," *Research in African Literatures* 28.4 (1997): 112-20. Rather than merely enumerating and writing about anthropological issues, Hountondji will prefer that African philosophers investigate the presuppositions underlying these anthropological issues. Expectedly, Hountondji is demanding originality. But how can mere analysis inspire originality in the absence of a foundation, of a prior synthesis? In presenting the worldview of the tribe as a philosophy—and not only as philosophy but also as an original and therefore truly African philosophy—ethno-philosophy asserts that it has married analysis with synthesis and has scored a victory for African philosophy. Therefore Hountondji's criticism is harsh, although justifiable.

[3] Kwasi Wiredu, "Toward Decolonizing African Philosophy and Religion," *African Studies Quarterly* 1.4 (1998), http://www.africa.ufl.edu/asq/v1/4/3.htm.

[4] See M.A. Makinde, "Whither Philosophy in Africa?" in Proceedings of the 20th World Council of Philosophy, Boston, USA, http://www.bu.edu/wcp/Papers/Afri/AfriMaki.htm.

[5] For the denunciation of Hegel's supposed denial of rationality to the Black African mind, see Olufemi Taiwo, "Exorcizing Hegel's Ghost: Africa's Challenge to Philosophy," *African Studies Quarterly* 1.4 (1998), http://www.africa.ufl.edu/asq/v1/4/2.htm. Like most Europeans of his day, Hegel considered Africa a dark continent and Black Africans

a mysterious set of people, possibly, nay, certainly, without rationality, without any real comprehension of sublime ideas such as those of God and law. At a loss for what to make of the African in his ignorance, Hegel confesses that with regard to what struck him as a "peculiarly African character," the category of Universality, with which the human mind connects all our ideas of the facts of the world, must be abandoned. See G.W.F. Hegel, *Philosophy of History*, trans. J. Sibree (New York: Prometheus Books, 1991), 93. African philosophers have generally responded with outrage to Hegel's erroneous conclusion. Taiwo's paper is a typical and eloquent example of this intellectual outrage. See also F.O.C. Njoku, *Essays in African Philosophy, Thought & Theology* (Owerri, Nigeria: Claretian Institute of Philosophy, 2002), 7-9.

[6] Taiwo, "Exorcizing Hegel's Ghost."

[7] Innocent Asouzu is a Catholic priest and a professor of philosophy at the University of Calabar, Nigeria. His published works include *Ibuarụ: The Heavy Burden of Philosophy Beyond African Philosophy* (Münster: Litverlag, 2007); *The Method and Principles of Complementary Reflection in and Beyond African Philosophy* (Münster: Litverlag, 2005); *Ibuanyidanda. New Complementary Ontology: Beyond World-Immanentism, Ethnocentric Reduction and Impositions* ((Münster: Litverlag, 2007); and *Ikwa Ogwe. Essential Readings in Complementary Reflection: A Systematic Methodological Approach* (Calabar, Nigeria: Saesprint Publishers, 2007). Introductory and other very adequate articles on his complementary reflection are available online at http://frasouzu.com/Issuesand Papers/SeminarPapers/ComplementaryReflection.htm.

[8] In a marked contrast to Olufemi Taiwo who has blamed intellectual racism for the lowly status of African philosophy, Asouzu believes African philosophical thinkers themselves have failed to make their philosophical tradition worthy of respect. See Asouzu, *Ibuarụ*, 292. With regard to the reprehensible intellectual laziness and over-dependence of the departments of philosophy of the various African universities on Western genius, M.A. Makinde laments the fact that African philosophy is barely taught in African universities and that the hoopla over whether African philosophy exists or not is at bottom a facetious exercise, chiefly a footnote to Western philosophy. See M.A. Makinde, "Teaching Philosophy in Africa," *Teaching Philosophy* 10.3 (September 1987): 235-36. What is tragic in this admission is that by "African Philosophy," Makinde actually means "Ethno-philosophy." In which case, there is really nothing to teach. It is then obvious that the teachers are not to be blamed for not teaching something that barely exists.

[9] See V.Y. Mudimbe, *The Invention of Africa: Gnosis, Philosophy, and the Order of Knowledge* (Bloomington, Indiana: Indiana University Press, 1988).

[10] See D.A. Masolo, *African Philosophy in Search of Identity* (Bloomington, Indiana: Indiana University Press, 1994), 2; Barry Hallen, "Contemporary Anglophone African Philosophy: A Survey," in *A Companion to African Philosophy*, ed. Kwasi Wiredu (Oxford: Blackwell Publishing Ltd, 2004), 118-19.

[11] See Martin Heidegger, *Being and Time*, trans. John Macquarrie and Edward Robinson (New York: Harper and Row, 1962). Division 1 of Part 1 particularly highlights Heidegger's idea of anxiety in *existential* terms. Anxiety points to the emptiness into which death plunges us. The only positive meaning of death is on the side of life which ironically is doomed in perpetuity as a preparation for death, in our resolute anticipation of future outcomes. Heidegger's implied agnosticism is carried further to the level of unapologetic atheism by Sartre who brings anxiety close to freedom without exactly granting them the same identity. Anxiety and freedom belong to human consciousness, and as belonging to consciousness anxiety convinces us of our terrible, because unbounded, freedom. This freedom being foundationless is nothingness, the nothingness of the being-for-itself (*être-pour-soi*). There is no God. Certainly being-in-itself (*être-en-soi*) cannot be God since it cannot found itself and is therefore pure positivity. See Jean-Paul Sartre, *Being and Nothingness*, trans. Hazel E. Barnes (New York: Pocket Books, 1966), Part 4.

Chapter 1: Introduction to Consolation Philosophy

[1] William E. Abraham, "Anton Wilhelm Amo," in *A Companion to African Philosophy*, ed. Kwasi Wiredu (Oxford: Blackwell Publishing Ltd, 2004), 191-199.

[2] Martin Heidegger, *An Introduction to Metaphysics* (New York: Anchor Books, 1961), 1.

[3] We agree with Njoku who notes that Tempels investigates Bantu philosophical worldviews with a Bergsonian temper. The influence of Teilhard de Chardin is even greater. See F.O.C. Njoku, Essays in *African Philosophy, Thought & Theology* (Owerri, Nigeria: Claretian Institute of Philosophy, 2002),17, 20. Asouzu has been particularly critical of Tempels for essentializing force in African ontology, thereby promoting a doctrine of exclusive ontological dynamism, one unique to Africa. See Innocent Asouzu, *Ibuanyidanda: New Complementary Ontology Beyond World-Immanentism, Ethnocentric Reduction and Impositions* (Münster: Litverlag, 2007), 176ff.

[4] M.A. Makinde, "Teaching Philosophy in Africa," *Teaching Philosophy* 10.3 (September 1987): 235f.

[5] Lucien Levy-Bruhl, *Primitive Mentality* (Paris: University of France Press, 1947), 17.

[6] D.A. Masolo, *African Philosophy in Search of Identity* (Bloomington, Indiana: Indiana University Press, 1994), 1.

[7] Njoku, *Essays*, 292-93.

[8] Lucius T. Outlaw, "Africana Philosophy: Origin and Prospects," in *A Companion to African Philosophy*, ed. Kwasi Wiredu (Oxford: Blackwell Publishing Ltd, 2004), 90.

[9] See John Murungi, "A Philosophical Path to African African Departures,"

Caribbean Journal of Philosophy 2.1 (2010), http://ojs.mona.uwi.edu/index.php/cjp/article/viewFile/2500/2324.htm. Murungi here harps on the homelessness of the African—even though he has an ancestral home in Kenya, unlike the African-American he has befriended as a diaspora African—the feeling of impotence that comes with not being in control of one's destiny in a world seemingly owned by the West. I think that Murungi over-idealizes Africa.

[10] Barry Hallen who lived among the Yoruba of Nigeria and taught philosophy in Nigerian universities worked with the late J.O. Sodipo. Their partnership produced *Knowledge, Belief and Witchcraft: Analytic Experiment in African Philosophy,* revised ed. (Stanford: Stanford University Press, 1997).

[11] J.O. Sodipo, "Philosophy in Africa Today," *Thought and Practice: A Journal of the Philosophical Association of Kenya* 2.2 (1975): 117.

[12] Jonathan O. Chimakonam, "Outline of African Logic for the Development of Thought, Science and Technology in Africa," *International Journal of Philosophy and Religion* 3.1 (2011): 107-108.

[13] See, for instance, Cheikh Anta Diop, *The African Origin of Civilization: Myth or Reality* (New York: Lawrence Hill Books, 1974); *Civilization or Barbarism* (New York: Lawrence Hill Books, 1991).

[14] See Books III-XII of Aristotle's *Metaphysics* for his teleological doctrines. The great Greek philosopher discusses the problem of God's existence in Book XII.

[15] Antony Flew, for instance, has written a lucid and excellent little book outlining the reasons for his conversion from atheism to deism. See Antony Flew, *There is a God: How the World's Most Notorious Atheist Changed His Mind* (New York: HarperCollins, 2007).

Chapter 2: Countdown to Consolation Philosophy

[1] Olufemi Taiwo, "Exorcizing Hegel's Ghost: Africa's Challenge to Philosophy," *African Studies Quarterly* 1.4 (1998), http://www.africa.ufl.edu/asq/v1/4/2.htm.

[2] Kwasi Wiredu, "Toward Decolonizing African Philosophy and Religion," *African Studies Quarterly* 1.4 (1998), http://www.africa.ufl.edu/asq/v1/4/3.htm.

[3] Theophile Obenga, "Egypt: Ancient History of African Philosophy," in *A Companion to African Philosophy*, ed. Kwasi Wiredu (Oxford: Blackwell Publishing Ltd, 2004), 47.

[4] See, for instance, C.B.N. Gade, "What is Ubuntu? Different Interpretations among South Africans of African Descent," *South African Journal of Philosophy* 31.3 (2012): 484–503.

[5] Julius Nyerere, *Ujamaa: Essays on Socialism* (Nairobi: Oxford University Press, 1968), 10–13.

[6] Nyerere, *Essays*, 12.

[7] See Innocent Onyewuenyi, *The African Origin of Greek Philosophy: An Exercise in Afrocentrism* (Nsukka, Nigeria: University of Nigeria Press, 1993). As the title of this book implies, it is unabashedly pro-Africa. It seeks to show that ancient Egyptian philosophical thought served as the prototype of ancient Greek philosophy. This is a controversial terrain. We refuse to be drawn into the fruitless argument. While it is almost certain that ancient Greece borrowed or "stole" ideas from ancient Egypt it cannot be doubted that Greek philosophical genius was always unique. For us it is enough to note that philosophy survived in the myths of ancient Egypt, qualifying the philosophical outlook of the ancient Egyptians as ethno-philosophy.

[8] Cheikh Anta Diop, *Civilization or Barbarism* (New York: Lawrence Hill Books, 1991), 357ff.

[9] Onyewuenyi, *Origin*, 252.

[10] Paulin Hountondji, "Knowledge as a Development Issue," in *A Companion to African Philosophy*, ed. Kwasi Wiredu (Oxford: Blackwell Publishing Ltd, 2004), 532.

[11] Kwame Gyekye, "The Concept of a Person," in *Philosophy and Choice*, ed. Kit R. Christenson (Mountain View, California: Mayfield Publishing Company, 1999), 216–17.

[12] See Gyekye, "The Concept of a Person," 217.

[13] Kwasi Wiredu, "The Concept of Mind with Particular Reference to the Language and Thought of the Akans," in *Contemporary Philosophy: A New Survey*, ed. Guttorm Floistad (Dordrecht: Martinus Nijhoff Publishers, 1987), 160–63.

[14] See O.A. Balogun, "Ori as the Sole Determinant of Human Person in Yoruba Traditional Thought: Further Comments" (paper presented at the Biennial Conference and Meeting of the Nigerian Philosophical Association held at the University of Calabar, Calabar, Nigeria, from October 8 to 11, 2008). Gbadegesin may be agreeing with us when he submits that the *okan* is understood both as the physical heart and the non-local mind. See Segun Gbadegesin, " 'Eniyan': The Yoruba Concept of a Person," in *Philosophy from Africa: A Text with Readings*, ed. P.H. Coetzee and A.P. Roux (Johannesburg: Thomson Publishing, 1998), 150ff.

[15] The following works by Paulin Hountodji more than reveal his dissatisfaction with ethno-philosophy. *African Philosophy: Myth and Reality*, 2nd ed. (Bloomington, Indiana: Indiana University Press, 1996); "From the Ethnosciences to Ethno-philosophy: Kwame Nkrumah's Thesis Project," *Research in African Literatures* 28.4 (1997): 112–20; *Philosophical Research in Africa: A Bibliographic Survey* (Cotonou: Inter-African Council for Philosophy, 1988); "The Pitfalls of Being Different," *Diogenes* 131 (Fall 1985): 46–56.

[16] On the general thrust of Hountondji's anti-ethnophilosophical polemic, Imbo

writes: "For Hountondji, African philosophy is addressed to Africans. Even as ethno-philosophy served the purposes of Europe in its colonisation of Africa, so should an African philosophy which is both critical and constructive serve the purposes of a contemporary Africa." See S.O. Imbo, *An Introduction to African Philosophy* (New York: Rowman & Littlefield Publishers, Inc., 1998), 24.

[17] In this regard Oladipo is guilty. He prescribes an action program for African philosophy that consists of solving the problem of adapting science and Western methods to the African environment to promote development for social progress in an increasingly multi-cultural world. See Olusegun Oladipo, *The Idea of African Philosophy*, 3rd ed. (Ibadan, Nigeria: Hope Publications, 2000), 114f. This amounts to giving philosophy powers it cannot claim legitimately. No matter how much we mathematicalize philosophy, as some philosophers in the analytic school do, it will never be a science. The appeal of philosophy is the appeal to reason on behalf of humankind. The objective of philosophy, like the objectives of religion, literature, the arts, and history, must remain a humanistic objective.

[18] See Marcel Griaule, *Conversations with Ogotemmeli* (Oxford: Oxford University Press, 1965).

[19] See Tsenay Serequeberhan, *The Hermeneutics of African Philosophy* (New York: Routledge, 1994).

[20] Kwasi Wiredu, "Toward Decolonizing African Philosophy and Religion," *African Studies Quarterly* 1.4 (1998), http://www.africa.ufl.edu/asq/v1/4/3.htm.

[21] Wiredu, "African Philosophy."

[22] For an example of the trend towards bare practice, see Oriare Nyarwath, "The Luo Care of Widows (Lako) and Contemporary Challenges," *Thought and Practice: A Journal of the Philosophical Association of Kenya* 4.1 (June 2012): 99–110.

[23] "No one can deny the fact that human beings are different in many respects and that they have localised conceptual schemes that determine the way they use certain words and ideas," writes Asouzu, still thinking of Wiredu. "However, they are different within a framework of mutual enrichment and mutual dependence in the genesis of their thoughts and ideas." See Innocent Asouzu, *Ibuarụ: The Heavy Burden of Philosophy Beyond African Philosophy* (Münster: Litverlag, 2007), 267.

[24] Kwasi Wiredu, *Cultural Universals and Particulars: An African Perspective* (Bloomington, Indiana: Indiana University Press, 1996), 137.

[25] "Whatever fault one may find with the articulation and content he gave to the conception [négritude]," writes Sodipo in admiration, "it is in my view to Leopold Senghor's eternal credit that he boldly even if poetically asserted the existence of a distinctly African conception of the universe and of a mode of existence founded upon that conception." See J.O. Sodipo, "Philosophy in Africa Today," *Thought and Practice: A Journal of the Philosophical Association of Kenya* 2.2 (1975): 117. We think that this

is a correct estimation of the metaphysical and epistemological worth of négritude as conceived by Senghor.

[26] See F.O.C. Njoku, *Essays in African Philosophy, Thought & Theology* (Owerri, Nigeria: Claretian Institute of Philosophy, 2002), 49.

[27] L.S. Senghor, "On Negrohood: Psychology of the African Negro," in *African Philosophy: Selected Readings*, ed. Albert Mosley (Englewood Cliff, New Jersey: Prentice Hall, 1995), 121.

[28] Njoku, *Essays*, 182–83.

[29] Senghor, "On Negrohood," 121.

[30] This question was first critically posed in an article entitled "Is African Philosophy Progressing?" *Filosofia Theoretica* 2.1 (June 2013): 239–273.

[31] See, for instance, Innocent Asouzu, *Ibuanyidanda: New Complementary Ontology Beyond World-Immanentism, Ethnocentric Reduction and Impositions* (Münster: Litverlag, 2007), 176ff.

[32] See Innocent Asouzu, *The Method and Principle of Complementary Reflection in and Beyond African Philosophy* (Münster: Litverlag, 2005), 78.

[33] Innocent Asouzu, "Ibuanyidanda and the Philosophy of Essence," *Filosofia Theoretica* 1.1 (December 2011): 97.

[34] Innocent Asouzu, The Complementary Comprehensive Noetic Alternative," http://frasouzu.com/IssuesandPapers/Seminar Papers/- The complementary comprehensive noetic alternative.htm.

[35] Asouzu, "Ibuanyidanda," 103.

[36] Asouzu, "Noetic Alternative."

[37] Asouzu, "Noetic Alternative."

[38] Asouzu, "Ibuanyidanda," 97.

[39] Asouzu, "Noetic Alternative."

[40] Asouzu, "Ibuanyidanda," 105.

[41] Asouzu, "Ibuanyidanda," 103.

[42] Asouzu, "Ibuanyidanda," 106.

Chapter 3: Consolationist Metaphysics

[1] See Henri Bergson, *Creative Evolution*, trans. Arthur Mitchell (New York: Henry Holt and Co., 1911), http://www.manybooks.net/title/bergsonh2616326163-8.pdf. See Chapter III & IV. Just as the idea of disorder indicates a subjective dissatisfaction with a perceived lack of order, so does the idea of nothingness or annihilation for a being

with memory imply the disappointment of finding something new in the place of an old object rather than a metaphysical void. We are dissatisfied with the substitution because we prefer the old object. This is what we interpret as annihilation. This Bergsonian treatment does not of course exhaust the theme of nothingness. For further analysis of this problem see Part Four. The section discusses nothingness as it features in the thought of Heidegger, Sartre, and this author.

[2] Bergson, *Creative Evolution*, 109.

[3] See Part One, Chapter 2, Sections 4 and 5 of this work for an in-depth analysis of Senghor's notion of the emotionality of the African and Asouzu's idea of complementary reflection in relation to the consolationist synthesis.

[4] See Martin Heidegger, *Being and Time*, trans. John Macquarrie and Edward Robinson (New York: Harper & Row, 1962), Division 1, vi, §§ 39–43, 225–55. The definition of human being as care puts the phenomenon of anxiety in proper perspective as the most unique fact of human consciousness, supplying some kind of basis, however tenuous, for an attempt to found space on time, since anxiety can no longer be separated from the consciousness of time.

[5] Jacques Loeb, *The Mechanistic Conception of Life* (Chicago: University of Chicago Press, 1912), 5ff.

[6] Ernst Haeckel, *The History of Creation*, trans. E.R. Lankester (London: H.S. King & Co., 1876), 318–48.

[7] Anthony Flew (with Roy A. Varghese), *There is a God* (New York: HarperCollins, 2007), 124.

[8] Flew, *There is a God*, 129.

[9] Bergson, *Creative Evolution*, 61.

[10] See Richard Dawkins, *The God Delusion* (London: Bantam, 2006) for his unrepentant atheistic viewpoint.

[11] See, for instance, Stephen Hawking, *A Brief History of Time* (New York: Bantam, 1988) and Erwin Schrödinger, *My View of the World* (Cambridge: Cambridge University Press, 1964).

[12] See Immanuel Kant, *Critique of Practical Reason*, in *Critique of Practical Reason and Other Works on the Theory of Ethics*, trans. T.K. Abbott. 4th revised edition (London: Longmans, Green and Co., 1889), Book II, Ch ii, v.

[13] Herbert Spencer, *Principles of Psychology* (London: Longman, Brown, Green and Longmans, 1855), Part 4, Ch viii, § 198, http://oll.libertyfund.org/title/1394.html.

[14] Spencer, *Psychology*, Part 3, Ch iv, § 120.

[15] Jean-Paul Sartre, *Being and Nothingness*, trans. Hazel E. Barnes (New York: Pocket Books, 1966), Part 4, Ch. 2, iii, 784.

[16] See Gideon Rosen and Cian Dorr, "Composition as a Fiction," in *The Blackwell Guide to Metaphysics*, ed. Richard M. Gale (Oxford: Blackwell Publishers Ltd, 2002), 161–62.

[17] Spencer, *Psychology*, Part 1, Ch ii, § 5.

Chapter 4: Consolationist Metaphysics and Epistemology

[1] Miguel de Unamuno, *Tragic Sense of Life*, trans. J.E. Crawford Flitch (New York: Dover Publications, Inc., 1954), ix, http://www.gutenberg.org/files/14636-h/14636-h.htm.

[2] Richard Swinburne, *The Existence of God* (Oxford: Clarendon, 2004), 152.

[3] Kwasi Wiredu, "Toward Decolonizing African Philosophy and Religion," *African Studies Quarterly* 1.4 (1998), http://www.africa.ufl.edu/asq/v1/4/3.htm.

Chapter 5: The Problem of Evil in the World

[1] See Albert Schweitzer, *Ethical Vision*, ed. Predrag Cicovacki (Oxford: Oxford University Press, 2009), 40.

[2] See the article "Lake Toba," *Wikipedia the Free Online Encyclopedia*, http://en.wikipedia.org/wiki/Lake_Toba.

[3] Pierre Teilhard de Chardin, *The Phenomenon of Man*, trans. Bernard Wall (New York: Harper, 1959). See the entire Epilogue.

Chapter 6: Recapitulation, Probability, and Summary

[1] See Isaiah Berlin, *Vico and Herder: Two Studies in the History of Ideas* (London: Chatto & Windus, 1980), 15.

[2] Berlin, *Vico and Herder*, 17.

[3] Berlin, *Vico and Herder*, 20.

[4] David Hume, *Treatise of Human Nature*, ed. L.A. Selby-Bigge (Oxford: Oxford University Press, 1888). See Book 1.

[5] Immanuel Kant, introduction to *Critique of Pure Reason*, trans. Norman Kemp Smith (London: Macmillan, 1929), 34.

[6] See G.E. Moore, "Proof of an External World," *Proceedings of the British Academy* 25 (1939): 273-300.

[7] See W.T. Stace, *A Critical History of Greek Philosophy* (London: Macmillan and Co., 1920), 104-113.

Chapter 7: The Human Phenomenon

[1] Battista Mondin, *Philosophical Anthropology*, trans. M.A. Cizdyn (Bangalore: Theological Publications in India, 1985), 34.

[2] George Wald, "Life and Mind in the Universe," in *Cosmos, Bios, Theos*, ed. Henry Morgenau and R.A. Varghese (La Salle, Illinois: Open Court, 1992), 218.

[3] John Leslie, "Modern Cosmology and the Creation of Life," in *Evolution and Creation*, ed. Ernan McMullin (Notre Dame: University of Notre Dame Press, 1985), 102.

Chapter 8: The Human Community

[1] See, for instance, G.E. Moore, "Proof of the External World," *Proceedings of the British Academy* 25 (1939): 273-300. Moore argues for the existence of the world as something given and therefore indubitable.

[2] After severely criticizing Kant, Hegel, Husserl, Heidegger, and the realist approach to the problem of the existence of the other, Sartre formulates his own solution using the instrument of the *look*. He is confident that the concept of the look carries us from absolute immanence to absolute transcendence. Sartre writes: "I must find not *reasons for believing* that the Other exists but the Other himself as not being me.... Therefore if he is *for us* this can be neither as a constitutive factor of our knowledge of the self, but as one who 'interests' our being, and that not as he contributes *a priori* to constitute our being but as he interests it concretely and 'ontically' in the empirical circumstances of our facticity." See Jean-Paul Sartre, *Being and Nothingness,* trans. Hazel E. Barnes (New York: Pocket Books, 1966), Part Three, Ch One, iii, 338-39. Sartre thinks that a factual necessity arises that condemns representation to superfluity. In directing my gaze at a person I objectify him by transcending his transcendence. The look establishes the other as a being given to me in a concrete situation, not abstractly, and therefore unquestionably.

[3] Friedrich Nietzsche, *Beyond Good and Evil*, trans. Helen Zimmern (London: George Allen & Unwin Ltd, 1967), 10.

Chapter 9: The Second Witness to Liberty

[1] See Martin Luther, *The Bondage of the Will*, trans. J.I. Packer and O.R. Johnston (London: James Clarke & Co Ltd, 1957).

[2] R.H.M. Elwes, *The Chief Works of Benedict de Spinoza* (New York: Dover, 1955), Vol. 2, Letter 62, 390.

[3] William James, "How Can We Explain Judgments of Regret?" in *Philosophy: History and Problems*, ed. Samuel Enoch Stumpf. 5th ed. (New York: McGraw-Hill, Inc., 1994), 749.

[4] See Robert Kane, *The Significance of Free Will* (New York: Oxford University Press, 1996); Robert Kane, ed., *Oxford Handbook on Free Will* (New York: Oxford University Press, 2002).

[5] See M.A. Makinde, "A Philosophical Analysis of the Yoruba Concept of *Ori* and Human Destiny," *International Studies in Philosophy* 17.1 (1985): 53-69; Segun Gbadegesin, "Destiny, Personality and the Ultimate Reality of Human Existence," *Ultimate Reality and Meaning* 7.3 (1984): 173-88.

[6] Schopenhauer constructed his magnificent system on the foundation of pessimism. He makes *will* the fundamental essence of life, the thing-in-itself. The pessimism of this German idealist, the most striking in philosophy, makes the groundless *will* a blind irrational force. Consequently, Schopenhauer arrives at a philosophy basically different from consolation philosophy, in spite of the many points of convergence of the German and Nigerian syntheses. See Arthur Schopenhauer, *The World as Will and Idea*, Vol. 1, trans. R.B. Haldane and J. Kemp (London: Kegan Paul, Trench, Trübner & Co., 1909). In particular see Book Two and Book Four.

Chapter 10: The Metaphysics of Morality

[1] John K. Roth, ed., *Ethics*, Vol. 1, revised edition. (Pasadena, California: Salem Press Inc., 2005), xi.

[2] Udo Etuk, *The New Humanism* (Uyo, Nigeria: Afahaide & Bros Publishers, 1999), 71.

[3] Arthur Schopenhauer, *The World as Will and Idea*, in *Masterworks of Philosophy*, Vol. 3, ed. S.E. Frost, Jr. (New York: McGraw-Hill Book Company, 1972), Part 1, Bk 2, 18.

[4] Alisdair MacIntyre, "The Rationality of Tradition," in *Moral Disagreements: Classic and Contemporary Readings*, ed. Christopher W. Gowans (New York: Routledge, 2000), 205f.

[5] Will Durant, *The Story of Philosophy* (New York: Simon & Schuster, 1926), 383.

Chapter 11: Anatomy of the Melancholy Being

[1] Friedrich Nietzsche, preface to *The Genealogy of Morals*, in *The Birth of Tragedy* and *The Genealogy of Morals*, trans. Francis Golffing (New York: Anchor Books, 1956), v, 153–54.

[2] Friedrich Nietzsche, *Beyond Good and Evil*, trans. Helen Zimmern (London: George Allen & Unwin Ltd, 1967), 105.

[3] Nietzsche, *Beyond Good and Evil*, 247.

[4] Nietzsche, *Genealogy*, Third Essay, vii, 242.

[5] For more details on biological and physical immortality see, for instance, Stephen S. Hall, *Merchants of Immortality: Chasing the Dream of Human Life Extension* (Boston, Massachusetts: Houghton Mifflin, 2003) and Michael R. Perry, *Forever for All: Moral Philosophy, Cryonics, and the Scientific Prospects for Immortality* (New York: Universal Publishers, 2000).

[6] Albert Camus, *The Myth of Sisyphus and Other Essays* (New York: Alfred A. Knopf, 1955), 3.

[7] Immanuel Kant, *Critique of Pure Reason*, trans. Norman Kemp Smith (London: Macmillan and Co. Ltd, 1929), Transcendental Dialectic, Bk. 2, Ch. i, 328.

Chapter 12: The Fundamental Harmony of Consolation Philosophy with the Basic Western Philosophical Imagination

[1] See M.A. Makinde, *African Philosophy: The Demise of a Controversy* (Ile-Ife, Nigeria: Obafemi Awolowo University Press, 2007), 26.

[2] Dario Composta, *History of Ancient Philosophy*, trans. M.A. Cizdyn (Bangalore: Theological Publications in India, 1990), 156.

[3] Plato, *Republic*, 508e-509a.

[4] W.T. Stace, *A Critical History of Greek Philosophy* (London: Macmillan and Co. Ltd, 1920), 111, http://manybooks.net/titles/stacew3341133411-8.pdf.

[5] Aristotle, *Nichomachean Ethics*, 1178b 29.

[6] Aristotle, *Metaphysics*, 1072a 30.

[7] Aristotle, *Metaphysics*, 999b 5-6.

[8] Charles Taylor, *Hegel* (Cambridge: Cambridge University Press, 1975), 89.

[9] G.W.F. Hegel, *The Science of Logic*, trans. W.H. Johnston and L.C. Struthers, in *The Philosophy of Hegel*, ed. Carl J. Friedrich (New York: Random House, Inc., 1953), 191–93.

[10] Taylor, *Hegel*, 105.

[11] Aristotle, *Categories*, 17a.

[12] See Composta, *History*, 388-90. While the highest being in Aristotle's metaphysics is simple and self-thinking, this being is conceived by Plotinus as so simple as to exclude the subject-object duality. The Plotinian vision presents a being that does not think, a mere unconscious principle of the universe (388).

[13] See Composta, *History*, 267.

[14] R.H.M. Elwes, *The Chief Works of Benedict de Spinoza*, Vol. 2 (New York: Dover, 1955), Letter 62, 390.

[15] T.S. Gregory, introduction to *Ethics* (and *On the Correction of the Understanding*), trans. Andrew Boyle (London: Dent, 1910), v.

[16] Gregory, introduction, vii-viii.

[17] Benedict Spinoza, *Ethics* (and *On the Correction of the Understanding*), trans. Andrew Boyle (London: Dent, 1910), Part Three, Prop xiii, 131.

[18] Spinoza, *Ethics*, Part Three, Prop xiii, 131.

[19] Spinoza, *Ethics*, Part Three, 139-40.

[20] Spinoza, preface, Part Four, 143.

[21] Spinoza, *Ethics*, Part Four, Prop xlvii, Note, 175.

[22] Spinoza, *Ethics*, Part Four, Prop i, Coroll., 176.

[23] Martin Heidegger, *Being and Time*, trans. John Macquarrie and Edward Robinson (New York: Harper & Row, 1962), Div Two, § 53, 308.

[24] Spinoza, *Ethics*, Part Four, Appendix, iv, 192.

[25] Spinoza, *Ethics*, Part Five, Prop xvii, 210.

[26] Spinoza, *Ethics*, Part Five, Prop xxxiii, 218-19.

[27] Spinoza, *Ethics*, Part Five, Prop xxxvi, 219.

[28] Spinoza, *Ethics*, Part Five, Prop xxxvi, 219.

[29] David Hume, *A Treatise of Human Nature*, 2nd edition, revised by P.H. Nidditch (Oxford: Oxford University Press, 1978), Bk 2, Part 3, § 3, 415.

[30] David Hume, *A Treatise of Human Nature*, ed. L.A. Selby-Bigge, 1st edition (Oxford: Oxford University Press, 1888), Bk 1, Part 3, § 3, 82.

[31] Hume, *Treatise*, 1st ed. Bk 1, Part 3, § 4, 86-88.

[32] Hume, *Treatise*, 1st ed. Bk 1, Part 3, § 5, 93.

[33] Hume, *Treatise*, 1st ed. Bk 1, Part 3, § 8, 103.

[34] Jonathan Bennett, *Kant's Dialectic* (New York: Cambridge University Press, 1974), 268.

[35] Immanuel Kant, *Critique of Pure Reason*, trans. Norman Kemp Smith (London: Macmillan and Co. Ltd, 1929), Transcendental Aesthetic, Part 2, ii, 96.

[36] Kant, *Critique*, Transcendental Analytic, Part 2, Div. 1, Bk ii, § 26, 173.

[37] Immanuel Kant, *Fundamental Principles of the Metaphysics of Ethics*, 10th edition, trans. T.K. Abbott (London: Longmans, Green & Co., 1946), § 3, 91.

[38] Bennett, *Kant's Dialectic*, 258.

[39] Kant, preface to *Critique of Pure Reason*, 7.

[40] Kant, *Critique*, Transcendental Dialectic, Part 2, Div 2, Bk ii, Ch ii, § 2, 409.

[41] Kant, *Critique*, 409.

[42] See Bennett, *Kant's Dialectic*, 202. Bennett adds that based on Kant's confession, that is, the submission that we cannot tell whether our temporal actions are due solely to freedom or natural causality, freedom may be associated with a deep psychosis and therefore not characteristic of psychologically healthy people. While a case of psychosis need not be invoked here, Bennett's interesting observation underlines my insistence that freedom in Kant's metaphysics is a vanishing ideal.

[43] According to Kant the notion of the *summum bonum* has two components, the *summum* which indicates perfection or excellence and the *bonum* which indicates something good. Thus we have something like the perfectly good. He identifies virtue as the supreme condition of the *summum bonum* while happiness, subordinated to virtue, completes virtue. Happiness should only be the reward for virtue. See Immanuel Kant, *Critique of Practical Reason*, in *Critique of Practical Reason and Other Works on the Theory of Ethics*, trans. T.K. Abbott (London: Longmans, Green & Co., 1889), Part 1, Bk 2, Ch 2, http://oll.libertyfund.org/title/360.html.

[44] K.C. Anyanwu, "African Religion as an Experienced Reality," *Thought and Practice: A Journal of the Philosophical Association of Kenya*, Vol. 2, No. 2 (1975): 153.

[45] Kant, *Critique*, Transcendental Analytic, Part 2, Div. 1, Bk ii, Ch iii, 257.

[46] Immanuel Kant, *Critique of Judgment*, trans. J.H. Bernard (Mineola, New York: Dover, 2005), Part 2, § 77, 192.

[47] Kant, *Critique*, Transcendental Dialectic, Part 2, Div. 2, Ch iii, Appendix, 568.

[48] Kant, *Critique of Judgment*, Part 2, § 83, Footnote, 212.

[49] G.W.F. Hegel, *Philosophy of Mind*, trans. William Wallace (Oxford: Clarendon Press, 1894), § 387, http://manybooks.net/titlehegelgeo3906439064-8.pdf.

[50] See F.H. Bradley, *Appearance and Reality: A Metaphysical Essay* (Oxford: Clarendon Press, 1930).

[51] Hegel, *Mind*, § 400, 76.

[52] See Stephen Houlgate, *Hegel, Nietzsche and the Criticism of Metaphysics* (Cambridge: Cambridge University Press, 1986).

[53] T.L. Sprigge, "Idealism," in *The Blackwell Guide to Metaphysics*, ed. Richard M. Gale (Oxford: Blackwell, 2002), 235.

[54] Martin Heidegger, *Being and Time*, trans. John Macquarrie and Edward Robinson (New York: Harper & Row, 1962), Part One, Div. Two, § 44, 262.

[55] Heidegger, introduction to *Being and Time*, ii, 63.

[56] Heidegger, *Being and Time*, Part One, Div. Two, ii, § 60, 343-44.

[57] Heidegger, *Being and Time*, Part One, Div. One, v, 30, 180.

[58] Heidegger, *Being and Time*, Part One, Div. One, vi, § 40, 230.

[59] Heidegger, *Being and Time*, Part One, Div. One, vi, § 40, 231.

[60] Heidegger, *Being and Time*, Part One, Div. Two, iv, § 69, 417.

[61] Heidegger, *Being and Time*, Part One, Div. Two, i, § 47, 284.

[62] Heidegger, *Being and Time*, Part One, Div. Two, i, § 50, 293-94.

[63] Heidegger, *Being and Time*, Part One, Div. Two, i, § 53, 308.

[64] Heidegger, *Being and Time*, Part One, Div. Two, iii, § 65, 377.

[65] Heidegger, *Being and Time*, Part One, Div. Two, iv, § 70, 418-19.

[66] Heidegger, *Being and Time*, Part One, Div. Two, v, § 72, 427.

[67] Martin Heidegger, *Existence and Being*, with introduction and analysis by Werner Brock (Chicago, Illinois: Henry Regnery Co., 1964), 330.

[68] Heidegger, *Existence and Being*, 336.

[69] Jean-Paul Sartre, *Being and Nothingness*, trans, Hazel E. Barnes (New York: Pocket Books, 1964), Part One, Ch One, i, 44.

[70] Sartre, introduction to *Being and Nothingness*, ii, 9.

[71] Sartre, *Being and Nothingness*, Part Four, Ch One, ii, 625.

[72] Sartre, *Being and Nothingness*, Part Four, Ch One, i, 563.

[73] Sartre, *Being and Nothingness*, Part Four, Ch One, i, 567.

[74] Sartre, *Being and Nothingness*, Part Four, Ch One, ii, 650.

[75] Sartre, *Being and Nothingness*, Part Four, Ch One, i, 570.

[76] Sartre, *Being and Nothingness*, Part One, Ch One, v, 71.

[77] Sartre, *Being and Nothingness*, Part One, Ch Two, ii, 107.

[78] Sartre, *Being and Nothingness*, Part Four, Ch One, ii. 682.

[79] Sartre, *Being and Nothingness*, Part Four, Ch One, ii, 699.

[80] Sartre, *Being and Nothingness*, Part Four, Ch One, ii, 784.

[81] Sartre, *Being and Nothingness*, Part Two, Ch One, iii, 140.

[82] Sartre, *Being and Nothingness*, Part Three, Ch One, iii, 338ff.

[83] Sartre, *Being and Nothingness*, Part Four, Ch Two, iii, 781.

[84] Martin Heidegger, *Existence and Being*, with introduction and analysis by Werner Brock (Chicago, Illinois: Henry Regnery Co., 1964), 343f.

[85] Sartre, *Being and Nothingness*, Part Three, Ch Two, ii, 445.

[86] Sören Kierkegaard, *Concluding Unscientific Postscript*, trans. David F. Swenson and Walter Lowrie (Princeton, New Jersey: Princeton University Press, 1968), Bk 2, Part 1, Ch 2, 101.

[87] Kierkegaard, *Postscript*, Bk 2, Part 2, Ch 4, § 2, 355.

[88] Sören Kierkegaard, "Fear and Trembling," in *Selections from the Writing of Kierkegaard*, ed. Lee M. Hollander (New York: Anchor Books, 1960), iv, 149.

[89] Kierkegaard, "Fear and Trembling," iv, 148f.

[90] Kierkegaard, "Fear and Trembling," iv, 139.

[91] Kierkegaard, "Fear and Trembling," iv, 142.

[92] Miguel de Unamuno, *Tragic Sense of Life*, trans. J.E. Crawford Flitch (New York: Dover, 1955), i, http://www.gutenberg.org/files/14636-h/14636-h.htm.

[93] Unamuno, *Tragic Sense*, x.

[94] Unamuno, *Tragic Sense*, x.

[95] Unamuno, *Tragic Sense*, viii.

[96] Unamuno, *Tragic Sense*, v.

[97] Unamuno, *Tragic Sense*, vi.

[98] Unamuno, *Tragic Sense*, vii.

[99] Unamuno, *Tragic Sense*, ix.

[100] Unamuno, *Tragic Sense*, vii.

[101] See Sören Kierkegaard, *Concluding Unscientific Postscript*, trans. David F. Swenson and Walter Lowrie (Princeton, New Jersey: Princeton University Press, 1968), Bk 2, Ch 2, 218. Kierkegaard does not explain exactly what he means by the statement that the immediate relation of man with God is paganism, but it seems he is referring to the tendency of the human mind to reify and personify ideas in the search for substantiality, the tendency to anthropomorphize occasioned by God's elusiveness or his non-materialization. In this sense primitive religions do not amaze us, with their worship of non-living objects such as stones, natural forces such as thunder, low life-forms such as trees, worship of ancestors, and other vehicles of diffused monotheism.

[102] The famous Kenyan scholar H. Odera Oruka engaged in field research that helped him identify independent indigenous thinkers he called sages, whose wisdom is not part of the collective tribal wisdom. See H. Odera Oruka, *Sage Philosophy and the Modern Debate on African Philosophy* (Leiden: Brill Publishers, 1990).

Conclusion

[1] Fayemi A. Kazeem, "H. Odera Oruka and the Question of Methodology in African Philosophy: A Critique," *Thought and Practice: A Journal of the Philosophical Association of Kenya* (Special Issue) 4.2 (December 2012): 185-204.

[2] See F.O.C. Njoku, *Essays in African Philosophy, Thought & Theology* (Owerri, Nigeria: Claretian Institute of Philosophy, 2002), 89-90.

[3] Jonathan O. Chimakonam, "Building African Logic as an Algorithm for Africa's Development" (paper presented at the Conference of the African Studies Institute of the University of Georgia on the theme *Africa and Its Diaspora: Expressions of Indigenous and Local Knowledge* held on November 8-10, 2012 at the University of Georgia, USA); "Principles of Indigenous African Logic: Towards Africa's Development and Restoration of African Identity" (paper presented at the 19th Annual Conference of the International Society for African Philosophy and Studies (ISAPS) held at the Department of Philosophy, Nnamdi Azikiwe University, Awka, Anambra, Nigeria from May 27 to 29, 2013).

Bibliography

Abraham, William E. *The Mind of Africa*. Chicago: Chicago University Press, 1962.

——. "Anton Wilhelm Amo." In *A Companion to African Philosophy*, edited by Kwasi Wiredu. 191–199. Oxford: Blackwell Publishing Ltd, 2004.

Agbakoba, J. C. A. "On the African Origin of Philosophy." *Uche* 10 (2004): 61–67.

Ameriks, Karl, ed. *The Cambridge Companion to German Idealism*. Cambridge: Cambridge University Press, 2000.

Anyanwu, K.C. "African Religion as an Experienced Reality." *Thought and Practice: A Journal of the Philosophical Association of Kenya* 2.2 (1975): 149–57.

Appiah, Anthony Kwame. *In My Father's House: Africa in the Philosophy of Culture*. New York: Oxford University Press, 1992.

Asouzu, Innocent. *Ibuarụ: The Heavy Burden of Philosophy Beyond African Philosophy*. Münster: Litverlag, 2007.

——. *The Method and Principles of Complementary Reflection in and Beyond African Philosophy*. Münster: Litverlag, 2005.

——. *Ibuanyidanda. New Complementary Ontology: Beyond World-Immanentism, Ethnocentric Reduction and Impositions*. Münster: Litverlag, 2007.

——. *Ikwa Ogwe. Essential Readings in Complementary Reflection: A Systematic Methodological Approach*. Calabar, Nigeria: Saesprint Publishers, 2007.

——. "Ibuanyidanda and the Philosophy of Essence." *Filosofia Theoretica* 1.1 (December 2011): 79–118.

Baier, Kurt. "Smart on Sensations." *Australasian Journal of Philosophy* 40 (1962): 57–68.

——. "Pains." *Australasian Journal of Philosophy* 40 (1962): 1–23.

Balogun, O.A. "Ori as the Sole Determinant of Human Person in Yoruba Traditional Thought: Further Comments." Paper presented at the Biennial Conference and Meeting of the Nigerian Philosophical Association held at the University of Calabar, Calabar, Nigeria, from October 8 to 11, 2008.

Bennett, Jonathan. *Kant's Dialectic*. New York: Cambridge University Press, 1974.

Bergson, Henri. *Creative Evolution*. Translated by Arthur Mitchell. New York: Henry Holt and Co., 1911.

Berlin, Isaiah. *Vico and Herder: Two Studies in the History of Ideas*. London: Chatto & Windus, 1980.

——. *Against the Current: Essays in the History of Ideas*, edited by Henry Hardy. New York: The Viking Press, 1980.

Bradley, F.H. *Appearance and Reality: A Metaphysical Essay*. Oxford: Clarendon Press, 1930.

Bronner, Stephen Eric, ed. *Twentieth Century Political Thought*. New York and London: Routledge, 1997.

Cahhone, Lawrence, ed. *From Modernism to Postmodernism: An Anthology*. Malden, Massachusetts: Blackwell Publishers, 1997.

Campbell, C.A. "Is 'Free Will' a Pseudo-Problem." In *Contemporary Ethical Theory*, edited by Joseph Margolis. 371–399. New York: Random House, 1966.

Camus, Albert. *The Myth of Sisyphus and Other Essays*. New York: Alfred A. Knopf, 1955.

Chardin, Pierre Teilhard de. *The Phenomenon of Man*. Translated by Bernard Wall. New York: Harper, 1959.

Chimakonam, Jonathan O. *Introducing African Science: Systematic and Philosophical Approach*. Indiana: Authorhouse, 2012.

——. "Building African Logic as an Algorithm for Africa's Development." Paper presented at the African Studies Institute Conference on the theme *Africa and Its Diaspora: Expressions of Indigenous and Local Knowledge* held at the University of Georgia, USA, from November 8–10, 2012.

——. "Principles of Indigenous African Logic: Towards Africa's Development and Restoration of African Identity." Paper presented at the 19th Annual Conference of the International Society for African Philosophy and Studies (ISAPS) held at the Department of Philosophy, Nnamdi Azikiwe University, Awka, Anambra, Nigeria from May 27 to May 29, 2013.

——. "Outline of African Logic for the Development of Thought, Science and Technology in Africa." *International Journal of Philosophy and Religion* 3.1 (2011): 93-114.

Coley, Noel G., and Vance M. D. Hall, eds. *Darwin to Einstein*. New York: Longman, Inc., 1980.

Composta, Dario. *History of Ancient Philosophy*. Translated by M.A. Cizdyn. Bangalore: Theological Publications in India, 1990.

Copleston, F. *A History of Philosophy*. Vol. IX. New York: Image Books, 1994.

Craig, W. L., and Q. Smith. *Theism, Atheism, and Big Bang Cosmology*. Oxford: The Clarendon Press, 1993.

Davies, Paul. *The Accidental Universe*. Cambridge: Cambridge University Press, 1982.

Dawkins, Richard. *The God Delusion*. London: Bantam, 2006.

Dennet, Daniel C. *Brainstorms: Philosophical Essays on Mind and Psychology*. Sussex: The Harvester Press Limited, 1981.

Diop, Cheikh Anta. *The African Origin of Civilization: Myth or Reality*. New York: Lawrence Hill Books, 1974.

——. *Civilization or Barbarism*. New York: Lawrence Hill Books, 1991.

Dolmage, Cecil G. *Astronomy of Today*. 3rd edition. London: Seeley and Co. Ltd, 1910.

Durant, Will. *The Story of Philosophy*. New York: Simon & Schuster, 1926.

Edeh, Emmanuel. *Towards an Igbo Metaphysics*. Chicago: Loyola University Press, 1999.

Elwes, R.H.M. *The Chief Works of Benedict de Spinoza*. Vol. 2. New York: Dover, 1955.

Etuk, Udo. *The New Humanism*. Uyo, Nigeria: Afahaide & Bros Publishers, 1999.

Ewing, A. C. *The Fundamental Questions of Philosophy*. London: Routledge and Kegan Paul, 1931.

Eze, Emmanuel, ed. *Postcolonial African Philosophy*. Oxford: Blackwell, 1997.

Fayemi A. Kazeem. "H. Odera Oruka and the Question of Methodology in African Philosophy: A Critique." *Thought and Practice: A Journal of the Philosophical Association of Kenya* (Special Issue) 4.2 (December 2012): 185–204.

Fischer, J.M., ed. *The Metaphysics of Death*. Stanford, California: Stanford University Press, 1993.

Flew, Antony. *There is a God: How the World's Most Notorious Atheist Changed His Mind*. New York: HarperCollins, 2007.

Frost, S.E., ed. *Masterworks of Philosophy*. Vol. 3. New York: McGraw-Hill Book Company, 1972.

Gade, C.B.N. "What is Ubuntu? Different Interpretations among South Africans of African Descent." *South African Journal of Philosophy* 31.3 (2012): 484–503.

Gange, Robert. *Origins and Destiny*. Dallas: Word Publishing, 1986.

Gbadegesin, Segun. *African Philosophy, Traditional Yoruba Philosophy and Contemporary African Realities*. Chicago: Gateway, 1991.

Griaule, Marcel. *Conversations with Ogotemmeli*. Oxford: Oxford University Press, 1965.

Gyekye, Kwame. *An Essay on African Philosophical Thought*. New York: Cambridge University Press, 1987.

——. "The Concept of a Person." In *Philosophy and Choice*, edited by Kit R. Christenson. 215–225. Mountain View, California: Mayfield Publishing Company, 1999.

——. *Tradition and Modernity: Reflections on the African Experience*. Oxford: Oxford University Press, 1997.

Haeckel, Ernst. *The History of Creation*. Translated by E.R. Lankester. London: H.S. King & Co., 1876.

Hall, Stephen S. *Merchants of Immortality: Chasing the Dream of Human Life Extension*. Boston, Massachusetts: Houghton Mifflin, 2003.

Hallen, Barry. *A Short History of African Philosophy*. Bloomington, Indiana: Indiana University Press, 2002.

——. *The Good, the Bad and the Beautiful: Discourse about Values in an African Culture*. Bloomington, Indiana: Indiana University Press, 2000.

Hallen, Barry, and J.O. Sodipo. *Knowledge, Belief and Witchcraft: Analytic Experiments in African Philosophy*. Revised edition. Stanford, California: Stanford University Press, 1997.

Hawking, Stephen. *A Brief History of Time*. New York: Bantam, 1988.

Hegel, G.W.F. *Philosophy of History*. Translated by J. Sibree. New York: Prometheus Books, 1991.

——. *The Science of Logic*. Translated by W.H. Johnston and L.C. Struthers. In *The Philosophy of Hegel*, edited by Carl J. Friedrich. New York: Random House, Inc., 1953.

Heidegger, Martin. *An Introduction to Metaphysics*. New York: Anchor Books, 1961.

——. *Being and Time*. Translated by John Macquarrie and Edward Robinson. New York: Harper and Row, 1962.

——. *Existence and Being*. With introduction by Werner Brock. Chicago: Henry Regnery Co., 1964.

Heim, Karl. *The World: Its Creation and Consummation*. Translated by Robert Smith. Edinburgh and London: Oliver and Boyd, 1962.

Hick, John. *Evil and the God of Love*. London: Macmillan, 1985.

Horton, Robin. *Patterns of Thought in Africa and the West*. Cambridge: Cambridge University Press, 1993.

Houlgate, Stephen. *Hegel, Nietzsche and the Criticism of Metaphysics*. Cambridge: Cambridge University Press, 1986.

Hountondji, Paulin. *African Philosophy: Myth and Reality*. 2nd edition. Bloomington, Indiana: Indiana University Press, 1996.

——. "Knowledge as a Development Issue." In *A Companion to African Philosophy*, edited by Kwasi Wiredu. 529–37. Oxford: Blackwell Publishing Ltd, 2004.

Hume, David. *Treatise of Human Nature*, edited by L.A. Selby-Bigge. Oxford: Oxford University Press, 1888.

——. *The Natural History of Religion*. London: A. and H. Bradlaugh Bonner, 1889.

——. *Enquiry Concerning Human Understanding*. In *Enquiries Concerning Human Understanding and Concerning the Principles of Morals*. 2nd edition, edited by L.A. Selby-Bigge. Oxford: Clarendon Press, 1902.

Imbo, S.O. *An Introduction to African Philosophy*. New York: Rowman & Littlefield Publishers, Inc., 1998.

James, W. *Essays in Philosophy*. Cambridge, Massachusetts: Harvard University Press, 1978.

Jowett, Benjamin. *The Dialogues of Plato*. Vol. 1–4. Oxford: Oxford University Press, 1892.

Kane, Robert. *The Significance of Free Will*. New York: Oxford University Press, 1996.

——. ed. *Oxford Handbook on Free Will*. New York: Oxford University Press, 2002.

Kant, Immanuel. *Critique of Practical Reason*. In *Critique of Practical Reason and Other Works on the Theory of Ethics*. 4th revised edition. Translated by T.K. Abbott. London: Longmans, Green and Co., 1889.

——. *Critique of Pure Reason*. Translated by Norman Kemp Smith. London: Macmillan and Co. Ltd, 1929.

——. *Critique of Judgment*. Translated by J.H. Bernard. Mineola, New York: Dover Publications, Inc., 2005.

——. *Fundamental Principles of the Metaphysics of Ethics*. 10th edition. Translated by T.K. Abbott. London: Longmans, Green & Co., 1946.

——.*Prolegomena and Metaphysical Foundations of Natural Sciences*. 3rd edition. Translated by Ernest Belfort Bax. London: George Bell and Sons, 1891.

——. *Religion Within the Limits of Reason Alone*. Translated by T.M. Greene and H.H. Hudson. New York: Harper & Row, 1960.

Kierkegaard, Sören. *Concluding Unscientific Postscript*. Translated by David F. Swenson and Walter Lowrie. Princeton, New Jersey: Princeton University Press, 1968.

——. "Fear and Trembling." In *Selections from the Writing of Kierkegaard*, edited by Lee M. Hollander. 119–52. New York: Anchor Books, 1960.

Korner, Stephan. *Metaphysics: Its Structures and Functions*. Cambridge: Cambridge University Press, 1984.

——. *Fundamental Questions of Philosophy*. Sussex: The Harvester Press, 1979.

Levy-Bruhl, Lucien. *Primitive Mentality*. Paris: University of France Press, 1947.

Lewis, Joseph. *An Atheist Manifesto*. 3rd edition. New York: The Freethought Press, 1958.

Locke, John. *Two Treatises on Government and a Letter Concerning Toleration*, edited by Ian Shapiro. New Haven and London: Yale University Press, 2003.

Loeb, Jacques. *The Mechanistic Conception of Life*. Chicago: University of Chicago Press, 1912.

Luther, Martin. *The Bondage of the Will*. Translated by J.I. Packer and O.R. Johnston. London: James Clarke & Co Ltd, 1957.

Makinde, M.A. *African Philosophy: The Demise of a Controversy*. Ile-Ife, Nigeria: Obafemi Awolowo University Press, 2007.

—. "Whither Philosophy in Africa?" In *Proceedings of the 20th World Council of Philosophy*, Boston, USA. http://www.bu.edu/wcp/Papers/Afri/AfriMaki.htm.

Marcel, Gabriel. *The Mystery of Being*. First series. Translated by G. S. Fraser. Chicago: Henry Regnery Co., 1960.

Masolo, D.A. *African Philosophy in Search of Identity*. Bloomington, Indiana: Indiana University Press, 1994.

Mbiti, J. S. *African Religions and Philosophy*. London: Heinemann, 1969.

—. *Concepts of God in Africa*. New York: Praeger, 1970.

McGin, C. *The Problem of Consciousness: Essays Towards a Resolution*. Oxford: Blackwell, 1991.

McMullin, Ernan, ed. *Evolution and Creation*. Notre Dame: University of Notre Dame Press, 1985.

Mondin, Battista. *A History of Mediaeval Philosophy*. Translated by M.A. Cizdyn. Bangalore: Theological Publications in India, 1991.

—. *Philosophical Anthropology*. Translated by M.A. Cizdyn. Bangalore: Theological Publications in India, 1985.

Mosley, Albert, ed. *African Philosophy: Selected Readings*. Englewood Cliff, New Jersey: Prentice Hall, 1995.

Mudimbe, V.Y. *The Idea of Africa*. Bloomington, Indiana: Indiana University Press, 1994.

—. *The Invention of Africa: Gnosis, Philosophy, and the Order of Knowledge*. Bloomington, Indiana: Indiana University Press, 1988.

Nietzsche, Friedrich. *Beyond Good and Evil*. Translated by Helen Zimmern. London: George Allen & Unwin Ltd, 1967.

—.*The Birth of Tragedy* and *The Genealogy of Morals*. Translated by Francis Golffing. New York: Anchor Books, 1956.

——. *The Antichrist*. Translated by H. L. Mencken. New York: Alfred A. Knopf, 1918.

Njoku, F.O.C. *Essays in African Philosophy, Thought & Theology*. Owerri, Nigeria: Claretian Institute of Philosophy, 2002.

Nkrumah, Kwame. *Consciencism*. London: Heinemann, 1964.

Nyerere, Julius. *Ujamaa: Essays on Socialism*. Nairobi: Oxford University Press, 1968.

Obenga, Theophile. "Egypt: Ancient History of African Philosophy." In *A Companion to African Philosophy*, edited by Kwasi Wiredu. 31–49. Oxford: Blackwell Publishing Ltd, 2004.

O'Connor, Timothy, ed. *Agents, Causes, and Events: Essays on Indeterminism and Free Will*. New York: Oxford University Press, 1995.

Oguejiofor, J. Obi. "Négritude as Hermeneutics: A Reinterpretation of Léopold Sédar Senghor's Philosophy." *American Catholic Philosophical Quarterly* 83.1 (2009): 79–94.

Oladipo, Olusegun. *Philosophy and the African Experience: The Contributions of Kwasi Wiredu*. Ibadan: Hope Publications, 1996.

——. *The Idea of African Philosophy*. 3rd edition. Ibadan, Nigeria: Hope Publications, 2000.

Onyewuenyi, Innocent. *The African Origin of Greek Philosophy: An Exercise in Afrocentrism*. Nsukka, Nigeria: University of Nigeria Press, 1993.

Oruka, H.O. *Sage Philosophy and the Modern Debate on African Philosophy*. Leiden: Brill Publishers, 1990.

Oruka, H.O., and D.A. Masolo, eds. *Philosophy and Cultures*. Nairobi: Bookwise Publishers, 1983.

Outlaw, Lucius T. "Africana Philosophy: Origin and Prospects." In *A Companion to African Philosophy*, edited by Kwasi Wiredu. 90–98. Oxford: Blackwell Publishing Ltd, 2004.

Pascal, Blaise. *Pensées*. Translated by A. J. Krailsheimer. Baltimore and Harmondsworth: Penguin Books, 1966.

Perry, Michael R. *Forever for All: Moral Philosophy, Cryonics, and the Scientific Prospects for Immortality*. New York: Universal Publishers, 2000.

Peterson, Michael L. *Reason and Religion: An Introduction to the Philosophy of Religion*. New York: Oxford University Press, 1991.

Plantinga, Alvin. *The Nature of Necessity*. Oxford: Clarendon Press, 1974.

——. *God, Freedom and Evil*. London: Allen &Unwin, 1975.

Plato. *Republic*. Translated by Benjamin Jowett. New York: Vintage Books, 1991.

Pringle-Pattison, A. S. *The Idea of God in the Light of Recent Philosophy*. Oxford: The Clarendon Press, 1917.

Rader, Melvin. *The Enduring Questions*. 2nd edition. New York: Holt, Rinehart,and Winston, 1969.

Radhakrishnan, Sarvepalli. *An Idealist View of Life*. London: Allen & Unwin, 1937.

Reichenbach, Bruce R. *Evil and a Good God*. New York: Fordham University Press, 1982.

Rosen, Gideon, and Cian Dorr. "Composition as a Fiction." In *The Blackwell Guide to Metaphysics*, edited by Richard M. Gale. 152–74. Oxford: Blackwell Publishers Ltd, 2002.

Rosen, Stanley. *The Mask of Enlightenment: Nietzsche's Zarathustra*. Cambridge: Cambridge University Press, 1995.

Ross, W.D. *Aristotle*. New York: Meridian Books, 1959.

Roth, John K., ed. *Ethics*. Vol. 1. Revised edition. Pasadena, California: Salem Press Inc., 2005.

Rousseau, Jean-Jacques. *The Social Contract*. Translated by Maurice Cranston. London: Penguin Books, 1968.

Rowe, William L. *Philosophy of Religion: An Introduction*. Belmont, California: Dickenson, 1978.

Russell, Bertrand. *Mysticism and Logic*. 11th impression. London: George Allen & Unwin, 1959.

Sartre, Jean-Paul. *Being and Nothingness*. Translated by Hazel E. Barnes. New York: Pocket Books, 1966.

Savitt, Steven F., ed. *Time's Arrow Today*. Cambridge: Cambridge University Press, 1997.

Schopenhauer, Arthur. *The World as Will and Idea*. Translated by R.B. Haldane and J. Kemp. Vol. 1. London: Kegan Paul, Trench, Trübner & Co., 1909.

——. *Parerga and Paralipomena*. Vol. 1 & 2. Translated by E.F.J. Payne. Oxford: Oxford University Press, 2000.

Schrödinger, Erwin. *My View of the World*. Cambridge: Cambridge University Press, 1964.

Schweitzer, Albert. *Ethical Vision*, edited by Predrag Cicovacki. Oxford: Oxford University Press, 2009.

Senghor, L.S. *On African Socialism*. Translated by Mercer Cook. London: Pall Mall Press, 1964.

——. "On Negrohood: Psychology of the African Negro." In *African Philosophy: Selected*

Readings, edited by Albert Mosley. 116–127. Englewood Cliff, New Jersey: Prentice Hall, 1995.

Serequeberhan, Tsenay, ed. *African Philosophy: The Essential Readings*. New York: Paragon House, 1991.

——. *The Hermeneutics of African Philosophy*. London: Routledge, 1994.

Smith, Quentin, and L. Nathan Oaklander. *Time, Change and Freedom*. London: Routledge, 1995.

Sodipo, J.O. "Philosophy in Africa Today." *Thought and Practice: Journal of the Philosophical Association of Kenya* (1975): 115–123.

Spencer, Herbert. *Principles of Psychology*. London: Longman, Brown, Green and Longmans, 1855.

Spinoza, Benedict. *Ethics* (and *On the Correction of the Understanding*). Translated by Andrew Boyle. London: Dent, 1910.

——. *Tractatus Theologico-Politicus*. Translated by R.H.M. Elwes. New York, Dover, 1955.

Sprigge, T.L. "Idealism." In *The Blackwell Guide to Metaphysics*, edited by Richard M. Gale. 219–41. Oxford: Blackwell, 2002.

Stace, W.T. *A Critical History of Greek Philosophy*. London: Macmillan and Co. Ltd, 1920.

Stumpf, Samuel Enoch. *Philosophy: History and Problems*. 5th edition. New York: McGraw-Hill, Inc., 1994.

Suárez, Francisco. *A Commentary on Aristotle's Metaphysics*. Translated by John P. Doyle. Milwaukee, Wisconsin: Marquette University Press, 2004.

Sumner, Claude. *Classical Ethiopian Philosophy*. Los Angeles: Adey Publishing Company, 1994.

Swinburne, Richard. *The Existence of God*. Oxford: Clarendon, 2004.

Taiwo, Olufemi. "Exorcizing Hegel's Ghost: Africa's Challenge to Philosophy." *African Studies Quarterly* 1.4 (1998). http://www.africa.ufl.edu/asq/v1/4/2.htm.

Taylor, Charles. *Hegel*. Cambridge: Cambridge University Press, 1975.

Tempels, Placide. *Bantu Philosophy*. Translated by Colin King. Paris: Presence Africaine, 1959.

Tennant, F. R. *Philosophical Theology*. Cambridge: Cambridge University Press, 1928.

Unamuno, Miguel de. *Tragic Sense of Life*. Translated by J.E. Crawford Flitch. New York: Dover Publications, Inc., 1954.

Veeschauwer, Herman-J de. *The Development of Kantian Thought*. Translated by A.R.C. Duncan. Edinburgh: Thomas Nelson and Sons Ltd, 1962.

Wiredu, Kwasi. *Cultural Universals and Particulars: An African Perspective*. Bloomington, Indiana: Indiana University Press, 1996.

—. "Toward Decolonizing African Philosophy and Religion." *African Studies Quarterly* 1.4 (1998). http://www.africa.ufl.edu/asq/v1/4/3.htm.

Wiredu, Kwasi and Kwame Gyekye. *Person and Community: Ghanaian Philosophical Studies*, 1. Washington DC: Council for Research in Values and Philosophy, 1992.

Wittgenstein, Ludwig. *Tractatus Logico-Philosophicus*. Translated by C.K. Ogden. New York: Harcourt, Brace & Co., 1922.

—. *Philosophical Investigations*. Translated by G.E.M. Anscombe. Oxford: Blackwell, 2001.

Wright, Richard A., ed. *African Philosophy: An Introduction*. 3rd edition. Lanham, Maryland: University Press of America, 1984.

Yaran, Cafer S. *Islamic Thought on the Existence of God*. Washington: Council for Research in Values and Philosophy, 2003.

Index

H

I

T

About the Author and General Editor

Ada Agada is based at the University of Nigeria Nsukka where he obtained his master's degree in philosophy. He specializes in African philosophy, existentialism and metaphysics. He has authored a number of articles on the subjects. He propounded the theory of consolationism in African philosophy. This treatise *Existence and Consolation: Reinventing Ontology, Gnosis and Values in African Philosophy* is the first articulation of the theory in a book form. His research and publication in the area of African philosophy have spanned years of unwavering interest. He is the author of this book.

Jonathan O. Chimakonam, Ph.D., teaches at the University of Calabar. He is the editor of *Filosofia Theoretica: Journal of African Philosophy, Culture and Religion*. He has contributed articles to many academic journals on African philosophy, logic, and systems of thought, with years of experience in these fields. He is the author of *Introducing African Science: Systematic and Philosophical Approach* (2012) and a co-editor of other books. He propounded the theory of Ezumezu logic and is currently working on a manuscript on the subject. His research interests span intercultural philosophy, bio-ethics, and philosophy of mathematics. He is the editor of *Atuolu Omalu: Some Unanswered Questions in African Philosophy* and a member of the Calabar School of Philosophy. He is the general editor of this book.

Advance Praise for this Book

"As Africa's global influence grows in the 21st century, the significance of that continent's philosophies rises as well. Ada Agada's Existence and Consolation supports that judgment. Writing in dialogue with key traditions in Western and African thought, ever mindful that life unfolds in particular situations and circumstances, Agada sheds important light on the contemporary human condition and insightfully envisions what people share and need to honor in every time and place."

—John K. Roth, Edward J. Sexton Professor Emeritus of Philosophy, Claremont McKenna College

"Agada introduces a set of concepts to African philosophy that are unique and original. He addresses mood (an orientation, affect, or attitude that drives thought), terror (our condition in a deterministic universe), and consolation (our response to terror), and weaves these into an intriguing and rich African theistic existential philosophy. Agada sees consolation as a fundamentally African ethic, extending the collective humanism implicit in proto-philosophies such as maat, ujamaa, ubuntu, ethnophilosophy, and especially negritude. Consolation philosophy begins with a phenomenology rooted in intersubjectivity, played out in a fatalist arena. This intersubjectivity undergirds communalism, which gives character to the context of ethical action in the face of anxiety and despair. This is the "melancholy being" who finds his roots in African community, who exists at the knife-edge of fate and freedom, and who finds consolation in ethically resolute action that faces the hope of transcendence.

Agada's philosophy is ambitious, responsive to the history of African and Western philosophy and cognizant of the realities of living in Africa. His existential project is well conceived and carefully explored. What is most exciting is that this account addresses significant elements of African life and thought, while at the same time making a robust contribution to world philosophy. It stands as a significant new contribution to the expanding literature on African forms of life and thought, and deserves a wide reading and careful thought."

—Bruce Janz, Professor of Philosophy, University of Central Florida

"A challenging and well-informed rereading of African philosophy to date that, combined with a fascinating retrieval and transformation of Senghor as well as with the intriguing thought of the contemporary Nigerian philosopher Asouzu, leads to an impressively comprehensive speculative account of the world and of human experience that balances a tragic sense of life with the joy of being: this is a "consolation philosophy" rooted in the African experience of the world."

—Professor Gerard Walmsley, Vice President/ Head of Philosophy, St. Augustine College of South Africa

"This work constitutes a sustained critique of major currents and orientations in African philosophy thus inaugurating a new order with the universal vision of consolation. It recaptures the ontology, gnosis and values determined by the weltanschauung of the African. Grounded in complementarity logic, the book provides Africa's constructive philosophy that acknowledges the solidarity of human quest. The message is new and clear—and the style irresistible."

—Professor O. A. Oyeshile, Department of Philosophy, University of Ibadan, Editor of *Philosophy, Culture and Society: An African Gaze*